An Introduction
to Guidance

An Introduction to Guidance

The Professional Counselor

Second Edition

E. L. Tolbert

University of Florida

Little, Brown and Company

BOSTON   TORONTO

Library of Congress Catalog Card No. 81-83312

ISBN 0-316-84992-8

9 8 7 6 5 4 3 2

HAL

Published simultaneously in Canada
by Little, Brown & Company (Canada) Limited

Printed in the United States of America

The first edition of this work by E. L. Tolbert was published in 1978 under the title *An Introduction to Guidance*.

ACKNOWLEDGMENTS

The excerpt on page 18 is from American School Counselor Association, "The Unique Role of the Elementary School Counselor," *Elementary School Guidance and Counseling*, vol. 12 (1978). Copyright 1978 American Personnel and Guidance Association. Reprinted with permission.

The excerpt on page 28 is from Martin L. Stamm and Blossom S. Nissman, *Improving Middle School Guidance: Practical Procedures for Counselors, Teachers, and Administrators* (Boston: Allyn and Bacon, 1979), p. 112. Reprinted by permission.

The excerpt on page 33 is from American School Counselor Association, "Developmental Guidance," *The School Counselor*, vol. 26 (1979). Copyright 1979 American Personnel and Guidance Association. Reprinted with permission.

The excerpt on page 36 is from American School Counselor Association, "ASCA Position Paper on Peer Counseling," *The School Counselor*, vol. 26 (1979). Copyright 1979 American Personnel and Guidance Association. Reprinted with permission.

The list on page 55 is from Commission on Professional Development, "Student Personnel Services in Higher Education," *Journal of College Student Personnel*, vol. 15 (1974). Copyright 1974 American Personnel and Guidance Association. Reprinted with permission.

Table 3-1 on page 60 is from Robert C. Troy and Thomas M. Magoon, "Activity Analysis in a University Counseling Center: Daily Time Recording of Time Estimates," *Journal of Counseling Psychology*, vol. 26 (1979).

Data in Table 3-2 on page 61 are from Charles J. Gelso, Janice M. Birk, Patrick W. Utz, and Anne E. Silver, "A Multigroup Evaluation of the Models and Functions of University Counseling Centers," *Journal of Counseling Psychology*, vol. 24 (1977).

(*continued on page 454*)

To Frances, Margaret, Jane, and Yves

Preface

The audience for this textbook is beginning counselor education students in a one-quarter or one-semester introductory course. Others such as administrators, teachers, student personnel workers, and community agency workers will find the book useful as an introduction to counseling services. Specific chapters and the experiential activities could be used for intensive workshops and in-service programs. Throughout this text the emphasis is on basic aspects of counseling and guidance in all settings.

The preface to the first edition began with the statement that the book "is designed to help students learn about the guidance profession and explore its suitability as a career . . ." This underlying intent has not changed, but the content and focus of the second edition have been altered in three important ways. First, all settings for professional counseling and guidance work — schools, colleges, universities, and community agencies and organizations — are examined. Not only is it important for professional counselors to know something about the work of colleagues in other settings, but it is also necessary to introduce beginning students to the whole array of guidance services. As a result, students can acquire information vital to deciding on a career in counseling and to choosing the setting in which to specialize. At this early stage of preparing to enter the profession it is also important for students to understand the process of helping others develop and fulfill their potential. Our goal in this book, and in a first course in counseling, is to lay the foundation for developing a strong sense of the profession and, of course, a feeling of professional identity.

The second major change in this second edition is its highlighting of the counseling needs of special populations. A discussion of working with the disabled is one example. Counselors in all agencies and institutions will almost inevitably work face to face with the disabled, with members of their families, with their prospective or actual employers, and with other significant persons who have the opportunity to promote the growth and development of members of this special population.

The third change is to the orientation of each chapter so that content will be appropriate for counselors in schools, colleges, and agencies. For example, issues about testing in one setting apply to all settings in which counselors work.

These changes in focus have resulted in new chapters on college and university settings, community agencies, and special populations. One chapter on school guidance and counseling services combines first edition chapters on consultation, support personnel, and new educational models. The total number of chapters has been reduced from fifteen to fourteen.

Chapter 1 reviews the status of the profession today, discusses occupations in counseling, and describes the rationale for the book's organization and content.

Chapter 2 introduces the reader to the work of the counselor in the elementary, middle/junior high, and high schools.

Chapter 3 covers the counselor in the college and university.

Chapter 4, the final settings chapter, deals with counseling in community agencies and institutions.

Chapter 5 presents a chronological account of the development of guidance, counseling, and personnel services.

Chapter 6 reviews the values base and the theoretical assumptions underlying counselor-provided helping services.

Chapter 7 covers the counselor's responsibilities for program building and management.

Chapter 8 discusses the counselor's face-to-face helping roles, summarizes major counseling theories, and describes some widely used techniques for individual and group work.

Chapter 9 surveys the characteristics and counseling needs of special populations.

Chapter 10 reviews issues and principles surrounding the use of information in the helping process and describes representative media and technology.

Chapter 11 covers the counselor's use of tests and measurements, including issues and problems involving the application of these instruments.

Chapter 12 provides a broad view of the counseling profession, emphasizing preparation standards, legal guidelines, ethical standards, credentialing, and organizations.

Chapter 13 examines the implications of accountability for counselors.

Chapter 14 identifies major trends and issues in the profession and makes predictions about the future.

The appendixes contain APGA counselor preparation standards, APGA ethical standards for counselors, a listing and description of APGA divisions, guidelines for a brief group-helping experience, and a counseling dialogue-test exercise.

Several special features of the book are designed to facilitate learning. Chapter summaries highlight major concepts. Research summaries focus on particular topics to illustrate the contributions of research to practice. Activities are provided to encourage experiential learning. Annotated reading lists at the end of each chapter guide the reader to sources of additional information. Illustrations add a visual dimension to significant concepts. An instructor's manual contains multiple choice questions, essay questions, and several teaching aids.

Many persons have contributed in one way or another to this book. Colleagues — those with whom the author is personally acquainted, those known only through brief and occasional correspondence, and those known solely through their writing in journals and books — have provided the substance and concepts upon which this book is built. Instructors who have used the first edition have been refreshingly candid in comments and suggestions — not always positive but always perceptive and helpful. Students, the ultimate jury, have made both possible and impossible suggestions to improve the book. The Little, Brown staff has been of tremendous assistance since the early planning of the revision. Mylan Jaixen and Dana Norton have with unflagging diligence helped decide what to add, subtract, clarify, or restate in order to move the manuscript along expeditiously to its final stages. I wish to thank J. L. Biggers, Texas Tech; John C. Jessell, Indiana State University; and Robert W. Read, Northeastern University, who provided perceptive and knowledgeable criticisms of the revised manuscript. I would like to express my appreciation to Margaret Tolbert, who read the entire manuscript and prepared illustrations that highlight major concepts in the text. Lastly, appreciation is expressed to Jane Tolbert Rouchaleau for her journalistic skill in editing the manuscript in its initial stages and for the indexing of the text.

E. L. Tolbert

Brief Contents

Contents

4 Counselors in Community Settings   73

5 Counseling, Guidance, and Personnel Services: How They Grew   99

6 Bases of Counseling, Guidance, and Personnel Services   129

7 Building Counseling, Guidance, and Student Personnel Programs   151

8 Counseling Individuals and Groups   177

9 The Counselor and Special Groups   217

10   The Counselor's Use of Information   247

11 The Counselor's Use of Measurements 271

12 The Counseling Profession 291

13 Accountability for Counselors   323

Chapter

1

Introduction

The profession of counseling is growing, changing, and increasing in sophistication. Three striking features stand out. Counselors now work in almost every helping setting — colleges, community agencies, schools, businesses, and private practice. They serve populations that range from preschool children through those in the retirement years. They use a wide array of techniques and kinds of technology, including working face-to-face with one individual, teaching skills to others to effect widespread changes, and using computers to assist individuals in decision making.

These changes reflect a sensitivity to the needs and directions of society, whether they be, for example, the developmental needs of elementary school pupils, the mental health problems of adults, or the employment problems of college students.

Two brief descriptions of counselors will help show how these new developments are affecting practice. One portrays the work of a counselor in higher education. The other is about a counselor in a community mental health agency.

Two Counselors at Work

Bill Smith works as one of four counselors in a college counseling center. Some years ago these counselors waited for students to come in for help. Now that has changed. In the course of one day, Bill's responsibilities take him all over the campus. He spends an hour talking to a student to help him deal with overwhelming anxiety. Next, he meets with a group of resident assistants learning techniques for communicating with students. In the afternoon he takes part in a group meeting to plan services for minorities on campus. Later, he engages in group counseling with four couples who are having marital problems. After that, he meets with a department head who wants to improve student advising services. Finally, during the evening he conducts the sixth meeting of an undergraduate class on life planning. This one day is not typical, but it is about as varied as any other day in the week.

Mary Jones is on the staff of a community mental health agency. On this particular day she works with a group of six individuals who are having considerable difficulty in coping with everyday interpersonal relations. Later, she meets with three persons for individual conferences. The first one is an adolescent who was referred for counseling by parents as being ungovernable. The second is an adult drug user. The third is a suicidal wife whose husband has left her. Still later, she visits a halfway house under the center's supervision to help plan a behavioral reinforcement program for residents. Finally, she visits a local school to make a presentation on alcohol abuse, part of an ongoing program at the school.

These two counselors are in different settings and assist different populations, but their problems and techniques are remarkably similar. Both Bill and Mary work face to face with individuals to help them express and understand feelings and develop effective living patterns. They both conduct groups, taking advantage of the interaction of group members to facilitate self-understanding, self-acceptance, and improved interpersonal relations. They help clients become more effective help providers. Bill is coaching residence hall advisers on communication, and Mary is aiding the halfway house supervisors to become more effective facilitators. Both are doing a type of teaching in the alcohol abuse and career planning courses.

These two examples provide only a glimpse of the profession of counseling as it is today. What, then, are other major features that characterize contemporary counseling?

The Counseling Profession Today

Certain clearly definable features illuminate the field of counseling. Each feature has significance for what you as a practitioner will do. Each is worth careful thought at this stage of your preparation. The following list identifies these contemporary characteristics:

1. The expanding role of the counselor.
2. Expanding opportunities for practice.
3. Increasing professionalization.
4. Increasing responsiveness to needs of society.
5. Responsibility for observable results.

The order of these points is not important; each has a direct effect on work. Each is related to all of the others.

Almost any setting is appropriate for counseling.

The Expanding Role of the Counselor

Counselors today do more than work with individuals in a one-to-one relationship. In the examples of Bill's and Mary's day, it is obvious that consulting, teaching, and group work are significant involvements. In contrast, only a few years ago counselors mainly counseled. Moreover, they usually remained in their offices for counselees to arrive, either through self-referral or that of others. In schools, counseling was often done by a "teacher-counselor" who taught part time and had several hours a day for providing individual assistance and related guidance activities. Now, however, the thrust of most functions is to spread the effects of the counselor's work far beyond what can be done by means of one-to-one help.

The expansion of the counselor's role operates in other ways that increase his or her involvement in all sorts of helping activities. Taking part in staff meetings to plan ways to help a pupil is not a new procedure, but the more systematic way this is done today is new. Using computer guidance systems, and instructing others in their use, is relatively new. Moreover, counselors also utilize a wide variety of new theories, techniques, strategies, and materials for individual and group work. The role expansion provided by this augmentation of theories and methods is demonstrated by the greater variety of approaches in use today. In addition, counselors today are frequently involved in program building in schools, colleges, and community settings. Their expertise in human development theory and their ability to facilitate group action make programming a natural role. Finally, the evaluation of services, while not new, has recently moved to the fore in importance for a number of reasons, both financial and humanistic.

Role expansion also involves the rationale for helping others. First, there is a developmental focus on planning and providing helping services. Emphasis is on those services that assist individuals to develop capacities, understand themselves, and move effectively from one developmental stage to the next. Moreover, counselors at each stage relate what they do to the work of other counselors at prior and subsequent stages. Second, the whole individual is the focus of help: Home, family, work, education, and personal qualities are all considered. Third, the counselor works as a member of a team of helpers. In the school, for example, the team includes teachers, administrators, and psychological and medical personnel. In the community mental health setting, the team may include psychiatrists, social workers, psychologists, and aides.

In each setting the counselor is responsible for the services that emphasize growth, self-discovery, and decision making. Moreover, the counselor uses strategies to reach as wide an audience as possible.

Expanding Opportunities for Practice

Counselors are ranging far beyond the limited settings of a few years ago. Aside from the high school, the college counseling center, and the rehabilitation agency, counselors were hardly visible in helping services. Today counselors are active in the elementary and middle or junior high schools and in the community college. They work in community mental health agencies, crisis centers, drug rehabilitation agencies, and mental hospitals. They are employed by private agencies that provide contractual services to business and industry, and serve as staff members in businesses and industries. Some are in private practice. Counselors are employed in countless other settings, such as law enforcement agencies and institutions, hospitals, employment agencies, halfway houses, residential centers for drug and alcohol abusers and those with emotional problems, and centers and nursing homes for older persons.

Counselors also work with many more groups than just the high school and college students of years past. In the preceding discussion of work settings, some special populations were identified, such as older persons and the handicapped. The range of clients has expanded to the extent that it now includes all ages — from preschool children to postretirement persons.

Services have also expanded to include groups and individuals with special needs. Minorities are one example. Blacks, native Americans, Hispanic Americans, and Asian Americans are major minority groups. The handicapped have already been mentioned, but the "exceptional" — in terms of unique talents and abilities — are also given more attention by counselors than in the past. In addition, counselors work with families in conflict, drug and alcohol abusers, those in crisis situations, and employees of public and private establishments. In short, the types of help counselors provide are being utilized by persons of all ages and by those who have virtually every type of problem, need, or difficulty.

Increasing Professionalization

A third group of significant characteristics involves professionalization. Great strides have been made in establishing preparation standards and ethical codes in the counseling profession (see Appendixes A and B). Licensure is perhaps the major current issue. Several states now provide for licensure of counselors, but most do not. Licensure is essential for counselors to enable them to protect the practice of their profession. Moreover, licensure has a direct bearing on the legal status of the profession. Adequate licensure should spell out the rights of counselors — for example, the right of confidentiality. Moreover, it would clarify the status of the counselor in legal matters such as liability in case of lawsuits and also in financial matters such as the right to receive payment for services from insurance companies (third-party payments).

Licensure and the legal status of counseling concern every member of the profession. They are two interrelated aspects that will shape the practice of counseling in the years ahead.

Increasing Responsiveness to Needs of Society

The counseling profession is not the only social service that is sensitive and responsive to society's needs and problems. It is, however, one of the major ones. This social sensitivity has been a major theme since the emergence of counseling. Its origin as part of a social reform movement attests to the social awareness of counselors. Current concern with problems such as those of older persons, the unemployed, the troubled family, the battered child, and the drug and alcohol abuser continue and expand the social-concern mission of counselors. New techniques and settings for services facilitate the delivery of assistance to those needing it. Crisis centers are available to help individuals with overwhelming problems gain immediate aid through telephone hotlines, counseling, and outreach teams. Community mental health centers emphasize assistance to mentally troubled persons in the community as opposed to placing them in large institutions. Counselors in schools and colleges help students learn to find work in an increasingly competitive job market. Counselors in elementary schools work with groups to help pupils cope with family dissolution, bereavement, and other traumas of childhood and youth.

You are no doubt aware of many if not most of the contemporary problems of our society. The news media daily highlight both old and new ones. The counseling profession makes no pretense of attending to all the ills and problems of our society. It is, however, one of the significant professions that recognizes and endeavors to alleviate social problems.

Responsibility for Observable Results

As counseling has emerged as a more visible profession, as new roles have developed, and as new target populations are reached, the pressure to provide evidence of the impact of service has increased. Other conditions, such as decreasing economic resources, have contributed to this demand for accountability. It is becoming increasingly clear that if programs are to continue to be funded we will have to show that we make a difference in the lives of those served. Moreover, the effects must be in terms of criteria that the public, budget makers, and administrators consider important.

Accountability must be a major factor in planning and providing services in all settings and for all target groups. Moreover, the most economical ways of providing services must be determined and used. If, for example, paraprofessionals can assemble information about educational opportunities for counselees or instruct counselees in the use of computer guidance systems, there is no need for the counselor to use his or her time on these tasks. If an expensive counseling center on a college campus can accommodate only 1 or 2 percent of the student body, changes need to be made so that assistance will be available to, and utilized by, a much wider population.

There are other aspects of counseling today that are important and that are, along with the ones already discussed, dealt with in much more detail in the chapters that follow. The five given, however, are the most salient ones.

Introduction to the Profession: A Point of View

The five major features of the profession discussed in the proceding section — expansion of role, increase in work settings, professionalization, sensitivity to needs of society, and accountability — serve as the basis for the point of view about the profession given in this book. The major elements of these features are discussed in the paragraphs that follow, in terms of how they affect preparation and practice.

Common Core of Preparation

All counselors share a common core of preparation. Regardless of specialization planned, all counselors have preparation in psychological and sociological foundations, the helping relationship, groups, career development, appraisal, research and evaluation, and professional aspects (see Appendix A). When you complete the program, you are a counselor *first*, and then a community agency counselor, an elementary school counselor, or a college counselor.

Specialization

The common core of preparation plus the specialization acquired through courses and practical experience equip the counselor to be proficient in a particular work setting. The specialization consists of learning about the specific work environment and adapting techniques to the target population. For example, the elementary school counselor learns about the elementary school, the characteristics of the pupils in this age group, and the necessary modifications of techniques to help these persons.

Flexibility

The ability to work effectively with different groups — age, sex, ethnic, racial, socioeconomic — is a third aspect of the contemporary counselor. Specialization is needed to learn about the characteristics of the particular group, but the basic core of preparation provides the foundation on which special-population treatment skills are built.

Versatility

Versatility with many techniques, particularly those that will reach large numbers of persons, is a fourth characteristic of the contemporary counselor. The counselor is knowledgeable about personality, learning, and helping techniques and can select those methods that best fit the particular situation. The one-to-one helping approach is often not the most productive or practical one, but many times it is necessary. The counselor is knowledgeable about what may work best and why. For example, the college-level counselor who wants to help a group of test-anxious students may use group counseling and bring in relaxation techniques while participants vicariously experience the threatening task.

Professionalization

Professionalization is a fifth aspect of the point of view about today's counselor. The counselor knows and abides by ethical standards and legal guidelines. He or she keeps up to date by being active in professional organizations, by reading, and by participating in classes and workshops. Fulfilling a professional role includes informing the public about counseling, building support for services, and insuring that only quality services are offered to the public.

Professionalization calls for a self-regulating, responsible, competent counselor. Professionals should be free to exercise judgment in matters of ethical practices, treatment methods and goals, and evaluation. The professional counselor insists on these conditions at work.

One additional and very significant aspect of professionalization is the team concept. As a team member, the counselor works closely with those in allied professions such as clinical psychology, social work, psychiatry, and school psychology. It is essential that the counselor be able to communicate his or her role to others and also that he or she understands the services and functions of these related professionals. In addition, the team often includes paraprofessionals, that is, nonprofessional personnel trained to carry out a specific function. Counselors establish the duties and supervise the work of paraprofessionals.

It is obvious from the foregoing discussion that fulfilling the role of the professional counselor is a demanding task. Professional status, however, has been energetically sought by counselors for many years. It is a high-water mark of achievement. Professional status must be supported by each of you who completes the program of preparation.

Social Sensitivity

A sixth aspect of the point of view has to do with the social sensitivity of the counselor. The professional counselor avoids a narrow parochialism and keeps in touch with national trends and needs as well as those in the community served (the school community, college campus, or politically defined community). A proactive rather than a reactive stance is essential. The counselor does not wait for problems to occur but is aware of conditions that may lead to them. An awareness of emerging needs, conflicts, and problems flows naturally from the regular input the counselor obtains from members of the target population.

Goal-directed Assistance

A seventh aspect of the point of view is that all assistance — whether individual, group, or institution-wide — is goal-directed. Help is supposed to assist the individual accomplish something that is socially and personally desirable and observable. Part of the counselor's responsibility is to evaluate what he or she has accomplished. If procedures do not work, changes are made. It should be possible to describe the impact of services on the lives of others; it should also be possible to specify how much the desired changes in individuals cost. In short, the counselor is accountable.

There are several other elements that make up the point of view of the counselor's work today that focus on the rationale for the helping process itself. First, there is a developmental emphasis that takes into account what has already happened and what the individual has to do next. Much attention is given to assisting the individual to build strengths for future tasks. Counseling services take into account the individual's total life span, rather than only the needs and concerns of a specific point in time. There are, however, specific areas in the developmental process when assistance is particularly critical, and these are given particular attention. Second, assistance of any kind takes into account the whole person; individuals are not compartmentalized into home, family, school, and work areas. Third, it is assumed that individuals can change, make better use of attributes than has been made, and find more rewarding life-styles than those previously engaged in. Fourth, the reality of the world must be taken into account when helping a person. Some illustrative realities are pupils' attitudes toward those with physical or mental handicaps, the availability of jobs in the community, and the intellectual demands of school programs. For example, personal conflicts that have led to drug abuse may be identified and resolved in counseling, but attitudes of employers and the community-at-large toward former drug users are realities to be considered.

The point of view of the counselor's work I have discussed above should help you understand the profession for which you are preparing. In addition, it serves as the rationale for the organization and content of this book.

Summary Concepts

The preparation of counselors equips them to provide assistance in almost any situation where human behavior is of concern. All counselors share a common foundation of knowledge and skills on which helping services are based. Specialization involves learning about and experiencing a particular setting and population. Modes of helping have been developed that aim to spread the effects of direct assistance by the counselor. A major technique is to help others improve their own helping competencies. Moreover, the time has arrived when it is essential to be able to present "hard data" to substantiate claims that services make a difference in individuals' lives. Counselors have sought the increased expectations that are implicit in expanded responsibilities. Such expectations are in keeping with increased professionalization.

Suggested Readings

Creamer, Don G., ed. *Student Development in Higher Education.* Cincinnati: American College Personnel Association, 1980.

> College counselors will likely work in student development programs and thus should learn about this concept and how it affects counselor preparation and practice. Furthermore, counselor education graduates often move into some student development function other than counseling per se. Chapter 1 gives a concise and readable account of the growing emphasis on student development.

Gysbers, Norman C. "Career Guidance at the Crossroads." In *New Imperatives for Guidance,* edited by Garry R. Walz and Libby Benjamin, pp 2–29. Ann Arbor, Mich.: ERIC Counseling and Personnel Services Clearinghouse, 1978.

> An insightful review of major issues faced in school guidance and counseling today. The developmental emphasis is clearly defined, and "guidelines" for progress by the profession are given.

Herr, Edwin L. *Guidance and Counseling in the Schools: The Past, Present, and Future.* Falls Church, Va.: American Personnel and Guidance Association, 1979.

> Part 2, pages 25–88, contains a comprehensive overview of the work of the counselor, elementary through high school. This is a more appropriate reading for Chapter 2, but a quick review of roles, functions, and results will be useful with this chapter.

Lewis, Judith A., and Lewis, Michael D. *Community Counseling: A Human Services Approach.* New York: John Wiley and Sons, 1977.

> Chapter 1 gives an overview of how counselors can work in community settings. A broad-range counselor approach is suggested. A valuable reference for an understanding of opportunities in the community setting.

Miller, Frank W.; Freuhling, James A.; and Lewis, Gloria J. *Guidance Principles and Services.* 3rd ed. Columbus, Ohio: Charles E. Merrill, 1978.

> The authors give their "Principles of Guidance" on page 14; a comparison with those given in the preceding section is suggested. Roles in various settings are contained in parts of Chapters 4–7.

Pietrofesa, John J.; Bernstain, Bianca; Minor, J. Anne; and Stanford, Susan. *Guidance: An Introduction.* Chicago: Rand McNally, 1980.

> Chapter 1 gives an excellent overview of the need for, and principles of, guidance. Pages 4–25 are particularly recommended.

Shertzer, Bruce, and Stone, Shelley C. *Fundamentals of Guidance.* 4th ed. Boston: Houghton Mifflin, 1981.

> Particularly valuable as a reference for guidance in the school setting. Other settings for work, however, are discussed in Chapter 4. Chapter 2 is recommended for an analysis of principles and developmental influences. Chapter 3 covers points of view about school guidance.

Warnath, Charles F., ed. *New Directions for College Counselors.* San Francisco: Jossey-Bass, 1973.

   The book covers a number of issues and trends related to counseling in higher education. Chapter 1, by Warnath, identifies changes that should take place in traditional college counseling centers.

Wirtz, Willard. *The Boundless Resource.* Washington, D.C.: The New Republic Book Company, 1975.

   The major focus of this book is on education and work, but pages 1–14 and 16–31 give vivid and currently relevant perspectives on the problems of young people looking forward to entering the world of work.

Wrenn, C. Gilbert. "Personnel Perspectives Past and Present." In *New Imperatives for Guidance,* edited by Garry R. Walz and Libby Benjamin, pp. 456–491. Ann Arbor, Mich.: ERIC Counseling and Personnel Services Clearinghouse, 1978.

   The whole section, including the opening pages on historical development, is excellent background, but the most relevant parts for this chapter are pages 470–490, which review "conditions" that support the need for counselors.

Chapter
2
Counselors in the School Setting

Counseling services in schools began early in this century and developed in a "backward" way, that is, from the upper grades down. The first counselors were in high schools. Much later, services very much like those at the high school level were instituted in junior high schools. Only fairly recently have counselors appeared in elementary schools and in the relatively new middle schools.

Why this growth of services that we characterize as backward, and what significance does this growth pattern have for the practice of counseling? First, there was a strong career guidance emphasis in the early period; the time for help was when the pupil left high school. The work-choice emphasis gave rise to a model of heavily cognitive assistance, usually one to one, and at a point in time. The weight of tradition still influences the work of counseling at the high school level and permeates many persons' perceptions of what counselors do.

The changes in the nature of the work of the counselor discussed in Chapter 1 began to appear several decades ago. As elementary school counseling emerged, the new model featuring a developmental emphasis, consultation, group work, as well as the use of school and community resources, gained widespread visibility and acceptance. Now the movement in the modernization of guidance is upward, that is, the concepts of elementary school counseling are filtering into the higher grades. Whereas practice has not always caught up with theory, there is some strong support for a developmental emphasis throughout the system, grades K through 12. Groups are replacing individuals in face-to-face modes of help. Consultation is used to provide assistance to the teacher, parent, and administrator.

Several vignettes illustrate the types of activities school counselors are engaged in today.

Three Counselors

Ralph Biggers is an elementary school counselor. He selected this setting because he likes to work with the 6–10-year age group, he feels that these are the critical years in development, and he is confident that he can organize a program as he wants it to be. On a typical day his major activities consist of observing several pupils in classrooms, consulting with two teachers, talking with two children individually, and conducting two group procedures with six pupils each. The observations are recorded in a systematic way and will be used in a staffing to determine if the pupils need to be in one of the programs for the handicapped. He consults with a second-grade teacher to work out a plan of reinforcement to change the behavior of a pupil who is extremely hyperactive. The other consultation is to identify pupils who can profit by participating in a group on how to make friends. Structured approaches are used for the two types of group work: four second graders take part in a DUSO (Developing Understanding of Self and Others) group; a fourth-grade class meets in a group called the Magic Circle, which uses a sequential affective education curriculum. These are a sampling of the counselor's major activities, but others are also being carried out.

Sarah Hill is one of two counselors in a large middle school, grades 5–8. The school is organized into three teams that consist of several teachers each and pupils of different grade levels. Sarah chose this level because she wants to work with pupils in the important transition phase between elementary and high school. In the course of several days she has worked with two small groups of pupils on building positive self-concepts, met with parents in an ongoing program to help them understand their children, and helped peer advisers learn communication skills so they can help in the orientation of incoming pupils. In addition, individual meetings were held with several pupils who present various problems — shyness, hostility, and difficulty concentrating on a task. Some time has also been spent in large-group activities on career exploration and interpersonal relations. While these activities take up most of the time during these few days, others also demand attention. A public relations talk to a community group, consultation with teachers on classroom problems, arranging for several employers to meet with a team for career exploration, and helping plan an individualized program for a handicapped pupil are examples. In many ways, her work is similar to that of the elementary school counselor but places more emphasis on exploration, interpersonal relations, and identity formation.

Jim Jones is a high school counselor who has worked long enough to see his job change radically. In past years he was mainly occupied with schedule-making conferences with pupils, helping them with college admissions, conducting individual sessions with those with personal problems and career questions, and administering the school testing programs. Now his time is spent quite differently. For one thing, he sees pupils individually for a much wider range of problems — intrapersonal conflicts, family problems, drug use, job seeking. For these conferences, he uses a much wider range of techniques than he formerly employed. In addition, he uses group counseling extensively for developmental as well as remedial needs. He consults with teachers on learning and behavior problems, conducts a peer advising training program, refers pupils to various community agencies such as a community mental health center, and coordinates a program on alcohol and drug abuse. He sees much of his work as remedial, but he also believes that he has given it a substantial developmental emphasis.

Each of these school counselors shares a number of similar activities in the course of the day. The levels of maturity of pupils, the school programs, and the school organizations differ, but the major functions are more alike than they are different. Each counselor is particularly concerned with evaluating the effects of services. Each is aware that accountability is a major factor in program continuity.

The Counselor in the Elementary School

Guidance programs in the elementary school have been in existence a relatively short time compared with those in the secondary schools, but they have shown remarkable growth in only a few years. They are more clear-cut and consistent than at the secondary level, partly because of their more recent arrival on the school scene and the simpler organization of schools at this level, and partly because of a clearer focus (e.g., counselors do not have to concern themselves with electives, choice of programs, job preparation, or college admission). But these conditions would not have led to an efficient and systematic pattern without the conceptualization of early leaders whose work set the stage for school programs today (Faust 1968).

Functions and Role of the Counselor

The elementary school guidance program usually involves a school-based counselor providing the services of counseling, consultation, and coordination (priorities vary). Further guidance responsibilities within these areas are diagnosis and referral. The counselor is in a key position to help identify pupils with special needs, disabilities, or handicaps and to refer those in need of special assistance (Cottingham 1969; Faust 1968; Patterson 1969a).

The role of the elementary school counselor is that of helper to pupils, teachers, and parents. To carry out this role, the counselor works face to face with pupils individually and in small groups on remedial and developmental needs, provides classroom guidance activities focusing on affective aspects of personality, and assists teachers in developing skill in use of these techniques. Consultation with teachers is designed to help them work effectively and positively with individuals and groups. Both individual conferences and group meetings with parents are used to help with problems and give information about guidance services. The counselor also coordinates services such as team help for learning deficiencies and referrals to out-of-school agencies. Counselors facilitate the developmental process by helping teachers, the primary person working with the child, to provide an effective educational program (American School Counselor Association 1978b).

Priorities in Setting Up Programs

Programs differ according to priorities established among the three basic services. Faust ranks consulting with teachers along with counseling as the first priority for help to teachers and pupils. Consulting with school administrators, parents, and others is placed at a lower level (Faust 1968, pp. 13–14, 41). Dinkmeyer (1971) recognized that the counselor must set up priorities, and recommends this order: first, working with administration; second, working with groups of teachers; third, counseling with children in groups; fourth, consultation with parents in groups; and fifth, individual counseling with children. The setting of priorities, once objectives are established, is a critical task; it indicates where to begin and the sequence of activities to be followed in implementing the program (Heddesheimer 1975, p. 29).

Tuma's report (1974) illustrates her use of the cube design in an elementary school developmental guidance program. The chief problem during her first year was gaining access to classrooms in order to initiate activities necessary for the program's success. To overcome this difficulty, she utilized the cube strategy to select the target population, the method of intervention, and purpose of intervention. She also employed the model proposed by Blocher and Rapoza to effect change in the human system (1972), in this case to gain teachers' cooperation. Thus, she defined services, identified potential clients, introduced new concepts to clients, and set up mutually agreed-upon goals. With teachers' acceptance, and with the help of the principal, the counselor succeeded in introducing a number of techniques and guidance strategies. By the end of her second year, she had established working relationships with nearly all staff members. Direct contact with small groups and individuals was part of the program, but the major emphasis was on classroom demonstrations and consultation with teachers.

Contemporary Problems

The work of the elementary school counselor originally covered a broad range of personal, social, and educational problems, but in recent years the scope has expanded even more. Some major ones are divorce, drug abuse, discrimination, two-career families and other changing family patterns, delinquency, child abuse, special needs of the handicapped, including those with learning difficulties, and problems of talented individuals. There are other areas of concern, but these vividly illustrate the wide array of problems that demand attention.

Additional contemporary problems are reflected in studies carried out in the elementary school. Long (1971) describes school phobia and suggests remedial steps a counselor can take, pointing out that the condition is difficult to deal with because it is often reinforced by actions of parents and others. The abuse of pupils by parents and guardians is another widespread problem. According to Forrer (1975), at least 700 children die every year from mistreatment and abuse by parents or guardians; approximately 60,000 cases of abuse were reported in 1974. Forrer concludes that while the danger of death or serious injury decreases as pupils grow older, the possibility of psychological damage is great. Christensen (1975) comments on the tendency to lump various minority groups together as if all had the same needs and stresses the importance of knowing the unique background of each group to counsel effectively. As an example, he describes Puerto Ricans' open demonstration of love, tolerance of children, and gregariousness. This group makes up a sizable minority; there are currently approximately 2 million Puerto Ricans living in the United States. Cross and Maldonado (1971) review the problems of Mexican Americans and describe how their values might differ from the counselor's own. The authors underline the importance of accepting individuals as unique and recognizing their cultural values and characteristics. Smith, Barnes, and Scales (1974) enumerate problems that arise in counseling blacks. Blacks seek greater identification with each other; they are developing an awareness of their rich and colorful heritage; and they communicate a great deal nonverbally.

The elementary school counselor's attention is coming to focus on children from disrupted families. Concern has been expressed in the past for the effects of stressful family conditions on children, but recent emphasis is more systematic and productive. A special issue of *Elementary School Guidance and Counseling* shows this involvement. Helping the pupil understand and accept the death of a family member is one example (Ryerson 1977). Dealing with the child of an incarcerated parent is another (Chaney, Linkenhoker, and Horne 1977). Counselors are developing new approaches for helping abused children (Griggs and Gale 1977), children of alcoholic parents (Hecht 1977), children of divorced parents (Wilkinson and Bleck 1977), foster children (Bard 1977), those who move frequently (Splete and Rasmussen 1977), and children from homes where a different language is spoken and a different culture is dominant (Inniss 1977).

In spite of the impression given by these studies that remediation occupies most of the counselor's time, the major emphasis is developmental. The salient features of today's counseling given in Chapter 1 illustrate this developmental focus. The brief descriptions at the beginning of this chapter portrays counselors primarily concerned with developmental services.

This developmental emphasis fits admirably with the purposes of education and the principles of human growth and development. Moreover, the position statements of the American School Counselor Association (1978b, 1979a) strongly support a developmental emphasis. For example, the following excerpt is from "The Unique Role of the Elementary School Counselor":

> Consistent with the philosophy of education, elementary school counseling concerns itself with children in the developmental process of maximizing their potential. The elementary counselor works within the educational framework and the child's total environment to enable each child to arrive at the identity and learn to make choices and decisions that lead to effective functioning as a worthwhile being. (American School Counselor Association 1978a, p. 200)

Special Tasks of the Counselor

The major functions of counseling, consulting, and coordinating of resources and services are widely accepted. Services, however, should be based on the needs of the particular school and community. There is plenty of flexibility in the ASCA model given above to accommodate local needs and to permit the establishment of priorities that attend to major school and community concerns.

The work of the elementary school counselor is shown in outline form in the preceding paragraphs. This brief discussion should give you a fairly general understanding of the counselor's focus for this level. Additional descriptions of several areas are presented to give you a more complete picture of some important areas of involvement. The first of these is counseling, the face-to-face helping process for individuals and groups. Counseling is without question a central function of counselors and deserves special attention. The second is consultation, also one of the major responsibilities of counselors. The third includes two groups of nonprofessional participants — peers and paraprofessionals. The use of pupils to help other pupils is a promising new approach that should be described in detail. The use of paraprofessionals is included because it is a type of differentiated staffing that may offer a way of extending services in times of limited budgets. It also provides a way of using indigenous personnel when working with special populations — for example, minorities.

Fourth, career education is singled out for additional discussion because it is a relatively new and innovative program to help pupils cope successfully in our technological society. The final topic for special emphasis is the handicapped. Services to this group is one of the newer responsibilities of counselors since the implementation of PL 94–142.

Counseling

Much of the counselor's time involves face-to-face work with counselees. The focus of help may be either developmental or remedial, but aside from emergencies and problems that require immediate remedial assistance, the elementary school counselor is mainly involved in providing developmental help.

One-to-one counseling may be carried out by verbal methods; by the use of play materials or drawing; or by means of other techniques that emphasize behavior more than conversation. In counseling by verbal means, the counselor adjusts his or her language and concepts to the level of the counselee and seeks to convey understanding, empathy, and positive regard. Efforts are made to build trust and to assist the counselee to talk. Expression of feeling is particularly important, as it helps to relieve suppressed emotions and opens the way to solving problems and learning new ways of behavior. In addition, setting goals helps the child change behaviors that are disruptive or ineffective. For example, a goal may be for the counselee to increase on-task behavior. Rewards, perhaps check marks on a chart, are given for increased on-task time.

Group counseling and classroom activities are used to assist pupils to accomplish all sorts of developmental goals. Making friends, communicating effectively with others, building self-confidence, and learning how to express feelings are typical goals. Besides those group activities with a developmental focus, however, remedial help is often provided. Children of divorced parents, those with behavior problems, or those with problems in self-perceptions, are examples of target groups.

Group counseling and classroom activities are typically carried out with a structured format. Ground rules are usually established, and activities or exercises are introduced and directed by the leader. Kits and prepared materials such as DUSO and the Magic Circle may be used.

Consultation

Consultation has a high priority in the work of the elementary school counselor. It not only provides assistance to a far greater number of children than individual or group work; it also helps others, particularly teach-

The counselor can reach greater numbers of people through consultation.

ers and parents, learn helping skills. A review of program descriptions and studies vividly illustrates the innovative applications that have been made.

Much of the assistance is provided to teachers to help them deal with pupils in the classroom. Engelhardt, Sulzer, and Alterkruse (1971) give an example of a counselor working out a reinforcement schedule with a teacher to strengthen positive behavior of a disruptive child. After establishing a baseline for the disruptive behavior, the reinforcement schedule was carried out and the undesirable behavior was sharply reduced. In another example (Kuzniar 1973), the consultee (the teacher requesting help) was advised to visit other classrooms; the counselor focused on positive aspects of the consultee's work and helped her develop a list of desired classroom behaviors, strategies for implementing them, and ways to reward pupil progress. In changing classroom management procedures, the teacher actually changed herself. The use of teacher groups has also been advocated as an effective strategy. Moreover, consultation provides an effective approach to help teachers develop skills to aid children who are experiencing bereavement or who are unable to deal with tension (McBeath 1980).

Consultation is also a productive way to work with parents. Meetings with parents can supplement information gained in teacher conferences and classroom observations for child-help strategy planning. In addition to direct work with children as part of the helping process, counselors work with individual parents, parent groups, or families to improve intrafamily communication and school adjustment (Macaluso 1976). Consultation may be with several families to achieve the same results — better communication within the family and better adaptability to the school program (Sauber 1975). The consultation approach to working with parents has shown positive results, but much of the current work has a remedial focus. A more productive approach is to combine relatively long-term consulting with pupil counseling, with special attention to parent-child communications and relationships between parent and pupil behavior. Positive reinforcement in the home is an essential component of this approach (Warner 1974).

Consultation may also be used with the school program or the total school system. Psychological education (Ivey and Alschuler 1973b) is one of the newer approaches to using consultation in the curriculum. It has, for example, been used for values clarification in the classroom. Improving the climate and operation of the institution may be the goals of consultation with staff members. In such a case, the organization has the problem; consultants' efforts improve communication, effect needed structural change, and modify conflict-causing situations (Murray and Schmuck 1972).

Paraprofessionals and Peers

There are many types of paraprofessionals (also often called support personnel). Peers, probably the most numerous, are pupils trained to work with pupils. Parents, retired persons, and others from the community may also take the role of paraprofessional, usually on a volunteer basis.

Peer counseling programs have been developed and shown good results. Three sixth-grade classes in Dryden Central School, New York (McCann 1975), took part in a peer-counselor training program. Pupil helpers were selected by class sociograms, i.e., measurements of social preferences. The counselor discussed the program with sixth-grade teachers and then met with classes to talk about helping and the work of peer counselors. Eight volunteers were selected, evenly divided by sex; all but one elected to continue after learning more about what was involved. In eight 1-hour primarily experiential training sessions, pupils were trained to listen, notice nonverbal communication, talk to others about problems and feelings, reflect feelings, develop options for problem situations, and demonstrate caring. After training, they worked in a drop-in center under the counselor's supervision. Results showed that both peer counselors and counselees benefited. Counselees expressed positive attitudes toward the program; peer counselors learned helping skills and developed positive attitudes toward being of service to others.

Other types of paraprofessionals work in the elementary school. Carlson and Pietrofesa (1971) describe a three-level organization. At the first level paraprofessionals perform routine clerical duties and build school-community relations. The middle level consists of guidance workers who concentrate on activities other than counseling. The Deerfield, Illinois, project (Carlson, Cavins, and Dinkmeyer 1969) utilized guidance assistants who had more training than the typical paraprofessional. Pasco County, Florida, used five occupational specialists in elementary career-education to develop and present career-oriented materials in Project CHOICE (Comprehensive Humanistic Oriented Implementation of Career Education); although college preparation is not required for the occupational specialists, all had bachelor's degrees.

An impressive use of paraprofessionals to improve career guidance for disadvantaged youth, grades K–12, is demonstrated by the Detroit Developmental Career Guidance Project (Leonard and Vriend 1975). Evaluations have shown that the work of community aides as liaison between school, home, and community is one of the major reasons for success of the program.

Counselor attitudes about working with paraprofessionals have tended to place these subprofessional helpers in a non-personal-contact, clerical role (Zimpfer, Frederickson, Salim, and Sanford 1971, p. 30). Counselors in programs in which lines of responsibility and roles are clearly described and followed, however, seem to exhibit a more positive attitude about the helping potential of paraprofessionals.

Career Education

The term "career education" is particularly relevant for the work role of the elementary school counselor. Its meaning goes far beyond preparation for a job — it involves the restructuring of American education, grades K–12. It is a developmental concept of the learning experience, in which school and community together help prepare the individual to cope successfully in our technological society. All aspects of life are covered in what Gysbers (1978, pp. 21–22) calls "Life Career Development."

At the elementary school level the emphasis is on developing career awareness: awareness of the place of work in one's life; values about work and about self; beginning competencies in areas such as planning and decision making; and knowledge of broad occupational categories. Career education is infused into the curriculum in a way that makes extensive use of the community in learning experiences that cover all life arenas.

The elementary school period is certainly not too early a stage in children's lives to give concentrated attention to career attitudes and values. Evidence shows that career values emerge in the elementary school (Cooker 1973) and that, by the end of the fifth grade, sex stereotyping has taken place and later becomes increasingly difficult to change (Leonard, Sather, Sheggrud, and Handel 1973). Moreover, research has shown that career education can raise the level of career maturity (Clapsaddle 1973) and that such community activities as field trips can facilitate the development of awareness even as early as the kindergarten level (Edington 1976). Other research supports the effectiveness of career education in the elementary school (Omvig, Tulloch, and Thomas 1975; Tolbert 1980, pp. 304–306).

The elementary school counselor has an important role to play in career education (Hansen 1978); consulting with teachers to assist them in planning activities that incorporate a developmental emphasis is the most important aspect of that role. Helping with program building also enables the counselor to put special career development skills and knowledge to good use. Coordinating the use of resources and counseling are also essential involvements; while time for face-to-face work may be limited, some assistance is given in this way, particularly in small groups and classroom-wide activities.

Working with the Handicapped

Until relatively recently, counselors have not been extensively involved with the handicapped. There are several reasons for this. Many handicapped individuals were in special classes or special schools under the supervision of special-education teachers. And usually school psychologists (particularly for diagnosis), rather than counselors, were involved with these individuals.

The situation has been changed radically by the Education for All Handicapped Children Act of 1975, Public Law 94–142 (Noble and Kampwirth 1979). This legislation requires that handicapped children be put in the least restrictive learning environment, a procedure usually referred to as *mainstreaming*. Furthermore, it necessitates an Individualized Educational Program (IEP) for each child. Other requirements, such as parent consultation, in-service education for staff members, and assessment of the limitations and the potential of handicapped children, cut across areas of counselor expertise.

The law is comprehensive in its definition of the handicapped. Included are the mentally retarded, the learning-disabled, the emotionally disturbed, the deaf, the speech-impaired, the visually impaired, the severe- and multiple-handicapped, and the orthopedically impaired. Thus, the range of individuals with whom the counselor works requires extensive knowledge and the ability to adapt skills to the unique capabilities and patterns of learning of individual pupils.

The counselor works with a team of professionals, such as the school psychologist and the special-education teacher, to assist in diagnosis, planning, and carrying out the individual programs; counsels pupils; consults with parents; and effects changes in staff and pupil attitudes toward the handicapped. Counselors recognize the need for their involvement with the handicapped but also indicate a need for assistance in developing implementation competencies (Lombana 1980).

An Elementary School Counselor Builds a Program

Carolyn Schwartz arrived at West End Elementary School after graduate school specialization in elementary school counseling and two years of work experience in an inner-city school. West End Elementary School is one of ten schools in a city of 50,000 population. It has 932 pupils and a staff of 32. Prior to her employment, the school did not have a counselor. Thus, she felt that she had the opportunity to structure the role according to her preferences.

A brief review of her activities and reactions during the early part of the school year illustrates some important aspects of the counselor's work.

During the preschool workshop meeting, the new counselor outlined her plans for carrying out her responsibilities. The first priority would be to determine needs. For this, she would meet with all the teachers individually to discuss services and get their perceptions of problems, and gather additional information from samples of parents and pupils. Results would be pulled together and presented to principal and faculty, along with a set of high-priority objectives based on needs.

The counselor said she would prepare a weekly schedule of what she would be doing, when, and where. The teachers and principal liked this plan, which sounded efficient and organized. They did not realize that this systematic planning would make the counselor unavailable for a host of other things like cafeteria and bus duty, clerical work, and substituting for absent teachers.

Activities the counselor had not brought up at the meeting were family counseling and work with handicapped pupils. She was still formulating her role in these two areas and felt it best to wait until she had a more crystallized statement to make. A first step will be to meet the school psychologist to develop cooperative working-relationships for services to the handicapped. At the same time, she will review several approaches used in family counseling and select the one that seems most suited to the local situation.

When school started, the counselor began immediately to put her plans into effect. By the end of the second month, she had accumulated enough data to suggest that some of the major problems were as follows:

Pupil Problems

- Don't like teachers. Teachers too strict.
- Don't have any friends here. This is an unfriendly school.
- Don't like this school. Wish I were back at my old school (those who transferred from other schools).
- Don't understand lessons. Failing in courses.
- Some people pick on you. Some people make you afraid.
- Feel left out of everything. Lonely.
- Some pupils are teachers' pets.

There were, of course, many positive comments, and the counselor emphasized them at the start of her summary to the school staff.

Problems Stated by Teachers

- Pupils easily upset and emotionally unstable.
- Pupils who disrupt the classroom and are constantly out of their seats.
- Children mistreated or deprived at home. Come to school without adequate meals and/or with signs of physical mistreatment.
- Hostility. Some children pick on others all the time. Make scapegoats of one or two pupils.
- Bad language. Use of profanity and obscenities.
- Pupils who do not know how to make friends or how to keep them. Some are lonely and isolated pupils.
- Some are very deficient in learning skills, particularly reading. May actually be unable to read or communicate with others verbally.

Problems as Viewed by Parents

- Children do not seem to be learning very much. They don't have any homework.
- Teachers pick on certain pupils, particularly those from minority groups and those from the lower socioeconomic sections of town.
- Racial conflicts. Apprehension about violence by minority-group members.
- Classrooms are too rowdy and unruly. Children say they cannot learn in classrooms because of disturbances.
- Teachers do not insist on good-quality work.
- Teachers insist on too high a quality of work and make many feel stupid.
- Difficult to talk with teachers, or teachers are mainly critical of pupils when conversations are held. Difficult for a parent to get information from the teacher or principal.

In presenting the report to the school staff, the counselor pointed out that this was how various groups *perceived* the situation, and not proof that things were this way.

Success and Failures.   For the first several months since the start of the year, the counselor sums up successes as follows:

- Contact has been made with all the teachers in the school. The counselor feels that she has communicated what she is trying to do. She realizes that some of the teachers are not really enthusiastic and that they will cooperate no more than minimally.
- The needs survey has sensitized many people — parents, teachers, pupils, administrators — to pressing problems in the school. Previously they had had only vague and uncomfortable feelings that something was wrong and that something needed to be done.
- Some successful cases have been worked out in the classroom using planned reinforcement-type activities.

The counselor would be the first to point out certain shortcomings. She does not regard the lack of complete acceptance by teachers as a failure; it is a typical situation and it would be unrealistic to expect 100 percent acceptance, at least this early. She plans much more work in this area in the future, but is realistic enough to accept the fact that she may never find enthusiastic support from all the teachers in the school.

Other problem areas are as follows:

- The public relations function. There has not been enough time to communicate the purposes of the counseling service to parents. (Public relations also includes work with teachers and pupils.) Very little has been done to contact and work with groups of parents and to let the community know more about the counseling program. This is a high-priority item for the rest of the year.
- The peer counseling program is at a standstill. The counselor had hoped to get it started early in the year, but teacher apathy and lack of time have prevented any progress.
- Guidance and counseling demonstrations in the classroom have not been failures, but they have not advanced very far. Most teachers are positive, but so far few visits have been made. This is the counselor's highest-priority item; she intends to set up a schedule of visits and try to get to each classroom or talk with each teacher at least once a month for the rest of the year.
- Accountability is a high priority even though there is currently very little pressure to set up objectives. The administration and teachers do not seem to be especially interested in identifying objectives, but the counselor is certain that by the end of the year questions will arise as to what has been accomplished. She is, therefore, de-

veloping a procedure to involve teachers and parents in establishing objectives and in deciding on how to assess progress.

- Counseling with parents is also an area that the counselor plans to develop. Tentative goals are to help parents in small groups bring out problems, learn how to communicate with children, and build productive strategies for positive discipline. Models such as Parent Study Groups (Dinkmeyer and McKay 1974) and Parent Effectiveness Training, P.E.T. (Gordon 1970), will be used. The counselor is particularly impressed with Dinkmeyer's STEP program, Systematic Training for Effective Parenting (Dinkmeyer and McKay 1976), which the school has recently acquired, and plans to put it to use.

The Middle/Junior High School

A discussion of work in junior high and middle schools reviews guidance in the middle years of school. Of the two types of program for early adolescents, the junior high school type is older and better known. But over the years it has come under fire for imitating senior high school programs, and guidance services have been subjected to similar criticism. The middle school, designed to replace the junior high school, is structuring guidance services that follow the trend from a former vocational-education emphasis to a new balanced program of psychological-personal-guidance and career education (McGlasson 1973, p. 26). More similar to programs on the elementary than the secondary level, the middle school program is developing its own identity.

A discussion of guidance in school years 6 through 9 could very well constitute a separate chapter — work at this level presents unique challenges unlike those in elementary and high school and merits specific attention. This is particularly true for the middle school but also applies for the junior high school. Unfortunately, junior high schools have in some cases tended to follow practices of the senior high school. The middle school guidance program, on the other hand, tends to resemble elementary school services and emphasizes group work, parent contacts, work with teachers to help them improve classroom climate and promote exploration of self and environment. But the middle school does need its own strategies and approaches.

The evolving role of the middle school counselor reflects the needs and problems of pupils at this stage, but not all professional issues are resolved. As Tindall says (referring also to the junior high school): "Many . . . counselors feel they do not have a special identity and place. They often feel they are [in] a smaller high school or a bigger elementary school and feel frustrated with the lack of training and information to perform a good job at the junior high/middle school level" (1976, p. 5). But there is a visible trend to strive for continuity from grades K to 12, giving the middle school the responsibility to promote the development of social, emotional, and physical growth, and assisting with educational planning and career development (Hill 1974, pp. 78–79). Specific goals and objectives need to be developed for this stage. Functions must be expanded beyond traditional individual and small-group assistance to include teaching teachers guidance techniques to help them understand and facilitate the growth of individuals in their classes, and preparing pupils to help their peers (Tindall, 1976, p. 5).

The intermediate school years used to be considered grades 7, 8, and 9, which make up the typical junior high school. More recently the middle school concept has emerged, covering grades 5, 6, and 7 or 6, 7, and 8. The elementary school may thus run from grades 1 to 4 or 1 to 5. In more traditional junior high school organizations, the 6 : 3 : 3 system includes 6 years of elementary school, 3 of junior high school, and 3 of senior high.

Both educational plans are aimed at meeting the needs of early adolescents. Research does not strongly support one over the other, but there are a number of reasons why the middle school concept has caught on and why it is beginning to replace the junior high school. It provides a program specifically aimed at the 10–14-year age group, and is characterized by flexibility and exploratory emphasis rather than the specialization typical of high school. Even the term "middle school" gives the new-type institution an identity of its own (Howard and Stoumbis 1970, p. 205), distinguishing it clearly from the high school. Methods and curriculum content take into account characteristics of the students' developmental stage. Pupils take responsibility for learning (Kohut 1976, p. 8). There is a widening of interests, and individuals are ready, with the security of adult guidance and supervision, to assume more self-direction and self-management (Hansen and Hearn 1971, p. 20). Whether or not the middle school replaces the junior high school and constitutes, as some claim, the major educational development of our times (Howard and Stoumbis 1970, p. 216), it does have features designed to make the transition from elementary to high school a period of growth.

The middle years present the counselor with an opportunity to focus almost entirely on development. Stamm and Nissman put it this way:

> The effective counselor supports the student's fundamental need to assert independence. The counselor must be able to provide the expertise in human growth and development as a supportive service to teachers and parents in understanding the special needs of this age group. Accepting this challenge, the school counselor needs to broaden the scope of his image to include that of staff member involved in all aspects of the learning process. (1979, p. 112)

Change is the underlying theme at this stage. "Children from age 10 through age 15 must endure more changes than they will for the rest of their lives. They are changing physically, sexually, mentally, socially, emotionally; in every way possible" (George 1979).

Even though the developmental emphasis is dominant, existing problems require attention. Middle school pupils have difficulties, among others, with career planning, communication, school achievement, and parent relations. Reports of treatments highlight typical needs and problems. For example, Hillman and Shields (1975) used consultation and positive reinforcement to increase seventh-grade boys' attending behavior and achievement. Deffenbacher and Kemper (1974) used desensitization to reduce test anxiety with a group of eleven boys and eleven girls in the sixth grade. Changes in grade point average (GPA) provided the measure of success. The counseling-group grades improved an average of .42, significant at the .001 level, and the increase was slightly greater for those who were failing prior to counseling. Though a limited study, it does indicate that counseling can reduce test anxiety, and it illustrates a procedure the teacher or counselor can learn in a relatively short time.

Counseling, consultation, the work of peers and paraprofessionals, career education, and work with the handicapped are discussed separately for the middle/junior high school just as they were for the elementary school. These five areas do not make up the total work of the counselor, but they are major responsibilities and thus merit special attention.

Counseling

Both individual and group counseling are widely used at this developmental level. More emphasis is placed on groups, as the social interaction inherent in this approach facilitates growth and problem solution. Verbal interaction can be employed effectively, although play materials such as puppets may be needed to promote expression of feelings. In both individual and group work, the counselor attempts to help pupils develop trust, to communicate effectively, to experience emotions, and to make choices. In group work, activities and exercises that provide the setting for new behaviors to be tried out are particularly useful. Contracts for specific behaviors are frequently employed. While individual work may at times be counselee-directed, there is usually a need for structure. The counselor selects the process to be used, sets up or helps set up ground rules, and keeps the counselee on task. There is, however, a place for free-flowing, unstructured, feeling-oriented counseling for some counselees.

Consultation

The consulting function is as important for the middle/junior high school level as it is for the elementary school. Cole (1979) identifies it as one of the four major components in a model for middle/junior high school guidance. It enables the counselor to affect the pupils' school and home environments in ways to facilitate the accomplishment of the developmental tasks that are particularly critical for these pupils. It is especially important to build a total school atmosphere in tune with needs and growth patterns of this age group. Consultation with parents covers a number of areas, including helping them learn about the growth patterns, needs, and conflicts of this age (American School Counselor Association 1978b).

Peers and Paraprofessionals

Volunteer and paid paraprofessionals can help the counselor expand helping services to include a far greater number of persons than would otherwise be possible. What has already been said about the use of paraprofessionals in the elementary school also applies at the middle/junior high school level, with the addition of more help in exploring career, leisure, and educational opportunities in the community, and program options in the high school. Moreover, peer facilitation can be useful at this level — pupils helping pupils to develop social skills, achieve group acceptance, and clarify attitudes about drug use. Through the consulting approach, counselors help others — pupils, parents, resource persons in the community — serve as paraprofessionals in the school guidance program.

Career Education

For a continuous and effective career education program, this school level must carry forward the awareness phase of the elementary school with an exploratory emphasis. This is the time of life when the young person is becoming more aware of his or her own preferences, capabilities, and other personal attributes and is learning about broad areas of work and education. There are choices to be made about high school courses. There is a vast range of careers to explore in the community. There are experiences to be provided in classrooms to expand students' career horizons and to help them gain insight into their personal preferences. There should be an information center in the school that facilitates such exploration with printed and other types of career and educational information.

As in the elementary school, the counselor's functions are to help teachers plan activities in line with pupils' developmental stages, to work with individuals and groups, and to participate in curriculum building. The counselor's expertise in career development theory and techniques makes him or her the best-qualified person in the school to assist teachers as they design activities and incorporate career education into the curriculum and the total school program.

Working with the Handicapped

Responsibilities that apply to the elementary school cover all school levels; the middle/junior high school counselor also participates in assessment, counseling with handicapped individuals and their parents, providing input into the curriculum-building process, and helping design the individualized educational programs. One of the major functions — one that makes particular use of human relations skills — is encouraging the development of a positive attitude toward the handicapped throughout the school. The attitudes of others, particularly peers, have a tremendous impact on the handicapped person's feelings about self and about belonging, yet many individuals (including some counselors) have an aversion toward those with handicaps and avoid contact with them. This period of the pupil's development is characterized by the numerous tasks that revolve around status in, and acceptance by, the peer group. Thus, the attitudes of others are very significant to the handicapped individual.

A Middle School Guidance Program

An example of guidance in the middle school illustrates some of the principles that have been given. The Don C. Allen Middle School is in a small city with a population of about 200,000. Recently there has been a change from the older 6:3:3 plan, partly because of a new building program, and partly because of financing. It was felt that it would be economical to have grades 6, 7, and 8 together on the same campus without the ninth grade. The new middle school has about 1,000 students and is considered to be a model institution for its age group.

The school has a number of innovative features. Pupils are divided into groups of about 100, each with a team of four teachers. Modular scheduling is used to break down groups according to pupil needs and to provide flexibility. The procedure has not been an unqualified success; teachers complain that it is difficult to keep up with pupils. Some problems have arisen with the learning center for individual, self-initiated work. Some pupils seem unable to accept responsibility for individual study.

Guidance is organized around teaching teams. A counselor is assigned half time to each team, with a full-time guidance coordinator supervising the program. Major activities of the counselors consist of work with individuals and small groups, consulting with parents, and guidance sessions in classrooms on topics like values clarification, career education, personal development, and exploration of feelings. The program has made an acknowledged and distinct contribution, helping the school to facilitate physical, intellectual, and personal growth of pupils.

The counselors have no difficulty convincing others that guidance is an essential part of the middle school program; the position is widely accepted. They have used the role statement published by the American School Counselor Association ("The Unique Role of the Middle/Junior High School Counselor" 1978*b*), which focuses on individual counseling, group counseling, peer counseling, sharing expertise with teachers, giving input to curriculum planning, parental consultation, utilizing community resources, and providing orientation both to the middle/junior high school and to the next educational level. Moreover, they have based their program, as recommended in the ASCA role statement, on the psychological and physiological characteristics of pupils at this developmental stage.

The High School

The counselor in the high school is faced with the conflicts of a rapidly evolving situation. One reason is that this is by far the oldest guidance role in the school; it predates the elementary and middle/junior levels by almost five decades. Thus, patterns of operation, although changing over the years, have tended to crystallize. Conflict has arisen because the demands of society, briefly reviewed in Chapter 1, have produced an almost overwhelming array of new functions for the counselor. Old methods, rationales, and roles no longer suffice. And the newer, more contemporary, and more comprehensive theory-based models for the two previous levels of school have illuminated the paths to new services and new strategies.

As Gysbers (1978) says, guidance today is at a crossroads — there are choices to be made about the direction it should take. This choice is between the traditional role of high school guidance as career assistance, or as "a program which deals with the developmental concerns of individuals as well as their immediate and/or crisis oriented needs" (p. 23). Following this second option leads to an approach that has equal status with the school's educational program and has clearly identified areas of responsibility in the educational process.

Wrenn (1978, pp. 470–487) elaborates on social, economic, and value changes that underline the importance of moving in the developmental comprehensive direction. The changing college population, particularly the influx of older students, new teaching media and styles of learning, and the changing family patterns and birthrates are representative. The counseling profession's response to these trends and demands is discussed in a colloquium (Goldman, Carroll, Forsyth, Muro, and Graff 1978) that analyzes, for all levels of school guidance, counselor identity, sources of support, public reactions, influences, and preparation — all critical factors in the status and progress of the profession. The issues raised and the participants' divergent opinions portray progress and strengths, but more often than not they throw into sharp relief the issues and problems that demand attention.

There are guidelines that clearly delineate what is done by the school counselor, why it is done, and what it should accomplish. The role statement of the American School Counselor Association (1977) identifies personal counseling as a major function. The counselor is also responsible, however, for consultation with staff members, for providing assistance to parents, for helping pupils develop self-understanding, and for informational services, referral, and public relations. The role statement specifies both the relationships and responsibilities of staff, parents, pupils, and the community. The emphasis is on a helping relationship that assists others to understand themselves, make their own decisions, utilize personal and community resources, and carry out plans successfully. Moreover, the assistance is provided by an up-to-date professional who observes ethical standards and who keeps abreast of conditions that call for new services and strategies. While all members of the staff are involved in helping pupils achieve self-understanding, the counselor is a leader in program building as well as a provider of specialized services.

Proactive and preventive themes supporting a developmental approach are particularly noteworthy. In the position statement of the American School Counselor Association, this emphasis is defined as follows:

> Developmental guidance is that component of the guidance efforts which fosters planned intervention within educational and other human development services programs at all points in the human life cycle to vigorously and actively facilitate the total development of the individual in all areas — personal, social, emotional, career, moral-ethical, cognitive, aesthetic — and to promote the integration of the several components into an individual life-style. (1979A, p. 270)

This definition, applying to all school levels, is particularly important as a guideline for the high school in forging a more comprehensive and sequential program.

The same five areas given special attention at the earlier school levels are also particularly significant for the high school. These areas do not constitute the total range of responsibilities of the contemporary counselor, but they are singled out because of their potential for expanding and revitalizing the role of the high school counselor.

Counseling

Traditionally, one-to-one counseling has been used extensively for high school pupils. In recent years, however, use of group counseling has increased tremendously and now is widely practiced. Some classroom-sized group applications are made, but not on the scale of that done in the earlier grades.

At the high school level, assistance through verbal interaction is usu-

ally the major strategy. Pupils at this level can identify and explore feelings, conceptualize, gain insight, and make choices with greater facility
than those in lower grades. High school counselees have had more varied
experiences, and they are often dealing with adult-type problems. Developmental tasks such as forming an identity, establishing some independence from home, and selecting educational and work goals need to be
accomplished.

Counselors use verbal techniques to build conditions that facilitate
self-understanding, growth, and decision-making. These conditions involve empathy, acceptance, and positive regard — the counselee is accepted and understood as a unique person. This facilitative climate helps
both in personal development and in solving problems that already exist.

The high school counselor's work with individuals and small groups
is sometimes complicated by problems entailed in getting pupils out of
classes. At the departmentalized high school level, teachers sometimes
object to releasing pupils, particularly for regular group counseling meetings. Self-referral is also difficult unless the school allows pupils to miss
classes or other scheduled activities in order to see the counselor. For counseling to be available when needed, it is essential that the school have a
policy that enables pupils to leave classes for group or individual appointments.

Willingness to use counseling services is closely related to the question of accessibility. Pupils' attitudes are critical determinants of usage.
Klopfer's (1977, pp. 110–111) study found (as have many others) that high
school pupils tend to view counseling positively. Her study, however, was
designed to test the effects of written and verbal orientations to counseling.
While methods of presenting information did not have different effects,
sex, race, and grade level *did* relate to responsiveness, regardless of presentation method. Underclassmen, girls, and blacks tended to be affected more
positively on a number of variables — the expectation that a counselor will
be helpful, for example. Results suggest that counselors must know how
they are perceived by pupils and should design orientation procedures for
specific target groups.

Consultation

Consulting has been a part of the work of the elementary and middle/
junior high school counselor for some time, but it is relatively new to the
high school. This is partly because of the effects of tradition. Now it is
given increasing emphasis, but extra efforts are needed to make services
known to parents, teachers, and administrators. More often than not, the
counselor will need to meet potential consultees more than halfway to
make consultation a vital part of the program. Examples show how this has
been accomplished in several school settings.

Building good relations with teachers is a productive way to begin. Dent (1974) describes a program in which counselors and teachers were members of a guidance team and worked closely together in handling problems relating to classroom guidance, career education, and communication. At first teachers were apprehensive about a guidance responsibility, but acceptance improved considerably with improved communication between teachers and counselors, and through cooperative activities such as developing career education units and building skills in values clarification. Engelhardt, Sulzer, and Alterkruse (1971) describe how a counselor worked out a reinforcement schedule with a teacher to strengthen positive behavior of a disruptive child. After establishing a baseline for the disruptive behavior, the reinforcement schedule was carried out and the undesirable behavior was sharply reduced. Kuzniar (1973) describes an approach in which a teacher requesting help was first sent to visit other classrooms to observe different classroom climates. The consultant and teacher worked together to develop lists of desired classroom activities, strategies for implementing them, and ways to reward pupil progress. The consultant started where the teacher was, avoided devoting too much attention to negative aspects of her work, and supported her in trying out new experiences. The teacher's changes in classroom management procedures reflected a change in the teacher herself.

The same method can be aimed at the school program or the total system. Psychological education (Ivey and Alschuler 1973b) is one of the newer approaches to using consultation in the curriculum, and it has been employed, for example, for values clarification in the classroom. Consultation with school staff members may be used to improve the climate and operation of the institution (Murray and Schmuck 1972). In such a strategy, the organization is taken to have the problem; consultants use their special skills to improve communication, effect structural changes, and modify norms to lessen dissonance.

Another well-designed consulting approach is the collaborative consultation applications of Carrington, Cleveland, and Ketterman (1978) and of Hansen and Keierleber (1978). In each situation, the consultant helped consultees identify and own their problems, plan solutions, and carry them out. In the first example, Carrington, Cleveland, and Ketterman used a 14-step structured approach to help school guidance departments set goals. In the second, a program was developed to lessen sex-role stereotyping in educational institutions.

Peers and Paraprofessionals

The types of paraprofessionals and peers used in the elementary and middle/junior high school are also used in the high school — community volunteers, paid workers, retired persons, and pupils. They perform an invaluable service in extending the impact of guidance far beyond that which the counselor could do without their assistance.

There are three basic requirements for working with paraprofessionals. First, a professional with a sound background in theory, competencies, and evaluative skills must set up all activities. Second, paraprofessionals must be trained to carry out specific functions (e.g., communication skills); following training, the activity of paraprofessionals must be supervised through staff meetings or individual conferences.

The ASCA position statement (1976) spells out guidelines for the effective use of paraprofessionals to free counselors for counseling and other demanding professional functions. Well-prepared and carefully selected paraprofessionals are used in ways such as the following:

- *for clerical work* (maintaining pupil records, helping pupils to complete information forms, etc.).
- *as resource persons* (e.g., to make contacts with community agencies, build the informational file, prepare materials for counselor use, and operate technological equipment).
- *as helpers in assessment* (e.g., carrying out the arrangements for administering and scoring tests).

Peer counseling programs, increasingly popular in recent years, are defined by the American School Counselor Association as follows:

> a variety of helping behaviors by non-professionals who undertake a helping role with others. Peer counseling includes one-to-one helping relationship, group leadership, discussion leadership, advisement, tutoring, and all activities of an interpersonal helping or assist-nature. A peer counselor refers to a person who assumes the role of a helping person with contemporaries. The term "peer" denotes a person who shares related values, experiences, life cycle, and is approximately the same age. (1979B, p. 273)

The same report emphasizes the importance of the professional counselor's responsibility for the selection, training, supervision, and evaluation of peer counselors. With adequate planning, this type of program can not only help the school and community but can also provide a growth experience for participants.

A number of programs utilizing peer counselors and other types of paraprofessionals have been established. Varenhorst (1974) describes the long-term, extensive peer counseling program at Palo Alto, California, that involved precounseling training and in-service supervision. Both junior and senior high students trained together in groups of ten or twelve in an eighteen-hour course covering communication skills, decision making, counseling strategies, and ethics. Initially, peer counselors were assigned tasks, usually at the request of teachers or counselors. Later, they chose assignments in line with preferences and estimated capabilities, often starting out with elementary pupils. This program has the unique feature of regular practicum supervisory meetings. Specially trained leaders come from various backgrounds, and include parents and school secretaries; many of them are paraprofessionals themselves. Varenhorst points out the difficulty of obtaining evidence of benefits to pupils, but subjective data on effects were positive, and there are plans to offer peer counseling as a credit course. SPICE (Sex Peer Information Center for Everyone), a pupil-operated information center, is part of a pilot program of the Student Family Living Sex Information Project in New York City. The pupils who staff the project centers have undergone extensive training in sex information, self-understanding, and communication skills; the program has had to anticipate and overcome many objections (Welbourne 1975). Volunteers as well as peers are widely used in career information centers (Jacobson 1972, 1975) to help pupils find information, maintain information files, and attract pupils to the service.

The occupational specialist, a position established by the Florida legislature (Panther 1972), has no graduate preparation but may take the place of counselors. There are occupational specialists in about two-thirds of the counties in the state (Raney 1975). Evidence suggests that the program produces positive results and shows it to be well accepted (Myrick and Wilkerson 1976). High school juniors selected by sociometric ratings were trained as peer counselors for group work with freshmen (Schweisheimer and Walberg 1976). The counseled pupils were educable mentally handicapped and others classified as potential dropouts. Peer counselors were trained in a thirty-hour program, and two peer counselors per group worked with pupils for a total of twenty hours. Results showed that attendance for the experimental group improved significantly; decisiveness (as seen, for example, in the intention to complete tasks) was also significantly higher (both at the .05 level, i.e., by chance only five times in one hundred). No differences were found in fourteen other variables. The authors attribute this finding partly to the newness of the program and partly to organizational problems. In another study, the effects of an eight-hour communications-type training program used with high school peer counselors was evaluated. Comparisons were made with an untrained control group on their ability to respond effectively as peer facilitators. Results were assessed by a communications questionnaire, role-playing ratings by trainers, and pupil evaluations in group sessions. Peer facilitators worked with almost the entire high school population in three 1-hour, small-group meetings. Results showed there were differences, significant at the .05 level, between the trained and untrained peer facilitators on written and role-playing evaluations; the differences favored the trained group.

goal setting ⟶

Career Education

As has been pointed out in earlier discussions of career education, this concept, based on career development theory, places all learning experiences in the whole context of a way of life (Hoyt 1975a). Career education covers the life span, from preschool years, and includes acquiring values and competencies and setting goals for both in-school and out-of-school experiences. The spread of this new concept has been rapid. It is being implemented in every state, and most states have held conferences on it for further study (Worthington 1974). Critics, however, find that the concept is based on unwarranted assumptions (Grubb and Lazerson 1975; Kroll 1976), primarily regarding the availability of challenging and suitable work for all in a free-enterprise, technologically advanced society.

Regardless of criticisms, the Association for Counselor Education and Supervision (Hansen 1978) has taken the position that all counselors should acquire knowledge and competency in career guidance and career education. Moreover, career education has been characterized as one of the significant developments of the profession in the past decade (Herr 1980).

There are a number of models of career education for high-school-age individuals. The school-based is the most widely implemented, but work has been done on other innovative ones designed for non-school settings (Tolbert 1980, pp. 286–300). Some idea of the diversity and creativity of programs is illustrated by the following examples.

In the school setting, the Orange County, California, program is a large-scale career education model. Three school districts joined to establish the Orange County Consortium Career Education Project (Hamilton 1975). Starting with a needs assessment of education K through community college, the program directors, assisted by teachers and counselors, introduced career education activities and concepts into the curriculum. Materials were developed for the fifteen occupational clusters identified by the U.S. Office of Education (broad groupings of occupations such as business, clerical, and construction). Teachers were paid incentive stipends to develop units, and part-time "facilitators" were set up in each school to help teachers obtain materials, establish resource centers, and provide career education experience. Counselors have been active in the program from the start and have been quite effective as resource persons. The Skyline Center in Dallas (Marland, Lichtenwald, and Burke 1975) divides its curriculum into twenty-eight clusters, each including several career families, e.g., business and management technology, aeronautics. Pupils' programs, consisting of a balance of academic and occupational education, are based on needs. School policy on curriculum is flexible and enables pupils to change from one cluster to another and to proceed at their own pace.

Evaluations, both large- and small-scale, have supported school-based career education as a viable educational model. Much more developmental and evaluative work needs to be done, however, to assess effects and to develop ways to bring all resources — school, community, employees, and family — together in effective working relationships.

A second model, Experience Based Career Education, (EBCE) uses the community as the learning environment and offers an innovative approach. It is for high school sophomores through seniors who, for one reason or another, do not profit from a traditional school program or who want more experience-related learning. Pupils participate in an individualized program that merges the worlds of work and school; they are based either in their own schools or in community learning centers. Pupils also participate in nonpaid work experiences in real-life settings to prepare for adult life ("EBCE" 1975). The primary setting for learning is the community. An EBCE student may conduct biological research and experiments (for science credit) while exploring a possible career in ecology (for career development credit). Student accountability and performance evaluations are given high priority; results so far are quite positive ("EBCE" 1975, pp. 10–11). More than sixty educational agencies in forty-six states are operating or planning to institute EBCE programs (*Update* 1977).

Other models focus on out-of-school individuals. They are the Home-Based approach (*Career Counseling for Adults: An Overview of the Home and Community Based Career Education Project*, 1975, p. 3) and Rural-Residential model (Worthington 1974, p. 28). These and similar models are examples of innovative community career education programs (Tolbert 1980, pp. 298–300, 303–304).

The pros and cons of career education have been hotly debated. Peterson and Park (1975) point out the critical place of values in career education — career education, though helpful in bridging the gulf between adolescence and maturity, may emphasize the values of the industrial system to the neglect of humanistic ones. Agne and Nash (1973) throw out four cautions: the concept of career education is basically conservative; it overemphasizes the status quo; it promotes an uncritical acceptance of the importance of work to maintain the system; and it develops work skills rather than the person. The concept is under suspicion of serving to divert capable blacks from attending college and exploit them as a labor pool for business and industry (Kearney and Clayton 1973). Labor has received many aspects of the concept with enthusiasm (Sessions 1975) but has expressed concern about narrowing opportunities, viewing individuals only as economic producers, and forcing them into premature occupational choices.

The counselor has a significant role to play in all levels of career education (Tolbert 1980, pp. 314–315). Counseling, consulting, and programming skills — the counselor's unique competencies — are put to use in working with teachers, community members, parents, and employers to build a comprehensive program.

Working with the Handicapped

The provisions of PL 94-142 apply to the high school level as well as to others discussed. While responsibilities such as counseling, assessment, influencing school climate, curriculum input, and participation in planning individualized programs are of continuing importance, there is an increased emphasis on work preparation and placement. Here community agency personnel, particularly rehabilitation counselors, are important team members. The school counselor is in a good position to evaluate work competencies and attitudes and to provide training in job-finding and job-maintenance skills. It is not a matter of developing new counseling skills and techniques, but rather of the adaptation of current ones to the needs of this special population.

George Miller High School

Near the center of town, George Miller High School is the city's oldest school and, with an enrollment of approximately 2,000, its largest. The other two high schools, Eastern and Western, each have student bodies of approximately 1,500. About 20 percent of the pupils are black and come from all over the city, while most of the others are from the sections the school served originally. The school population used to be made up of middle-class, college-bound pupils, but now represents the total spectrum with respect to socioeconomic and intellectual background and motivation, and their number greatly exceeds the 1,600 for which the facilities were designed. Some years ago, before integration, about 80 percent went on to college; the figure today is nearer 30 percent. Another 20 percent do some work at the community college or voc-tech center. Usually about 80 percent of a class entering George Miller choose the college preparatory program and state career goals in high-prestige and professional areas. About 40 percent end up, after several program changes, in the general curriculum. Girls tend to name the traditional female occupations as career goals.

The dropout rate prior to graduation is about 30 percent of the entering ninth graders. A number of other pupils might be classed as potential dropouts — they are frequently late or absent, very deficient in one or more subjects, and do little more than go through the motions of doing their schoolwork. Some staff members refer to the dropouts as "pushouts," because many who leave are subtly urged to by teachers and administration. Having them go is an accepted solution for academic and behavior problems.

George Miller has supportive psychological, social work, and medical pupil personnel services at the district level. There is a guidance director who moves very cautiously. He advises school counselors, "Do the scheduling, even if it gets in the way. You have to start where the people are." Counselors don't agree but have followed the advice, hoping for eventual policy changes. A new director of career education has been appointed to set up new programs in the city's schools; his major efforts have been directed at teachers, as he feels, with some justification, that counselors are less than enthusiastic about career guidance.

The Guidance Staff.   The guidance staff is balanced according to sex and race, a point the principal refers to with pride when affirmative action is brought up. Furthermore, the staff represents a wide range in age, type of preparation, and approach to helping.

Sam Jones, senior in age and experience, has a long history of teaching, administrative work, coaching, and counseling. Certified in guidance through summer college work some years earlier, he feels that he keeps up to date by reading journals, attending local meetings and workshops, and taking occasional evening courses at the university. He has the title of *Coordinator*, which has never been defined and which does not require him to coordinate anything. His approach to guidance and counseling emphasizes one-to-one contact, and he considers himself a good listener who knows how to use the current expressions to communicate.

Mrs. Jayne Joyner also arrived at counseling via a circuitous route, including home economics, teaching, home-demonstration work, and elementary school teaching. She moved into the job through two NDEA (National Defense Education Act) summer institutes where enrollees, supported with generous stipends, devoted their full time to the study of guidance. Her approach could be best described as "come on strong"; she thinks of herself as a positive person. She gives pep talks to pupils, keeps in close contact with parents and teachers, and is on the go all day. This is how she describes her point of view: "Action guidance. That's the way I do it. Go where the kids are. Keep in touch."

Pat Smith and Will Sharp represent youth and modern trends. Pat, a white female, has had no previous work experience of any kind. Will, the young black male counselor, has just completed an intensive preparation program, after a variety of the typical low-level jobs open to minority persons. Like Pat, he has had no teaching experience. Will's Afro, Pat's long hair, and what is interpreted as a permissive attitude toward drugs, sex, gays, dress, and pupil demonstrations have resulted in mild suspicion on the part of older teachers and some parents. They realize that in the two years they have been at the school they have become more like the teaching and administrative staff. This bothers them, but pleases the principal and most of the teachers.

Pat and Will need not worry too much about turning into teaching or administrative types; they have the support of other professionals in maintaining guidance roles.

Two paraprofessionals and a secretary complete the guidance staff. Mary Carter, one of the two paraprofessionals, moved into her job from a secretarial desk in the principal's office.

Two recent developments herald improvement in the guidance program. One has already been mentioned — the superintendent's stated policy to give high priority to improving secondary school guidance. A second is a growing concern among counselors about a number of old and new problems that have recently become more visible: lack of communication in the school, racial incidents, use of drugs, sexual permissiveness, gays coming out, poor achievement, dropouts, and lack of career plans. Teachers have become more vocal with suggestions that guidance workers do something about these problems, and have also been referring pupils more frequently and requesting help with problems. Comments such as "Something needs to be done," and "Guidance counselors don't know what we're up against," are being heard more often.

Specifically, the superintendent has insisted on setting up a district-wide series of monthly meetings to upgrade guidance services. The first, focusing on the question of accountability, was held during the preschool workshop. This meeting made clear that there was only fragmentary information about problems and needs; the superintendent concluded that the first order of business should be a needs survey, a recently popular procedure in his administrative circles. The counselors saw this as a threat rather than as an essential step, but because it was required, plans to conduct the needs survey were developed during the preschool workshop.

In addition to the needs survey, the guidance staff has made an informal evaluation of successes and failures. They feel that registration conferences have helped many pupils think about life plans and given pupils the sense that at least one person in the school takes a personal interest. They believe they have helped many pupils *avoid* drug problems, dropping out, and becoming entangled in other difficulties. While they readily admit having had extensive personal contact with only a few of the 500 assigned to each counselor, they are convinced that there is a spread of effect from the ones they have seen to others; for example, in reducing racial conflicts. They realize that many of these results cannot be documented to demonstrate their effectiveness.

Counselors feel their greatest failures to have been with pupils to whom they could not devote enough time, particularly those who wanted to talk about conflicts at home, career plans, feelings of loneliness, dropping out, and trouble getting along with others. In addition, there were groups of pupils who wanted to improve their ability to communicate, develop self-confidence, or master effective social behavior. Most of these pupils were never reached.

Summary Concepts

Counseling in schools has a developmental emphasis and contributes to the educational process — particularly in affective and life planning aspects. Helping services are based on needs of pupils, and techniques are adapted to their stage of maturity. Even with a developmental emphasis, however, remedial and problem-solving services must be provided. In addition to the developmental focus, counseling services today are characterized by procedures to spread their effects beyond those resulting from direct help to one person. Consulting with teachers and parents is one of the most effective approaches to expanding impacts on both school and community.

Innovativeness and flexibility in both role and approach have become increasingly important for counselors because of responsibility for new populations and programs. Career education is one of the newer programs. The handicapped constitute the most recent population with which counselors are involved. Effectiveness of services has always been a professional concern of counselors, but recently accountability has become an important determinant in funding of services.

Examples of Research on a Topic
Consultation in the Elementary School

Consultation has been highly recommended as an elementary school counselor function. But what does research reveal about its effectiveness? A review of some studies should help to answer this question.

The first studies involve consulting with teachers to help them reduce disruptive classroom behavior.

Mitchell and Crowell (1973) used behavior modification to reduce disruptive behavior in art classes. Randolph and Saba (1973) describe procedures to change behavior through modeling and consulting, in which teachers reinforced desired performance. Briskin and Anderson (1973) show how pupils can be used as contingency managers. Six boys in sixth grade were recruited to reduce disruptive behavior of third graders and were trained in six half-hour sessions to administer *time-out procedure* and to give positive reinforcement for appropriate behavior. (The time-out procedure involved removing pupils from the class when their behavior was disruptive.) The pupil was reinforced if not sent for time-out. Others, including the teacher and principal, provided support and encouragement for the work of the sixth graders. The contingency management approach resulted in a sharp decrease in disruptive behavior. Hiltzheimer and Gumaer (1979) report how a teacher and counselor developed a reinforcement schedule to reduce fighting and other disruptive behavior in an inner-city fourth grade. One indication of results was that in a period of a little over a month fighting episodes were reduced from about 3 in an hour to 3 in 13 days. Pound and Roberts (1978) describe how a counselor and a sixth-grade teacher used self-management procedures to help a pupil increase achievement in arithmetic. One specific outcome was a 60 percent increase in completed assignments.

Consulting with parents has also been studied extensively; some results of investigations are given next. Shaw (1968) found that parents show very positive attitudes toward group consulting and demonstrated good attendance at meetings. Frazier and Matthes (1975) compared two parent-consulting methods and concluded that both affected parents' behaviors and attitudes. The behaviors of children with parents in treatment and children with parents in a control group, however, showed no differences. Guzzetta (1976) reported on the results of a parents' program investigating the effects of a three-week mini-course (six hours of meetings; four of actual group work) on "Communication with Your Teenager." Thirty-seven of the group were mothers; fathers, therefore, were not included in the statistical analysis.

The study involved three treatment groups and a control group. Each group of parents received structured learning in empathy; their children participated as follows:

- Group 1: Children did not participate.
- Group 2: Children participated separately.
- Group 3: Children participated with parents.

Results were as follows:

- All three treatment groups were significantly higher (.01 level) than the control group on two measures of empathy.
- The treatment groups were identical in terms of transfer of training, although parents whose children participated in the training with them, and whose treatment situation therefore most closely resembled real life, attained higher levels of empathy. Guzzetta points out, however, that display of empathy in role-playing episodes designed to measure transfer may not accurately reflect what would happen in the home.

An example of research comparing different consultation methods was reported by Palmo and Kuzniar (1972). The study compared three treatment methods involving group counseling, consulting and counseling, and consulting alone:

Twelve sessions of group counseling for pupils, three at-home consulting sessions with parents, and twelve consulting meetings with teachers.

A control group met with a counselor but did not engage in counseling activities.

Compared with the control group, all treatments groups improved significantly (.05 level). The group that showed the greatest improvement was the parent-teacher consulting group (no. 3). The difference was significant at the .05 level.

While this is a limited number of studies and typically small-scale ones, the results tend to support consultation as a valuable function for the elementary school counselor.

Do you agree with this conclusion? What additional evidence is needed to provide stronger support? How would you apply these results in a school?

Examples of Research on a Topic
Group Work in the Middle/Junior High School

The following studies involve some kind of group work — half a dozen pupils up to class size. As you read them, evaluate the evidence in support of using group approaches with pupils at this level. Also note the variety of needs and problems covered in group work.

The first subtopic involves group work to help middle school girls be less subjected to sex-role stereotyping and to become more androgynous, i.e., to incorporate in ideal selves socially valued characteristics of both genders (Clark-Stedman and Wolleat 1979). A series of eight structured small-group meetings was used. Results showed, however, that the group procedure did not have a statistically significant effect on the experimental group's sex-role attitudes and perceptions. The experimenters' observations of the groups in action provided some subjective evidence to support the position that changes were taking place, although they did not reach the established level of statistical significance with the measuring instruments used.

Group counseling has also been used to improve self-concept. Three studies of this type are summarized next. DeEsch (1979) reports on a structured approach of about a dozen sessions to reduce disruptive behavior by pupils in grades seven through ten. Five to seven pupils were in each group. Self-concepts of group members improved, and disruptive behavior was significantly reduced. Moreover, academic performance improved. In another study (Kaiser and Sillin 1977), self-concept improvement was achieved in a class-sized group counseling program for sixth graders. Meetings involved structured group work followed by counselor-led discussions. Otte and Sharpe (1979) describe a semester-long combined group, classroom, and hands-on occupational experience for seventh-grade inner-city pupils.

Among the gains made by pupils there was a significant increase in self-esteem. (Other results are reported in another section of this review.)

Group work has also been used for practically all of the other problems and needs of pupils at this level. Concerns about death and dying, study skills, divorced parents, stress, test anxiety, and career development are examples. Robinson (1978) describes a "death and dying" unit approximately two weeks long conducted as part of a developmental counseling class for seventh graders. Designed to reduce negative attitudes and anxiety about death, the group was rated as successful by participants. Moreover, positive responses about death and dying increased substantially. Cole (1979) describes a four-session study skills group for middle school pupils focusing on time management that was rated as helpful by both participants and teachers. Wilkinson and Bleck (1977) describe an eight-session group for children affected by divorce (used with upper-elementary-grade pupils) that received very positive evaluations from participants; for example, more than four-fifths said they had learned about their own feelings and those of others. Relaxation training was used with intermediate-grade pupils to promote body awareness and teach tension-coping techniques. Evaluation suggested that coping skills had been increased and that pupils were applying what they had learned (Rossman and Kahnweiler 1977). Systematic desensitization was used with test-anxious sixth graders to help them improve school grades. Results showed significant increases in achievement by pupils, including those who had been failing.

Career development group work covers a variety of areas. Typical ones involve occupational knowledge, modeling, stereotyping, and career maturity. Inner-city seventh graders in the previously reported study by Otte and Sharpe (1979) showed a significant increase in knowledge of preparation and personality traits associated with occupations. A videotaped example of information-seeking behavior influenced ninth-grade girls to significantly increase variety and frequency of career information seeking (Motsch 1980). An eleven-session group counseling program proved to be effective in reducing occupational stereotyping by junior high school girls (Cramer, Wise, and Colburn 1977). Rural junior high school pupils increased significantly on several dimensions of career maturity after five 1-hour sessions with the vocational exploration group, a structured program for exploration of the world of work in terms of needs and competencies (Yates, Johnson, and Johnson 1979).

These reports vary in comprehensiveness and controls; some are small-scale, local studies. Moreover, specific methods and counselor characteristics are not discussed in this brief summary. You do not know all of the techniques, personalities, and procedures involved in the studies. Taken as a whole, however, what could you conclude about the value of group counseling in the middle/junior high school?

In our judgment, this sample illustrates the wide range of applications of group work at this level as well as providing some evidence of the effectiveness of the approach. Do you agree?

What is one way you could use these results in the school?

Examples of Research on a Topic
How Others Perceive the High School Counselor

The way others view the counselor is of considerable importance to the individual worker and the profession. Several studies on these perceptions are briefly summarized next. As you look over these summaries, see if there are consistent patterns or trends. What do the findings suggest for a work role?

Hart and Prince (1970) found that principals and other administrators have similar expectations of counselors. They questioned Utah high school principals on counselors' responsibilities and compared responses with opinions of counselor-educators. The results showed complete disagreement at the .05 significant level even for principals who had taken counseling courses or had worked as counselors. Principals felt that counselors should:

- Be involved in discipline (mainly the principals without counseling courses or experience).
- Carry out clerical duties.
- Give little emphasis to help with personal-emotional problems.
- Share confidential information.
- Be given many duties not related to counseling.

Other studies support these findings of discrepancies between counselors' roles and principals' expectations (Boller 1973; Buckner 1975). But agreement exists on certain specific duties. Maser (1971) found substantial accord on many counseling functions, e.g., helping the potential dropout and assisting pupils to assess strengths and limitations. Most evidence points to administrators' emphasis on clerical, disciplinary, and nonguidance functions.

Teachers in a study by Stinzi and Hutcheson (1972) indicated that they felt:

1. Counselors should support them.
2. Counselors should help teachers with discipline problems, and even administer discipline.
3. Counselors should help with scheduling.

Other research cites lack of agreement over appropriate roles (Riese and Stoner 1969), lack of opportunity to perform counseling functions

(Trotzer and Kassera 1971), and lack of counselors' understanding of their roles (Buckner 1975) as causes of counselor problems.

Pupil attitudes are critical for appropriate use of counseling services. Heilfron's (1960) study, although carried out some years ago, gives results that appear to be relevant if the traditional rather than the developmental role is emphasized.

A group of 107 high school students were given a series of brief case studies describing pupils with various problems and needs and asked to indicate the amount of counseling, including outside referrals, they would consider appropriate. This is a sample case:

"Athlete. A natural athlete. Even at this grade level is the star of all athletic events held in the school. Has average intellectual ability and grades are generally average also. Has pleasing personality."

A total of 14 brief case descriptions were used, including such types as "bright," "failing," and "gauche."

The results indicated that pupils see counseling as a service for the odd and obviously maladjusted, and that no one whose social performance is adequate needs it.

Project Talent data were used to analyze other facets of pupil utilization of counselors. Shapiro and Asher (1972) studied the assistance high school pupils received in planning. Results showed that:

- Pupils from higher-income families are likelier to see counselors.
- Less than half the pupils of both sexes discussed plans with a counselor.
- Girls planning to marry early are less likely to discuss plans with a counselor, even if academic achievement is high.
- Counselors spend little time with counselees from backgrounds unlike their own, e.g., those of low socioeconomic status, the non-college-bound, and those with difficulty in communication.

Leviton (1977) found that only about a fourth of the students in one system would take problems of career indecision and poor work to the school counselor, while fewer than one in twenty-five would seek the counselor's help for personal problems. At the same time, pupils gave high-importance rankings to guidance functions providing career and educational counseling.

Another aspect of perceptions of the counselor is represented by the relative importance of criteria guidance supervisors say they would use in hiring guidance personnel (Beale and Bost 1979). Experience in school counseling, recommendations of the practicum supervisor, and teaching experience in the system were the top three. Work experience outside education was fourth.

Most of these studies were done in specific schools, school districts, or regions, so that results could not safely be generalized to include all schools. While regional and local variations must be considered, the studies suggest themes that appear to have wide applicability. What would you say these themes are? Do you consider them important? How do they affect your attitudes about work in this setting?

Experiential Activities

1. Feelings About Pupils' Problems and Needs

One person or a small group can do this exercise. In a classroom of twelve or more students, subgroups of three or four may be used.

Choose the two types of pupils with problems you would most like to work with and the two you would least prefer. Then take turns explaining why you feel the way you do, as if you were talking to a pupil in one of these groups. Have the others comment on what your statements convey about your work preferences.

Does the experience give you new insights about yourself? Share them with others. (If the exercise is done alone, think through the explanation in your head, but write your new insights down.)

2. Perceptions of the Counseling Role

In a small group, have one member play a counselor (elementary, middle, or high school) explaining the counseling role to a pupil, parents, or teachers. Other group members play the people receiving information.

At the end of the presentation, ask group members to comment on how clearly the role was communicated. Ask the "counselor" to describe how the role play felt.

3. Working with Paraprofessionals

As a counselor in the school, you have been assigned two paraprofessionals to help you in your work. Both have had a brief preparation program in communication skills, administering group tests, and leading group discussions. Their previous experience includes completing high school and some miscellaneous work. They are in their early thirties. One is male (white), the other female (black). Both are anxious about acceptance and do not feel very competent to handle expected tasks. They want helpful supervision and in-service preparation.

Role play your first meeting with your new paraprofessionals. After about five minutes stop and review the session, covering the following questions:

- What were your feelings while talking to the support persons?
- Did you respond to their needs? (e.g., anxiety about acceptance by school staff and pupils, lack of confidence in abilities, desire for on-the-job training.)
- How much responsibility did you give them?
- What would you do differently the next time?

Rotate roles and repeat.

If paraprofessionals are available, include them in the role play, both as themselves and as counselors.

4. Practicing Consulting

Role play a situation in which one person serves as a counselor, another as a consultee, and a third as the "third person." The consultee and third person first decide on the problem. Next, the consultee asks the counselor for help.

If possible, record the consulting session.

After about five minutes, have all three persons review the session. Use these questions as guides: Did the counselor try to understand the circumstances surrounding the problem? How well did the consultation focus on the third person? Was a plan of action formulated?

Suggested Readings

American School Counselor Association. "The Role of the Secondary School Counselor." *School Counselor* 24, no. 4 (1977), pp. 228–234. The updated role statement gives a clear and helpful exposition of counselor relationships and responsibilities.

————. "The Unique Role of the Middle/Junior High School Counselor." *Elementary School Guidance and Counseling* 12, no. 3 (1978), pp. 203–205.

The official role statement covering the rationale, relationships, and functions of the counselor at this level.

————. "The Unique Role of the Elementary School Counselor." *Elementary School Guidance and Counseling* 12, no. 3 (1978), pp. 200–202.

The official role statement that spells out in succinct fashion the part counselors and others play in the school guidance program.

Capuzzi, Dave. "From the Editor's Desk." *School Counselor* 28, no. 3 (1981), pp. 158–159.

A special issue of the *School Counselor* on family counseling. This and the special issue of *Elementary School Guidance and Counseling* (see McComb, listed later in this section) are the best available references on school counselors' involvement in this important new service. The guest editor suggests the sequence for readings in the journal.

Foster, Charles R.; Fitzgerald, Paul W.; and Beal, Rubye M. *Modern Guidance Practices in Teaching.* Springfield, Ill. Charles C. Thomas, 1980.

Helpful for the counselor in understanding how the teacher can participate in the school guidance program. Chapter 1 is recommended for a brief overview. Chapter 2 provides a useful discussion of classroom opportunities for guidance.

Goldman, Leo; Carroll, Marguerite R. (Peg); Forsyth, Louise B.; Muro, James; and Graff, Franklyn A. "How Are We Doing in School Guidance? The Moody Colloquium." *School Counselor* 25, no. 5 (1978), pp. 307–325.

A wide-ranging discussion of issues and trends by leaders in the guidance field. Highly recommended for a broad view of status, direction, and controversial issues of the profession.

Herr, Edwin L. *Guidance and Counseling in the Schools: The Past, Present, and Future.* Falls Church, Va.: American Personnel and Guidance Association, 1979.

A comprehensive review and analysis of major themes of school guidance prepared from the results of a three-phase procedure involving national participation. Part 2, covering the current situation, elementary through high school, is highly recommended reading for this chapter.

Hoyt, Kenneth B. *An Introduction to Career Education.* Washington, D.C.: U.S. Government Printing Office, 1975.

The first comprehensive definition of career education by the U.S. Office of Education. The counselor's role is clearly identified.

McComb, Bette. "Guest Editor's Introduction." *Elementary School Guidance and Counseling* 15, no. 3 (1981), pp. 180–181.

The guest editor's introduction to a special issue on family counseling. This is an emerging area of service for school counselors and one that is given excellent coverage in this issue and the special issue of the *School Counselor* (edited by Capuzzi, listed earlier in this section).

Pietrofesa, John J.; Bernstain, Bianca; Minor, Jo Anne; and Stanford, Susan. *Guidance: An Introduction.* Chicago: Rand McNally, 1980.

Chapter 2, on the pupil personnel team, is recommended. It covers not only counselors but other professionals such as the school psychologist and the school social worker. The functioning of the team is covered on pages 61–76.

Shertzer, Bruce, and Stone, Shelley C. *Fundamentals of Guidance.* 4th ed. Boston: Houghton Mifflin, 1981.

School guidance programs are covered in Chapter 3 and on pages 95–100. Particularly valuable as a review of current models and for employment trends for school counselors.

Stamm, Martin L., and Nissman, Blossom S. *Improving Middle School Guidance.* Boston: Allyn and Bacon, 1979.

Chapter 4 presents an interesting and well-designed model for middle school guidance. Chapter 8 gives a vivid account of the counselor at work.

Walz, Garry R., and Benjamin, Libby, eds. *New Imperatives for Guidance.* Ann Arbor, Mich.: ERIC Counseling and Personnel Services Clearinghouse, 1978.

A valuable and highly recommended reference for all parts of this chapter. The Foreword, pages i–vii, sets the stage with the overview of concerns faced by the profession. All chapters are helpful, but the more appropriate ones are: Chapter 1, "Issues"; Chapter 5, "Rural Schools"; Chapter 6, "Elementary Guidance"; and Chapter 12, "Development and Needs."

Zimpfer, David; Frederickson, Ronald; Salim, Mitchell; and Sanford, Alpheus. *Support Personnel in School Guidance Programs.* Washington, D.C.: American Personnel and Guidance Association, 1971.

A monograph of the APGA Guidance and Counseling Series providing the most comprehensive review available of support personnel. Highly recommended.

Chapter

3

Counselors in the College and University Setting

Student personnel services cover all the nonacademic educational experiences in the institution. Counseling is one, but only one of these services. Counseling has as its specific mission the provision of personal assistance to individuals and small groups. Counselors usually work in a centralized location offering both office and outreach assistance. The overall goal of counseling and the other student personnel services is the development of students.

In the context of student development, counselors carry out a number of helping functions besides counseling. They may, for example, also teach and build programs. Moreover, those prepared to do counseling may also work in other student personnel services, such as financial aid or placement. The purposes and helping focus of such services provide a setting in which the counselor can use professional skills in contacts with students and colleagues.

Counselors at Work

At the beginning of Chapter 1, we had a brief glimpse of college counselor Bill Smith at work. He counsels; he teaches facilitative skills to others; he takes part in program building. He also does a number of other things such as orientating new students, assessing student attitudes, and supervising students preparing to be counselors.

Several other counselors work in the institution's student personnel services but not in the counseling center. Glenn Hansen teaches full time in the counselor education program. Ruth Burns directs a special program for minorities. Although much of her time is devoted to coordinating campus services and resources, she also does a great deal of face-to-face work with minority students. Sandra Givens is an assistant student personnel dean who works with campus social organizations. The facilitative skills she brings to her work are frequently put to good use in helping students establish positive, constructive objectives for their campus social activities and in assisting them to set up and manage these activities.

Not all student personnel workers on the campus are counselors, but a number are. These counselors find that the student development focus of the student personnel program provides an excellent climate for implementing a counseling point of view.

Some Significant Trends in Higher Education

College populations are changing. The 1980s and 1990s are predicted to be a period of decreasing enrollments in four-year colleges, particularly for the young high school graduate. Increased costs and a declining birthrate are two causes of the trend. The community college, however, is enjoying a boom in attendance.

The change is more than quantitative, however. Diverse groups with varied backgrounds and nontraditional attitudes about the methods and purposes of education have begun to appear on the scene. Emerging patterns of values show up on the campus as they have in the larger community. The changing economy affects both the reasons students attend college and their career plans.

Both quantitative and qualitative changes in student populations require new approaches to helping services. These approaches are discussed and illustrated in sections that follow.

Student Personnel Services

The actual range of services that can be classified as supervised by the chief student personnel office extends far beyond counseling per se. These areas are classified by Pinsky and Marks (1980) as including: admissions and records, counseling services, health services, financial aid services, and placement services. With few exceptions, students, faculty members, and academic administrators tend to agree that these are important services for the university. Other evidence suggests that student personnel offices at two- and four-year institutions have somewhat similar responsibilities, particularly in counseling-related and developmental areas, and that there has been a sharp increase in responsibilities since the early 1960s. In career planning and placement, financial aid, and student activities, the degree of responsibility has increased more than 30 percent. During the past 17 or 18 years, in fact, there has been a substantial overall increase in responsibilities (Brodzinski 1980).

It is clear that student personnel work encompasses a wide array of services, some of which are closely related to the counselor's special competencies and some of which are not. In both the four-year and the community college, the emphasis is on services that facilitate student development (Jonassen and Stripling 1977; Nolan and Paradise 1979).

Trends in Student Personnel Services

Student development is the widely accepted rationale today for student personnel services. The meaning of this concept is of paramount importance to the counselor because it gives direction and purpose to his or her varied tasks. Its importance for rejuvenating helping-approaches in higher education can hardly be exaggerated.

Traditionally, student personnel work has been viewed as providing an array of services, through a "teacher-scholar" (Schmidt 1975) relationship, and as preparation for life (Williamson and Biggs 1975). But a different emphasis has emerged in which the focus is on student development, a model in which the student personnel worker and students are collaborators, and "the student must accept at least equal responsibility with the teacher for the quality of the learning content, process and product" (Crookston 1975, p. 369). It makes sense to assume that one learns democratic content and process in settings where both of these are ways of living and learning.

This student development point of view has several general characteristics that set the tone for campus services:

1. The orientation is developmental.
2. Self-direction is the goal of the student.
3. Students are collaborators in the process.
4. Any one of several theoretical approaches to human development can be used as a framework for implementation. (Commission on Professional Development 1974, p. 74)

In this approach, the content experts — experts on what is to be developed — are the faculty. The process experts are student development specialists; these specialists help students as individuals, as groups, and as organizations to fully develop and gain "increasing mastery of their own self-direction and fulfillment" (Commission on Professional Development 1974, p. 77).

This approach and the foregoing definitions have generated questions and criticisms; clarifications have been suggested. Williamson and Biggs (1975) raise the possibility that a new, flexible, needs-based model such as this might itself become rigid and bureaucratic in time. Parker (1974) points out that this new approach lacks sufficiently specific meaning, goals, and steps to be translatable into programs. He sees the need for a stage theory involving specific tasks to be mastered and appropriate levels for such tasks to be accomplished. Parker and Morrill (1974) argue for specific programming in a proactive student personnel service built on existing and emerging needs of students as alternatives to a global student development model.

The student development approach to college personnel work takes into account institutional influences that affect the student. These influences have been identified as objectives of the institution, size, curriculum, residence hall arrangements, faculty and administration, and student culture (Miller and Richardson 1978). Moreover, conditions today — budget limitations, extended faculty roles, changing views about the monetary values of a college education, and the attraction of competing institutions — tend to necessitate a developmental model attuned to the needs of students enrolled in higher education, including an integration of the student personnel and the academic community (Harvey 1976). Closer relationships with faculty in planning and program development — recognizing that student development is not the exclusive province of student personnel workers — represents the highest level of staff development approach (Canon 1976).

Not only is it suggested that student personnel workers collaborate with faculty in expanding the concept of student development, but it is also recommended that personnel workers move into instructional fields by leading the way in reforming instruction (Nash, Saurman, and Sousa 1976). Utilizing humanistic learning theory, student personnel staff can help faculty to provide meaningful and appropriate instruction for students, particularly the "new learners" who bring nontraditional backgrounds of information and learning styles to the campus. Moreover, the teaching expertise of student personnel workers, "mastered, mostly as a consequence of on-the-job, trial and error training, has been such basic teaching skills as listening, empathy, group leadership, values clarification, intervention techniques, and attending-responding-understanding-acting behaviors" (Nash, Saurman, and Sousa 1976, p. 246). These skills, along with the underlying humanistic psychology, enable the student personnel workers to aid faculty in developing approaches as well as enabling themselves to interact directly with students in a developmental relationship.

There is a wealth of evidence that lends strong support to the student development model for student personnel services. Moreover, there is support for the position that student personnel administrators would like to implement more developmental functions. But, since administrators also wish to implement more nondevelopmental functions, a question arises about the most effective use of limited resources for the greatest possible effect on the college community (Gamsky and Oleshamsky 1980). This issue is one that will have to be dealt with in the years ahead.

Counselors in Student Development Programs

From the discussion of the student development model for student personnel services, it is quite clear that counselors must understand and support the concept and also participate in its implementation as they carry out their diverse tasks. (In later sections in this chapter some specific counselor functions are discussed.) Aside from the more traditional counseling competencies, such as consultation and working with individuals and small groups, the student development counselor will utilize the community-building skills described by Mable, Terry, and Duvall (1977) involving both unity of purpose for the organization and individual development. Counselors facilitate the sharing of goals among community members; the sharing of responsibilities; and the sharing of communications (giving and receiving communications from others in the community). Organizational development (OD) competencies are recommended for implementing the changes that will need to be made, but practitioners should also be knowledgeable about other types of change strategies (Blaesser 1978).

Competencies are discussed in the process-outcome model for the preparation of student development specialists. Spooner (1979) describes how this model helps students develop the skills needed — those already mentioned in the discussion of student development — through the implementation of a model involving experiences in assessment, goal setting, and carrying out change processes with individuals, groups, and organizations. In this process, the student personnel worker assumes the various roles of researcher, consultant, instructor, and administrator. The model portrays the competencies needed, the clients served, and the roles the counselor should be able to assume. Not all counselors will need to use all of these skills, but to be able to participate fully in new approaches to helping on the college campus, mastering them is recommended.

The "New" Student

The terms "new" and "nontraditional" are frequently used in describing changes in college population, particularly during the 1980s. Cross (1980) says the term "new" is frequently used to identify individuals who were underrepresented on campuses during the 1950s. Ethnic minorities, those with low income, women, low achievers, adults (including part-time students), and the handicapped fall within this classification. College attendance by these groups has shown substantial increases, and the future will no doubt involve even greater participation rates.

This is not to imply that all colleges will be crowded with new types of students, that all colleges will be equally affected, or that traditional students will become an insignificant factor in higher education. There will still be a substantial number of traditional students. Although in the late

1960s there were optimistic predictions that the percentage of high school graduates attending college would rise steadily in the next several decades, it dropped from 55 percent at that time to 47 percent in 1979. Moreover, 50 percent of all college students attend college part time, and 48 percent are over 22 years old (Brodzinski 1979).

Campus changes brought about by new needs and demands of traditional students and characteristics of "new" attenders are having, and will continue to have, a profound impact on student personnel services. New models will have to be developed to provide services that proactively attend to all students' expectations and needs. The student development model appears to have the capability of meeting these new demands.

A further look at the characteristics of students throws additional light on the task faced by student personnel workers. Cross (1980) divides the new students into two groups: "New Students" and "Nontraditional Students." Her definitions of these classifications illustrate the problems of colleges and of student personnel services. New students are those that would not be considered good college bets and might not be admitted without special admissions requirements. Regardless of ethnic group or socioeconomic status, they have performed poorly in school and need help in basic academic skills, in motivation, and in learning how to get along in an educational institution.

Nontraditional students are those adults who have had successful educational experiences but who are attending school part time while also working. They require a different kind of assistance from that of new students. The number of nontraditional students is increasing, and as lifelong education grows in popularity in the years ahead, they will be a tremendous influence. Cross (1980) makes the prediction that by the year 2000 there will be a striking resurgence of full-time student enrollment in higher education and that the number of part-time students will also continue to increase.

Adult students, both full and part-time, are a very significant group to consider in student personnel planning. The number is impressive — those 25 years of age and older are estimated to comprise about one third of the national undergraduate enrollment. Moreover, they differ from the 18–22-year-olds in a number of ways: in level of maturity, sense of identity, involvement in work, and goal orientation (Kasworm 1980). Achievement is higher, probably because of self-direction and goal orientation (Von der Embse and Childs 1979). There are other characteristics that should be considered, such as the use of college services and the perceptions of the value of these services. Moreover, usage differs for age groupings of older students; those in their 50s and 60s, for example, often seem to have more reservations than younger persons about using counseling services.

The handicapped constitute another group that needs special services. Federal legislation has paved the way for making classrooms and other facilities accessible to them, but more than structural improvements are needed to make the campus a good learning environment for the handicapped. Acceptance and understanding of these students by staff and students is essential. Moreover, student personnel workers, like their counterparts in schools, need to understand the effects of disabilities and to be able to adapt counseling and other services to the needs of the disabled.

The college population experiences all the trends, problems, and crises present in community life. Student personnel workers are involved with substance abuse, emotional problems, marital and couples conflicts, financial difficulties, minority issues, and conflicts in day-to-day work. Student personnel workers plan for orientation of new students, assist in placing those leaving the institution, set up programs for reentry students, participate in building housing services and establishing regulations, and carry out a host of other responsibilities. The key factor is that each of these services, as well as the total student development program, should be based on the needs of students — new, nontraditional, and traditional.

The Functions of Counselors

One of the major functions of counselors is face-to-face work with individuals and small groups; the term "counseling" covers these activities. But, as is apparent from the previous discussion of the services of the student personnel office and from the definition of the term "student development," the counselor does much more. Activities such as consulting, career guidance, living-learning programs, faculty advising, and peer counseling also make use of the counselor's unique professional talents. Quite often the counseling center is the base of operations for counselors who engage in these varied activities.

The Counseling Center

Counseling centers and counselors who work in them have been in the vortex of currents and pressures that emerged in the early 1960s and that have continued to exert a profound influence. Prior to changes that resulted, counseling center staffs for the most part worked one to one, utilizing a clinical approach with typical, relatively healthy college students to help them with social relations, life plans, institution adaptability, and identification and use of resources. When student unrest erupted in the late 1960s and demands for more relevant college programs were heard, counseling centers began to change. The initial thrust was to move away from the clinical model and to institute remedial, preventive, and developmental programs that included consultation, skills development groups, the training of paraprofessionals, and the use of crisis intervention (Foreman 1977). Further developments, stimulated in part by accountability pressures, have led to more concern with outreach activities, career development, reentry assistance, sex equality, minority problems, and relationship help for couples. Troy and Magoon's survey (1979) of one institution is illustrative of the activities carried out. These are shown in Table 3-1. It is revealing to note that no percentages were given for the following survey items: developmental counseling services, improvement of campus ecology, or development of new personnel resources. The study primarily involved the development of an instrument for analyzing counseling center activities, but its results shed light on the activities of the college counseling center.

What counselors, other campus personnel, and students rate as important for counseling center functions reveals not only what is considered to be appropriate but also opinions of these various groups about degree of appropriateness. According to counselor preferences, the activities shown in Table 3-2 appear to be important in the order given.

In cases where ratings were tied, all functions are given the same ranking. These results are for large institutions (more than 10,000 students); they clearly indicate the importance of individual counseling/therapy, although consultation gets a fairly high rating. Interestingly enough, counseling center staffs, dormitory assistants who work in a coun-

Table 3-1
COUNSELING CENTER FUNCTIONS

Activity	Percentage of Weekly Hours
Counseling — remedial and rehabilitative	30
Administration, maintenance, and development	24
Instruction, training, and supervision (including counseling and supervision)	16
Off-campus professional services (community and professional orgs.)	7
Research	7
Alternative treatment modes	6
Campus consultation	3
Accountability procedures	2

Source: Troy, Warwick C., and Magoon, Thomas M. "Activity Analysis in a University Counseling Center: Daily Time Recording or Time Estimates." Journal of Counseling Psychology 26, No. 1 (1979): 58–63. Reprinted by permission.

Table 3-2
COUNSELOR RATINGS OF IMPORTANCE OF COUNSELING
CENTER FUNCTIONS

Activity	Order of Importance
Short-term counseling/therapy (up to 12 sessions)	1st
Individual personal counseling/therapy	2nd
Group therapy/counseling	2nd
Educational/vocational counseling	2nd
Consultation with residence hall assistants, faculty, etc.	2nd
Supervision of doctoral students	2nd
Counseling/therapy for students with normal personal/social problems	3rd
Study-skills counseling/training	4th
Consultation with administrators	6th
Counseling research	7th
Student development research	7th
Reading instruction	8th
Long-term counseling/therapy (year or more)	9th
Counseling/therapy for students with severe psychological problems	10th
Tutoring for special course	11th

Source: Gelso Charles, Birk, Janice, Utz, Patrick W., and Silver, Anne E. "A Multigroup Evaluation of the Models and Functions of University Counseling Centers." *Journal of Counseling Psychology* 24, No. 4 (1977): 338–348. Reprinted by permission.

selinglike role, and student personnel administrators rated an overall "consultation model" as more appropriate than did students, faculty, and university administrators. Moreover, counselors felt that vocational-educational counseling was highly appropriate even though not done as extensively as they believed it should be.

Community college counseling services, while manned by counselors who need competencies similar to those in 4-year colleges, are oriented to students who differ in many ways from those in the 4-year institutions. Thus, as Young and Harris (1977) point out, counseling in the community college should be interdependent (among students, counselors, and the institution), interactive, proactive, and client-centered. The student development emphasis pervades the counselor's work as he or she anticipates student needs — educational, social, and personal — and plans ways to meet these needs before they become problems (Nolan and Paradise 1979).

Counselors in community colleges may fill more diverse roles than those working in medium- or large-sized 4-year institutions, mainly because of the small size of the community college (Nolan and Paradise 1979). In these smaller colleges, counselors may recruit, provide admissions counseling, register students, work with student organizations, and carry out placement. Miller's (1979) survey of some northeastern institutions reveals that all had a formal counseling service and most gave it the title "counseling center." Typical functions found were academic, career, personal/emotional counseling; transfer counseling; testing; services for the handicapped; help for learning difficulties; crisis intervention; group counseling; services for mature students; and peer counseling.

Litwack's (1978) survey, covering a broader geographical area, gives a similar picture of counseling services. Counseling — career and personal/social — ranked first and second respectively. The next five, in order of responsibility, were: academic advising, testing, orientation, college and community liaison, and admissions counseling. Establishing development programs ranked 15th for current responsibilities and only one point higher for future responsibilities. Counselors are expected to assume increasing responsibility for college and community liaison and group counseling.

It is evident that counseling centers put considerable emphasis on the traditional services of individual counseling and testing, but there is also evidence that more consulting, group, and outreach functions are recognized as important. Certainly more campus-wide developmental services are needed if student development is to be a reality. Miller (1979) suggests that community college counselors may move in the direction of helping faculty provide more effective learning situations, by recognizing that direct services, while essential, may no longer be sufficient.

The same campus-wide impact is considered to be essential for the survival of 4-year college counseling centers (Foreman 1977). Moreover, there is a need for these centers to become income producers (e.g., through acquiring research grants, teaching, conducting workshops, becoming involved in student health programs, and participating in community mental health programs). Some of these functions fit well with a student development approach, whereas others lead to a therapeutic-remedial focus. Preventive and developmental services could also be a substantial part of the mental health functions of the centers.

Consulting and Outreach

As has been pointed out, counselors in the campus counseling center engage in consultation and outreach programs. Other, related roles are those of change agent, ombudsman, and organization development specialist — through each of which the counselor has an impact on the larger environment. The central role is that of the consultant, more often than not involving an outreach approach. Moreover, the consultant is basically a change agent, using his or her influence to improve conditions that in turn contribute to the growth and development of students. The consultant may use organizational developmental strategies to help the institution solve problems and develop more effective operating procedures.

Some illustrations of existing types of consultation underline the importance of this role for the student development approach. "Born Free" (Hansen and Keierleber 1978) is a program designed to reduce sex-role stereotyping in educational institutions. The college counselors, acting as consultants, worked with consultees in the consultees' own environment, helping them to identify, define, and take responsibility for their problems. Second, the consultants helped the staff of the consultee institution plan and implement services for students. Basing their actions on the assumptions that consultees would likely make more use of materials they prepare themselves, the consulting staff assisted consultees in developing aids such as videotapes.

A consultation and outreach approach was used by Domke, Winkelpleck, and Westefeld (1980) to implement proactive consultation with residence hall personnel. A formalized program was developed, commencing with a survey to determine the kinds of consultation residence hall personnel wanted. These data were used in planning interventions. Services were then made known to target groups by contacts and printed material (e.g., a quarterly newsletter). After a contact for assistance was made, there was an effort to identify and define the real need and to agree on goals. Interventions were planned, and choices of strategies were made; the consultation was then conducted and evaluated. In another example, a dyadic model was used to provide consultation in dormitories (Westbrook, Johnson, Hunt, Leonard, Boyd, and McDermott 1978). Counseling center consultants were paired with resident directors for the development of projects. Guidelines for working relationships were established, and steps in the consulting process were defined.

Other examples of actual projects or suggested models show applications to classroom teaching methods, working with the campus environment as the client, and implementing an outreach ombudsman role. Parker and Lawson (1978) describe counselor consultation in helping a faculty match teaching methods with students' learning styles. In another approach, strategies to affect the total campus are suggested — consulting, organization development, and change-agent skills. Assessment might suggest the use of a midsemester break to reduce stress, for example (Conyne, Banning, Clack, Corrazzini, Heubner, Keating, and Wrenn 1979). Chaney and Hurst (1980) point out limitations of the traditional ombudsman role of waiting for complaints and suggest a prevention and growth-producing one that involves four target groups: the individual, the primary group, the associational group, and the institution. The outreach ombudsman could participate in the orientation of new students or involve parents in the solution of a problem.

Consultation is increasingly seen as one of the essential services of the counseling center. It is one of the best ways to bring the center into the mainstream of campus life and to contribute to the student development program.

Career Development

While career guidance has always been one of the mainstays of college counseling, it has typically had low visibility compared with personal and social assistance — the type referred to as therapeutic. It has of course had central importance to counselors who work in the career placement center, but much of the emphasis has been on placement carried out by bringing recruiters and students together.

This picture has changed drastically. Counseling centers now offer career-oriented counseling — individual and group — and quite frequently provide workshops, courses, and special programs aimed at facilitating students' career development. Moreover, many career placement centers, once focusing mainly on job placement in the last year of the students' academic programs, now extend their services downward to offer career development activities to freshmen.

There is broad-based support for increasing the visibility of career guidance and career development programs on the campus. These concepts fit well with the student development approach (Harvey 1976). Career development has accumulated both a theoretical and a research base that serve as guides for programming. The expressed needs of students reflect a concern about preparation for successful coping in a technological society. Ard and Hyder's (1978) study of students in one institution reflects a desire for job-seeking skills and for information about specific careers and gaining self-understanding. In addition, professional associations are giving increased weight to adequate preparation in career development for counselors (Hansen 1978). Technology, such as the use of career guidance computers, has been developed to facilitate the career guidance service. Budgetary factors have also played a part; career guidance is usually viewed as necessary when funds for student personnel services are allocated (Bishop 1979).

Several trends are emerging in response to increased concern about career development. Although there are few examples of what could be called *career education*, specific college-wide programs abound. Parker (1974) describes how a small liberal arts college instituted a broad-scale career development program starting with freshmen orientation and extending through the job-seeking stage. A second trend involves the provision of all kinds of career short-term programs and workshops. The dual-career family workshop reported by Kahnweiler and Kahnweiler (1980) is an example. Students considering a dual-career life-style were offered a three-phase workshop that involved factual information about dual-career families, interaction with models and a dual-career family, and discussion of questions that led students to focus on their own lives.

A third trend — an example of new organizational structures for student personnel services — is to combine counseling and career services (Bishop 1979). To date, only a few institutions report this pattern, but it is one that integrates elements that need to be brought together to make career planning and placement a total developmental process.

Living-Learning Centers

Opportunities for counselors exist in all kinds of campus housing, not only those designated as living-learning centers. These special centers, however, combine housing with planned educational and social programs and aim for the maximum student development possible from this aspect of campus life. Counselors (student personnel with interest and preparation in housing) work as professional staff in housing units, providing counseling, referral to resources such as the counseling center, planning programs, and supervising the work of staff members including student paraprofessionals.

The goals of a living-learning residence hall program illustrate how this type of housing arrangement contributes to the total education process (Buckner 1977).

1. Raise students' levels of educational and cultural awareness.
2. Provide the opportunity to explore educational and career interests.
3. Facilitate informal contacts with faculty and staff.
4. Contribute to development through group interactions and opportunities for leadership experiences.
5. Help plan and engage in productive leisure experiences.
6. Develop a sense of community.
7. Make counseling services available.

Several studies show that the effects of housing educational plans with comprehensive goals have been positive (Buckner 1977) (Magnarella 1979).

Moreover, where a total program does not exist, both in-house staff and those from the counseling center have provided a variety of generally well received programs in such areas as assertiveness training, career development, and sexual and ethnic stereotyping.

Student Advising

College advising has long been viewed by some as scheduling, with perhaps some advice-giving. Now, however, a number of factors have pushed this often neglected function into the limelight and have emphasized its central importance in student development. According to Abel (1980), the reasons for this development are the increased complexity of institutions of higher education, the shrinking enrollments, and the diversity of student populations — new and nontraditional students are just two subgroups that demand more active advising.

In spite of these reasons and in spite of the fact that a modern concept of advising contributes to the student development approach, a study of collective-bargaining agreements between faculty and administration revealed that approximately half of them did not even mention academic advising as a faculty responsibility. Two-year colleges exceeded 4-year colleges in providing remuneration for advising, but 4-year colleges were more likely to describe adviser responsibilities in detail (Teague and Grites 1980).

Academic advising can help students develop positive attitudes toward the institution and can, in the process, decrease drop-out rates. Helping students plan programs, evaluate progress, and identify special learn-

College advising is sorely needed but not always effectively provided.

ing needs are essential features of advising (Abel 1980). Moreover, advisers should be familiar with appropriate campus resources, such as the counseling center, and make referrals when needed.

Delivery systems for advising present interesting and varied patterns (Abel 1980; Verner and Krupka 1980). Some institutions have advising centers staffed by specialists for students in the first two years. Centralized advising staffs are provided by others. In still others, paraprofessionals are used for specific groups, such as undecided students and those needing help with study skills. Institutional housing personnel may serve as advisers for particular aspects of educational and personal concerns.

In order to fulfill the developmental role so important in a student development program, advisers need preparation. Counselors as well as other student personnel workers play an important role in such activities as teaching communications skills and presenting career development concepts (Gordon 1980). Workshops for advisers provided by counselors are well received and improve the quality of help provided (Johnson and Pinkney 1980). Nonetheless, the evaluation of advising and the clarification of the adviser's role as perceived by all concerned does need much more study; these are areas in which student personnel workers can provide an important service (Hornbuckle, Mahoney, and Borgard 1979; Russel and Sullivan 1979).

Peer Counselors in the Student Personnel Program

In many of the preceding paragraphs, peers have been mentioned as members of student personnel services. Peers make up the majority of paraprofessionals at the college and university levels, carrying out specific, supervised functions in everything from computer guidance systems, to how-to-study programs, to orientation and student-group facilitation. They help with outreach, particularly to individuals similar to themselves. Housing makes much use of peers for a variety of activities; for example, hall supervision.

Although peer counselors or peer advisers have been prepared to perform specific tasks, they do not possess the qualifications and preparation of counselor education students who are serving to gain practicum experience. These students are not considered to be "peers" as the term is defined here.

Counselors play a critical role in the training and supervision of peers. Some elementary techniques from all the counselor's areas of expertise can be shared with peers; attending skills, group facilitation, testing, career guidance, technology, and information are examples. Peers are able to learn specific communication skills (Danish, D'Augelli, and Brock 1976). Moreover, there is evidence to suggest that paraprofessionals are more effective if they are facing and successfully coping with situations their clients are encountering (Creaser and Carsello 1979). It is particularly important, however, that specific steps be taken to recognize the paraprofessionals' contributions to the service and to help them in communicating with professional staff members (Heitzmann 1979). Supervision is a continuous process that not only facilitates monitoring the effectiveness of the paraprofessionals' work but also provides them with personal and professional growth experiences.

The varieties of use are illustrated by ongoing programs. Community colleges use peers for specific functions such as freshman orientation, academic advisement, and part-time counseling supervised by the professional staff (Miller 1979). Counseling for a variety of problems is reported for a university setting, with peers preferred over professional counselors for some types of problems (Getz and Miles 1978). Paraprofessionals made regular assessments of the campus environment, collecting data that were used to enhance the attractiveness to students of various campus services (e.g., the college union) (May and Rademacher 1980). In another institution, peer academic advisers supplemented the work of regular faculty advisers, scheduling regular office hours and receiving credit for their work (Gnepp, Keating, and Masters 1980). Students conducted a special summer orientation for new black enrollees, meeting expressed needs not covered in the regular orientation program.

Evidence that may be derived from current campus conditions — reduced financial resources, increased student diversity, need for outreach, importance of a campus-wide developmental approach — indicate that peers have a solid place in the student personnel program. Professional counselors will have major responsibilities for selection, preparation, and supervision of many of the paraprofessionals that serve on college campuses and will play a central role in training involving human relations skills.

Summary Concepts

Student personnel services focus on the nonacademic aspects of the educational program in colleges and universities. Thus, these services should be especially sensitive to the needs, problems, and developmental concerns of students. The student development concept provides a rationale for orienting all services to contribute to the growth of students in self-direction. As changes take place in both the number and type of college admissions, student personnel services encounter new demands and challenges. Counselors, by virtue of their preparation and professional role, are well suited to play a vital part in the student development program. The expanded role of counselors, including consultation, teaching, and programming, is a radical change from the traditional counseling center concept of one-to-one assistance. The human relations, planning, and facilitative competencies of counselors equip them to fill many other positions in student personnel services. The movement of new and nontraditional populations into higher-education settings and the emphasis on student development enhance the need for counselors who possess a wide range of helping competencies.

Examples of Research on a Topic
Perceptions of Student Personnel Services

Perceptions of student personnel services by student, faculty, administration, and student personnel workers are of paramount significance for counselors considering this work setting. As you read the following summaries, what do you understand to be the major perceptions of student personnel work? How do these fit with your own views of this work setting?

Pinsky and Marks (1980) report on student, administration, and faculty perceptions of 10 student personnel services at Iowa State University. (Student personnel workers' perceptions were not included.) Data were collected on importance, quality, and knowledge of provisions of each service. Students, administrators, and faculty agreed on the importance of: admissions and records, counseling, health, housing and food, student activities, and financial aid. Administrators ranked disciplinary services and minority and international student services higher than did students. Students gave financial and placement services their highest ratings; financial aid was also the highest-ranked service in importance by faculty and administration. Both faculty and administration rated the quality of services higher than students did. Knowledge of services by all groups was less than desirable.

Another study (Hendry 1977) assessed students', noninstructional staff's (including student personnel workers), and instructional staff's perceptions of quality of student services at five Alberta, Canada, colleges. A partial summary of quality of services is shown in Table 3-3.

What trends and themes do these studies reveal about perceptions of student personnel services? Do your conclusions have any effects on your attitudes about working in student personnel services? What additional information would you like to have?

Table 3-3

STAFF AND STUDENT RATINGS OF QUALITY OF
STUDENT PERSONNEL SERVICES

Function	Instructors	Noninstructors	Students
Recreational activity	1	7	1
Student counseling	1	2	2
Student advising	5	5	3
Basic skill development	10	9	4
Student registration	12	14	5
Student records	9	15	7
Career information	16	19	8
Basic skill diagnosis	20	10	9
Preadmission information	7	4	10

Source: Hendry, Andrew M., "Student Services in Five Alberta Colleges: A Measure of Quality." *Journal of College Student Personnel,* vol. 18 (1977). Copyright 1977 American Personnel and Guidance Association. Reprinted with Permission.

Experiential Activities

The campus offers an ideal setting for experiential activities for learning about your reactions to student personnel services. Four types of activities are suggested:

1. Simulations

Organize the class into a student personnel service for a real or hypothetical institution and specify services that will be offered. Divide students into groups representing each service. Present a problem or need and ask each group to plan a strategy for handling it. For example, one problem could be a large number of "undecided" students. Another could be students' complaints about advising. A third might be additional services needed by older or minority students.

2. Direct Contact with Student Personnel Services

Visit each of the services on campus and talk with the director and staff members. (It is suggested that small groups visit different services and pool results rather than overloading directors with numerous individual interviews.) Ask about the functions, future plans, rewards, and frustrations of the work. It may also help to find out how the director and staff members arrived at their present positions.

Arrange to spend a day or so in the setting, "shadowing" the staff as much as possible. Try to learn about what happens and to understand the climate and tempo of the work setting. Extended volunteer service may be possible. When the time comes for practicum and intern choices, these experiences will be of inestimable assistance.

3. Panel Discussions

Invite student personnel workers to meet with the class to discuss their specialties. Prepare questions in advance so that important topics will not be overlooked and so that the discussion will not fade out.

4. Surveys of Students

Conduct informal surveys of undergraduate students to find out how important they consider services to be, the services' effectiveness, how much they know about them, and what help they would like services to provide. Use either brief checklists or interviews. This is not a "scientific" poll, but it will provide insight into the consumers' point of view.

Other experiential activities may suggest themselves. For example, invite a group of students — freshmen, minority, older, and others — to meet with the class to present their perceptions of services. Moreover, certain experiences will be more appropriate for specific institutions.

Suggested Readings

Creamer, Don G., ed. *Student Development in Higher Education.* Cincinnati: American College Personnel Association, 1980.

> An in-depth coverage of student development in institutions of higher education. Chapter 1 is recommended for a brief introduction of the concept.

Delworth, Ursula, and Hanson, Gary R., eds. *Student Services.* San Francisco: Jossey-Bass, 1980.

> A comprehensive and vivid portrayal of all aspects of the work of the counselor as well as other student personnel specialists in higher-education settings. Most chapters will be of value as additional reading. Chapter 3, on current trends, is suggested as a start.

Giroux, Roy F.; Biggs, Donald A.; Hoffman, Alan M.; and Pietrofesa, John J., eds. *College Student Development Revisited: Programs, Issues, and Practices.* Rev. ed. Falls Church, Va.: American Personnel and Guidance Association, 1979.

> A comprehensive reference containing reprints of articles from the *Journal of College Student Personnel*. Recommended as a convenient source of readings on topics of current significance.

Miller, Theodore K., and Prince, Judith S. *The Future of Student Affairs.* San Francisco: Jossey-Bass, 1976.

    An excellent reference on newer concepts of student development in higher education. Chapter 1, on the rationale for student development, is recommended.

Ostroth, D. David. "Competencies for Entry-level Professionals: What Do Employers Look for When Hiring New Staff?" *Journal of College Student Personnel* 22, no. 1 (1981), pp. 5– 11.

    The report on a nation-wide survey of employers' preferences of competencies for entry-level student personnel services positions. The results suggest that counselor-type competencies are essential.

Packwood, William T., ed. *College Student Personnel Services.* Springfield, Ill.: Charles C. Thomas, 1977.

    Particularly valuable as an overview of all student personnel services. Chapter 16 is devoted to junior college services. For each service (with a few exceptions), history, definition, organization, programs, personnel, and research are covered.

Warnath, Charles F., ed. *New Directions for College Counselors.* San Francisco: Jossey-Bass, 1973.

    A valuable collection of articles on the counselor's changing role in the higher-education setting. Chapter 1, by Warnath, is recommended as an overview of problems and needed changes.

Chapter
4
Counselors in Community Settings

The most striking development in the counseling profession in recent years is the movement of counselors into community agencies. Masters'-level workers' entry into broad-based community mental health agencies is one example, and is perhaps the most significant of all. The same trend is also apparent for doctoral-level counselors who have not only filled direct-service positions but who have also moved into supervisory and administrative roles.

Counselors work in the many specific programs of the comprehensive community mental health agency where they encounter the entire age-range of psychological problems. They also are employed in a myriad of other services and programs. Major areas are: crisis centers, residential treatment centers, the criminal justice system, business and industry, and private offices. Many of these opportunities are relatively new. For many years, however, counselors have worked in the more traditional services such as employment offices and rehabilitation.

Community counseling services, particularly comprehensive mental health programs, reflect the public's awareness of the need for, and the value of, these facilities. Moreover, state and federal policy affect the shape and extent of services. Regardless of policy changes emanating from state and federal levels, however, extensive community counseling services are almost certain to continue.

Three Counselors at Work

Susan Brown is employed in the outpatient service of a community mental health agency. She has a master's degree in counseling and has taken some additional courses in group and family counseling. She may work with children and adults, but most of her clients are adolescents or older. She likes the community mental health setting both because she finds great satisfaction in working with the different types of persons in need of help and because of the variety of job functions this work involves. For example, she is meeting individually with a number of clients who present problems of emotional immaturity, drug use, and hostility. She is conducting two therapy groups for adults whose interpersonal relations deficiency cause job and family problems. Several of her clients are taking medication, and she has referred them to the staff psychiatrist to see if dosages should be changed. These referrals also call for a conference with the psychiatrist. She has a referral from the local crisis center waiting for her now. Since the crisis center has dealt with the emergency situation, she will take the individual on for regular therapeutic sessions. Later in the week she will hold a family counseling session with a family that she is working with on an ongoing basis. She will also work with a local school on the implementation of Public Law 94-142, the Education for All Handicapped Children Act. This school-agency collaboration involves evaluation of psychological functioning and providing remedial treatment. Several pupils who have been placed in a special class for the emotionally handicapped are now being seen for regular therapeutic sessions at the community mental health center. Other responsibilities of the counselor involve staffings on clients being seen by agency counselors, public relations, evaluation of services, and community consultation.

At the same agency Saul Renner is an outreach counselor who visits homebound clients and families who are unable to come to his office. His work takes him to trailer parks, isolated rural homes, and other out-of-the-way places. Many of his clients are older persons for whom his visit is the major event of the week.

Carol Cooper is a counselor on the staff of a special project for delinquent and predelinquent children and adolescents. She works closely with the local parole officer in identifying clients who have been in trouble with the law. She keeps in contact with school counselors to identify pupils who are truant, failing their courses, and frequently involved in disciplinary problems. Referrals are made by law enforcement personnel, and participation is required of juvenile offenders. The counseling, however, is independent of the parole system. Individual counseling, group counseling, academic tutoring, and home visits are used in the treatment process.

These community agency counselors are only three of the many types that could be described. Their clients and activities provide a small sampling of the varied target populations and procedures used by counselors in community settings.

Counseling Services in the Community

Only a decade ago the concept of community psychology came into existence (Zax and Specter 1974, p. 1). The focus of this approach to helping in the community recognizes the environmental factors that lead to problems and the steps that can be taken to alleviate them; thus the helper, whatever his or her background and preparation may be, actively seeks to analyze conditions in the community, to modify or change destructive conditions, and to enlist the help of organizations and persons to provide assistance. In some ways, community psychology reflects the characteristics of a broad approach to community mental health.

In a sense, the concept of community psychology is similar to that of student development on the campus. Both emphasize positive development, the identification and analysis of social forces that have negative effects, and the planning of interventions to improve the environment.

The significance of the concept of community psychology for counselors is that it leads to functions and strategies that fit well with what the counselor is equipped to do. It moves workers away from the clinical-therapeutic model of waiting for problems to be brought in and allows them to treat one person or a small group of persons at a time. One way of illustrating this point is to refer to the three types of prevention conceptualized by Gerald Caplan from guidelines used in the public health field: primary, secondary, and tertiary prevention (Rappaport 1977, pp. 63–66). Primary prevention attempts to alleviate negative social conditions in the community *before* they can cause problems. Secondary prevention reduces the prevalence of problems through early detection and treatment; it is a wide-ranging effort rather than one that provides help only for those individuals who are already in difficulty. Tertiary prevention is a large-scale effort aimed at individuals who have full-blown emotional problems; with this type of prevention, the total community is improved as problems of these individuals are reduced. This last type most closely resembles traditional remedial assistance, but there is more emphasis on leaving individuals in the community and treating them rather than institutionalizing them.

Further evidence of the value of the concept of community psychology for counselors is illustrated by the parallel model of community counseling formulated by Lewis and Lewis (1977, pp. 3–5). Their concept brings together trends in counseling and psychology to provide a basis for a new counseling role that recognizes helpful and harmful effects of the community, the need for a variety of helping strategies, the importance of developmental and preventive approaches, and a cooperative team effort among helpers. New concepts of helping services are clearly embodied in the community psychologist and the community counselor roles and functions, parallel to similar movements in school and college counseling.

The four facets of community counseling specified by Lewis and Lewis (1977, p. 17) further illustrate functions counselors can perform. They use the terms *experiential* to mean services provided directly to individuals and *environmental* to indicate those that focus on the community. Moreover, experiential services can be intensive, that is, for specific individuals or groups in need of them, or *extensive,* for educational programs for the community-at-large. Environmental programs may also be extensive — involving community change — and intensive — changing the environment of a particular individual or group.

What does all this mean for the individual who is considering work in one or another community setting? First, although it is true that not all counselors in the community carry out the broad roles described here, the trends as exemplified in community psychology and community counseling do point to a wide variety of opportunities in an activist, developmental, broad-based type of work. Second, it underlines the need for a preparation program that not only helps the prospective counselor develop individual and group counseling skills but that also provides preparation for consulting, community action strategies, organizational development, training, and team work with other professionals. A thorough knowledge of the nature of community resources and skill in working with them, in developing helping strategies and making referrals, are also invaluable.

It is clear that the major differences in school, college, and community work is the setting, the persons worked with, the needs encountered — not the helping processes. The model proposed by Lewis and Lewis (1977, p. 3) and illustrated in Table 4-1 is for "communities" that, for example, could be educational institutions as well as areas suggested by the usual meaning of the term *community*. Thus, the key to inventorying your own

Table 4-1
FOUR FACETS OF COMMUNITY COUNSELING

	Extensive	Intensive
Experiential	Educational programs	Creation of self-help and volunteer programs for special populations
	Training in helping skills	
	Assistance to self-help groups and programs	Facing and preventing crises
		Accessible counseling services: volunteer, paraprofessional, and professional
Environmental	Community planning and development	Linkage with a helping network
		Consultation with other helpers
	Community action for change	
		Advocacy on behalf of individuals and groups

Source: Lewis, Judith A., and Lewis, Michael D. *Community Counseling: A Human Services Approach.* New York: Wiley, 1977. Reprinted by permission.

attitudes about this specialization is information about, and experiences in, agencies and services. The following sections describe a number of the more typical work settings, identifying the functions carried out and the clients served.

Users of Community Services

In addition to individuals, users of services may be institutions, organizations, the total community, or parts of the total community. Even so, it is important to look at some types of individual clients who make use of counseling services; client characteristics illustrate many of the kinds of problems and needs that confront the counselor. Later sections of this chapter, which describe settings designed for specific types, suggest additional problems. To round out these sources, this section reviews some general characteristics of typical help seekers.

Some characteristics of clients who contact agencies have appeared consistently in research (Gourash 1978). They tend to be comparatively young, white, educated, middle class, and female. They are usually looking for support in the form of advice, reassurance, and comfort. In general those who seek help had initially turned to the social network (friends, family, relatives, and others the individual knows) and requested professional help as a last resort. The social network serves a number of helping functions, including influencing the individual to seek professional assistance. Social class seems to be disappearing as a factor in determining who requests counseling, although education does continue to be a determinant. Moreover, there has been an increase in the number of help seekers who define a problem in mental health terms. There have been changes, too, in the sources, of help used; the proportion using a mental health professional (e.g., a psychiatrist, a psychologist, a marriage counselor) has increased substantially (Kulka, Veroff, and Douvan 1979).

Other research has suggested that social class differences play a part in individuals' preference for a particular helping approach. Asser (1978) found that the lower the social class, the more likely both males and females were to use didactic assistance (advice, problem solution). Higher-social-class individuals, particularly females, preferred a negotiating style (more like counseling). The implications are that psychological services are used more by higher social classes and that, even if readily available, lower-class individuals would be less likely to request help from those types of services, at least in their traditional forms.

The support network is an important factor not only in help seeking, but also in coping with daily life in the community. It is important for the client to refer himself or herself rather than have someone else do it (Walsh and Melton 1978), yet the network of support can be a significant factor in community adjustment, particularly for chronic patients (Froland,

Brodsky, Olson, and Stewart 1979). Strengthening these networks may be productive strategy for counselors. Compared with the general population, treatment groups' social networks are smaller and show less stability.

The few studies reported here do not constitute a comprehensive description of the clientele served by community agencies. They do, however, identify factors that play a part in facilitating or hindering the use of community counseling services. Although the clientele is growing in size, the potential clientele is much larger. The scope of the services has been expanded by new definitions of emotional problems, so that, as Zax and Specter (1974, p. 14) say, "this broadening has led to a commitment on the part of the mental health field to a staggering high percentage of the general population."

Community Counselors: Employment and Preparation

It is difficult to estimate the number of community counselors at work today. One survey indicates that in 1976 there were approximately 20,500 psychologists and psychological service workers (the latter so identified because of subdoctoral preparation) in public and private mental health facilities (Committee on Health Insurance 1979, pp. 8–9). In addition, during the years 1972–76, the number of full-time positions increased by 62 percent. But these figures do not reveal *how many* of these counselors were in community work, or whether or not the services were community-based. A recent survey reveals that more than 10,000 counselors work in federally funded community mental health centers (*Mental Health Counselor's Fact Sheet . . .* 1980). Although precise counts are not available, it is apparent that a sizable number work in these settings.

A better indication of counselor interest in community work (if not actual employment) is provided by the membership growth of the new American Mental Health Counselors Association, a division of the American Personnel and Guidance Association (APGA) (Breasure 1980, p. 2). Membership in this division, which was not even chartered until the late 1970s is now above 4,000, making this new division already fourth in size in the APGA. All members may not be working in community counseling, but as this division is for mental health, agency, and pastoral counselors, it is likely that a sizable number are.

While community counseling is a new and popular specialty and while many career opportunities are in evidence, more work has to be done to insure that employers understand the capabilities of counselors, that licensure requirements can be satisfied, and that counselor education programs have guidelines for setting up preparation programs. For one thing, community mental health directors do not seem to be aware either of who community counselors are or of what they are qualified to do

(Randolph 1978). In addition, there is not a great deal of evidence that these directors accurately perceive the role of the community psychologist, a situation not limited to administrators of community mental health centers (Randolph 1978; Super 1977).

Preparation programs for community counselors are relatively new, but some substantial progress has been made in identifying needed elements. Numerous programs are already offered, and many institutions have as priority the establishment of a community counseling option. Courses offered tend to be in line with what preparation program directors think should be included, but there are some differences, between what department chairpersons and community mental health center directors rate as important. For example, research, statistics, and career development are given a much lower rating by community center directors than by preparation program chairpersons (Stadler and Stahl 1979). Courses taken by counseling psychologists also differ in some ways from the center directors' recommendations (Banikiotes 1977). There is not as much of the "community psychology" approach in the responses of community mental health directors as one would expect; this is a factor to be reckoned with by community counselors or counseling psychologists who plan to work in community agencies.

One aspect of the preparation program deserving special mention has to do with accountability. Wheeler's (1980b) study suggests that although mental health counselors may be prepared in traditional research and statistical methods, they are lacking in program evaluation skills. Well-designed and well-executed program evaluation may spell the difference between funding and termination of programs. Recent statements of program competencies specify evaluation skills that should be mastered by those in programs approved by the American Mental Health Counselors Association.

Occupational opportunities appear to be available for community counselors in community agency work. Wheeler's (1980b) survey of the membership of the American Mental Health Counselors Association, although completed before the recent sharp increase in this membership, revealed that more than one-third were working in community mental health agencies. Banikiotes' (1977) survey indicated that about one-fifth of counseling psychologists worked in community mental health centers.

In both of these studies, additional community settings employed many counselors, making the total community percentages larger than those given for mental health agencies. Moreover, Banikiotes' (1977) and Stadler and Stahl's (1979) studies suggest that there are few counselors who are unable to find jobs. Data do not show that all those interested in community settings found work in those settings, but it is reasonable to assume that a large proportion did.

Settings for Counselors

These settings for community counselors include: community mental health centers, services for crises or emergencies, institutions for residential care (hospitals, mental hospitals, nursing homes, residential settings for the handicapped, halfway houses), penal institutions, work-placement services, business and industry, and private practice. There is some overlapping in this classification (e.g., community mental health centers may provide other services such as crisis centers). Furthermore, not all community opportunities are covered, among them are: special government projects, housing, recreational facilities for older persons, drug and alcohol centers designed for extended treatment, and pastoral counseling in religious institutions. Those described do provide an overview of potential employment opportunities.

The Community Mental Health Agency

This setting is probably the most comprehensive of all those available in the community in clients, variety of interventions, and specialties represented by staffs. The present concept of community mental health centers has been in effect for almost two decades and may be affected to some degree by federal action on mental health strategies (Herbert 1979). In any case, it appears to be likely that the concept of a comprehensive community mental health program will continue to be central to mental health care plans, although results have not met expectations anticipated when this approach to community mental health was first organized.

Types of Services Provided.   Legislation in the mid-1960s resulted in guidelines for comprehensive community health centers (Rappaport 1977, p. 56). Five services were regarded as essential: inpatient care for those requiring full hospitalization, outpatient service for adults and children, partial care in day or night hospitals, 24-hour emergency services, and consultation and education. Optional, recommended services were: diagnostic services, social and vocational rehabilitation programs, pre- and posthospital care, preparation for mental health workers, and research and evaluation. These guidelines illustrate the broad coverage that centers were to have.

Analysis of Services.   A rundown of the types of services provided gives an idea of the comprehensiveness of programs and the kinds of functions one might perform in this type of agency. A particularly helpful way to look at services is from the standpoint of how well the concept of community psychology is being implemented; Miller, Mazade, Muller, and Andrulis (1978) illustrate implementation by their classification of

Type I, reactive (given after the problem has been recognized), and Type II, proactive (preventive and educative). These types are further broken down by services offered to the individual, the family, and the community (see Table 4-2). A summary of the status and trends in these groupings reveals some interesting facts from the standpoint of the potential community mental health worker.

One very important point revealed by the results shown in Table 4-2 is the proportion of time devoted to individual Type I reactive services; but it is also significant that this proportion has decreased and is expected to decrease even more. Type II, individual services such as growth groups and assertiveness training, show a fairly stable trend.

Work with families, both reactive (such as family therapy, marriage counseling) and proactive (such as parent effectiveness education) show a definite upward trend, with the remedial (reactive) services requiring by far the larger amount of time. Community services (not broken down in terms of reactive and proactive) also show a substantial increase. An example of a Type I reactive community service is helping to relocate workers after a plant closing; an example of a Type II proactive service is improving interagency coordination.

These data give general patterns of activities that agree to some extent with the priorities found by Randolph (1978) in his survey of community mental health centers. The latter study does not reflect the trend toward a broad human services approach shown by Miller, Mazade, Muller, and Andrulis (1978), however. The above discussion does not identify specific services. For a more complete picture of these services, data from the study by Miller, Mazade, Muller, and Andrulis (1978) and one by Bloom and Parad (1978) are particularly helpful.

Table 4-3 shows only the percentage of centers offering specific services and the expected increase or decrease for the next several years. (Note: this list of services is drawn from a total of 53 and is presented to illustrate the variety, not the complete range, of services.)

The listing provided in Table 4-3 does not show all of the activities

Table 4-2
PERCENTAGE OF HOURS DEVOTED TO TYPES OF SERVICES

	Past (3 years ago)	Present	Future (next 3 years, approximately)
Individual, Type I	48.8	41.6	36.0
Individual, Type II	17.5	18.3	17.8
Family, Type I	19.5	21.7	23.0
Family, Type II	4.5	5.7	7.3
Community	9.7	12.7	15.9

Table 4-3
CURRENT AND PROJECTED SERVICES OF COMMUNITY MENTAL
HEALTH CENTERS

Type	Service	Percent Offering	Percent Expecting to Offer in 3 Years
Individual Type I, Reactive	Psychotherapy	93.6	78.6
	Aftercare (with medication)	83.1	71.1
	Halfway houses	24.9	48.6
	Hospitalization	50.3	50.9
	Drug abuse clinics	42.8	46.2
	Programs for child abuse and neglect	30.1	41.0
	Rape counseling	24.3	30.6
	Crisis intervention therapy	82.7	73.4
Individual Type II, Proactive	Personal growth groups	38.2	41.6
	Resocialization programs	52.6	50.9
	Mental health diagnostic screening	88.4	76.3
	Case finding (outreach efforts)	61.3	57.8
	Assertiveness training	20.2	23.1
	Peer group counseling for teens	39.3	37.0
	"Case consultation" to other professionals	86.1	74.0

carried out in a community mental health center, but it does give a picture of the variety and importance of services. Furthermore, the listing does not include data from the original table that reveal phenomenal growth in mental health services in the early 1970s. There is a leveling-off process for many services after a growth spurt in this period. For example, the number of resocialization programs jumped from 26.6 to 52.6 in three years, although that number is expected to decline slightly in the next several years. It is significant to note that many programs for which increases are predicted emphasize outreach, group, and community developmental and preventive assistance.

Bloom and Parad's (1978) study of psychologists' activities in community mental health centers shows that most time is spent in providing clinical and related services — therapy, report writing, staff conferences.

Table 4-3 (continued)

Type	Service	Percent Offering	Percent Expecting to Offer in 3 Years
Families Type I, Reactive	Family psychotherapy	92.5	78.6
	Marriage counseling	87.9	72.8
	Group psychotherapy	81.1	71.7
	School social work services	41.0	33.5
	Day care	40.5	39.7
Families Type II, Proactive	Parent effectiveness training	42.8	52.0
	Group work with Scouts, YMCA, etc.	11.0	16.2
	"Parents without Partners" programs	9.8	20.8
	Family crisis police teams	7.5	27.7
Community	Community education: problems of living, e.g., drug abuse	72.8	63.6
	Facilitating collaboration toward developing interagency programs	63.6	60.1
	Program development consultation to agencies	66.5	61.3

Source: Adapted from Francis T. Miller, Noel A. Mazade, Sally Muller, and Dennis Andrulis, "Trends in Community Mental Health Programming," *American Journal of Community Psychology* 6, no. 2 (1978), pp. 194–195. Reprinted by permission of Plenum Publishing Corporation.

The average hours per week for individual treatment (8–12) was the largest single time-usage. All community activities used an average of only 6.29 hours per week. Psychologists showed considerable variability; for example, the maximum time spent on mental health consultation was 22 hours per week, but the average time was 2.81 hours. The authors point out that although relatively little time was devoted to activities that implement newer concepts of community mental health, the amount of time actually used in this area represents a substantial increase over that in previous years. Moreover, psychologists expressed considerable interest in additional education in community-oriented mental health activities. On the negative side, little time was devoted to research and program evaluation. The little that was done was carried out primarily by the younger psychologists.

Community mental health centers can provide a startling array of counseling services.

Traditional Versus Modern Approaches.   The above surveys give a broad picture of the work of the community mental health center but do not reveal attitudes of counselors about traditional versus more modern emphases. A study by Robin and Wagenfeld (1977) suggests that psychologists who perceive their role as an activist one, such as those who favor indirect services in the community, experience role discrepancy in agencies. While more than one half of the psychologists and other workers surveyed experienced this role discrepancy, it is possible to infer from these data as well as from those presented earlier that many community mental health centers do not embrace a community action approach. Moreover, as the authors suggest, the role problems that exist may be leading to role differentiation in which the more traditionally oriented staff works with severely maladjusted individuals, and psychologists deal with the more global family and community problems in an activist, change-agent approach.

With this overview of community mental health agencies as background, a look at some particular services will help to illuminate the functions of the counselor in this setting.

Organizational Approaches.   Consulting with other community agencies is one of the proactive strategies that community mental health agencies can use to good advantage. Werner (1978) describes how a mental health agency followed a six-level model in helping another agency increase staff skills in such areas as interviewing, case management, and planning and implementing in-service education. Consultation began with consultee agency referrals for addiction. Shortcomings in the way these referrals were made gave mental health center staff members the opportunity to initiate case consultations, first for the clients, then for focus on consultee-staff members' skills. The consultee agency not only developed the skills mentioned as well as others, but it also undertook to deal with emergency problems in the community such as child abuse cases and lack of services for the elderly. The long-term results illustrate how a community mental health agency can effect community-wide changes through consultation.

The organization of a crisis intervention program, aimed at reducing the rate of institutionalizations, is reported by Delaney, Seidman, and Willis (1978). For all requests for hospitalization coming into the office, a team visited the locale of the crisis, such as a bar, a home, or a jail. One of the elements in the process was the development of a therapeutic relationship and an accepting attitude toward treatment. A definite reduction in state hospital admissions resulted.

A number of innovative programs sponsored by hospitals and mental health centers are described by Zax and Specter (1974, pp. 74–78). One is the day hospital, which provides observation of behavior and aids gradual transition back into the community. The resources of the family can also be marshaled for treatment. A second type is the night hospital, which is a haven for the individual who can work but who is not ready to return to the community on a full-time basis. A third example is home treatment services, available on a 24-hour basis, to evaluate and treat the mentally ill. Drugs and psychotherapy are used for treatment.

Miller (1974, pp. 58–61) describes a city mental health center that was formed from a confederation of private agencies that had been providing mental health services. The range of services meets federal requirements for a comprehensive community mental health program. Services are as follows:

1. Emergency services: child and adult.
2. Outpatient services: child and adult.
3. Inpatient and partial hospitalization: child and adult.
4. Rehabilitation services: adult (nondrug), child, and adolescent.
5. Drug treatment services: outpatient and residential.
6. Casework and family counseling.
7. Maternity services for unwed mothers.
8. Telephone suicide prevention service.
9. Home visitation.
10. Community consultation.

11. Education and training.
12. Research and evaluation.

The services of another community mental health center give a more detailed portrayal of the types of activities that may be carried out.

1. *Outreach Program.* This program includes outreach services such as outpatient services for homebound clients, single-contact home visits, and consultation and education in rural areas.
2. *Consultation and Education Program.* This program provides education, consultation, and coordination with all the other divisions; but it is also the major prevention effort for the community. Programs are directed to special target groups as the needs arise.
3. *Adult Clinic Services.* Services offered to those 18 years of age and older include, among others, individual therapy, group therapy, couples and family therapy, mental health evaluations, medication evaluation, and aftercare following psychiatric hospitalization. Consultation with other community agencies and institutions is also provided by this office.
4. *Child, Youth, and Family Services.* Services provided include outpatient group, individual, and family psychotherapy; chemotherapy; and mental health evaluations. Inpatient services are provided by arrangements with local hospitals, and aftercare is supplied by the outpatient service. In addition, a residential treatment program is available for a small group of adolescents, and a summer camp is run for children 12 years of age and under. Consultation and education programs are also provided.
5. *Gerontology Program.* This program offers outpatient services for those 55 years of age and older. Consultation and educational services are also provided. Typical treatments are individual, group, and family therapy. The primary goal of this service is to delay long-term institutionalization of older persons for as long as possible. Both rural and urban groups are served in the day-treatment aspect.
6. *Alcohol Program.* Prevention, education, and treatment are provided for those with problems relating to alcohol use and abuse. An outpatient service supplies psychotherapy, crisis intervention, and chemotherapies. Psychological evaluations and consultation are also part of the service.

This community mental health center also gives practicum and internship experiences for students in counselor education. Staff members in the center serve as consultants and supervisors, focusing on the specific program services.

The comprehensive mental health center, staffed by a variety of mental health professionals and offering an array of services, illustrates the multitude of roles that community counselors can play. Some of the specific mental health services taken up in sections that follow, although closely related to those that are the comprehensive community center, further illustrate the diverse specialties available.

Emergency Assistance Centers

Various types of crisis or emergency assistance services are provided in many communities. In the above discussion of community mental health centers, it was pointed out that 24-hour-a-day emergency services are usually available. Often, however, separate community services are set up to deal with crisis needs. Typical ones deal with suicide prevention, rape, battered wives, drug abuse, alcohol abuse, and runaways; others may be established to meet crises arising in particular communities, such as a large influx of refugees or mass unemployment.

These settings are frequently managed by a counselor, with perhaps several professional staff members, depending on the size of the operation. A crisis center providing emergency and short-term counseling and 24-hour hot line telephone service may have several professional counselors for overall supervision, training, and individual and group counseling. Most of the staff may be volunteers, particularly those manning the telephones. Thus, training is a major counselor responsibility. In addition, teams may operate out of the center to follow up on crisis calls. A high level of skill is essential in dealing with persons in acute emergencies — such as suicidal persons — so professional and highly trained volunteers are essential.

Centers established primarily to assist rape victims are frequently staffed by counselors who not only help the individual with the emotional stresses at the time but also provide support and follow-up (Freiberg and Birdwell 1978, pp. 266–268). Volunteers may also be a part of the staff, and thus training is a counselor function. The effects of rape have been analyzed and counseling approaches have been developed to help the victim deal with the trauma (Capuzzi and Hensley 1979).

Services that include counseling, shelter, and legal assistance have been set up in some communities to assist battered wives. Quite often the individual seeking help is in need of concentrated assistance to deal with self-attitudes and decision making (Heppner 1978).

Drug and alcohol treatment programs are part of comprehensive community health centers, but special emergency programs may be established. A center might be designed to serve on a 24-hour basis for both walk-ins and referrals for drug overdose or acute alcohol problems. Paraprofessionals, trained and supervised by professional counselors, may constitute the majority of the staff. Emergency counseling and referral are standard treatments; in some cases, extended counseling is provided.

Emergency shelters are often required for runaways or for children who, for one reason or another, must be removed from the home. Wheeler (1980a) describes a child shelter in which counselors conduct intake interviews, plan programs for those admitted, work with families on avoiding crises, and coordinate therapeutic efforts with community agencies. A community service of this type not only gives emergency care to children in trouble but also provides preventive assistance for families in the community.

Counselors in Residential Institutions

General hospitals, mental hospitals, nursing homes, institutions for the mentally retarded, and similar settings offer numerous opportunities for counselors. There are great variations among institutions; some make extensive use of counselors, whereas others may offer little opportunity for professional functions.

The mental hospital is often an example of limited use. In some large institutions, the emphasis may be on maintenance aided by extensive use of drugs, with relatively minor and often ineffective efforts devoted to returning patients to the community. There is considerable negative criticism of these types of institutions (Rappaport 1977, pp. 273–274). Reports resulting from the Mental Health Study Act of the early 1960s recommend reducing the number of persons in state mental hospitals. To this end, a number of innovative plans have been developed and tried out with the aim of upgrading hospital therapeutic effectiveness and lowering their population (Rappaport 1977, pp. 274–288; Zax and Specter 1974, pp. 81–112). The "Lodge" program is an example. A reference group was established in the hospital to function as an organized unit within the institution. This group was later returned to the community to function as a unit. Results showed that both the in-hospital and the community phases were effective. Individuals in Lodge groups housed together functioned better in the community, remained in the community longer, and were employed longer than those in the control groups who received traditional aftercare.

Establishing a therapeutic community with older persons in a mental hospital (Gatz, Siegler, and Dibner 1979) involved extensive staff interaction with patients in building competencies for self-care and rehabilitation. While a number of difficulties were experienced — for example, some patients could not keep up production standards for a workshop project designed to bring in funds — staff did provide higher-quality care. The above-described programs illustrate how helpers can use diverse strategies in a mental hospital.

Counselor opportunities in general hospitals have increased in recent years. Veterans Administration hospitals employ counseling psychologists, but special requirements such as licensure must be met (see Chapter 12). There are many other opportunities for working with patients and families. Functions include career planning and placement assistance, consultation for other staff members, and training. May (1977) describes a number of cases for which psychological assistance was requested, such as helping a patient lose weight and working with an amputee who must change occupations because of the loss of a limb. Counseling with the seriously or terminally ill patient is another service that is receiving much-needed attention. This type of assistance may be provided in a hospital setting or in a hospice.

The hospice, a unique setting designed to meet both the medical and psychological needs of the terminally ill, "provides pain relief, symptom control, and emotional support to a person with a disease whose course medical intervention cannot stop" (Cheikin 1979, p. 186). Support is also given to the patient's family by the hospice team of which the counselor is a member. The counselor, as Cheikin (1979) points out, is prepared to deal with the emotional needs of both the patient and the family; this fact, coupled with the counselor's separation from the medical and financial services, makes possible a unique counselor-patient relationship. In addition, consultation and training can be of help to other staff members in dealing with the stress of hospice work (Gray-loft 1980).

Institutions for the mentally retarded may employ counselors to provide group and individual assistance to residents, to help plan programs of activities, and to train paraprofessionals who provide supervision in housing units. Career planning assistance may be needed for residents who work in the community in sheltered workshops or regular employment. Screening, classifying, and recommending assignments for new residents may also be counselor responsibilities. Moreover, counseling services are helpful to families in understanding and accepting the retarded member.

Criminal Justice System

In Chapter 1 there was a brief review of the types of jobs available in penal institutions. Actually, the possibilities in this general area are much more extensive than was indicated. Counselors have skills that can be used in all the components of the criminal justice system — law enforcement, administration of justice, and correctional agencies.

The role of the counselor dealing directly with inmates is fairly traditional. Although evidence of effectiveness of traditional practices is not very impressive, the setting in which the work is done and the typical levels of counselor skills found may very well be inhibiting factors. Those who serve as correctional counselors need preparation for this task as well as basic counseling skills (Page and Shearer 1980). In addition, the needs of specific offender groups (e.g., women) need to be understood (Brodsky 1979). Newer methods show promise of effectiveness (Eckstein 1981; Ross and Gendreau 1980, Ch. 1).

Beyond this the counselor working in the correctional system needs to be a change agent, a consultant, a trainer, and a bridge to the community. Wittmer, Lanier, and Parker (1976) describe a program that helped prison guards develop race relations skills. The program was well-received by participants. A group program, "concept therapy," run by counselor-trained inmate leaders appeared to be very effective in rehabilitating offenders. Effective planning with institutional authority and community contacts for inmates, including a halfway house, job placement, and legal assistance, contributed to the positive results of the project. A rational-behavior type of therapy was found to be helpful in changing basic behavior patterns of inmates in work-release programs. This therapy focuses on behavior in interpersonal relations, money management, and leisure-time activities — all of which show a close relationship to further criminal activity (Smith, Petko, Jenkins, and Warner 1979).

There are other areas in the criminal justice system that offer opportunities for counselors. Establishing positive links between the offender and the free society; that is, community-based corrections such as probation, can be used at any place in the criminal justice process (Dye and Sansouci 1974). Diversion programs provide the opportunity for alternatives to incarceration and may involve counseling as well as other developmental skill-building activities (Jasmine 1974). A program of this type involved a counseling staff in a police department's youth section (Collingwood, Williams, and Douds 1976). The program also includes human relations skills for the police officers. Juveniles who participated in the counseling program showed a much lower recidivism rate than a control group. At least part of the credit for the success of the program was attributed to the fact that professional counselors were employed by the police department.

Lee and Klopfer (1978) underline the need for multiple approaches to helping juvenile delinquents. The CREST Program (Clinical Regional Support Terms), an outreach service for youthful offenders, has revealed that counselors and the court system should work together to decide the assistance each child needs on a case-by-case basis. Help can be any or all five of the following types: adjustment, facilitation, growth counseling, advocacy, and environmental change.

Opportunities for counselors cover the whole range of the criminal justice system. For each type of work, the basic counselor preparation background is essential, but additional preparation, particularly direct experiential involvement in the setting, is essential.

Services for Older Persons

There has been a marked increase in occupational opportunities in programs directed toward the needs of older persons. Quite recently a publication of the American Personnel and Guidance Association described preparation of counselors for this specialty (Ganikos, Grady, and Olson 1980). This is in sharp contrast to the state of the gerontological field given in the fall 1976 special issue of the *Occupational Outlook Quarterly* (1976), which made almost no mention of "counselors." Now counselors serve not only in community mental health agency programs for older persons but also in public housing, in industrial retirement programs, in nursing homes, and in numerous other settings. Counselors also study the needs of older persons, consult with and train helpers including paraprofessionals, and take part in planning comprehensive programs attuned to specific needs.

The counseling of older persons is clearly receiving much more attention than it did in past years. Much more research needs to be done on the effectiveness of various therapeutic approaches (Sparacino 1979), but much essential information is already available; analyses of needs provide guidelines for attitudes about counseling, for example (Blake 1975; Ward 1977).

Nursing homes present an opportunity for a number of counseling or counselor-organized services. In addition to individual and small-group work, counselors develop treatment methods such as reality orientation to reduce confusion (Schwenk 1979). Counselors have also organized programs and arranged for the use of community resources, as in bringing in high school students to interact with older persons (Wallach, Kelley, and Abrahams 1979). Skill training by structured learning therapy has helped older persons (in this case, psychiatric inpatients) learn skills to facilitate social interactions in the community (Lopez 1980). Except in the most custodial type of nursing home, there is a variety of functions the counselor is well suited to provide or manage.

Public housing for the elderly can benefit from the same types of services — counseling, consulting, and training. Stevens's (1973) account of how she developed strategies for assessing needs, getting to know residents, gaining their trust, and bringing in community resources, illustrates important steps for counselors to take in this setting. The problem experienced by the elderly and the value of specific procedures such as assertiveness training are illustrated by Leung and Eargle (1980).

Retirement counseling, although offered in a number of nonprofit settings and agencies, is increasingly made available by business and industry ("In Preretirement Planning Enthusiasm Is Counseling Key" 1979). Programs have been prepared to meet psychological needs as well as those that are financial and health-related (see Chapter 9).

Services for older persons will certainly expand, both in agencies and institutions already doing work in this area and in new settings yet to be developed. Such expansions will provide many new employment opportunities for counselors.

Job Training, Placement, and Rehabilitation Settings

For counselors who prefer to be involved in services that focus on occupational assistance, the community provides a wide range of settings. The major ones were identified in Chapter 1 as the state employment service, state vocational rehabilitation service, CETA (Comprehensive Education and Training Act), and the Job Corps. There are also private employment agencies, but the number of opportunities they offer are quite small compared with the state services.

The state employment service is part of the Federal-State Employment Service System under the Wagner-Peyser Act of 1933. It is the largest employment service in the country today (Fantaci 1973; *Placement Services* 1977, pp. 75–77). One or more professional counselors and a number of other specialists in the agency work with clients. Economic and case-load pressures may affect the time available for counseling that focuses on self-understanding and decision-making, but the emphasis is on a type of assistance that utilizes the counselor's unique competencies: helping the client develop an understanding of abilities, limitations, values; assisting him or her in planning strategies for reaching goals; and facilitating client use of information about the environment and job opportunities in a developmental way. Moreover, the counselor has at hand a sophisticated set of aids that can indicate needed workers in any part of the country.

The Employment Service covers all working ages, socioeconomic levels, and types of handicap. Special emphasis is put on youth programs and assistance for the disadvantaged.

The federal-state rehabilitation program is the largest employer of rehabilitation counselors in the country today. As has been noted, however, professional rehabilitation counselors work in a number of other settings such as hospitals and community centers. In the past, the work has centered on remediation of physical disabilities and placement for those judged to be good prospects for employment. Now, however, the guidelines for who is eligible for services has been broadened so that a greatly increased range of persons may be served, including those with mental handicaps, emotional problems, and drug abuse problems. The goals of rehabilitation are being reevaluated; there is considerable support for including enriched living and enhancement of the client's life and work. The passage of PL 94-142 (education for handicapped children) has opened up new imperatives for cooperation between school and rehabilitation counselors (American School Counselor Association and American Rehabilitation Counseling Association 1979; Riggar and Riggar 1978). All indications are that this is a field that will continue to offer a large number of employment opportunities for counselors.

Industry and Business

Two types of employment opportunities exist for counselors who provide services to business and industrial establishments — counseling and personnel positions within the organization and consulting as a staff member of a private agency. Although neither of these opportunities has offered extensive job opportunities in the past, the in-house employment outlook appears to be promising.

There are several reasons for the changing situation. One (mentioned in Chapter 1) is that as growth in opportunities in the educational sector has slowed, counselors have begun to look elsewhere for suitable work settings. Analysis of the business and industrial settings has resulted in the identification of a number of applications of counseling skills in these settings (Cristiani and Cristiani 1979). There has been an increase in concern about work alienation and a decline in productivity; there is a growing recognition among business and industrial leaders that career development, in addition to the more traditional mental health services (e.g., therapy for alcoholism), has the potential to contribute to worker interest in, and enthusiasm for, the job. Legislation concerning the handicapped, minority-group members, and others has also given impetus to the provision of counseling services.

The career development approach is a comparative newcomer to the scene; there has been a general acceptance of the need for providing therapeutic assistance for some time, although counselors are outnumbered by other professionals in provisions of this function (Lovenheim 1979).

Another reason for the opening up of opportunities in the private sector stems from increased concern about older persons. There has been a steady growth in preretirement assistance ("In Preretirement Planning Enthusiasm Is Counseling Key" 1979; Ullman 1976). In addition, business and industrial organizations have recognized that there are economic and public relations values in programs of this type.

Probably the most significant factor of all in opening the way for counselors to move into business and industry is the increasing professionalization of counselors — the ability to design and execute programs that get at the pressing problems faced by employers. Helping with concerns such as emotional and family problems and alcoholism utilize therapeutic skills (Bentel 1980), but counselor competencies are much broader than skills such as these. The term *human development* is a useful one to indicate a wide range of services, including career development, stress management, communications skills, and training (Knowdell 1980;

Osipow 1979; Cristiani and Cristiani 1979). There is evidence that this broader application of counseling services in business and industry is making some headway, but there should be opportunities for much greater counselor involvement (Griffith 1980; Kladnik 1979).

The consulting route, that is, employment in an outside organization that provides services to business and industry, offers increasing opportunities. In some cases, counselors employed in educational institutions work on a consulting or short-term, in-house basis (Lipsett 1980; Papalia and Moore 1979) or move from education to full-time business employment (Necessary 1979). Others have found employment in consulting firms that provide services, including personnel screening on a contract basis to business and industry. Some of these firms also include placement services for executive-level and specialized scientific and technical personnel. This is a special type of private practice in which the client is an establishment buying services or an individual looking for high-level job opportunities.

Private Practice

The term *private practice* often evokes an image of a counselor ensconced in an office suite, complete with secretary, diplomas, and couch. Clients come in for individual or group treatment, very much as it is often shown on TV. An approximation of this is a reality for some counselors, but the percentage is small. The problems of licensure (see Chapter 12), building a clientele, and overhead have to be dealt with. Moreover, free services drain off some of the potential clients.

Traditional counseling as well as some of the newer approaches, however, give the counselor something to sell to meet critical needs — marriage counseling, assertiveness training, behavior modification, career development, and stress management, to name a few. Contracts may be made with educational, governmental, or private organizations to provide specific services (e.g., assessing occupational handicaps). If and when third-party payments are available to counselors, many new opportunities will emerge (e.g., from health-care programs).

Opportunities in private practice exist if the individual is willing to face the uncertainties involved. As Tanney (1979) says, it takes considerable self-confidence to make the move. Many help seekers choose a private counselor in preference to a free or relatively inexpensive public service; this choice says something about the financial resources of the client and the type of clientele. Furthermore, as new concerns and needs emerge, private practitioners can move in on them promptly and offer services; Edwards and Bloland (1980) describe their private practice for leisure counseling. One approach to starting a practice is for a counselor in a community agency or an educational institution to devote part time to private practice (if employment institution rules allow it) and gradually move into full-time work if the market is adequate.

Summary Concepts

Community services, particularly the comprehensive community mental health agency, offer counselors a fertile new field of endeavor. Some opportunities are limited to those with doctoral-level preparation, but master's-level counselors have comprised the bulk of service providers in agencies and institutions and will continue to do so. Credentialing, particularly licensure, will likely be a critical factor in job accessibility for those at both levels. In a sense, all counselors are community counselors; they recognize and utilize the forces and resources of the individual's environment. Ideally, the community — school, neighborhood, and city — can be changed to promote positive growth. Often, however, the focus must be on the individual with problems and what will help him or her cope with negative conditions. The variety of target populations, the problems that members present, and the needs of communities are so varied that almost any counselor work preference can be met. While direct individual assistance is a significant part of the community task, group work, consultation, training, program building, and supervision of paraprofessionals are growing in importance. These large-effect techniques have the potential to enhance the counselor's impact, particularly for developmental goals. New methods that reach large numbers, that produce results, and that make the most economical use of personnel and material resources are critical for the profession. Accountability is as much, if not more, a factor to be dealt with in the community setting as it is in schools and higher-education institutions.

Examples of Research on a Topic
Who Seeks Help in Community Services?

Research on help seekers of community services and characteristics of areas from which they come reveal patterns of problems and needs that have important implications for counselors who are considering working in this setting. As you read the following summaries, some of which have been given earlier, identify patterns or problems and other client characteristics. (Refer to pages 77–78 for additional details on these studies.)

Those who seek help tend to be younger; female; white; looking for comfort, reassurance, and advice; have first solicited assistance from family and friends; and have come for professional help as a last resort. The social network — family members, friends, and co-workers — are influential in referral. Those who seek help tend to be satisfied with results, although actual positive effects of the assistance may not be clear-cut (Gourash 1978). At one time social class was considered to be an influential determinant (the higher the class, the more likely the use), but this trend is changing (Kulka, Veroff, and Douvan 1979).

The way the problem is defined by the individual has a relationship to help seeking. Those who define their problems in mental health terms are more likely to use professional services. Furthermore, among those so defining their problems, the higher the psychological distress, the more likely they will seek help (Kulka, Veroff, and Douvan 1979).

The kind of help sought also reveals information about clients (Asser 1978). Those of a lower social class (as indicated by education and occupation) tended to prefer a didactic (helper gives instruction, advice; client displays little autonomy) rather than a negotiating approach (client exhibits need for autonomy and takes responsibility for definition and solution of the problem). While males of higher social class expressed a preference for both approaches, those of lower social classes had a clear-cut preference for the didactic. The preferences by social class were more clear-cut for females. No age or racial differences were found.

Surveys of communities' needs for mental health services also suggest some of the characteristics of those who are likely to be clients. For one thing, individuals in high-need areas tend to have a limited and unstable social network; for example, the social network is smaller in size, and there are fewer long-term friends (Froland, Brodsky, Olson, and Stewart 1979). They also tend to be less affluent, in lower-status occupations, at lower educational levels, have lower ratings in quality-of-life factors, are from families showing relatively high instability, and are lower in positive affect (Zautra and Simons 1978).

What general characteristics of help seekers can you infer from these brief summaries? How do you feel about working with clients who have these characteristics?

Experiential Activities

Most communities have many if not all of the agencies and institutions discussed in this chapter. Experiential activities that provide direct exposure to settings, staff functions, and clients will be the most profitable. Role playing and simulation will be useful, but to a lesser degree. The following, in order of least to most contact, are suggested:

1. Role Playing

Select a particular agency and, dividing the class into small groups, assign each group the task of specifying the services that will be provided and the types of clients served.

Process the activity by asking students to share feelings about working in the particular setting and serving the identified target group. Then ask each of the above groups to select the agency or service of most interest to group members.

Next, assign each group the task of describing a hypothetical client. Ask each group to share descriptions with the class. Discuss the suitability of the service for the client.

2. Panel Discussion

Invite representatives of community agencies to take part in a panel discussion about their programs. Include some attention to entry jobs for which class members qualify upon graduation. (It is suggested that questions be prepared ahead of time to insure that important points are covered.)

3. Agency Visits and More Extended Experiences

Ask small groups of students to visit selected agencies and report on their impressions to the class. It is recommended that a list of agencies agreeing to visits be prepared prior to class selections. In addition, it is suggested that questions be formulated prior to visits.

If it is possible, have class members spend a day in agencies of interest, learning as much as possible about the general atmosphere and tempo, staff functions, type of clients and problems they present, and qualifications of counselors. Ask class members to share information and impressions. A volunteer experience, lasting for a week or more, is the most intensive way to learn about the setting and one's reactions to it. Furthermore, this type of experience will help identify one or more agencies for practicum and internship later in the program.

Suggested Readings

Goodyear, Rodney K. "Counselors as Community Psychologists." *Personnel and Guidance Journal* 54, no. 10 (1976), pp. 512–516.

A lucid and helpful discussion, with examples, of how the counselor can provide the three levels of prevention identified in this chapter.

Lewis, Judith A., and Lewis, Michael D. *Community Counseling: A Human Services Approach.* New York: John Wiley and Sons, 1977.

The whole book is particularly useful for learning about counseling in the community. (The concept of community counseling as used here applies to work in any setting.) The author's model of experiential (individual) and environmental (community) services, further broken down into extensive and intensive levels, illustrates community approaches to meet a wide range of needs. Chapter 1 describes the community counseling approach and is a good place to start.

Mann, Philip A. *Community Psychology.* New York: The Free Press, 1978

Chapter 1 gives an interesting and informative account of how the concept of community psychology developed, pointing out social conditions that led to the position that new models and methods were needed in mental health. Discussions of many of the other settings included in this chapter may be found by using the index.

Miller, Donald H. *Community Mental Health.* Lexington, Mass.: Lexington Books, 1974.

A case study of a community mental health service describing users, types of services, and results. Early chapters summarize research on mental health agencies; for example, Chapter 3 contains a discussion of definitions, causes, and treatment of mental illness. Chapter 5 provides a description of the services and service area of the case study center.

Miller, Frank W.; Fruehling, James; and Lewis, Gloria J. *Guidance Principles and Services.* 3rd ed. Columbus, Ohio: Charles E. Merrill, 1978.

Chapter 7 includes brief but helpful descriptions of a number of community counseling settings such as correctional, business and industry, rehabilitation, and employment.

Rappaport, Julian. *Community Psychology.* New York: Holt, Rinehart and Winston, 1977.

An extremely thorough and comprehensive analysis of the concept of community psychology and its various ramifications for services. Chapter 1 on the development of community psychology, is the most useful one as a start. It is suggested that the reader look for other chapters of interest. For example, Chapter 9 contains accounts of innovative programs and studies, and Chapter 10 outlines suggestions for changes in the criminal justice system. Descriptions and evaluations of nearly all the community agencies and institutions discussed in this chapter may be found in the book.

Ross, Robert R., and Gendreau, Paul, eds. *Effective Correctional Treatment.* Toronto: Butterworth and Company, 1980.

Descriptions of a number of programs and studies that illustrate successful work in criminal justice settings. Chapter 1 is recommended as an overview of programs that have had positive results.

Zax, Melvin, and Specter, Gerald. *An Introduction to Community Psychology.* New York: John Wiley and Sons, 1974.

A complete and clear presentation of the concept of community psychology. Chapter 2, on development of the community approach and prevention models, is recommended. Chapter 12 includes discussions of innovative community programs.

Chapter
5
Counseling, Guidance, and Personnel Services: How They Grew

Learning about the development of counseling services helps one appreciate the rich and turbulent past, understand the present, and predict and prepare for the future. This chapter looks back over the past eight or so decades, identifying events, personalities, and social forces that have shaped the profession of counseling as we know it today.

Gaining Insight from a Study of the Past

Counseling and guidance were not always as they are today. Questions may be raised about the development of each aspect; answers to these questions take one back over the 60- or 70-year period of the development of guidance. Why, for example, is guidance considered to be a school function rather than a community-based service as in many European countries that served as models for so much in our educational system? How did the concept originate? Who conceptualized it and what generated its momentum? What are the origins of a developmental emphasis? How did testing become a function of guidance and counseling? What shaped the approaches to counseling that we see today, primarily emphasizing subjective aspects of a person? What gave rise to the present concern about subgroups, accountability, and strategies to spread the effects of guidance?

Questions may also be raised about the development of guidance and counseling services at different educational levels. Why is elementary school guidance different from guidance at the secondary level, and why did it begin so much later? What shaped the approach to guidance in the transitional years between elementary and secondary school? What trends are evident in college personnel work? How did community counseling develop?

Questions such as the above do not constitute an outline for a review of the history of guidance counseling and student personnel work; they do focus attention on the threads in its development and alert the reader to the persons and events that lead us where we are today. They help point to relationships among seemingly disparate events that have interacted to produce a rationale and strategies for guidance and counseling services.

An understanding of history is particularly important for a profession that unlike teaching, law, or medicine, for example, has no official historical identity. Tracing the development of guidance and counseling illustrates the search for an identity that has been and still is a major problem confronting those who work in the field.

The chronological development of counseling services, with the exception of the first 2,000 years, is portrayed in the pages that follow in phases identified by events, major movements, or professional developments.

Organizing the Past

One way of viewing history is to take a chronological perspective and move through time identifying persons, events, and conditions that have led to the present state of affairs. This procedure not only shows the major stages or epochs into which history falls but conveys an understanding of the interactions of the times; for example, how economic conditions influenced the conceptualizations of helping priorities. Not only are the overriding influences of time apparent, but the broadening or dwindling threads running throughout history are apparent.

There are other ways to organize history to promote understanding. One is to use themes (e.g., government assistance, legislation). The development of each theme is traced and its influences evaluated. History thus becomes a set of subhistories. Still another way is to begin with major, highly visible current conditions. One may concentrate on dealing with feelings in counseling, the function of consulting with others, or the types of counselor preparation now in use. There are, of course, other ways of presenting the past, but the three given are the most widely used.

Each method of analyzing history has its unique values. Each facilitates insights for the individual's understanding of his or her profession. The first — chronological — enables one to understand the dynamic interrelationships and sequences of factors, to appreciate how these interrelationships have brought us to the present, and to make inferences about future developments from them.

By use of the chronological approach, a number of major periods may be identified. The period labels used here do not characterize the only influences, but they do reflect major ones that have had a profound impact on the developing guidance movement. These periods are:

- Origins in social reform movement.
- The impact of testing.
- The impact of the depression.
- The new counseling.
- The National Defense Education Act (NDEA) and Guidance.
- Expanding the concept of guidance.
- Counseling at the crossroads.

Following a brief review of the earliest precursors of the guidance movement, these phases are discussed. The events in the major stream reflect contributing factors to all settings; special events in developments in elementary school, colleges, and community mental health agencies are covered in separate sections following the broad historical review. It should be emphasized that each of these special settings has its roots in the mainstream of the development of guidance and counseling.

The First Years

Records show that Egyptian society was concerned with guidance as early as 2500 B.C. (Borow 1964, p. 46). Plato recognized the value to society of differing work for differing abilities (Borow 1964, p. 46; Zytowski 1967). Roman parents helped boys and girls identify capacities through the use of role models and occupational exploration (Meyer 1965, pp. 35, 37). These early efforts reflect an interest in helping youth to plan, choose, and develop.

Events in the past 400–500 years show guidance beginning to emerge as an organized service. Publications became available in the 1400s soon after Gutenberg invented printing. Bishop Rodrigo Sanchez prepared a book on guidance for both secular and religious occupations entitled *The Mirror of Men's Lives.* It was in Latin, the language of scholars, and so probably did not serve the general public (Zytowski 1972). The number of books on guidance increased rapidly during the sixteenth, seventeenth, and eighteenth centuries (Brewer 1942, Ch. 2). Zytowski (1972) identified some 400 that described occupations, but were as much for general information as for guidance. Titles are strikingly different from ours today. A book published in 1575 by a Spanish author, Juan Huarte, is called *The Examination of Man's Wits,* and one published in 1585 by an Italian, Tomaso Garzoni, is entitled *The Universal Plaza of All the Professions of the World.* This book qualifies as the sixteenth-century version of the *Occupational Outlook Handbook,* a U.S. Department of Labor biennial publication, the best-known current reference on careers.

During the 1800s, publications began to appear in the United States. Whittock's *The Complete Book of Trades: or a Parent's Guide and Youth's*

Instruction was, according to Zytowski (1972), the first with a title to indicate it was designed for guidance. Brewer (1942, pp. 21–41) describes a number of books by American as well as foreign authors that provided occupational and leisure guidance.

Much of what is known about early efforts at guidance is contained in publications such as those named above. How these documents were used and the attitudes and goals of the users may only be guessed, but certainly part of the purpose was to help people understand themselves better and gain a more realistic perception of opportunities.

Awareness of Need
for Career Planning Assistance

Conditions around the turn of the century set the stage for the development of guidance. As Aubrey writes, "It arose in the dawning of the 20th Century as one of several movements answering the upheaval and turmoil created by the Industrial Revolution" (1977, p. 288). Leaders emerged to institute and upgrade help for young people faced with the new industrial movement and wanting to live productive lives and escape from poverty and wretched working conditions.

Among these early leaders, George Merrill, Eli Weaver, Anna Reed, and Jesse B. Davis stand out. Each of these early leaders was associated with an educational institution, even though the roots of guidance were in community agencies. Merrill's program in the California School of Mechanical Arts in 1895 included work samples, program selection, placement, and follow-up, but strangely enough, he did not consider his work to be guidance (Brewer 1942, p. 49). Weaver, a teacher and later principal at Boy's High School in Brooklyn, originated a program for placing boys in summer part-time work related to their school programs and provided occupational information in courses. Critics condemned the placement aspect, apparently oblivious of the guidance value of exploration. His book, *Choosing a Career,* was published in 1906, and his approach was widely followed in New York City schools at the time. In many ways his work resembled that of the West Coast leader, Anna Y. Reed. She gave more emphasis to in-school guidance, and her programs reflected methods utilized in business and industry. Both Reed and Weaver operated on the principles of "social Darwinism" (Rockwell and Rothney 1961), believing in evolution through competition and natural selection within the established world-of-work structure.

Jesse B. Davis, like many other early leaders in vocational guidance, exemplified the tenets of the social reform movement. His work was well known; he was a tireless lecturer and teacher, applying the "calling" concept to vocational life in very much the same way as it is used in the ministry and emphasizing work as serving humanity (Rockwell and Rothney 1961). He instituted guidance classes on moral values and occupational study (Miller 1961, p. 150). Davis played a major role in the beginnings of guidance. Shertzer and Stone (1974, p. 22) suggest that counseling may have begun with his ten years as a class counselor helping pupils with educational and vocational problems at Central High School in Detroit. Later, as principal of Grand Rapids High School, he employed counselors to work with pupils from the seventh grade on (Odell 1973; Shertzer and Stone 1974, p. 22).

Other streams fed into guidance, notably measurement and clinical treatment of learning difficulties. Binet, concerned about retardation in French schools, collaborated with Simon to develop a mental ability scale for classifying children (Miller 1961, p. 152). The 1905 scale was revised several times and later introduced into the United States. Louis M. Terman developed the best-known version, the Stanford-Binet Scale. At Columbia University, James McKeen Catell, influenced by German psychologist William Wundt and English biologist Francis Galton (Williamson 1965, p. 64), began work on the measurement of students' abilities. Lightner Witmer established the first psychological clinic for the study of student difficulties at the University of Pennsylvania (Borow 1964, p. 48) and is credited with developing modern concepts of counseling (Williamson 1965, p. 87).

Around the turn of the century, guidance was part of the broad movement of social reform; the movement's social and economic values were combined in schools in a unitary concept of vocational guidance and vocational education. The settlement house movement and the National Society for the Promotion of Industrial Education (NSPIE) were instrumental in shaping guidance and moving it into the schools (Stephens 1970, p. 5). But another influence was at work. While many of the early efforts were directed to introducing guidance as another subject into the curriculum, as Aubrey (1977) points out, it was the beginning of Progressivism in American education instituted by Horace Mann and John Dewey that insured the visibility of guidance in the schools. More pronounced influences of the Progressive Education Movement were to follow, but Aubrey (1977) characterizes Davis as an important example of American Progressivism in education. The ties with vocational education were close at this time; both were considered part of a larger helping strategy; separation eventually came, but at a later date.

Origins in Social Reform Movement

Conditions in urban centers in the early 1900s generated national pressure for wide social reform and set the stage for Frank Parsons's remarkable achievement in formulating the concepts that were the beginnings of present-day guidance (Shertzer and Stone 1974, p. 24). While guidance was not his invention, the establishment of his Vocational Bureau in the Boston Civic Service House was the most significant event in its development in the past seven or eight decades, and his work overshadowed that of his contemporaries.

Parsons was a social reformer whose philosophy of mutualism amounted to gradual socialism. Ahead of his time, he advocated many reforms, such as methods of selecting congressmen, women's right to vote, and a progressive income tax, which have since been realized (Rockwell and Rothney 1961). Parsons's concepts about guidance as revealed through his work and activities are remarkably up to date. Biggs (1963) points out that Parsons emphasized all-around development, continuity of guidance from childhood through adulthood, the need for professionally trained counselors, referral resources, follow-up, and evaluation (early signs of accountability!).

Parsons's personal experiences and the appalling living and working conditions of immigrants, particularly children, fed his zeal for social reform and led to an involvement in helping activities that continued until his death. He lost his job as an engineer in the panic of 1873. His liberal views brought him into conflict with big business, and railroad interests forced him out of his teaching position at Kansas State College in 1899. To effect reform in the industrial system and improve working conditions he became involved in activities of the Boston Civic Service House. He set up what was appropriately called the Breadwinner's Institute and then went on to establish the counseling service known as the Vocational Bureau. In a lecture on the "Ideal City," in which he described the help needed by young people in the choice of a vocation, Parsons developed the rationale for counseling. The talk aroused much interest, and many young people requested interviews with him. By 1907 a plan for a counseling office was prepared, and the bureau opened formally in January, 1908 (Brewer 1942, p. 59). It was, in effect, an early example of community counseling.

It is difficult today to visualize the social and economic conditions of Parsons's times. Children started looking for full-time work at age 14. Less than 10 percent of 17-year-olds graduated from high school, even though high school was regarded as the gateway to success. Parsons's efforts were directed at the lowest and most disadvantaged level in society — the 14-year-olds from underprivileged immigrant families, who made up the potential child labor force (Ginzberg 1971, p. 24).

Parsons's counseling principles are in many ways still sound. He advised choosing a vocation rather than merely looking for a job and urged young people to acquire a wide knowledge of occupations so as to avoid falling into the first convenient job opening. He gave considerable weight to expert advice but knew the value of basing predictions on research. Written self-analysis is still in use today, particularly in job search strategies. Parsons dominated the guidance work of his time with his innovative techniques. He died in 1908; his book, *Choosing a Vocation*, was published posthumously in May 1909. The work of the center continued under David Stone Wheeler, and similar guidance services were almost immediately established in Boston schools (Brewer 1942, pp. 65–66).

Some developments in other fields with which Parsons was not acquainted were overlooked, though they were later to have a profound impact on guidance and counseling. G. Stanley Hall brought Sigmund Freud to this country to lecture, and United States psychologists discovered psychoanalysis. The new personality theory and therapy had far-flung repercussions, affecting institutions as diverse as the theater and child clinics, but it did not affect school counseling during the next ten or twenty years (Miller 1961, p. 167).

In contrast the mental hygiene movement was getting under way, stimulated by Clifford Beer's book, *A Mind that Found Itself*, his account of a three-year confinement in mental hospitals. His activities led to the organization of the Connecticut Society for Mental Hygiene (Miller 1964, pp. 8–9), which was followed by the establishment of the group that is now known as the National Association for Mental Health. Over the years this organization has been increasingly active in promoting school and community counseling programs (Shertzer and Stone 1974, p. 26) and in drawing attention to affective aspects of guidance.

Aside from Parsons's use of the assessment concept, psychological testing at this time had little direct impact on the school guidance movement. Neither clinical nor group tests were used before World War I. Typically, guidance workers were cautious or negative about testing, and the pronounced effect it was later to have was not yet apparent.

This period of social reform was marked by great strides in guidance organizations and the spread of services into schools. The Boston Vocational Bureau and Chamber of Commerce organized the first national conference in Boston in 1910; its meetings attracted wide interest among employees, employers, social workers, and educators. It was a broadly supported, humanitarian crusade (Miller 1964, p. 5). A second national conference was called in New York in 1912.

The third national conference is of special significance. It was at this meeting, held in 1913 in Grand Rapids, Michigan, that the National Vocational Guidance Association, or NVGA, was founded. (Some thirty years later, it merged with other organizations to form the American Personnel and Guidance Association.) In 1927, the organization's professional publication was given the new name *The Vocational Journal*, which was later changed to *Occupations*, indicating how vocational counselors dominated the APGA.

The Vocational Bureau was turned over to the Division of Education at Harvard University in 1917 and continued to prepare guidance workers under the title "Bureau of Vocational Guidance" (Brewer 1942, pp. 74–75).

Later, and continuing until the 1940s, its work was taken over by the National Occupational Conference, the U.S. Office of Education, and the NVGA (Brewer 1942, p. 75).

During the latter part of this period, guidance was making phenomenal inroads into schools, and a number of city school systems set up programs. Weaver's work in New York spread from coast to coast — from Philadelphia to Los Angeles (Miller 1961, p. 150). The Smith-Hughes Act in 1917, designed to promote vocational education, stimulated interest in placement and follow-up, but its funds could not be used for guidance until later (Miller 1964, p. 7–8). Education had accepted guidance wholeheartedly. In fact, the beginnings of school guidance reflected the concern of Progressive Education for building a more humane and productive life (Cremin 1965, p. 4). But conflicts were beginning to emerge. Barry and Wolf (1957, p. 29) observe that the 1918 Cardinal Principles of Secondary Education furthered the split between vocational guidance and general guidance, even though during and well past this period guidance was viewed as broadly, rather than narrowly, vocational (Miller 1961, p. 151).

The Impact of Testing

The decade of the 1920s witnessed a tremendous growth of measurements of all kinds, stimulated by the unprecedented use of tests in World War I to classify and assign draftees. The confidence generated by the scientific allure of such instruments gave guidance status and respectability and infused its development with new life. But excessive dependence on testing is blamed for blinding guidance leaders to other potentially significant developments.

The time was ripe for a technique with the look of a precise technology, and widespread use had made the public familiar with its instruments. The army Alpha- and Beta-group intelligence tests (the latter for illiterates) were developed through the combined efforts of the Psychological Committee of the National Research Council and the army's Committee on Classification of Personnel (Borow 1964, p. 51). By 1918 almost 2 million persons had been given one of these intelligence tests (Miller 1961, p. 154). The army Alpha and Beta tests were quickly converted into the civilian Otis IQ tests and enthusiastically embraced by the emerging NVGA membership as the ideal complement to Parsons's "self-assessment" emphasis. Brewer credits these activities with having an effect on vocational guidance, although the emphasis of military testing was on selection (1942, p. 9). Input into the guidance movement at this time came from the armed forces, business, and education (Paterson 1938).

Clark Hull's work at the University of Wisconsin on predicting occu-

The expansion of testing arose from the extensive use of tests for personnel classification during World War I.

pational success anticipated modern computer technology (Borow 1964, p. 53). Hull hoped that by the use of tests and job analysis guidance could be made a science of matching men and jobs (Ginzberg 1971, p. 30). His landmark book, *Aptitude Testing,* was published in 1928, but results of his work led him to give up the idea of achieving a job-success prediction system with tests (Williamson 1965, p. 103).

Interest measurement got started late in this period. E. K. Strong published the Strong Vocational Interest Blank in 1927 (Borow 1964, p. 52), following earlier work on interest measurement by James Burt, Bruce V. Moore, and Walter V. Bingham at the Carnegie Institute of Technology (Crites 1969, p. 5). Several approaches to interest measurement grew out of the institute's seminars, but Strong's has been the most extensively studied and used.

Many effects of developments in military personnel work were felt in the postwar years. Assessment instruments, including high school and college achievement tests and cumulative record cards, were made available to schools (Paterson 1938, p. 39), and the Committee on Cooperative Experiments in Student Personnel (established in 1923) of the American Council on Education (founded in 1918) promoted use of the new materials and techniques.

Guidance with a vocational emphasis was spreading rapidly; during this period, it was probably at least taken under consideration by every system in the land. Seventeen large city systems set up programs in addition to those already established (Brewer 1942, pp. 100, 104). Legislation and leaders in the field reinforced the vocational thrust. The Smith-Hughes Act was not to have a clear-cut impact until later, but the Rehabilitation Act of 1918 was eventually placed under the jurisdiction of the Federal Board of Vocational Education (Borow 1964, p. 52). In his book, *The Psychology of Vocational Adjustment* (1925), Harry D. Kitson, a leading counselor-educator, emphasized that guidance is a specialized, professional occupation, and "not just for amateurs" (Brewer 1942, p. 88). He was influential in shaping the nature of both school guidance and the professional preparation of counselors.

Counselors and guidance workers were unaware of the emotional conflicts and tensions of the period, and failed for one reason or another to utilize insights from mental hygiene and psychotherapy (Miller 1964, pp. 8–9). Nor did they make use of the research of industrial psychologists pointing to the importance of workers' attitudes (Borow 1964, p. 367). For example, a significant study that added a new term to the vocabulary of counselors — the Hawthorne effect — was done in an industrial plant. Elton Mayo and a team of Harvard research workers analyzed the relationship of environmental conditions to production at the Hawthorne (Chicago) plant of the Western Electric Company and found to their surprise that the status and recognition of the workers they studied had a greater effect on output than physical surroundings and work scheduling (Miller and Form 1951, p. 50). The term "Hawthorne effect" has come to mean an effect that follows from being part of a study rather than from actual treatment.

Clinical methods for helping individuals were beginning to emerge; child study clinics, developing from the pioneering work of G. Stanley Hall, opened in a number of cities during the 1920s. Their approach emphasized detailed study of individual development starting with the very early years (Shertzer and Stone 1974, p. 24). Vitales began applying clinical techniques to vocational guidance by integrating Witmer's clinical approach with psychological measurement (Williamson 1965, p. 87).

At this time, guidance services were firmly entrenched in schools. These services had a strong vocational and testing identity and had not yet felt the impact of mental health developments.

The Impact of the Depression

Three characteristics of the time from 1929 to 1940 were of particular importance to the field of guidance and counseling. First, it was the period of the teacher-counselor. Second, it witnessed a substantial infusion of federal support for guidance and placement services. Third, the testing-information-giving model was beginning to give way to a more psychologically oriented approach.

Teacher-counselors divided their time between teaching and guidance work, devoting a half day to each. Preparation might be minimal; positions were filled with little regard for qualification. In fact, there was no consensus about personal qualifications, preparation, and duties. As a result of this lack of role distinction and the increasingly complex school curriculum that evolved to service all pupils, administrators tended to define counselors as implementors of school curriculum, which resulted in a multitude of ever increasing clerical tasks. Emphasis was on giving pupils information about occupations; little attention was paid to a clinical approach (Miller 1973, pp. 9–10). The professional counselor, with a background in interview methods, assessment, and mental health, had not yet arrived. There were some attempts to develop strategies for working with the total person, but typically the traditional guidance patterns remained in force; conflicts about new patterns v. traditional ones were still unresolved (Barry and Wolf 1957, p. 32), and ties with vocational education were still strong (Miller 1961, p. 167).

The economic depression caused initial setbacks in guidance, but the nation-wide need for services soon stimulated substantial advances in the profession. Up to about the middle 1930s, there was severe retrenchment, but the long-range effect was marked expansion (Barry and Wolf 1957, pp. 29–30). In 1939, there were 2,286 school counselors employed at least halftime in 1,297 schools in 702 cities in 46 of the 48 states (Odell 1973, p. 151). Brewer lists 24 large-scale programs organized during this period and identifies 22 different titles for guidance workers in 52 departments, with "guidance" being the modal one (Brewer 1942, pp. 104–105).

The depression years witnessed a sequence of federal programs and projects to reduce unemployment; their impact on school guidance varied. The CCC (Civilian Conservation Corps), established in 1933 to provide work for unemployed youth, amounted to a competing educational system, serving about 260,000 young people (Miller 1961, pp. 159–160). Two years later the NYA (National Youth Administration) was established and continued its activities into the 1940s, providing income and career guidance to approximately 2,677,000 young persons (Miller 1961, p. 160). The effects of these programs on school guidance is difficult to assess, but both focused on occupational exploration, and the NYA gave guidance workers the opportunity to gain job experience (Miller 1961, p. 161).

The same year that the CCC was instituted, the Wagner-Peyser Act established the U.S. Employment Service for youth and handicapped adults (Ginzberg 1971, p. 28) with a wide-ranging program of testing, counseling, research, and publication (Miller 1961, p. 161). As additional guidance needs became apparent, services were expanded to include all persons who required career planning and placement help (Ginzberg 1971,

p. 28). This legislation provided for out-of-school guidance; additional federal action expanded school guidance but at the same time narrowed its focus. The George-Deen Act of 1936 amended the earlier George-Barden Act so that funds could be used for guidance (Miller 1961, p. 162).

A number of other projects and programs were to have a lasting impact on guidance and counseling. In 1938 the Occupational Information and Guidance Service was established in the Division of Vocational Education of the U.S. Office of Education (Borow 1964, pp. 55–56). Under Harry Jager (Shertzer and Stone 1974, p. 27), it used funds provided by Vocational Education to promote school guidance and counseling. In 1939, the first edition of the *DOT* (*Dictionary of Occupational Titles*) was published by the U.S. Employment Service. The Occupational Outlook Service was established in the Bureau of Labor Statistics in 1940 and published the first *Occupational Outlook Handbook* in 1949 (Ginzberg 1971, p. 201). *DOT* and the *Handbook* have become basic references in school, college, and agency counseling.

Of various other programs initiated in response to the depression, two of the most potent in terms of their impact on school guidance were MESRI (Minnesota Employment Stabilization Research Institute), set up by the University of Minnesota, and the American Youth Commission, established by the American Council on Education. The former conducted research on employment and unemployment; the latter concentrated on problems of youth. MESRI's team of economists, engineers, social workers, medical personnel, and psychologists learned a great deal about the employment problems of adults and reported the findings as *Men, Women, and Jobs,* by Paterson, Darley, and Elliott (Miller 1961, p. 159) and other publications. The project developed tests that have been extensively used in guidance and counseling at all levels.

The work of the American Youth Commission revealed much about the social and vocational problems of the young. Publications of the project such as *Youth Tell Their Story* and *Matching Youth and Jobs,* by Howard Bell, reported that in the late 1930s nearly 4,000,000 youths between 15 and 24 were neither in school nor employed. These studies, like MESRI's, were based on the belief that better vocational guidance would result in better job adjustment.

In the 1930s, the Progressive Education Association carried out a particularly innovative project supporting new guidance concepts. The Eight-Year Study broadened the concept of guidance and emphasized groups and curriculum changes, approaches that conflicted with the current adaptations of Parsons's work (Miller 1961, pp. 165–166). As Aubrey (1977) indicates, the school counselor stood for the Progressive Education Movement in schools (child-centered, experienced-based), which was more a matter of theory than practice. Guidance professed the wish to concern itself with development of the total person; day-to-day work in the schools fell far short of this goal. But without the support of the Progressive Education Movement, there would probably not have been any counselors in schools at all.

During this period, the guidance model of matching traits with occupational requirements began to lose ground, but it was still a strong influence until well into the 1950s. Aubrey (1977) attributes its demise to its inability to adapt to the new demands of helping individuals with total developmental and adjustment needs. A new approach based on personality dynamics, developmental patterns, and affective communication was gathering strength.

The New Counseling

Carl R. Rogers's book, *Counseling and Psychotherapy* (1942), triggered a revolution in all forms of counseling. His client-centered approach broadened the concept of counseling, emphasized the counseling relationship rather than diagnosis and information, and opened up therapeutic practice to those without medical or psychoanalytic training. In this period, counselors began to focus on pupils' own perceptions of needs (Odell 1973, p. 152). The clinical emphasis, leaving out assessment, was now an integral feature of guidance (Miller 1961, pp. 167–168), and a closer relationship with psychology was established. The NDEA institutes in the late 1950s and the 1960s greatly expanded the nondirective impact (see section on NDEA). Prior to the NDEA, Rogers's work had little impact on counseling in most settings.

While Rogers's work had some influence on the face-to-face helping situation and changed the style of work with individuals and small groups, the research of Eli Ginzberg, Donald E. Super, and others offered new perspectives on the developmental process and the way individuals formulate and implement career goals. Ginzberg introduced his theory of vocational development at the NVGA Convention in the early 1950s; Super began the Career Patterns Study in 1951. These developments led to new concepts for preparing school counselors and organizing school guidance programs. But researchers of the period were most fascinated with finding new ways to explore feelings and providing therapeutically oriented help rather than with discovering ways to facilitate vocational development. As Aubrey (1977) says, Rogers's impact tended to obscure other techniques and approaches and to restrict the focus to counseling.

Another new approach, based on psychology, contributed to the eclipse of the Parsonian trait-factor method and widened the gap between guidance and vocational education. In 1941 psychologists began working in the Employment Service, the War Manpower Commission, and U.S. Air Force Personnel Research Units. Many counselors and counselor-educators served in these agencies and brought new techniques back to school counseling. Tests, notably the AGCT (Army General Classification Test), were developed, and occupational aptitude norms were set up (Ginzberg 1971, p. 32).

In 1944 the Veterans Administration established centers to provide counseling for those receiving benefits under the GI Bill, which provided for training and education for all veterans. Many counselors were trained in VA-supported counseling services on college campuses and, because of the financial support of the GI Bill, were able to go on for more advanced preparation. The Veterans Administration did much to broaden and professionalize the role of the vocational counselor. For example, the vocational adviser of earlier VA programs was not a full-fledged counselor, but in 1951 the VA established the position of counseling psychologist, in line with newer concepts from psychology and related disciplines (Borow 1964, p. 60; Miller 1964, p. 15).

Indirectly, the influx of veterans in colleges gave counseling and college placement programs another boost. Many schools added counselors to their staffs to help graduates gain admission to competitive institutions of higher education. The effects of this emphasis were felt for many years after the initial postwar period.

For some time there had been criticism of the teacher-counselor role with its splitting of responsibility between classroom instruction and guidance. Federal support gave leaders the opportunity to promote the employment of full-time school counselors. Jager used his powerful position to urge state guidance supervisors to improve certification programs for school counselors. His aim was to establish the school counselor as a full-time worker by advocating the role of the teacher-plus, that is, a teacher with graduate training (Hoyt 1974, p. 503). In order to identify the special skills needed to implement this concept, reports on counseling competencies were prepared as bases for the institution of reimbursable programs and certification. These reports set the pattern for postwar school counseling and counselor preparation until the late 1950s. New rehabilitation counselor and employment counselor programs were strongly influenced by this model, but there was little effect on counseling psychology programs in psychology departments (Hoyt 1974, p. 504).

School and college counseling also benefited from federal action to upgrade rehabilitation counselors. In 1955 the Office of Vocational Rehabilitation began providing training grants for these specialties (Borow 1964, p. 61). Support to departments and students in a no-strings program led indirectly to better preparation for school counselors. Indeed, some graduates of these new programs eventually did work as school and college counselors.

Publication of journals, books, and psychological measurements in the 1940s and 1950s added sophistication to counselors' theory and practice, and made available up-to-date information for occupational planning. *The Occupational Outlook Handbook,* Strong's *Vocational Interest of Men and Women,* and the U.S. Employment Service's *General Aptitude Test Battery* (building on some of the MESRI tests) are outstanding examples. A new periodical, the *Journal of Counseling Psychology,* published research and theoretical articles for counselors.

The professional status of the counselor was aided immensely by the expansion of already-existing organizations and the initiation of new ones. Developments reflect a broader approach to helping and a further recognition of the need for a team approach. In 1951, the newly formed American Personnel and Guidance Association took over the journal of NVGA (National Vocational Guidance Association), *Occupations,* and gave it the new title *Personnel and Guidance Journal* (Siegel 1972, p. 518). The new organization brought together the NVGA (the oldest association of its kind), the American College Personnel Association, the Association for Counselor Education and Supervision, and the Student Personnel Association for Teacher Education. The new group numbered about 6,000, more than half previously NVGA members (Barry and Wolf 1957, p. 104). In 1953, a year after it was formed, the American School Counselor Association became a division of the APGA. In 1947 the American Psychological Association established division 17, Counseling and Guidance, which took an active interest in school counseling and, although not a major school counselor organization, had an influence on counselor preparation (Barry and Wolf 1957, p. 95).

A Supreme Court decision during the 1950s set the stage for the challenges of this decade. The Plessy Doctrine of "separate but equal" was rejected, and the process of integration, marked by conflict and resistance, began. From the start, guidance workers were in the middle of developments, but typically, counselors' background and training left them unprepared to deal with different racial groups and the resulting tensions. Major changes had to be instituted in counselor education programs to provide the understanding and skills for working effectively with minority groups. Awareness and concern about minority-group differences probably got a real start during this time.

National Defense Education Act (NDEA) and Guidance

During the late 1950s, the American people were confident of the superiority of American education and guidance, but their complacency was rudely shattered by Russia's successful Sputnik launch in 1957. The National Defense Education Act of 1958 was designed to remedy shortcomings in our educational system and to produce more scientific talent through testing and counseling. The goal was to catch up in science; guidance was to play a strategic role in achieving it. Funds were provided first for high school counseling, but by 1964, amendments had extended support from elementary schools through junior colleges and technical institutions. During the first five years, about 13,000 counselors were trained in summer- or year-long NDEA institute programs (Borow 1964, p. 62).

Several components of NDEA are of special importance. Title V-B, supporting counselor preparation through counseling and guidance institutes, was the greatest landmark in the history of counselor education. By 1967, over $58 million had been spent on training more than 14,000 counselors in short-term (usually summer) institutes and nearly 5,000 in year-long institutes (Hoyt 1974, pp. 504, 506). Title V-A strengthened and expanded state guidance services. Provisions for the reimbursement of counselors' salaries dramatically increased the number of counselors employed in schools. In the late 1960s funding was cut substantially, and counselor preparation was incorporated in other education acts.

There is no question that school counseling profited at least quantitatively from NDEA, but it is not yet possible to assess the full effects. Some evaluations have been made and two major reports give positive conclusions (Tyler 1960; Pierson 1965). But some feel that it caused many of today's problems. One striking result was that the number of full-time counselors in secondary schools increased from 12,000 in 1958–59 to over 29,000 in 1963–64 (Odell 1973, p. 152). The reimbursement made possible counselor-pupil load ratios of 1 : 400 or 1 : 500 and facilitated the establishment of a developmental model of guidance from kindergarten through high school and beyond (Herr 1974, p. 41). Since assistance provided by the act went to states and counselor education programs through two separate sections (V-A and V-B), differences about the counselor preparation arose, and remained unresolved (Hoyt 1974, pp. 506–507). State counselor certification standards did not match the requirements of counselor preparation institutions.

The 1962 MDTA (Manpower Development Training Act) provided for training of unemployed and underemployed (Borow 1964, p. 62). Because of rapidly increasing unemployment in 1963, emphasis shifted from those displaced from work by economic and technological change to the disadvantaged (Ginzberg 1971, pp. 16–17). Project CAUSE (Counselor Adviser University Summer Education Program) of the U.S. Department of Labor provided for the preparation of guidance support personnel (Hoyt 1974, p. 507). The Vocational Education Act of 1963 and the 1968 amendments emphasized guidance for vocational planning; however, they had very little impact on school guidance (Hoyt 1974, p. 508).

Three major publications at this time dramatically moved forward the broad acceptance of guidance services. C. Gilbert Wrenn's book, *The Counselor in a Changing World,* the report of the Commission on Guidance in American Schools, defined the current status of school counseling and made far-reaching recommendations for economic, social, and occupational change in the world of counseling (Borow 1964, p. 62). Two other books, *The American High School Today* (1959) and *Slums and Suburbs* (1961) by James B. Conant, strongly supported guidance services and highlighted the need of disadvantaged inner-city youth. These three publications reached audiences far beyond the profession and generated wide support for school guidance.

The period was marked by the development of new approaches used in the intensive NDEA institutes. The influences of psychology and client-centered counseling increased, and group counseling became popular for counselees in need of help as well as counselors in training. Odell (1973, p. 152) describes this stage as focusing on counselee-perceived needs and counselors' personal characteristics as opposed to theoretical orientations, and notes a drive toward professionalization.

Special attention was paid to preparation standards and role statements, and after the NDEA was passed concern about these aspects surfaced on a national scale (Hoyt 1974, p. 509; Hill 1968). The most significant document of the time, the *Statement of Policy for Secondary School Counselors* (Odell 1975, p. 152), was prepared by the ASCA (American School Counselor Association) in 1964. The ACES (Association for Counselor Education and Supervision) published standards for counselor education in 1964, which were revised after tryout and distributed in 1967. These reports supported a two-year training program for counselors with practical work to develop skills. At about this time, ASCA became the largest division of APGA, symbolizing the change from vocational guidance (NVGA) to a more specialized but broader role of school counseling. Other divisions existed but were smaller. There was no mental health counselor division in the APGA at this time.

Expanding the Concept of Guidance

Perhaps the most appropriate label for the period from 1969 to the mid-1970s might be "the age of accountability." Odell (1973 pp. 152–153) has characterized it as a time of innovation in which some groups recommend new roles, others question the need for counselors, and still others vehemently support them. Aubrey (1977) identifies the trend of searching for a system to unify helping persons with common purposes. It is unquestionably a time for building comprehensive approaches to solving problems and fulfilling needs. With the help of a continuous assessment of the desires of those served, guidance can be provided when and where it is needed. But it is a time when realistic priorities must be established, and energy is being expended with care.

Emphasis on Career Education

The period might be characterized as a return to Parsons, Weaver, and the turn-of-the-century concepts in an updated, modernized, developmental, theoretically based, technologically sophisticated approach — career education. Some vestiges of Progressive Education are visible in the efforts to spread guidance throughout school and in the concern for the individual's total development. There are common themes, such as questions regarding counseling as therapy, work with minorities, licensing, specialist v. generalist, the counselor as change agent, the role of the consultant, and group work. Career education stands out from the others representing psychological education to facilitate personal development.

In the early 1970s Sidney P. Marland introduced the new concept of career education to stimulate vocational development in public schools and to help pupils learn to cope successfully in a technological society (Cramer 1974, p. 401). Marland, then commissioner of education, used discretionary and other funds to launch state efforts and establish research and demonstration projects (Herr 1974, p. 53). The National Institute of Education (NIE) has recently taken over responsibility for the program, which the Office of Education originally outlined in order to stimulate grass-roots definitions and state developments (*Career Education* 1971), while at the same time supporting large-scale research and development programs in major cities. In a later policy statement, the Education Office defined the concept and outlined goals, suggesting responsibilities for school, home, and community (Hoyt 1975a) and spelling out the key role of the counselor.

The school-based, career education model, involving the total individual and geared to stages in vocational development, has gained wide support among laypersons and educators but has also met with some resistance. Many blacks and other minority-group members see it as a way to build a supply of cheap labor and reduce upward mobility. Opposition has come also from labor unions and advocates of a broad liberal education. This model appears to offer school counselors a unique chance to expand their role (Cramer 1974, pp. 410–411; Hoyt 1974, pp. 523–524; Odell 1973, p. 155), but it remains to be seen whether counselors will participate effectively in this new educational approach.

Career education is only one sign of a growing interest in career planning and decision making. The multifaceted concept has three variations besides the school-based model already mentioned: the experience-based, home-based, and special-residential models (Herr 1974, pp. 48–53).

41	novice	11-12	50 brest	42
43		11-12	50 brest	44
45	novice	13-Over	50 brest	46
47		13-over	50 brest	48
49	novice	8 under	25 fly	50
51		8 under	25 fly	52
53	novice	9-10	25 fly	54
55		9-10	50 fly	56
57	novice	11-12	25 fly	58
59		11-12	50 fly	60
61	novice	13-over	25 fly	62
63		13-over	50 fly	64
65		8 under	100 IM.	66
67		9-10	100 IM.	68
69		11-12	100 IM.	70
71	novice	13-over	100 IM.	72
73		13-Over	100 IM.	74

FUN RELAYS   FUN RELAYS   FUN RELAYS

We will need parents to help run the swim meet and to help encourage all our swimmers.

NOVICE- swimmers that have just started up with the team this season.

BLUE AND GOLD INTERSQUAD MEET

When: Thursday October 21
       4:00 warmups 4:30 meet begins
       Lake Oswego Pool

ORDER OF EVENTS

Girls						Boys
1	novice	8 under	25	free		2
3	novice	8 under	25	free		4
5	novice	9-10	50	free		6
7	novice	9-10	50	free		8
9	novice	11-12	50	free		10
11	novice	11-12	50	free		12
13	novice	13-over	50	free		14
15	novice	13-over	50	free		16
17	novice	8 under	25	back		18
19	novice	8 under	25	back		20
21	novice	9-10	50	back		22
23	novice	9-10	50	back		24
25	novice	11-12	50	back		26
27	novice	11-12	50	back		28
29	novice	13-over	50	back		30
31	novice	13-over	50	back		32
33	novice	8 under	25	brest		34
35	novice	8 under	25	brest		36
37	novice	9-10	50	brest		38
39	novice	9-10	50	brest		40

CETA (Comprehensive Education and Training Act) emphasizes guidance, training, and job placement for those out of work. Moreover, the education amendments of 1976 (Alford 1977) promote guidance assistance and career education through educational guidance centers for adults and programs to help counselors and teachers learn about occupations.

The decade has also seen an increasing concern for the rights of individuals. The widely publicized Buckley Amendment (see Chapter 12) safeguards the confidentiality of records, and Title IX of the educational amendment of 1972 prohibits discrimination on the basis of sex. New programs to provide jobs for the unemployed, particularly the young, are in planning.

We have been experiencing a leveling off of job opportunities in many fields, including counseling. Birth statistics, which are the basis for projecting the size of schools, allow predictions about the numbers of counselors who under present ratios will be needed in the future. (Another question is whether more counselors will be employed to obtain more reasonable counselor-pupil ratios.) A major concern is the discrepancy between the number needed under present employment rates and the number currently being prepared.

New Methods and New Roles

Besides accountability, career education, and protection of personal information, the period was marked by a host of new procedures to increase the impact of the counselor's work. The effects of NDEA institutes were becoming more pervasive — individual and group counseling with an affect focus gained ground in school and higher-education settings. Later in this chapter, in the account of developments in the elementary school and the community agency, we will see counselors began establishing a place for themselves in these settings at this time. Computer guidance systems began to be used with increasing frequency. While the search for identity continued, parameters became more clear-cut. The unique competencies of the person bearing the title "counselor" became better understood, at least within the profession.

Counseling Services at the Crossroads

This characterization of the current status of counseling and guidance is reflected in a recent special 25th anniversary issue of the *Personnel and Guidance Journal* (Sue 1977) and by Gysbers (1978, pp. 2–3) in his perceptive analysis of current dilemmas. The terminology is borrowed by the author to apply to the decade of the 1980s. There are divergent paths that can be taken in schools, colleges, and community settings. In some cases, the crossroads have been passed and the direction taken, (e.g., working with new populations, moving into community settings). Perhaps it is actually more of an evolutionary process than a choice of one or another disparate direction — changes take place, modifications are made, new forms emerge, but directions tend to remain consistent. It is apparent that questions such as the following are still to be answered.

At the elementary school level, how much emphasis should be put upon career education? Should counselors play more active roles, or is career education solely a function of classroom teachers? How can the demands of working with the handicapped be handled while at the same time services must be provided to other pupils? In addition, how much of the counseling resources should be devoted to expanding the effects of counseling and guidance? More important than these specific questions are central ones that involve the influencing of public opinion — public relations, accountability, political activism. It is clear that counselors must be concerned about adequate supports when budgets are prepared in an increasingly competitive climate. How politically active should counselors be? What kind of evaluative evidence gives the best basis for support?

These same questions apply to middle/junior high and high school. But at the upper level, more insistent questions arise about bridging the gap between school and work. What resources should be devoted to this critical process, particularly for special groups such as the handicapped, the disadvantaged, and minorities?

Questions may also be raised about the model for secondary school counseling services. How will services be designed to cope with tightened budgets? For example, how much consulting, psychological education, and peer advising will be possible?

The college level, too, has problems of financial support, accountability, and implementation of new models to meet changing student demands. How well will the student development approach be infused in college personnel work, and how effective will it be in meeting the needs of the variety of students who are arriving on campuses and in adapting to shifting enrollment patterns?

One factor in the move to community agency counseling and the exploration of others (e.g., business and industry) has been changes in opportunities for counselors in educational settings. These settings offer considerable promise, particularly the community one, but how much of the profession's resources in personnel and preparation programs should be devoted to these new directions? Credentialing will obviously be a factor, but two unknowns overshadow all those mentioned — energy availability and consumption and national mental health policy and programs. The cost and availability of energy (from whatever source) will not only have an impact on what counselors do but will also affect the number and availability of helpers to a significant extent. National health policy will have a more specific effect on community counseling, since it will dictate the form and extent of local community counseling services.

There is, of course, a continuity to counseling services that virtually insures that some currently significant directions will continue. But in the 1980s there are choices yet to be made and directions that will lead to new services and roles.

Guidance in the Elementary School

Guidance had a much later start in elementary schools than in secondary schools. William Burnham was the first to see guidance in the elementary school as more than remediation, testing, and diagnosis; his book, *Great Teachers and Mental Health* (1926), established him as the precursor of elementary school counseling (Faust 1968, pp. 11–12).

Burnham translated his developmental concepts into practices emphasizing the affective and cognitive components of the teacher's work. The 1930 White House Conference, influenced by Burnham, used the term "mental hygiene," which has since been replaced by "developmental guidance." But elementary school guidance got nowhere from the 1930s through the 1950s, partly because the depression turned attention to vocational assistance (Faust 1968, pp. 15, 17, 21).

The 1960s saw significant new developments. As late as 1965 there were no accurate counts of counselors, but five years later their number was established as almost 8,000 (Dinkmeyer 1973, p. 172). The new elementary school counselor emerged, now that the NDEA institutes could include elementary programs; and institute proposals reflected new concepts of elementary school work (Faust 1968, pp. 25–26, 61).

A variation of the elementary school counselor role, identified as "child behavior consultant," was developed by IRCOPPS (International Research Commission on Pupil Personnel Services) (Seidman et al., 1970). The five-year program, starting in 1963, included representatives from thirteen professional groups and was influential in shaping the role of the modern elementary school counselor.

The decade of the 1970s was a period of continuing progress. There is a widely accepted model, a professional journal (*Elementary School Guidance and Counseling*, founded in 1965), and a substantial group of practitioners. In 1973–74 there were 6,929 counselors in elementary schools and 17,537 serving both the elementary and secondary levels (National Center for Educational Statistics, U.S. Department of Health, Education, and Welfare 1973–74). Current estimates of the number of elementary school counselors are in the neighborhood of 10,000 (Dinkmeyer 1973, p. 172; Shertzer and Stone 1981, p. 98). With goals and model questions settled, at least for the time being, much of the literature is devoted to techniques, procedures, needs of special groups, rights of children (Rotter and Crunk 1975), career education and career development (Leonard and Splete 1975; Splete 1980), and building support through public relations (Bluhm and Anderson 1976). Recent trends include the use of family counseling approaches (Capuzzi 1981).

The Development of Guidance for Middle/Junior High Schools

Accounts of the development of guidance in the public school do not often give much space to the middle grades, even though school reorganization was discussed extensively around the turn of the century and the first junior high schools were established in the early 1900s. In the 1920s, the central role of guidance was an important feature of this new school plan (Johnson, Busacker, and Bowman 1961, pp. 3, 14–15). But guidance at this level followed the high school model, using teacher-counselors, teacher participation, and with counseling, group work, and testing the major functions. More recently, as the middle school has emerged, guidance for this level has gained a more clear-cut identity; statements have stressed its transitional and exploratory role. Strategies are similar to those used at other levels, particularly that of the elementary school.

The junior high school came into existence as a reaction against the 8 : 4 system (Barnes 1974, p. 150), to better take into account the individual differences of pupils, to provide for career exploration, to promote counseling and guidance, and to accommodate the needs of early adolescents (Kindred, ed., 1968, p. 25). The new concept seemed to imply a strong guidance and counseling function. In fact, early origins can be traced to the reform movements promising social and economic efficiency (Stephens 1974, p. 14). The first designated junior high school was Indianola Junior High School in Columbus, Ohio, opened in 1909 (Lounsbury 1974, p. 5), but by the 1930s the junior high school had become an accepted part of the American school system (Lounsbury 1974, p. 5).

In its early years the junior high school adopted guidance patterns from those developing in the high school, using class advisers and vocational counselors. Unfortunately, this system was more suitable for the high school level and did not meet the special needs of junior high pupils. Later, through the influence of psychologist G. Stanley Hall and the Cardinal Principles of Education, the narrow educational and vocational scope broadened to include the whole range of needs of the individual (Howard and Stoumbis 1970, pp. 57–58).

Growth in the number both of institutions and guidance services has been substantial. For example, over a ten-year period from the middle

1950s to the middle 1960s, the number of junior high schools more than doubled, and the percentage of those having an organized guidance program increased from 61 to 91 percent (Lounsbury and Douglass 1974, pp. 168, 176).

The middle school gained a place in the educational system because of the way the junior high school developed rather than because it was originally conceptualized (Alexander et al., 1969, p. 4). If the junior high school had continued to serve as a bridge between the self-contained classrooms of the elementary school and the subject-field organization of high school, provided exploratory experiences for high school planning, and offered comprehensive guidance, there would have been no need for a change to the middle school (Compton 1974, p. 198). While there are still a large number of junior high schools in operation today, the 1960s could be called the decade of the middle school (Brough and Hamm 1974, p. 179).

Over the years, guidance services have been regarded as essential parts of both middle and junior high school programs, and some authorities feel that some of the best guidance anywhere is to be found at this level (Barnes 1974, p. 154). But guidance will have to move out of the office and help teachers in the classroom; the program must be spread throughout the school, using consulting, teacher participation, training, and community outreach. The timely model proposed by Hansen and Hearn (1971, p. 305) illustrates current thinking. They set up four levels of guidance roles and responsibilities within the middle school. The first two, meeting immediate and long-range needs, are primarily the teacher's responsibility. Counselors share in helping with long-range needs and have major responsibility for the third, consulting with other staff members. The fourth level, long-term treatment, is the responsibility of the school psychologist. Major emphasis is on the counselor as a consultant, but there are other responsibilities, among them counseling with individuals and groups, coordinating activities like staff conferences, and providing in-service education for teachers.

Guidance at the College Level

A brief review of the developments at the post-high-school level illustrates similarities and differences in public and higher education. While the settings are unlike in many ways, rather striking parallels are apparent in trends like the team approach, outreach, prevention, and training to enable others to carry out guidance functions.

In the early 1900s guidance at the college level was not affected by factors that stimulated developments in the public secondary school. Only a few could attend college. The German influence contributed to a wide gap between students and faculty; adaptations of the English tutorial system placed the focus on academic development (Brewer 1942, p. 237). College personnel work (comparable to pupil personnel work in schools) originated with the work of deans of women. By 1910, they had a variety of helping responsibilities, including vocational counseling. Deans of men arrived on campus somewhat later and served mainly as disciplinarians (Barry and Wolf 1957, pp. 19–20). Educational guidance at the University of Chicago in 1905 focused on students' personal qualities and the selection of programs (Brewer 1942, p. 237). A 1912 survey identified many examples of educational guidance, but there were also few programs of vocational guidance. Some colleges held vocational conferences once a year; women's colleges were more active in this service than men's (Brewer 1942, pp. 242–243, 245–246).

During the 1920s college personnel work was feeling the effects of studies and developments stimulated by World War I (Barry and Wolf 1957, p. 21; Williamson 1965, p. 100). New types of tests were made available for guidance, admissions, and placement; more attention was focused on mental hygiene. Specialists began to develop, and by the 1920s beginnings had been made in formulating purposes and specifying activities (Paterson 1938, p. 39; Barry and Wolf 1957, p. 22). In 1924 the National Association of Appointment Secretaries, later renamed the American College Personnel Association, was organized (Borow 1964, p. 52). A few institutions offered occupations courses and vocational counseling; a greater number provided placement services (Brewer 1942, pp. 244–249). The college population was not heterogeneous as it is today; the proportion of 18- to 21-year-olds in college in 1900–1910 was approximately 5 percent; by 1924 it had climbed only to 10 percent (Ginzberg 1971, p. 27).

During the 1930s guidance at the college level continued to expand and search for directions. During the depression, both its status and acceptance rose, partly because enrollments increased and student groups were becoming more heterogeneous (Barry and Wolf 1957, p. 23). By the end of the decade college enrollments reached about 16 percent of 18- to 21-year-olds (Ginzberg 1971, p. 27). Concern was growing about the nature and function of college personnel work. Debates resulted in the Clothier Report on principles and functions (1932) and the ACE publication, *Student Personnel Point of View,* which recommended an array of separate services for students (Barry and Wolf 1957, pp. 23–25). Both the American Council on Education and the American College Personnel Association were active in policy development (Borow 1964, p. 52).[1]

During the 1940s, 1950s, and early 1960s, student personnel workers continued to study and evaluate the traditional services: counseling, collecting and providing information, and exploratory activities for students

---

[1] The latter organization emerged during the 1930s from the National Association of Appointment Secretaries.

(Barry and Wolf 1957, p. 138). Williamson (1961, pp. 29–32), regarding student personnel work from this point of view, advanced the concept of personnel work as a way of individualizing education. Major doubts and conflicts about the purpose and value of the service did not arise until later.

The present modifications of college personnel work began in the late 1960s. Critical voices were heard (Warnath 1973a, pp. 2–3). Personnel workers were caught up in campus demonstrations; wave after wave of new problems developed, many due to the Vietnam War (Kincaid and Kincaid 1971, pp. 727–735). But even with the greater needs of students, college personnel work was described as a collection of separate services, lacking in professional identity and consistent point of view (Penney 1969, p. 961). The rapid growth of community colleges was well under way, and the budget crunch that would soon confront all levels of education was just around the corner.

The pressures, conflicts, and economic problems of the 1970s have affected all levels of counseling and guidance, but have had their greatest impact on services in higher education. Budgets for counseling and personnel services have been cut. Traditional counseling models have been sharply criticized (Warnath 1973a, pp. 18–20; Williamson and Biggs 1975, pp. 7–10). New approaches to student development are being tried out; collaborative work with students, peer counseling, and outreach are popular current strategies. There is evidence that these will gain the firm support that earlier programs once enjoyed and will lead to the establishment of college personnel services as a major function of higher education. The anticipated decline in college enrollment may affect both programs and employment opportunities for counselors in training. New models for higher education, although still mostly small scale, suggest alternative types of guidance and counseling services.

Counseling Services for Community Mental Health

The roots of community mental health counseling services have been identified in the discussion of history on pages 105–108. Early developments in clinical methods and actions to promote mental health are examples of these developments. Freud is credited with opening up the mental health field to broader services (Zax and Specter 1974, pp. 16–17). Other events discussed earlier (e.g., World War I) had pronounced effects on the development of clinical services. The National Mental Health Act of 1946 creating the National Institute of Mental Health also gave impetus to psychological services in the community and the training of psychologists. Whereas the earlier emphasis was on doctoral-level practitioners, more recent policy has expanded opportunities to include master's-level workers. This expansion resulted from an awareness that needs of various groups could not be met by the traditionally prepared doctoral-level clinician. Moreover, there was an obvious need to utilize minority-group members as counselors and to include paraprofessionals on staffs.

The passage of the Mental Health Study Act in 1955 led to a series of actions, among the most noteworthy being the recommendation to reduce the population in state mental hospitals. A further influence of the report was the passage of the "Kennedy Bill" in 1963. This legislation called for the establishment of comprehensive community mental health centers (discussed in Chapter 4). These centers were designed to serve specific geographical areas with comprehensive mental health care. The emphasis was on early detection and treatment of problems in the community and reduction of institutional populations. Counselors provided a wide range of services (see Chapter 4 for examples). Opportunities expanded for the generalist counselor — one prepared to offer individual and group help, consultation, outreach, and to be active in prevention in the community.

In the past decade, the status of community counselors, particularly those at the master's level, has been enhanced by the establishment of the American Mental Health Counselors Association as a division of the American Personnel and Guidance Association. Moreover, the American Mental Health Counselors Association provides certification of counselors through the National Academy of Certified Clinical Mental Health Counselors.

Using History to Look into the Future

It is difficult to show cause-effect relationships in the history of guidance and counseling, but by identifying related events one can understand the present and predict the future. The conditions that gave rise to Parsons's work are an example. Parsons was not alone in his recognition of problems and concern, but his experience and philosophy had prepared him for constructive action. The proposals he developed were designed to meet the needs he recognized. This pattern has been repeated over and over through the years as in the depression, World War II, and after Sputnik. Regardless of names or labels, there will be a demand for services to help people make the most of their lives; demand will increase as human needs increase.

Those who conceptualize the future role of guidance should keep in close touch with opinions of many different factions. It is tempting to think that in the future counseling will take the ideal shape guidance workers would prefer, but predictions can be misleading. A few years ago predictions were made calling for a great increase in the number of counselors; relatively little attention was given to evaluation. At the time no one questioned effectiveness. Now the picture has changed; economic conditions have cut budgets. Questions about results, previously ignored, are being asked, but data for answering them are lacking. Accountability is not a new problem — Brewer raised it more than three decades ago (1942, pp. 294–295) — but completely unexpected social and economic conditions have thrust it to the foreground.

History tells us that there is continuity in the development of guidance and counseling work, but that progress is not linear. Today some elements of the earliest models still remain or have been revived: People still need information about the environment; a concerned and interested listener still can help. With the present being so different from the past and the future sure to be more novel still, some may feel that the past is no guide. Guidance and counseling workers in any period may have felt this to be so, but history shows that there are periods of rapid advances, of stagnation, and of retrenchment. Smug satisfaction has given way to anxiety and bewilderment. History suggests that we shall see more of these conditions, but it gives some guidelines for coping with them.

Summary Concepts

If one is to understand the present status of the counseling profession and be able to predict future developments, an awareness of history is essential. Social, economic, and political factors interact to produce a milieu that exerts a profound impact on the shape of guidance and counseling services. The insights of leaders in the profession reflected in theories, techniques, research, and services also interact with the prevailing social climate to foster a particular type of assistance. A review of major phases in the development of counseling since the early part of this century offers support for this position. The problems faced by counselors today are to discern the major emerging influences, to take steps to capitalize on positive forces, and to work to counteract the negative ones.

Suggested Readings

Aubrey, Roger F. "Historical Development of Guidance and Counseling and Implications for the Future." *Personnel and Guidance Journal* 55, no. 6 (1977), pp. 288–295.

    A well-organized and very readable account of the development of guidance and counseling providing insight into the status of the profession today and into directions it may take in the future.

Brewer, John M. *History of Vocational Guidance.* New York: Harper and Bros., 1942.
    The standard reference on history up to 1942. Chapters 5 and 6 on Parsons and the reprint of his first and only report (Appendix, pp. 303–307) are recommended reading.

Fenske, Robert H. "Historical Foundations." In *Student Services,* edited by Ursula Delworth and Gary R. Hanson, pp. 3–24. San Francisco: Jossey-Bass, 1980.
    An interesting and detailed account of the development of student services at the college and university levels. A recommended reference concerned with factors and events that have led to the current student development emphasis.

Giroux, Roy F.; Biggs, Donald A.; Hoffman, Alan M.; and Pietrofesa, John J., eds. *College Student Development Revisited: Programs, Issues, and Practices.* Rev. ed. Falls Church, Va.: American Personnel and Guidance Association, 1979.
    The Introduction (pp. 14–24), and sections in Chapter 1, "Historical Perspective and Definition," provide a helpful review of the development of student personnel work in higher education.

Gysbers, Norman C. "Career Guidance at the Crossroads." In *New Imperatives for Guidance,* edited by Garry R. Walz and Libby Benjamin, pp. 1–29. Ann Arbor, Mich.: ERIC Counseling and Personnel Services, 1978.
    An insightful account of the major influences that have led to the present status of counseling. While the focus is on the school, most points are relevant for all settings. The directions suggested are well worth serious consideration, particularly by counselors in educational institutions.

Herr, Edwin L. *Guidance and Counseling in the Schools.* Falls Church, Va.: American Personnel and Guidance Association, 1979, pp. 1–24.
    A concise and informative history (partly in outline form) of the development of guidance in the schools with an analysis of contemporary forces and trends.

Hollis, Joseph W. "Guidance and Counseling in Schools: An Historical Approach." In *The Status of Guidance and Counseling in the Nation's Schools,* American Personnel and Guidance Association, pp. 1–16. Washington, D.C.: American Personnel and Guidance Association, not dated.
    One of the position papers prepared for the Association's "Status of Guidance and Counseling Project," providing a concise account of persons and events influencing the development of school counseling.

Miller, Carroll H. *Foundations of Guidance.* New York: Harper and Bros., 1961.
    This book, together with chapters in Borow's (ed.) *Man in a World at Work,* "Vocational Guidance in the Perspective of Cultural Change," pp. 3–23, and Borow's (ed.) *Career Guidance for a New Age,* "Historical and Recent Perspectives on Work and Vocational Guidance," pp. 3–40, establish Miller as the major historian on the guidance movement. The scope of his writing is broader than the term "vocational" implies.

"Pioneers in Guidance" articles in the *Personnel and Guidance Journal.*
    A series of articles based on interviews with leaders in counseling and guidance. These reports augment one's understanding of the profession by depicting not only the problems, issues, and trends over the decades but also the impacts these particular individuals had on the profession. See E. G. Williamson, vol. 54, no. 2 (1975), pp. 77–87; Robert Hoppock, vol. 54, no. 5 (1976), pp. 273–279; Esther Lloyd-Jones, vol. 54, no. 9 (1976), pp. 473–480;

Gilbert Wrenn, vol. 55, no. 2 (1976), pp. 75–85; Leona Tyler, vol. 55, no. 8 (1977), pp. 451–459; Donald Super, vol. 56, no. 10 (1978), pp. 585–592. Two additional interviews reported in the journal, while not in this series, are valuable in terms of the development of the profession: Dugald Arbuckle, vol. 58, no. 1 (1979), pp. 39–45; John Holland, vol. 58, no. 6 (1980), pp. 406–414.

Rappaport, Julian. *Community Psychology.* New York: Holt, Rinehart and Winston, 1977, pp. 12–16.

A lucid and concise review of the development of community psychology. The roots of community mental health counseling are apparent in the growth of this comprehensive approach to understanding and helping individuals and families.

Reed, Anna Y. *Guidance and Personnel Services in Education.* Ithaca, N.Y.: Cornell University Press, 1944.

A comprehensive account of the development of guidance and student personnel work. Part 1 covers events up to 1916; "Retrospect" (pp. 457–472) gives an authoritative and concise review of the period up to and including World War II. The author's "Prospect" section makes interesting reading as the passage of time allows the reader to check the accuracy of predictions.

Stephens, W. Richard. *Special Social Reform and the Origins of Vocational Guidance.* Washington, D.C.: National Vocational Guidance Association, 1970.

While the title suggests a narrow focus, the book covers general school guidance. The thoughtful analysis of factors leading to the present school model shows how the past can illuminate the present.

Wrenn, C. Gilbert. "Personal Perspectives — Past and Present." In *New Imperatives for Guidance,* edited by Garry R. Walz and Libby Benjamin, pp. 456–491. Ann Arbor, Mich.: ERIC Counseling and Personnel Services, 1978.

A brief but engaging personal account of Wrenn's perceptions of the development of counseling is contained on pages 459–469.

Zytowski, Donald G. "Four Hundred Years Before Parsons." *Personnel and Guidance Journal* 50, no. 6 (1972), pp. 443–450.

An interesting account with illustrations of early guidance publications that provide a readable record of past efforts.

Chapter

6

Bases of Counseling, Guidance, and Personnel Services

Helping services exist within a cultural context and draw goals and practices from that context. Cultural diversity and freedom to choose are hallmarks of our system. They epitomize the values that cut across all helping services. Science provides the means for reaching goals. Services are conceptualized and implemented in terms of these three basic elements — cultural values, social science principles, and validated techniques.

This chapter highlights the major features of the cultural context, the societal values, and social science theory. Values — which emanate from the philosophical stance of the counselor — point to what is worthwhile. Social science theories provide the ways to achieve the desired goals.

These foundations not only provide bases for services but constitute the knowledge essential for the counselor (see Appendix A, pages 368–369). This chapter is therefore primarily intended to review concepts to demonstrate their relationships to counseling services. It is aimed at helping you relate what you have learned in other courses to the design of services and the practice of counseling, guidance, and personnel work. It points to the needed knowledge base but does not attempt to supply it.

Culture, Values, and Theory

In this section, first the effects of culture on counseling and guidance are reviewed to highlight aspects of concern of the helping profession. Second, the role of values in the counselor's work is reviewed, and value dilemmas are identified. Third, on a theoretical level, representative principles of learning and personality development are summarized to show how psychological models can provide guidelines for helping activities. These models contribute to the counseling approaches that are described in Chapter 8, where the emphasis is not on theoretical concepts but on how these conceptualizations are put into practice.

Effects of Culture
on Guidance and Counseling

The larger setting of guidance determines its philosophy, the nature of its services, and the objectives it establishes; and the democratic principles underlying our form of government determine the nature of guidance in our country. The Declaration of Independence supports values of life, liberty, and the pursuit of happiness. The Constitution, too, emphasizes the importance of the individual, particularly through the Bill of Rights. The philosophical position set forth in these documents demands a service devoted to the full development of the individual. All command their own destiny. Rights imply obligations; people must be able to act constructively. Freedom of choice involves an awareness of options.

In practice, there have been shortcomings in insuring all the opportunities to choose, develop, and grow; deficiencies were discussed in Chapter 5. But history reveals a continuing effort by government through legislative, judicial, and executive action to implement democratic principles. Concerned groups and political leaders have brought public pressure to bear on deviations from democratic principles; voters have typically responded to improve conditions.

Governmental economic policy has a profound effect on freedom and choice. Regulations directed at business and industry, labor legislation, and monetary policy are examples. Positive actions like unemployment insurance, employment services, aid to the handicapped, and special training and work programs for minorities illustrate social concern.

Direct support to educational and guidance programs is another sign of underlying values. Program support usually arises in response to national emergencies or problems such as discrimination, need for scientific talent, education of veterans, or work for the unemployed. Direct legal action has been used to expand opportunities — for example, through desegregation.

Balancing the individual's rights with the requirements of the society poses difficulties for any democracy. Society is not static; needs change. What is necessary for the survival of the nation may not, at the moment, be in the best interests of the individual. This dilemma comes up again and again; solutions often generate hostility or resistance. There are no simple, quick solutions. Guidance workers must consider the values discussed next in this chapter to get their bearings and formulate a personal rationale for their activity.

The study of the family, the community, institutions, and other facets of group life provides bases for working with pupils and parents, providing outreach services, and making changes in the school and community environment. The family is a major concern of guidance workers. Counselors need to be aware of its changing role to understand young people, work with parents, and plan parent-oriented guidance activities. The middle class espouses, among other things, education, delay of rewards, and a small number of children; but values differ for families in other subcultures. The trend toward a nuclear family under one roof and away from an extended family has profound implications for guidance. As more wives have taken work outside the home, the family situation has changed; day-care centers are often used for child care. Mobility of families, the increase of commercial entertainment (TV, record players), and the automobile have reduced the importance of the home as the family's social and recreational center. Many responsibilities formerly taken care of by the home have shifted to the school. The predicted energy shortages are certain to reverse or alter some trends in family life. What will happen, for example, when it is no longer practical to drive to school or to have two or three cars in a family?

Community life has direct implications for guidance. The traditional community has declined as society has become urbanized (McKee 1969, p. 201). The movement of families to the suburbs has speeded the deterioration of the inner city. The difficulties faced by those who remain there — crime, drugs, unemployment — pose formidable challenges for guidance workers. Obviously, one task will be to build closer relations with community life and to adopt strategies that involve outreach, paraprofessionals, and expanded use of school and community resources and facilities.

Much of the school guidance program involves groups — small counseling groups, large guidance groups, training activities with classroom-sized groups. Principles of group behavior are important bases for guidance. Age plays a part in group participation; six-year-olds, for example, can do very little cooperative work in groups, but older children can go by regulations and interact as teams (Jersild, Telford, and Sawrey 1975, p. 267). Groups based on social stratification establish life-styles and attitudes (McKee 1969, p. 248), but not all group members are the same, nor do they fit a stereotype. Principles of group behavior are essential as background knowledge for the counselor or guidance worker, particularly when dealing with prejudice and discrimination.

Social organizations, religious, fraternal, educational and political institutions, the family, and the community all exert powerful influences on members' attitudes, opportunities, and life-styles. (The attitudes of teachers, for example, tend to differ from those of semiskilled plant operators.) A single individual may be a member of a number of groups through work, recreation, social, religious, labor organizations, and political party. Each calls for a different role. But institutions can be changed. The campus unrest during the 1960s is an example of collective action to alter institutions. One outcome for educators, particularly those in student personnel work, was a recognition of the critical role rumors play in touching off disorder, and the need for a rumor-control center.

The cultural context of guidance affects all aspects of the work of the counselor — goals, processes, rationale, target groups. In an environment that is rigid, authoritarian, and hostile to individual development and freedom, there would be no need or place for guidance as we know it.

Values Underlying Guidance Work

Values are philosophical positions not directly testable by research. If, for example, you say, "I believe that persons are inherently good," you are stating a value. I may recount numerous incidents of harmful acts, and attempt to show you that you are wrong — and that persons are usually bad — but very likely you will not change your opinion. It is deep-seated, resistant to change, and very important to you, that is, if it is really a value rather than a superficially held opinion.

The subject of values has always been a deep concern of guidance workers, but attention has varied over the years. Beck's analysis (1963) is a landmark in the search for the philosophical position of guidance. Interest

The counselor is faced with philosophical questions on a daily basis.

in the ethical standards of the profession is increasing (see Chapter 12). These standards, as Smith and Peterson (1977) point out, represent the underlying belief of members of the profession in the value and dignity of the individual.

Levels of Values

Values today play an increasingly vital role; guidance workers are facing more pressing conflicts and ambiguities than ever before. Smith and Peterson (1977) provide an extremely helpful discussion of the levels of values in society and identify the kinds of conflicts the counselor must deal with. The most general level, the "universals," is made up of values of profound importance to all; for example, right and wrong. The next level consists of "specialties," which are relevant to only a part of society; for instance, the values of a social class or subcultural group. At the third level are "alternatives," variations from the usual societal modes requiring choices. This last category is usually where changes occur; if universals are subjected to controversy, society tends to lose cohesiveness and established patterns deteriorate.

Smith and Peterson go on to identify a number of areas of conflict that cut across all three levels. Prominent among these are: the place of the counselor's values in the helping relationship; regulation of practitioners; adequacy of preparation; changes in sexual mores and differing views of marriage; and the meaning and purpose of life. There are others, but the point is clear from those given — conflicting trends reach to the most basic levels of our society's values.

Need for a Value Base

The counselor must have a value base for dealing with issues and pressures and as a guide for the daily responsibilities of counseling and other guidance tasks. Some suggested elements of this base are:

- For a full understanding, the counselor must view the counselee as a total person.
- You can know the counselee's personal world only to the extent that the counselee is willing to share it.
- Each counselee is motivated by a positive growth force.
- To develop fully, everyone needs others and needs to feel needed.
- All people have the freedom to choose what they are and will be.
- To develop fully, each person must accept responsibility for his or her choices.

The counselor thus views each counselee as a unique, valued, and independent person. Beck's comprehensive statement (1963, pp. 145–147) emphasizes further the need to maintain and enhance the self, and the potential for positive development if barriers and limitations are removed. These statements give the counselor's work a comprehensive and profound philosophical foundation.

A more down-to-earth statement of values may be drawn from ethical codes. Smith and Peterson (1977) suggest the following central concepts:

- The counselor values the uniqueness, worth, dignity, and potential of each individual.
- The counselor respects the rights of the individual to make choices. (An exception would be choices that are potentially destructive to the counselee and others.)
- The counselor provides an effective service to society based upon the first two value statements.

Values and Judgment

The values supporting counseling and guidance appear to be clear-cut, reasonable, and appropriate. But actually dealing with individuals is another matter. Personal situations usually involve complexities that make a quick solution impossible; needs of the individual frequently are in conflict with those of others or of society, and judgment is difficult. A counselee who is using drugs, for example, may be anxious to kick the habit through counseling, but school regulations require that drug use be reported for disciplinary action. The counselor may feel that there is a good chance to help the counselee if parents, school administrators, and police can be kept out of the case for a short time. How do counselors reconcile respect for the individual with responsibility to society? If they appear to "protect" drug users, will others be encouraged to regard drug use as acceptable? Is the counselor who turns a pupil in neglecting responsibility to the individual?

The counselor must answer philosophical questions every day and make decisions about the most effective types of help. Suppose the counselor is faced with Mark, a resistant student who is performing below expectations, is from a very difficult home situation, and is suspected of bringing drugs to the campus. What philosophical questions need to be answered? How do answers determine the methods of intervention? Here are some examples:

- Should Mark's behavior be changed? Do you have some standard of "good" and "bad," and if so, on what is it based? If you decide that behavior should be altered, will you use a process that, for example, permits him to decide what he wants to do or one that more or less dictates what the changes will be?

- Should he be required to participate in counseling? Suppose he does not want your help? Will you leave participation up to him? What if the dean requires him to enter counseling even though he doesn't want to? Would you work with him?
- What is the source of his needs? Can you decide what is best for him? Are there "absolutes" good for all? If so, where do they come from?
- What is the place of college and community standards in working with the student? Should he be required to live by them? Does he, for example, *have* to get better marks? Which is more important, the individual or the organization?
- Suppose he does participate in counseling. How will you select an approach? Each personality theory and each counseling approach (discussed in Chapter 8) makes certain assumptions about human nature. Some give weight to a positive growth force in the individual; others attribute much individual behavior to the effects of society.
- Who is responsible for his behavior? The family? The community? The student himself? Is he able to make decisions and change, or is his behavior determined?

When the philosophical questions are answered, the counselor looks to theory   psychological, sociological — to answer questions *how?* Theories discussed later in this chapter deal with how individuals learn, develop, and find rewarding life-styles. Chapter 8 identifies methods of counseling, which are largely based on these theoretical positions. Counseling techniques, also discussed in Chapter 8, enable the counselor to put the theory of helping into practice.

Learning and Personality Development

Psychological aspects of the individual are by far the most important for the counselor. Physiological factors play an important role but do not exert the strongest influence. Physical size, build, and other such characteristics have some slight relationship to personality and can produce major patterns in interaction with other conditions. The obese boy may avoid sports, where he is always outclassed, and turn to less physically demanding social activities or hobbies. But he *could* also choose to continue in sports. The way the person views the characteristic makes a major difference. In the school years, size, appearance, and physical ability are extremely important and exert a great influence on a person's self-concept. For the individual with a physical disability, the impairment may be a very significant determinant in self-perception and views of the world. It is the perceptions, however, that are of paramount concern to the counselor.

Various models of learning and personality development shed light on reasons for behavior and include implications for helping procedures. Those briefly summarized in the following sections are among the most useful, but they by no means exhaust the list.

Actual learning takes place by a number of processes that can be set up in guidance and counseling situations. One of the best known is pairing of stimuli to give previously unrewarded behavior motivational value. Behavior is built in this way every day. Suppose, for example, that an elementary pupil who is frightened by hostile, loud, threatening persons has a teacher who is loud and abrasive, and rules the class by sheer voice power. After a few days, the pupil begins to be afraid of previously non-threatening persons, objects, and events — teachers in general, schoolwork, going to school — having established an association between them and the feared person.

The same child may demonstrate another type of learning. Suppose, for example, that in trying various types of coping responses, the child gets up and walks around the room and discovers that the teacher becomes baffled and changes her style of discipline. A type of rewarded behavior has emerged, more or less by chance, and gains strength.

Social learning makes use of these types and also involves thinking processes for selecting a stimulus and a response to it. The environment has a pronounced effect, but people can reinforce their own behavior individually. A person can choose a model and maintain a consistent behavior of thinking, "I am acting the same as the person I admire." Guidance programs have used this process to promote new behaviors like openness in group discussions or searching for occupational information. The powerful effect of modeling can be seen every day in schools. It is one cause of concern about phenomena like TV violence.

Social learning is apparent in everyday activities. In interactions, first with parents and then in a wider circle, the individual builds a pattern of responses to obtain rewards like affection, acceptance, material goods, and learns to provide self-rewards in the absence of others, thus giving behavior a continuity. This view of personality also stresses the importance of models to identify with and copy. The environment is crucial as the source of rewards, behavior patterns, and models. Through behavior the individual builds up expectations; unanticipated results are likely to cause difficulty unless new or productive responses are found. For example, the child previously rewarded for an open, friendly manner may be baffled by suspicious and hostile classmates in a new school. The college student who is rejected by peers might very well consider himself or herself an outcast. The retiree may begin to feel useless without the status of productive worker.

The counselor can use concepts from learning theory to understand the individual's current behavior and to plan ways to promote new behaviors. If, for example, self-defeating behaviors have been learned, productive ones to replace them can also be learned.

Developmental Stages and Patterns

Human development tends to proceed along identifiable stages and to portray specific characteristics at each stage, although there are a number of dimensions to development, and not one global model that fits all. In the sections that follow, a number of models of human development are reviewed.

Intellectual Development

There are a number of concepts that explore how the individual develops intellectually. One of the most significant ones has been formulated by Jean Piaget. He views cognitive development as a series of ordered stages. At age six or seven, the child can think about things in logical or organized ways and classify objects; the ability to classify increases gradually in the later teens. Around 11 or 12, adult-type thought processes begin to develop; new abstract abilities are used extensively in arguing, debating, and discussing complex subjects. Children begin to develop personal theories of how their actions affect others and what will happen as a consequence of their behavior (Geiwitz 1976, pp. 296–299). Differing intellectual capacities determine how people deal with everyday problems and issues, and a young child does not have the same thought processes as an older one.

The process of intellectual development as conceptualized by Piaget, and by other theorists as well, has implications for programming guidance activities and for face-to-face work. For example, according to Piaget a child in the middle school could be expected to foresee consequences of actions and to test the validity of solutions to problems.

The stages of moral development have been identified by Kohlberg (Geiwitz 1976, pp. 320–324). There are three levels of two stages each. In level 1, the *preconventional* level, the individual forms a judgment of what is right or wrong without any basic reason for the choice. The first stage in this level involves obedience and the avoidance of punishment. The second, more advanced stage involves satisfaction of one's own desire or action expected to elicit reward from others. Seven-year-olds tend to respond at this level, and particularly at its second stage.

Level 2 is identified as *conventional*. In stage 3, the first stage of level 2, the urge is to portray oneself as good or pleasing to others. In stage 4, which is characterized by an orientation toward law and order, the individual supports the established way of doing things. Sixteen-year-olds in the research typically respond at this level, and particularly at stage 4, which is the most typical developmental stage of all persons studied.

Level 3, the highest level, is called the *postconventional*. It involves judgments that imply autonomy and principle. Stage 5, the first stage on this level, involves awareness of the need of society for order and regulation — these are essential. But there is an awareness too that rules may be changed by an orderly process. Research shows that individuals at stage 4 in high school tend to move up to the next stage if they did not go to college, while college entrants regress to stage 2. The challenges of the academic setting seem to overwhelm stage 4 judgments, but students are often not yet ready for the next higher level. Such regression is temporary.

Only a few individuals in the research reached stage 6, and it is assumed to be rare in the general population. It involves the application of self-chosen universal ethical principles that promote the greatest good for the greatest number.

Stages represent a step-by-step progression, with regression only as mentioned earlier. They correspond roughly to ages, but the relationship varies with groups and cultures (Brown and Herrnstein 1975, pp. 310–324; Geiwitz 1976, pp. 320–329).

Social Development

Social life also develops through identifiable stages. One way to look at social maturity is in terms of psychological crises as formulated by Erik Erikson (see Table 6-1). Each of these crises must be brought to a positive solution in order to attain the corresponding virtue (Goethals and Klos 1976, pp. 12–13). It is also apparent that interpersonal relations are critical factors in the resolution of the psychological crises. The consequence of not successfully working through the crisis is shown in the middle column of Table 6-1. For adolescence, failure results in role confusion.

Table 6-1
ERIKSON'S STAGES OF SOCIAL DEVELOPMENT

Age	Psychological Crisis	Virtue
1	Trust v. mistrust	Hope
2	Autonomy v. shame, doubt	Willpower
3 to 5	Initiative v. guilt	Purpose
6 to onset of puberty	Industry v. inferiority	Competence
Adolescence	Identity v. role confusion	Fidelity
Early adulthood	Generativity v. stagnation	Care
Old age	Integration v. despair	Wisdom

Chickering (Rodgers 1980, pp. 45–49) uses Erikson's theory as a basis of his model for college student development, covering ages 17–25. Between these ages, seven "vectors" (Chickering's term for developmental tasks) are significant in one's life. Representative ones are developing competence and managing emotions. As Chickering's concepts are much more specific than Erikson's, they are particularly useful for work with college populations; in setting up goals for student development programming, for example.

Developmental Tasks.   Looking at general development, a well-known framework (Havighurst 1972, pp. 1–98) identifies tasks at a series of age levels, and involving physical, psychological, and cultural factors. The six stages are: infancy and early childhood, middle childhood from about 6 to 12, adolescence from around 12 to 18 years, early adulthood, middle age, and later maturity. At each stage tasks must be mastered in order to move to the next stage. The six to ten tasks at each stage cannot be summarized here, but a brief description of each period illustrates the significance of the concept for guidance and counseling strategies.

The emphasis of the period of *infancy* and *early childhood* is upon instrumental behavior — learning to walk, talk, and relate to parents; there is also an incipient ability to judge right and wrong. *Middle childhood* is characterized by moving out from home-centered life to peer-group activities, increasing ability to communicate, awareness of role, and development of values. The *adolescent period* is marked by getting ready for adulthood, developing sex roles, building relationships with peers of both sexes, gaining emotional independence from parents, and increasing readiness for occupational selection and preparation. The period of *early adulthood* usually involves major events — marriage, starting a family, choosing an occupation. It is a unique period in that the individual moves from a relatively structured life to one that is often ambiguous and confusing. Later, in the period from approximately the middle 20s well into the 40s, the major tasks revolve around occupational and social achievement and stability. Still later, one should be able to gain satisfaction from accomplishments.

The identifications of tasks to be accomplished are specific enough to provide useful guidelines for building guidance and personnel programs as well as for goal setting for individual and group counseling. But the socioeconomic status of target groups must be taken into account in the use of Havighurst's developmental tasks, and his task statements provide for this adaptation.

Development may also be viewed according to Freudian theory as a series of stages through which the individual passes in biological maturation. In the first, the oral stage, focus is on oral satisfaction. The ease with which the child gets what he or she wants is important in later personality.

In the second and third years, called the anal stage, toilet training is the major task to be mastered; it is the first major source of conflict with parents, and the solution affects the development of autonomy, independence, and tendencies to control others. Still later there is the phallic stage, which is the early beginnings of normal sexual development. At this stage, the child experiences erotic and possessive feelings toward the parent of the opposite sex. The solution of this triangle has a lasting effect on personality and later interpersonal relations. If, for example, the father is extremely threatening and the mother very loving, the child may not be able to form normal social and marital relations later (Geiwitz 1976, pp. 304–313). Rivalry between children is based on the same dynamics; the child is jealous of the affection shown for his or her siblings by the parent of the opposite sex (Brown and Herrnstein 1975, p. 548). The Freudian approach puts particularly strong emphasis on the early years for the formation of adolescent and adult personality. The young person of high school age needs to reject a former dependent role and turn toward peers of the opposite sex, a process that can be helped or hindered by early parental attitudes.

Following along the same Freudian psychoanalytic approach, the structure of personality is composed of a source of energy, basically sexual and aggressive (*id*), an aspect that deals with the real world (*ego*), and the conscience (*superego*). Primitive basic drives are converted to socially acceptable behavior by the ego, while the superego judges whether the actions are good or bad. The individual who has a need to dominate others may work hard to make the best marks on a test, and thus meet the need in a socially acceptable way.

There are a number of variations in psychoanalytical theory that conceptualize human development. One that is widely used today is derived from the work of Alfred Adler. His personality theory and therapeutic approach have recently been espoused by Rudolph Dreikurs. A major postulate of the approach is that behavior is aimed mainly at coping with inferiority feelings. The individual's attempts to gain power are determinants of behavior. Furthermore, it is important for the individual to become aware that he or she can make choices of ways to attain power and recognition. The position of the child in the family has an impact on development and the types of behavior exhibited. As the individual moves through life, he or she selects goals that reflect his or her attitudes about relations with others. Problems arise because of learned distorted perceptions of self and others.

Insights about developmental processes derived from the various psychoanalytic positions have had an enormous influence on current counseling thought and practice. Typically, counselors would not use orthodox psychoanalytical theory or treatment methods, but they often do employ the models of those theorists who were members of, or were influenced by, the psychoanalytic school.

Career Development

In conceptualizing the individual's career life, it is helpful to think in terms of development. For example, as one grows older, one learns more about occupations, about personal preferences and abilities, and about the place and meaning of work in our culture. At points in time choices are made, and whereas these choices may appear to be isolated events, they are actually products of previous development. In a sense, development is largely a series of choices.

A number of theories have been formulated to explain the development and choice processes. Super's theory is one that gives considerable weight to developmental factors; there are others that embody a similar emphasis. David Tiedeman has conceptualized career decision making as an orderly series of six steps utilized as one builds an ego identity. He also links the developmental process to Erikson's psychosocial crises, indicating times when major decisions must be made. John Holland, another theorist, postulates six personality types (realistic, investigative, artistic, social, enterprising, and conventional). Career development is the process of searching for the environment that best matches one's personality type. The personality type of the individual is a result of the interaction of his or her personal attributes with the environment from the earliest years (see Herr and Cramer 1979, Ch. 4, for a discussion of these and other theories).

Super proposes five stages covering the entire life span (Super and Bohn 1970, pp. 136–137). From birth to about age 14, the child goes through the *growth stage*, which includes successive substages dominated by fantasy choices, next by interests, and a final one where abilities are the major focus. Next comes the *exploration stage*, covering the decade of life from middle teens to about the middle twenties, and involving first tentative choices, then efforts to move into desired work, and finally by a tryout of the chosen occupation.

Following the entry into what appears to be a suitable type of work, the phase of *establishment* continues for the next 20 or 30 years, until about the middle forties. The early part of this stage is usually devoted to verifying the suitability of the choice and making any needed changes. Following a generally satisfying placement, efforts are devoted to becoming established in the occupation.

Developmental tasks for the exploratory and establishment phases are (Super 1969, p. 4):

- Settling on an occupation as desirable and appropriate.
- Formulating a clear idea of what the occupation involves and how it meets one's needs.
- Putting plans into effect (getting the job).
- Becoming settled in the work.
- Achieving status and security.
- Moving ahead in the occupation.

Phases in both career development and developmental tasks show that certain decisions, plans, and new learning are related to life stages. For example, a student who should be exploring possible occupations would not profit from assistance in narrowing preferences with the purpose of making a specific choice.

These theories of career choice and development provide bases for selection of services for specific ages and educational settings. In addition, the decision processes serve as guidelines for counseling techniques as well as for use with computer guidance systems as a basis for programs to facilitate the use of self and occupational information.

Other Developmental Theories

Some developmental theories of particular value to counselors are summarized in Examples of Research on a Topic, pages 144–146. A review of these theories is recommended along with this section.

Self-Theory Approach

Another view of personality development focuses on the striving toward growth and self-actualization, toward becoming the best person one can. Key concepts are the basic drives and goals that account for behavior. In Maslow's version of this theory there is a hierarchy of needs. At the lower levels are those that must be met for survival, such as food and shelter. Next are safety and security, followed by love, affection, and the sense of belonging. Higher yet on the hierarchy are the needs involving self-esteem: respect for self and pride in accomplishments. Finally, there is the stage of self-actualization, which consists of being the best one can be and promoting the best for the society. Lower-order needs must be met before moving to higher levels, and the individual may regress to lower levels from time to time. Protection and enhancement of the *self* (self-identity, self-image) is central to this concept of personality. Conflicts can arise between what one wishes to do to make the most of potential (to become self-actualized) and the need to enhance the self through positive reactions from others. One may feel pressured into a role incongruent with the self, with a resulting gap between what one would like to be and what one is.

Using a self-theory approach, problems can be resolved when individuals feel safe enough to share their world with someone else and feel that threat to the self is low enough actually to consider alternative attitudes or behaviors and to face the feelings of adequacy or inadequacy that may arise. A person may be representing a personable, competent, successful ideal, while the real self is weak, irritable, narrow, anxious. The undesirable characteristics may be so threatening that the person cannot admit they exist. Change can take place when people face the way they really are, compare what is and what is desired, and bring the two closer together. The process helps the individual be more natural, spontaneous, and effective in all aspects of life. Situations in which the person can learn more about reactions of others, bring out feelings, and gain more realistic self-perception can facilitate the development of new and productive ways of dealing with oneself and the world. Many types of counseling and guidance activities, including growth groups and human potential programs, use this general approach to help people become happier, more productive, and more responsive to their own needs.

Building Your Own Intervention Style

Guidelines for selecting practices to implement values are found in the social sciences. The major reason for examining the theoretical bases is to provide a foundation for an effective counseling program. How it is done depends upon the individual guidance worker. One strategy is first to identify your philosophical beliefs and then draw on the social sciences to establish what to do and what to expect to achieve.

A helpful way to look at the process is described by Strickland (1969). He uses the term *philosophy* to denote the counselor's values and attitudes. (What is important? What is desirable? What is the nature and purpose of a human being?) *Theory* refers to the general plan for helping ("If I do this, the counselee will do that"). Theory emerges from, and is consistent with, philosophy. If I believe that the individual is by nature seeking self-enhancement, then I will use a relationship that helps free positive forces for effective use. *Practice*, in turn, is derived from theory and consists of the techniques used to implement it; the helping relationship to free positive forces may be, for example, implemented by demonstrating interest, concern, and understanding.

The starting place is to formulate your own values, attitudes, and beliefs. What do you believe about yourself? About others? What are they like? What do they want to do? What is the good life? The answers do not have to reflect one particular philosophical orientation (Tolbert 1972, p. 95), but they should be consistent. It would not make sense, for example, to say that individuals are of equal importance and operate on the assumption that some deserve more help than others.

The next step is to draw theoretical elements from the social sciences discussed earlier — psychology, sociology, and economics. These major sources of theory are used in subsequent chapters on counseling, group work, assessment, and other services. Research and theory do not prove unequivocally that any one method is better than others — no science provides final, fixed laws. Research and theory make a better base than intuition or trial and error; still, it is true that the counselor builds a store of experience that can often serve as a useful guide. Sue (1975c) has clarified the issue by pointing out the essential nature of a research base for the profession while acknowledging the value of experience and intuition. Research is not the complete answer, but it is one essential element.

Returning to the problem of improving practice, suppose you want to improve the general climate in your school. Through interviews, surveys, and personal observation, you have verified the existence of tension, hostility, and a lack of communication in the school. The obvious signs are absenteeism, vandalism, disciplinary problems, and low achievement. Drawing on psychology and sociology, you set up a plan, try it out, and evaluate results. The plan is itself a tentative theory. You have used theory to improve practice in two ways. First, you have used material from the social services for guidelines; second, you have organized your own plan into a theory-practice model.

Summary Concepts

The values of the society are reflected in the type of human services provided. If some measure of freedom of choice did not exist, there would be no point in helping individuals make choices. The cultural context of services has a tremendous impact on the nature and goals of guidance, counseling, and personnel services. The philosophical position of the counselor determines his or her style of helping and also the counselor's expectations of what counselee growth will consist of. These philosophical assumptions or values about the individual that focus on freedom, personal responsibility for choices, and respect appear to be essential for the helper.

The values $\longrightarrow$ theory $\longrightarrow$ practice paradigm illustrates how social science theory flows from values and provides ways to help individuals achieve their goals. Insights about helping procedures may be derived from theories of personality, learning, and development. The counselor brings together those concepts that are useful to him or her and organizes them into a workable rationale for counseling, consulting, and program building.

Examples of Research on a Topic
Developmental Stages

Developmental stages provide important bases of counseling. Patterns in career development, developmental tasks, and psychological crises, among others, have already been mentioned. Other research and theorizing that have important implications for counselors have been reported by Gould, Levinson, Sears, and Grunebaum. After reading the following brief summaries, what do you see as major counseling emphases for the various age periods covered?

Gould (1975) used a series of questions that covered major life concerns to assess developmental changes in more than 500 middle-class males and females, aged 16 to 60. Identifiable stages with unique characteristics were found. The results support the position that one's personality is not developed by the 20s but continues to change at least until the sixth decade. The early assurance of the 20s is to some extent replaced by an awareness of a lack of finances to accomplish the things one wishes to do. During the 40s, there is an awareness that time is passing, and major changes in one's career are difficult. The 50s are marked by increased self-acceptance and coming to terms with accomplishments and aspirations. There are other factors, but these reflect the continuous changes marking adult development.

Levinson's (Levinson 1977; Levinson, Darrow, Klein, Levinson, and McKee 1976) research on the psychological development of men, using 40 individuals for intensive study and a number of written accounts of individuals' lives, has revealed a series of stages and transitional phases that illustrate changing goals, needs, values, relationships, and behaviors. First there is the early adult transition in the upper teens and early 20s. Entering the adult world characterizes the 20s. Toward the end of this period a transition phase begins in which the early life structure is revised — it is a time to start in new directions if it is ever to be done. For some, this is a smooth transition; for others, it amounts to a crisis, affecting personal perceptions, marriage, work, and life-style. Following the transition period, the second adult life structure is formed at 32 or 33 and lasts until about the end of the 30s. It is a period of striving to build a life. Toward the end of this period, beginning about age 36–37, the individual moves into a stage designated by the acronym, BOOM (becoming one's own man) in which he is fully adult with the rewards and demands of this status. Following this period, there is the midlife transition that bridges the period from early to middle adulthood. The individual raises questions about the previous life structure and searches for personal meanings and values.

Other stages follow. Opportunities to change and grow continue to appear; the ones given here are the major stages that have been studied.

Grunebaum (1979) summarizes research on development suggesting that in the middle and later years wives may move away from a dependent and nurturant role toward a more assertive one, while husbands may do just the opposite. One result of this change in balance may be the husband's feelings of loss or threat. Sears (1977), in analyzing longitudinal data from Terman's study of gifted children, found that factors characterizing life satisfactions in the 30s continued to be present throughout the next three decades of life. These factors, involving the affective aspects of the individual — feelings of self-worth, enjoyment of the battle for achievement, feelings of having used abilities — were more important than more objective ones such as high-level preparation, financial success, and status.

The results of these and similar developmental studies represent preliminary statements and are somewhat like progress reports on continuing investigations. They do, however, provide a framework for understanding the developmental process.

Describe the counseling emphases you consider to be appropriate for the stages identified in these studies. At which level would you prefer to work?

Experiential Activities

Helpful activities are those in which students gain insight into how values, attitudes, and developmental stages affect their behavior and that of others with whom they plan to work. It is also important to infer how these factors lead to helping activities. In this way a connection will be apparent between this chapter and the chapters concerned with services that come later.

1. Clarifying Values

Students list ten values that each holds, in order of personal importance. Then they rank these values by the way they contribute to economic/social success. Discuss the results of the two rankings, either in small groups or with the whole class.

2. Making Value Decisions

A capable pupil, Mary, has been skipping afternoon classes and is threatened with suspension. You have talked with her and found her truancy allows her to work part time in a lunchroom. She has lied about her age to get the job. She says that she is helping out at home; her father is unemployed; her mother needs medical care; and unemployment payments have run out. If her parents know that she is working, they will force her to stop. In that case, she says she will drop out of school and work full time, even though her ambition is to continue at least through two years of community college. (Cooperative education is not a possibility.) She has given you this information with the assurance that you will keep it confidential.

What would you do?

What values underlie your decision?

What is the basis for your decision? Check the following list of moral criteria (based on Kohlberg in Geiwitz 1976, pp. 320–324). Note that the list does not refer to the decision itself but to your reasons for it.

- What you consider to be right or wrong, particularly to avoid difficulty or punishment.
- How much it suits you, i.e., fits in with your personal desires.
- What you think a "good" person should do according to school policy.
- Your recognition that there need to be rules and regulations.
- Your belief that rules and laws represent the consensus of the majority while recognizing that laws can be changed.
- Your belief about a higher principle of what is ethically correct.

3. Developmental Stages

In small groups, discuss events, interests, behaviors, and attitudes that appear to characterize developmental stages for group members. (For example, at what ages did members begin to be aware of community influences and persons as contrasted with home influences? At what ages did members begin to think seriously about what they would like as a career?) List the stages along with two or three specific needs that were present and that caused difficulties. Discuss the applicability of the stages, i.e., how well they fit all group members.

4. Self-Concept

Using small groups, ask each individual to list five adjectives that are descriptive of him or her. Then have one person collect and read each list aloud. Ask group members to identify the writer. Discuss reasons for choices.

5. Learning Theory

In small groups, discuss the learning theory your parents used.

Suggested Readings

Aubrey, Roger F. "Technology of Counseling and the Science of Behavior: A Rapprochement." *Personnel and Guidance Journal* 58, no. 5 (1980), pp. 318–327.

A highly recommended reading that shows convincingly the critical importance of bases in the social sciences and the humanities. The reader should be impressed by extensive evidence marshaled to show why counselors in all settings have much to gain from a study of the disciplines that provide a foundation for counseling, guidance, and personnel work. (Note: This is the guest editor's article in a special issue on "Counseling and the Behavioral

Sciences." Several others are listed here, but the whole issue is particularly useful for this chapter.)

Blocher, Donald H. "Some Implications of Recent Research in Social and Developmental Psychology for Counseling Practice." *Personnel and Guidance Journal* 58, no. 5 (1980), pp. 334–336.

A brief but very helpful reading on how recent psychological research can be used to build a counseling model. An example of strategy construction is given.

Brown, Roger, and Herrnstein, Richard J. *Psychology.* Boston: Little, Brown, 1975.

An excellent source of theory and research illustrating psychological bases of guidance. Chapter 11, on personality, is especially recommended.

Free, Christine G., and Tiedeman, David V. "Counseling and Comprehension of the Economics of Change." *Personnel and Guidance Journal* 58, no. 5 (1980), pp. 358–367.

A insightful article that discusses how the science of economics can broaden the counselor's perspective on his or her work.

Goethals, George W., and Klos, Dennis S. *Experiencing Youth.* 2nd ed. Boston: Little, Brown, 1976.

Twenty-seven vivid first-person accounts of the lives of college students, analyzed from various theoretical approaches, e.g., those of Freud and Erikson. While the subjects are beyond high school, the accounts cover the developmental process during childhood and early adolescence.

Heath, Douglas H. "Wanted: A Comprehensive Model of Healthy Development." *Personnel and Guidance Journal* 58, no. 5 (1980), pp. 391–399.

A stimulating if somewhat tentative model of the development of the healthy person. The author brings together an impressive amount of research to support a model that has important implications for counselors.

Hennessy, Thomas C. "Introduction to the Special Issue, 'Values and the Counselor.'" *Personnel and Guidance Journal* 58, no. 9 (1980), pp. 557–558.

The introductory article in a special issue on the place of values in the helping profession. Excellent as an overview of questions and issues. (The whole issue is particularly relevant for this chapter.)

Kegan, Robert Graham. "The Evolving Self: A Process Conception for Ego Psychology." *The Counseling Psychologist* 8, no. 2 (1979), pp. 5–34.

A stimulating and complex article that brings together several theoretical streams and applies them to cases. Valuable with this chapter as an example of using theory to guide interventions.

Kohlberg, Lawrence, and Wasserman, Elsa R. "The Cognitive-Developmental Approach and the Practicing Counselor: An Opportunity for Counselors to Rethink Their Roles." *Personnel and Guidance Journal* 58, no. 9 (1980), pp. 559–567. (See also the article by Rest.)

A lucid and interesting presentation of Kohlberg's approach to the identification of stages of moral development, including ways of implementing moral development concepts in schools and other settings. Ivey's comments in "The Counselor as Psychoeducational Consultant: Toward a Value-Centered Advocacy Model" (pp. 567–568) further substantiate the potential of this approach.

Loevinger, Jane. "Some Thoughts on Ego Development and Counseling." *Personnel and Guidance Journal* 58, no. 5 (1980), pp. 389–390. (See also the article by Swensen.)

A commentary on Swensen's discussion of ego development by an out-standing authority on this approach to personality development.

Miller, Carroll H. *Foundations of Guidance.* New York: Harper and Bros., 1961.

The classic on foundations of guidance, covering major cultural, economic, and psychological factors. The author surveys and synthesizes research in psychology, sociology, and other areas. Any chapter will add depth to the reader's understanding of guidance.

Miller, Theodore K., and Prince, Judith S. *The Future of Student Affairs.* San Francisco: Jossey-Bass, 1976.

Rest, James R. "Moral Judgment Research and the Cognitive-Developmental Approach to Moral Education." *Personnel and Guidance Journal* 58, no. 9 (1980), pp. 602–605.

The author presents evidence to support a developmental process for moral judgment and gives suggestions for program building. This is a valuable article, particularly in connection with the one by Kohlberg and Wasserman.

Rodgers, Robert F. "Theories Underlying Student Development." In *Student Development in Higher Education,* edited by Don C. Creamer, pp. 10–95. Cincinnati: American College Personnel Association, 1980.

A well-developed exposition of theoretical bases of a student development emphasis in college student personnel services. A valuable reference for those interested in higher education.

Schlossberg, Nancy K., and Entine, Alan D. "Guest Editor's Preface." *The Counseling Psychologist* 6, no. 1 (1976), p. 2.

The "Preface" introduces a series of articles and studies on developmental stages, helping strategies, and related topics. Section 1, "Adult Development," contains articles of particular relevance for this chapter.

Smith, Darrell, and Peterson, James A. "Counseling for Values in a Time of Perspective." *Personnel and Guidance Journal* 55, no. 6 (1977), pp. 309–318.

A vivid presentation of the value issues the counselor must deal with. The article is particularly helpful for readers beginning to identify where they stand on counseling values.

Swensen, Clifford H. "Ego Development as a General Model for Counseling and Psychotherapy." *Personnel and Guidance Journal* 58, no. 5 (1980) pp. 382–388. (See also the article by Loevinger.)

The research and theory on ego development is synthesized to show how this can be a productive approach to planning helping strategies. A valuable reading for understanding this rationale.

Tyler, Leona E. "Theoretical Principles Underlying the Counseling Process." *Journal of Counseling Psychology* 5, no. 1 (1958), pp. 3–8.

The author describes how she collects techniques, principles, and values from a variety of fields and uses them to build an approach to counseling. An excellent illustration of the point of view of this chapter. Pepinsky's comment (pp. 8–10) underlines the difficulties of building a rigorous theory as opposed to a general rationale.

Widick, Carole; Knefelkamp, Lee; and Parker, Clyde A. "Student Development." In *Student Services,* edited by Ursula Delworth and Gary R. Hanson, pp. 75–116. San Francisco: Jossey-Bass, 1980.

Chapter
7
Building Counseling, Guidance, and Student Personnel Programs

You can build a program in any setting by using similar principles. A school, college, or community agency is a social institution; staff members must work together to achieve goals. Effective operations of the program depend upon attitudes, motivations, competencies, and teamwork. Moreover, goals must be perceived by staff as meaningful and attainable.

It is not enough for the staff to be an effectively functioning social system, however. The program must focus on the needs of the target population, with the most pressing needs receiving top priority. In addition, there must be discernible benefits to those served. The program is accountable for producing results.

Fortunately, there are a number of well-developed procedures for building programs that are both organizationally sound and capable of having an impact on those served. In this chapter, a general program-building procedure is described, and there is special emphasis on techniques of goal setting. Evaluation is touched upon briefly but is covered in detail in Chapter 13.

The Counselor's Role in Program Building

All counselors have some responsibility for program building. As a counselor you may not be directly involved at first — the school, college, or agency program may already be in place and functioning. But before long, you will inevitably become involved in answering such questions as: Which services are needed? How may approaches be altered? How may personnel be shifted to improve efficiency? How may program support be justified? Moreover, either alone or with other staff members, you may actually be initiating an entirely new program. But perhaps your most important responsibility will be changing, modifying, or expanding existing programs to meet new and emerging needs, such as reaching disadvantaged unemployed high school dropouts, providing services for changing college populations, or establishing helping relationships with emotionally maladjusted individuals in the community.

What should you know about program development and management, and what skills should you master? The first course can provide only an overview of the areas; later courses and experiences in the program build knowledge and competency. The major areas taken up in sections that follow highlight the essential elements.

Regardless of the setting in which you work, you will be faced with the need to contribute effectively to the organization, to keep your skill up to date, and to help insure that your organization has a positive impact on those served. Effective programming is the key to these goals; it is the best way to insure continuation of the service.

The Process of Program Planning

Phases of Planning

The steps involved in program planning are identified and discussed in the sections that follow. The planning process is cumulative; each phase leads into, and is a prerequisite to, the next one.

Organizational Approval and Support.   The management and coordination of program planning is a primary consideration. Staff members who are participating in the process first need to have the approval and support of the organization or agency to begin the process. They also must have a background of planning and management competencies as well as an understanding of theories on which the program will be based, such as, pupil or student development.

Formulating the Program Rationale.   Those involved should be aware of the steps in program planning, from looking at the philosophical assumptions underlying the program, to evaluation and modification. Determining what the program should do (goals), why, for whom, and in what setting are initial considerations. Models of human behavior and development are considerations here. Are you concerned about the effective development of elementary school pupils? The social and personal growth of college students? The mental health of community members? This stage not only gives a focus to planning but provides guidelines for selecting a psychological model or models of human growth and development to serve as a foundation for the program. The needs of the target group are assessed using the model as a guide for formulating questions.

Needs Assessment.   Needs of the target group are assessed by data-gathering techniques such as use of questionnaires and interviews. The input of other concerned persons may be obtained; for example, teachers, parents, and employers have valuable information to provide about needs of pupils.

Formulating Goals and Objectives.   At this point, you have the data on which to base the broad goals of the program. Furthermore, you are able to put these goals in order of importance. For instance, you may decide that in keeping with rationale and needs, community college students should develop a flexible approach to facing future changes; college students should be able to cope successfully with the pressures and demands of a new environment; midlife career changers should be able to plan job-getting strategies. Goals stated in these terms are too broad and too general to permit assessment; they are, however, the sources of the specific outcomes you wish to attain.

These specific outcomes — the *objectives* of the program — are formulated in terms that make evaluation possible. Both process and product objectives may be established (see goals and objectives in later sections of this chapter). These objectives are the guides for determining what you should do and for assessing how well you have done it. Objectives must be stated in ways that allow observation of results.

At this point, you know in specific terms what you want to accomplish, those whom you want your program to benefit, and how they will demonstrate program effects. In the college student development program, your objective might be that students know about campus resources such as counseling services or remedial and how-to-study programs. This is a relatively simple objective and can be easily checked, but it is extremely important. Another objective could be in the area of students' sense of community; the objective might be reduction of prejudice, an increase in minority participation in college activities, an improved evaluation of dormitory programs, or an increase in the quality of life planning skills. In the community mental health agency, an objective in the area of improved family life could be the reduction of rates of children's truancy, marital conflict, and divorce. All these objectives are assessable in terms of observable events or conditions. While other outcomes — increased sensitivity to others, a more positive outlook, avoidance of drug use — may result from services and may be difficult to assess, a way must be found to translate them into objectives that can be measured to help give credibility to program effects. Some counselors may feel that formulating a number of specific objectives will distort the humanistic concerns of counseling services, but practical considerations demand that it be done. Without substantiating data, it is unlikely that programs will be supported on the basis of assertions that they "help people."

Functions.   Having established objectives, the next step is to select or devise functions to achieve them: counseling, testing, and orientation are typical functions. The program descriptions in Chapters 2, 3, and 4 illustrate strategies used in various settings. At the elementary school level, for example, group counseling may be provided to enable pupils to improve their communications skills. At the high school level, individual counseling may function as a strategy to help pupils resolve personal problems. At the college level, peer advising may be a means of helping students adjust to the campus environment. In the community mental health agency, outreach counseling may be used to help those who are unable to come to the agency. Consultation may be beneficial in altering destructive community conditions or in assisting community members to become helpers. The functions selected should be ones the staff can provide or learn to provide, although it may be necessary to employ some personnel to provide services that are outside the competency of the staff.

Resources.   At this stage of planning it is necessary to consider other resources such as facilities, equipment, time, and financial support available for providing the intervention strategies. If, for example, the time is not available to see each counselee for a number of individual sessions, alternative approaches will have to be adopted. If a computer guidance system is needed, the cost of the technology will have to be considered.

At this time it is also important to investigate what is already being done. It is quite often the case that others in an agency or institution are already providing services that relate to program objectives.

Staffing.   The next step, staffing, calls for assignment of responsibilities in keeping with competencies and preferences. Staff development may be needed to enable personnel to update existing skills and learn new ones. Staff development may also be used to improve the efficiency of the organization, prevent burnout, and enhance organizational climate. Guidelines for selecting and upgrading staff members are discussed later in this chapter.

Evaluation.   The next step is to decide who will do the evaluation, how it will be done, and how the results will be used. The objectives set up earlier provide the basis for estimating how well you are doing what you have set out to do. It is essential that the total evaluation process be built into the program plan; otherwise, evaluation might be incomplete (e.g., essential data might not be collected at the only time they are available). Without specific provisions, such data might be left out altogether.

Using results of evaluation to remedy deficiencies and improve the program is a process that takes place after results are in, but setting up procedures for carrying out these activities is part of the planning process.

Since results may be threatening to staff, efforts should be made to insure that evaluation data are viewed as helpful in upgrading services rather than for providing evaluation of individuals.

Preparing the Budget.   Throughout the planning process, budgetary provisions must be considered, but part of the final plan should be a detailed budget showing all types of costs, including personnel, supplies and materials, space, and utilities. In some settings, such as schools, space and utilities may not be thought of as costs since they are usually part of the existing building and are provided routinely. But these items should be included so that the total cost of the operation can be determined.

Implementing and Evaluating the Program.   All the parts of the program have now been developed, and financial resources have been obtained. The next step is to put the program into operation and evaluate its effectiveness. An analysis of results may show that changes are needed. If so, they are made. Evaluation does not stop with the initial trial of the program; it is a continuous process.

While the preceding steps give a general outline of the program-planning process; there are other approaches that specify more precise directions. One of the best known is the systems approach.

The Systems Approach to Program Planning

The systems approach is a method of organizing parts of a program (system) so that each part contributes to the general mission; the approach also specifies relations among elements. There are provisions for continuous evaluation to determine the effectiveness of the total system as well as of each subsystem. The approach does not determine program priorities, functions, and target populations, but it provides systematic procedures for identifying and reaching them.

The flowchart in Figure 7-1 shows the systems process. The major elements are somewhat similar to the steps given earlier. A comparison is given in Table 7-1.

To clarify the comparisons, the major systems units in Figure 7-1 are defined. First, there is an analysis of the environment and the target groups. This is essentially a needs survey. Second, from needs, problems are specified. For example, pupils may require help in developing positive social relations with each other, or fitting courses to career plans. Third, program goals and objectives are set up. Goals are general statements of what is to be accomplished; objectives are specific behaviors that can be observed and assessed. Objectives are particularly important; there is no way to estimate the effectiveness of the system if results cannot be measured. Fourth, all information, resources, and staff are organized into a

Figure 7-1 Counseling and guidance program development system model.

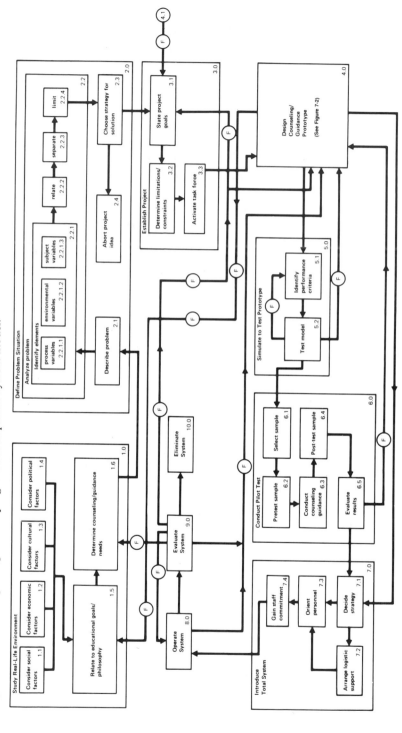

Source: From R. E. Hosford and T. A. Ryan, "Systems Design in the Development of Counseling and Guidance Programs," *Personnel and Guidance Journal* 49, no. 3 (1970), p. 226. Copyright 1970 American Personnel and Guidance Association. Reprinted with permission.

Activity	Hours	Dollars
Conferences with Olive	38	532
Conferences with mother	3	42
Conferences with teachers	2	28
	Total	602

(Krumboltz 1974, p. 642)

In a comment about the case the counselor says, "I'm sure I helped Olive overcome her depression but the most effective technique, I think, was assigning her to help a new transfer student. The new transfer student became her best friend. Many other hours I spent with Olive seem wasted" (Krumboltz 1974, p. 645).

Dimensions of Counselor Functioning

Another model that can serve as an aid in program planning, the *dimensions of counselor functioning cube*, is shown in Figure 7-3. This is not a guide for the total planning process, but it identifies major elements to be considered — target groups, purposes, and strategies.

Figure 7-3   Dimensions of counselor functioning.

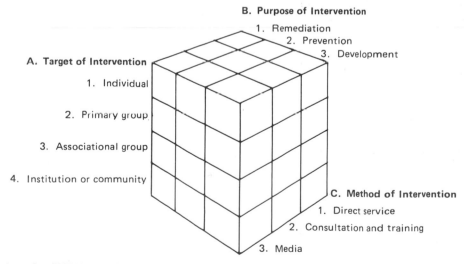

Source: From W. H. Morrill, E. R. Oetting, and J. C. Hurst, "Dimensions of Counselor Functioning," *Personnel and Guidance Journal* 52, no. 6 (1974), p. 370. Copyright 1974 W. H. Morrill, E. R. Oetting, and J. C. Hurst. Reprinted with permission.

Table 7-1
A COMPARISON OF TWO SYSTEMS MODELS

Hosford and Ryan Systems Model	Steps Given Earlier in This Chapter
1.0 Study real-life environment	organizational approval and support formulating the program rationale needs assessment
2.0 Define problem situation	(covered in "needs" assessment)
3.0 Establish project goals	formulating goals and objectives
4.0 Design counseling/guidance program prototype	functions resources staffing evaluation preparing the budget
5.0 Simulate to test program prototype	no comparable step
6.0 Pilot test model	no comparable step
7.0 Introduce system	implementing and evaluating the program
8.0 Operate system	same as above
9.0 Evaluate system	same as above
10.0 Eliminate system	(covered in "implementing and evaluating the program")

guidance plan or program (usually referred to as a model). Fifth, the model is tested. This may be done by such methods as computer simulation or the use of a small selection of pupils. Needed modifications are made. Sixth, the model is instituted. Systematic evaluation is carried out. Outdated or ineffective parts (or the total program) are replaced. (The *F* in Figure 7-1 indicates feedback for evaluating and modifying subsystems.)

The two procedures are relatively similar in the overall process, but the systems model has the advantage of being far more specific, showing alternative steps, and giving needed emphasis to feedback. Moreover, the systems approach clearly gives more weight to pilot testing and evaluating the system.

Figure 7-2 gives additional details for section 4.0 in Figure 7-1 (design counseling/guidance prototype). It illustrates systems steps in program design. The "Design C/G unit, sequences" make up the program. Carrying out this step involves a comparison of the costs and effectiveness of different helping strategies.

The systems approach provides a unique program, characterized by

Figure 7-2   Counseling/guidance programs prototype.

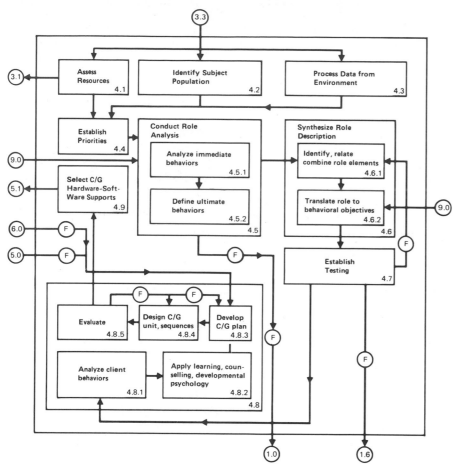

measurable objectives, clear-cut ways of achieving them, and evaluation in terms of effects on pupils. The model meets the accountability requirement and provides information on relative costs of strategies (Krumboltz 1974). The Los Angeles, California, plan for pupil personnel services is an example of this approach (Mitchell and Saum 1972, pp. 75–91; Sullivan and O'Hare 1971, pp. 1–6).

Planning, Program, Budgeting Systems (PPBS)

Another program-planning procedure ties program services and results to costs. Shaw (1973, pp. 336–337) points out that the systems approach and PPBS are interrelated. In many ways the program-building steps are the same, but PPBS approach adds the process of relating program costs to results. This process requires clear-cut objectives that can be used to show effects. In addition, there is a comparison of functions to determine which one is the most effective in reaching outcomes. The comparative importance of objectives also must be considered (e.g., an insignificant objective may receive little or no funds even if it is quite inexpensive).

When costs (salary of counselor, overhead, materials) are brought into program planning to relate results to the most effective procedures, an accountability model is being employed. Thus, if students can make as good choices of college majors in group sessions as they can in individual sessions, the group method would be preferable. (The *primary* reason for using groups, however, is not to save money.)

Consulting is obviously one function that has particularly good potential for cost-effectiveness. If aides in a mental health program can learn how to build a therapeutic climate that prepares individuals for return to the community as rapidly as individual therapist conferences do, the cost-benefits of the aide procedure are obvious. Krumboltz's (1974) illustration of how a counselor can keep a costs-results account of work is probably the best example of a relatively simple way of being accountable. One example from his article showing the actual cost and results of working with a severely depressed girl is as follows:

Problem Identification:

Olive's mother phoned: Olive depressed, talking vaguely of suicide, no friends.

Method:

Analysis of social reinforcers for Olive; social skill training; assigned Olive to help new transfer student.

Outcome:

Olive increased frequency of initiating social contact from 0/month to 4/month; reports having one good friend vs 0; mother reports Olive's depression gone — suicide talk from 1/month before referral to 0/month for 3 consecutive months.

The *A* dimension contains four target groups ranging from the individual to the institution or community. The specific purpose of counseling assistance falls in the *B* dimension; purposes range from remediation for existing problems to training and development. (Psychological education is an example of training.) The method of intervention is shown on the *C* dimension.

This efficient model makes a unique contribution by helping counselors clarify their work. The target-group dimension, for example, includes the individual; the primary group, such as family; the association group, such as a class or club; and the institution or community. The classification of purposes of intervention into remedial help, prevention, and development facilitates the choice of an appropriate method. ("Developmental intervention" is a technical term; it describes methods aiming to encourage growth, build strengths, and prepare for meeting needs.) The third dimension of the cube, showing methods of intervention, relates to the way help is provided. There are three approaches — direct face-to-face help, indirect assistance by consultation and preparing others to work with counselees, and the use of medialike computers and programmed materials. All of the activities of service are based on choices from elements in the three dimensions. A complete plan includes objectives, assessment methods, and coordinating procedures.

Goals and Objectives

No one element of the counseling program is expendable, but goals and objectives are without doubt the most critical for success. Counselors are realizing without them programs are often terminated when expenditures are reviewed for budget cuts. The public is insisting on an accounting for the use of funds and evidence that an agency justifies its existence; services that cannot document results are dropped.

Goals and objectives communicate what the service is attempting to accomplish and enable progress in meeting objectives to be judged. Functions like counseling and consulting are important, of course; without them nothing would be accomplished. But goals and objectives provide the ultimate justification for the total guidance program. Still, despite its importance, this aspect of the program typically gets little attention.

Definitions

One major problem in defining goals and objectives of a guidance program is confusion about terms. Widely used definitions are as follows:

Goals.   General statements of what is to be accomplished. They do not provide a basis for assessment of progress. This is an example of a goal statement from a school guidance plan: "To help pupils develop positive feelings about themselves." How can positive feelings be measured? What do we mean by positive feelings? How can we tell if pupils have developed them? How much do they have to develop for us to judge our efforts successful? Obviously, something more is needed to serve as a guide for planning and evaluation.

Objectives.   Sometimes called "specific goals," these state explicitly what we hope to accomplish. A good statement of an objective indicates what skill, attitude, or value is to be learned, who will learn it, how it will be demonstrated, and how much is needed to represent success on the part of the pupil. The two following statements are examples:

1. College students make the most of educational opportunities at the school.
2. Help entering freshmen choose a program consistent with stated goals and demonstrated ability in which they perform satisfactorily for the year.

Which one gives guidelines for action and provides for evaluation? Obviously the second. The example is oversimplified; better-developed ones are given later, but this one does show the basic difference between a vague, general objective and a specific one. Objectives provide the means to estimate attainment of goals; usually several objectives are needed for each goal.

Process Objectives.   These are objectives in terms of process (for example: counselors will see all tenth graders; counselors will confer with all teachers every two weeks). Such objectives are valuable if they are logical consequences of appropriate vehicles for change and have a basis in theory, but they tell little about pupil outcome.

Outcome Objectives.   This type is illustrated in the examples; it describes what is supposed to happen as a result of guidance. Process objectives can be translated into outcome objectives. If, as a result of counselor conferences, teachers initiate one new group technique each week, the result is an outcome objective for the counselor — it indicates what happens as a result of services. For the teacher, however, it is a process objective.

Performance Objectives.   The most useful type, though there is argument over how suitable such objectives are for counselors (Gubser 1974). Guidance and counseling should make a difference in people's lives, but counselors do not agree on the type of evidence and the methods needed to measure its effect. Can significant individual growth such as developing a sense of identity be put in objectively measurable terms? Is it possible to assess how many pupils have stopped using drugs because of the guidance program? (Accountability is discussed in detail in Chapter 13.)

Setting Up Goals and Objectives

Setting up goals and objectives is a clear-cut process and relatively simple to carry out. There are a number of useful guides that can help (Sullivan and O'Hare 1971; Mitchell and Saum, eds., 1972).

Goals and objectives are based on needs; needs assessment is therefore the first step. This includes all persons concerned: What problems do they face? What do they hope to achieve? What do they think the school or agency should do?

The greatest difficulty often seems to come at the end point of translating needs data into goals and objectives. There is a tendency to make objectives so broad that they are impossible to carry out and evaluate (e.g., "Help all pupils to make optimum use of potential"). There is also a tendency to substitute functions for objectives (e.g., "Provide group experiences for students"). There is also a tendency to establish objectives to cover everything. Usually priorities have to be set up and some important needs must be left out. Philosophy, goals, and objectives have an important relationship. Philosophy tells what is true, good, and real; needs tell what people feel they lack for a good life. Needs can conflict with values; for example, some pupils want preferential treatment. It is necessary, therefore, to check goals and objectives against the philosophy of the program and to present the projected program activities against these goals and objectives.

A philosophy should contain statements such as the following excerpts from *Perspectives on Secondary Guidance* (Lombana 1977, p. 1):

> Secondary school guidance services exist to provide assistance to students as they attempt to cope with the difficult, often puzzling, and complex problems associated with educational, personal, and vocational development. Facilitative in character, guidance services are planned, developed, and implemented on the basis of student-referenced assumptions:
> that each student is a unique individual capable of achieving self-direction in problem-solving and decision-making;
> that each student has a right to full acceptance and opportunity for personal development within the school milieu;
> that each student has a responsibility to seek fulfillment through maximum participation in the educational and career guidance programs in the school.

Writing of Goals and Objectives

The SPOP (Situation, Population, Outcome, Process) approach developed by a task force of the Bureau of Pupil Personnel Services of the California State Department of Education illustrates a systematic and effective way to spell out the specific accomplishments individuals are expected to attain. Each objective statement indicates the following (Sullivan and O'Hare 1971, pp. 16–21):

- Situation: describes the target group.
- Population
- Outcome: the desired behavior and expected level.
- Process: how the desired behavior will be learned.

The model further classifies objectives on three dimensions: educational level; educational, social, vocational needs; and action, awareness, or accommodation.

Staffing the Program

Utilizing the skills of the existing staff has already been mentioned in program development, particularly in deciding about who will carry out which functions or implement which helping strategies. There are several additional procedures that can be used to enhance the effectiveness of staffing. These procedures include job descriptions, staff development, differentiated staffing, utilization of unique talents, opening lines of communication, organizing a representative staff, and providing for effective management of the program. Both the initial selection and the ongoing conditions for work have an impact on staff productivity.

Staff Participation in Program Building

Before discussing these factors, mention should be made of the effects of staff participation in program building. Although at times reactions may be negative, there is value in having those who will actually carry out the program take part in building it as well as in evaluating the results. If this is done, it is likely that there will be more personal involvement and commitment in seeing that strategies work than if the program were set up by outsiders. At the same time, it should be pointed out that consultation from outside the organization may help agency staff identify target-population problems that might have been missed and reveal organizational difficulties that, for one reason or another, have been overlooked. It is suggested that the main, continuing responsibilities for program planning and management be handled by the local staff and that outside consultation be used for specific problems that appear to be outside the ability of the local staff to solve because of lack of technical knowhow or because it will not be possible to maintain organizational cohesiveness and good working relationships.

Job Descriptions

Carefully thought out, mutually acceptable job descriptions should be prepared for every staff position, including paraprofessionals and clerical personnel. In addition to spelling out the responsibilities of each position, the description should indicate relationships to other personnel — direct supervision by or for the job-holder, advisory relationships, and reports by or to the person occupying the position. The description should also indicate the qualifications needed for the position and lines of advancement to and from it. (The detailed educational, experience, and other qualifications used for employment may be in a separate list designed for hiring purposes.) The description should be free of bias of any kind.

Well-developed job descriptions can do much to reduce intra-agency conflicts, overlapping functions, and duplication of effort. Continuous monitoring of actual functions is needed, however; the best job descriptions that can be written will not guarantee that conflicts and misunderstandings will not occur in day-to-day practice.

Staff Development

Staff development is an invaluable program component to insure that services are up to date, well designed, and appropriate. Training may be used to help staff members learn new skills (e.g., group counseling). It can also be used to assist them to update areas of expertise (e.g., how to interpret new occupational interest inventories). Staff development can also be valuable in helping build good working relationships among staff members, improving institutional morale and effectiveness, and lessening the likelihood of counselor burnout. This aspect has to be carefully done; many well-intended efforts in this direction have the opposite effect. Overkill is a danger; too much "staff development" can build resistance.

What is labeled "staff development" sometimes amounts to little more than presenting staff members with administrative regulations and rules. Such tasks as these may need to be done, but a recitation of regulations does not constitute staff development.

Staff Differentiation

Differentiated staffing is one way to facilitate the best possible use of talents. In any setting there are functions that must be performed by the professionals (e.g., individual and group counseling). There are others than can be broken down into relatively simple tasks and carried out by paraprofessionals. For example, paraprofessionals can provide information about services to prospective counselors; they can administer and score some group tests and inventories; they can contact persons in the community in order to motivate them to seek help; and they can operate crisis telephone services. Indigenous personnel may be particularly effective in providing specific services to groups of which they are a member (e.g., disadvantaged, minority). In these ways, paraprofessionals can both extend the reach of services far beyond what would otherwise be possible and enable counselors to devote their time to professional services. The same principle holds for the secretarial staff. Duties and responsibilities should be assigned so that counselors do not have to use their time for clerical work. The concept can be extended in the professional direction by designating one or more of the counselors as consultants to others. These consultants, by virtue of extensive experience and training, can be of help to newer and less experienced staff members.

The Question of Specialization

Staffing raises the question of the specialist versus the generalist. Should all counselors in the school, college, or agency perform all duties — that is, counsel all types of individuals? On the other hand, should specialization enable each one to do what he or she prefers and can do best? (See Shaw 1973, pp. 45–46, for another interpretation of specialist v. generalist. He uses the term *generalist* to cover indirect help, e.g., consultation.) For example, an agency counselor who is particularly effective in group counseling would have the opportunity to do much of the small-group work; a secondary school counselor who is knowledgeable about college admissions may be given extra time to concentrate on this service. The same question arises for presenting problems (e.g., substance abuse, marital conflict, deep-seated feelings of inadequacy). In staff specialization use is made of particular talents and interests of staff members. On the other hand, staff members may become too specialized to be aware of the total scope of the setting; they may build small "empires" and not be able to assist each other in case conferences. A staffing approach that involves all staff members in all types of cases is recommended. Staff development offers a way to help each member develop needed competencies for service-wide involvement.

Communication Among Staff

Open lines of communication among all staff members, including clerical and paraprofessional workers, are essential for a smooth-running organization. Quite often these lines run down but not up; for instance, paraprofessionals may not have the opportunity to express their views about supervision, duties, and advancement opportunities. Lateral communication, however, is not automatically present. Misunderstandings may frequently arise about who does what; clear-cut job descriptions can help resolve problems, but productive interactions call for continuous monitoring of communication effectiveness.

Staffing and the Target Population

Those responsible for staffing need to be aware of legislation in such areas as affirmative action in order to select and reward personnel in keeping with guidelines and policies. But, more than merely following regulations, directors might do well to consider the nature of the target populations and look at staffs from their points of view. While building a staff with proportional representation to the population served is not advocated here (it *could* be in violation of laws), it is suggested that the helping service have at least some representatives of ethnic, racial, or other categories that characterize the population served. Numerous potential counselees have expressed this point of view to this author; that is, the service is more approachable by persons if a staff member like them is visible.

Staff Effectiveness

Effective staff performance depends on the quality of work done by each member and the workability of relationships in day-to-day operations. Problems arise because of poor communication, dissatisfied staff members, ineffective administration, and a host of other reasons. Organization development (OD) is a relatively new approach to reducing problems and improving the effectiveness of organizations. Definitions of OD vary, but Huse cites a useful one: organization development is "A long range effort to improve an organization's problem-solving and renewal process, particularly through a more effective and collaborative management of the organization culture. . . . with the assistance of a change agent, or catalyst and the use of theory and technology of applied behavioral science, including action research" (1975, p. 13). This definition implies that first there is an awareness of the need for change. Data are usually collected through interviews, surveys, or other means. Then an outside consultant (who may have been the one who collected the data about problems) utilizes counseling, consulting, group work, or other means to effect change.

OD at Work

An example of a limited organization development project is one that was carried out in a counseling and guidance agency. There were a total of

To provide effective services, the staff must work well together on a daily basis.

20 staff members, including clerical workers and paraprofessionals. Some signs of discontent paved the way for a job satisfaction survey by an outside consultant. Results pointed to several problem areas: poor communication from the top down, feelings that extra efforts were not rewarded, and uncertainty about agency policies. A series of group meetings was set up to deal with problems; for example, one group meeting was used to elicit from staff members all possible solutions to the communication problem and then to select the feasible ones. The group procedure used also stimulated interaction among employees and provided a therapeutic experience for participants.

Organization development may focus on changing individuals, modifying the structure of the organization, or both. For example, if there are no lines of advancement for employees, a first step in improving efficiency may be to change the organizational structure to correct the situation.

Organizational development makes use of many of the competencies counselors possess. A review of the steps in the process makes this clear:

1. Problem identification. At this stage, someone with power and influence in an organization becomes concerned about a problem that OD may be helpful in solving.

2. Consultation with a behavioral scientist expert. Behavioral scientists are not always necessary but can be helpful in the following steps.

3. *Data gathering and preliminary diagnosis (by the consultant).*
This stage usually involves someone from outside the unit who can be
more objective. The basic methods of data gathering include interviews, questionnaires, sensing, observation, and organizational performance data such as turnover, absenteeism, and other measures of
effectiveness (Sellitz, Jahoda, Deutsch & Cook 1959). Preliminary diagnosis is tremendously important to ensure that the project is successful;
many OD projects have failed because the wrong approach was used.
Beckhard (1970; Huse 1975, p. 105) has developed a typology for data
gathering and preliminary diagnosis that, if followed, can ensure that
the diagnostic stage has been properly done.

4. *Feedback to key client of group.* OD should be a collaborative
effort. After the preliminary data gathering and diagnosis, the individual or team that has gathered the basic data sits down with the client,
usually in a group or work-team meeting and presents the data together
with a preliminary diagnosis. This allows the client organization to
agree or disagree with the data collected and to move into the next
step.

5. *Joint diagnosis of the problem.* At this stage, the group discusses
the feedback and goes on to determine whether this is a real problem
on which the organization or group intends to work. The basic data
have come from the client group but now are presented to the group for
validation and further diagnosis. This is very different from what
Schein (1969) has called the "doctor-patient" model, in which the consultant comes in, makes a diagnosis, and prescribes a solution.

6. *Action.* Next, the consultant and the client system jointly agree
on further action to be taken. This collaborative approach allows the
specific OD intervention to avoid violation of the current culture, values, and norms of the client system.

7. *Data gathering after action.* Since OD is a cyclical process, data
must also be gathered *after* the action has been taken in order to monitor, measure, and determine the effects of the action, and then to feed
the results back to the client system. This stage leads directly to rediag-
nosis and new action. Thus, the process is a cyclical one that continues
until there is mutual agreement that the OD project or process should
be terminated. (Huse 1978, p. 404)

Higher education has generally tended to resist the utilization of
organization development, but it has been put into operation in individual institutions. Borland (1980, Ch. 9) gives a comprehensive discussion of
applications to student development programs and points out that with
the increasing demands for accountability and the reduction in student
personnel services "the utilization of organization development intervention strategies are a professional imperative for the effective implementation of the concept of student development" (1980, p. 207).

Regardless of the setting, the selection and supervision of staff is an
important task for program developers and managers. Fortunately, there
are a number of well-developed procedures such as those already de-

scribed that counselors can use when they have program responsibility or when they participate in activities such as committee work for recommending procedures to the program manager.

Summary Concepts

The beginning student may consider program building to be in the distant future, but every counselor will be involved in it to some degree. Participation may amount only to being a part of the program development process, but many will find themselves quickly placed in positions of leadership. There are several strategies that will greatly facilitate the program-building process and that will enable the service to be accountable.

Goals and objectives are closely tied in with accountability; the specification in concrete terms of what the service aims to accomplish is essential if hard data on results are to be obtained. Staffing and managing the service can be greatly facilitated if directors and staff members employ the human relations skills of counseling. All of the elements of programming — from the first conceptualization of the need for it to the final evaluation and modification — are done with accountability in mind.

Examples of Research on a Topic
Impacts of Helping Programs

Relatively little program-wide evaluation has been done; studies have usually centered on a specific service (e.g., counseling). Evaluations of accrediting agencies are exceptions to this situation. Usually, however, the focus of these evaluations is on qualifications of staff members, case loads, and presence of equipment and facilities rather than on effects on those served. Several studies are discussed next to illustrate effects of programs or parts of programs. As you read them, formulate your conclusions about the demonstrated effectiveness of counseling programs.

Several large-scale studies provide information on the value of guidance services in schools. Rothney's (1958) longitudinal study emphasized counseling by study staff members but included other activities such as working with teachers and curriculum committees. A total of 890 sophomores from four Wisconsin high schools took part in the eight-year study. Pupils were divided into experimental and control groups, and effects of the special counseling and guidance were checked at graduation and two and one half and five years afterward. Results showed that, during the period of study, the group provided with guidance (mainly counseling) was superior to the control group on a number of significant variables. Even in an additional follow-up ten years after graduation, the results favored the experimental group, although differences had become smaller (Tyler 1969, p. 232). The long-term results showed that guidance, using the services model, does have beneficial effects.

An earlier study by Rothney and Roens (1952) used regular junior high school guidance services for 129 eighth graders in three schools. Both experimental and control groups were composed of pupils identified as either superior or needing help. Evaluation was based on follow-ups at the end of five years of school and after one year of post-high-school experiences. Results showed that the staff of professional counselors working intensively with pupils and teachers had positive effects; pupils learned to plan effectively for realistic goals and acquired productive, more effective styles of interpersonal behavior. This study, too, illustrates the services model and emphasizes the need for teachers to participate in the program.

A study with college students also supports guidance services. Campbell (1965) followed up students who had participated in a research project at the University of Minnesota twenty-five years earlier. The long-term results revealed that counseled students had achieved at a higher level and had demonstrated more effective ways of coping with problems. The helping approach used was somewhat like the services model.

Gamsky (1970) reports on an evaluation of the services model. Data consisted of teachers' judgments of help to referred pupils. Results were quite positive; teachers noted substantial improvement and learned, moreover, how to understand and deal with pupil behavior.

The Mesa (not dated) and the Grossmont Union High School district (Jacobson and Mitchell 1975) utilized various aspects of a systems approach in their programs. Early preliminary evaluations of the Mesa accountability program showed substantial benefits from use of the model and provided data for revising procedures and materials.

The study by Perovich and Mierzwa (1980) is illustrative of the type that investigates specific counseling services. In this study, the focus was on identifying the most effective procedure to use in increasing vocational maturity and self-esteem of college students. Two treatment groups, one focusing on career information in an interactive group procedure and the other utilizing an encounter and T-group format (i.e., emphasizing interaction, communication, and group dynamics), and a control group were used. Results showed that both experimental groups had significant effects (at the .05 level) on dimensions of career maturity, i.e., maturity, exploration, and decision making, but only the one focusing on career information in a group setting had a significant effect on self-esteem and planning.

The "Lodge" program (Zax and Specter 1974, p. 105) mentioned earlier (see Chapter 4) is an example of an extensive community agency evaluation program. Small autonomous problem-solving groups were formed in a mental hospital to enable patients to learn self-management and to assist each other in resolving personal difficulties. To a significant degree, members of the autonomous groups left the institution sooner than those receiving traditional treatment, although follow-up revealed that the same proportions of both groups were later readmitted. The addition of a "lodge" type of group living for discharged patients, however, enhanced their ability to remain in the community longer and to be employed for a greater period of time than those involved in traditional aftercare.

A program to help older persons develop effective day-to-day interpersonal functioning compared three methods of group training — behavioral role play, social group work, and problem solving (Rosenfeld 1978, pp. 73–74). Those who had participated in the behavioral role-play training benefited most, according to immediate assessment. While questions may be raised about certain aspects of the design and generalization of results, the study provides evidence that older persons can be taught to be more effective in the tasks of everyday living.

On the basis of this sampling of studies, what do you conclude about the impact of counseling programs? Is it clear-cut enough to justify such programs? How could the research be even more effective in achieving such justification?

Experiential Activities

Two kinds of experiential activities are suggested for this chapter: simulated program planning and evaluation of actual programs. The following are examples:

1. Simulating Program Planning

Using small groups, assign each a setting (elementary school, secondary school, college, community agency) for program planning. Ask each group to first prepare a brief description of the setting and identify staff members. Group members give a short summary of what steps the staff would take to build the program.

2. Solving Program Management Problems

Prepare a program description, including brief descriptions of personalities of staff members. Also, identify a problem that is being encountered in the program. Ask class members to play the staff roles to find a solution to the problem. Process the role playing to identify dynamics of problem solutions.

3. Analyzing a Program

Obtain a description of a program from an educational institution or community agency. Also, obtain information about program elements discussed in this chapter (e.g., how needs were determined, staff development). Then, either in class or in small groups, ask students to identify program strengths and weaknesses and suggest improvements.

4. Presentation and Discussion of a Program

Either visit an agency or educational institution or invite one or more staff members to meet with the class to describe their program. Select questions ahead of time to cover areas of class interest (e.g., how inter-staff-member communication is facilitated, methods of conflict resolution, use of objectives).

Suggested Readings

Blimline, Carol A., ed. *Innovations in Counseling Services.* Falls Church, Va.: International Association of Counseling Services, not dated.

 An excellent collection of descriptions of innovative programs with a how-to-do-it emphasis. Many settings are covered. The table of contents should be consulted for programs of interest.

Borland, David T. "Organization Development: A Professional Imperative." In *Student Development in Higher Education,* edited by Dan G. Creamer, pp. 205–227. Cincinnati: American College Personnel Association, 1980.

 A valuable reference on organization development and its potential contribution to building and managing student development programs.

Burtnett, Francis E.; Collison, Brooke B.; and Segrist, Allen E. "The Comprehensive Involvement of the School Counselor in Career Education." In *The School Counselor's Involvement in Career Education,* edited by Francis E. Burtnett, pp. 131–135. Falls Church, Va.: American Personnel and Guidance Association, 1980.

 While the book is on career education, principles can be applied to the total school counseling program. The chapter cited above as reference is a valuable reading on program development.

Cerlotta, Beverly. "The Systems Approach: A Technique for Establishing Counseling and Guidance Programs." *Personnel and Guidance Journal* 57, no. 8 (1979), pp. 412–414.

 A brief, very helpful discussion of the use of the systems approach to program building in educational and agency settings.

Creamer, Don G., ed. *Student Development in Higher Education.* Cincinnati: ACPA Media, University of Cincinnati, 1980.

    A thorough and up-to-date reference on building student development programs in colleges. The Introduction by Creamer, pages 1–7, will give the reader directions in selecting sections of interest.

Giroux, Roy F.; Biggs, Donald A.; Hoffman, Alan M.; and Pietrofesa, John J., eds. *College Student Development Revisited: Programs, Issues, and Practices.* Falls Church, Va.: American Personnel and Guidance Association, 1979.

    A collection of journal articles covering all aspects of student development at the college level. The Introduction (pp. 14–24) provides an overview of the programming considerations. Services are covered in 19 articles in Chapter 5.

Hill, George E. *Management and Improvement of Guidance.* 2nd ed. Englewood Cliffs, N.J.: Prentice-Hall, 1974.

    Chapter 7, "Definition of Guidance Functions of Teachers and Others," describes the teacher's role in detail, covers other staff members, and gives a helpful point of view about the parts parents and pupils can play.

Hosford, Ray E., and Ryan, T. Antionette. "Systems Design in the Development of Counseling and Guidance Programs." *Personnel and Guidance Journal* 49, no. 3 (1970), pp. 221–230.

    An excellent presentation of the systems approach in building guidance programs. The discussion in this chapter utilizes concepts from this article.

Huse, Edgar F. *Organization Development and Change.* New York: West Publishing Company, 1975.

    A very useful reference on all aspects of organization development. The examples of use of OD with a junior high school (pp. 370–390) and a manufacturing plant (pp. 355–369) give vivid pictures of how this approach can aid various types of organizations in resolving problems.

Jacobson, Thomas J., and Mitchell, Anita M. "How to Develop a District Master Plan for Career Guidance and Counseling." *Vocational Guidance Quarterly* 25, no. 3 (1977), pp. 195–202.

    An excellent discussion of steps in program building. Principles can be applied to any setting.

Krumboltz, John D. "An Accountability Model for Counselors." *Personnel and Guidance Journal* 52, no. 10 (1974), pp. 639–646.

    An excellent discussion of the types of objectives needed in guidance and procedures for computing cost-effectiveness of services.

Kurpius, DeWayne. "An Introduction to Consultation II." *Personnel and Guidance Journal* 56, no. 7 (1978), p. 394.

    The guest editor's introduction to a special issue of the journal that features a number of articles of particular value for this chapter. The article by Huse, on organization development, is a good starting place.

Lewis, Judith A., and Lewis, Michael D. *Community Counseling: A Human Services Approach.* New York: John Wiley and Sons, 1977.

    A particularly valuable reference on program planning in many settings. Chapter 6, on community-based planning with procedures and examples, is recommended, but others are also relevant.

Miller, Theodore K., and Prince, Judith S. *The Future of Student Affairs.* San Francisco: Jossey-Bass, 1976.

Setting goals and objectives is covered in Chapter 2. Chapter 8 discusses the development of programs in the college and university. Particularly useful as an application of systems development principles to this setting. Chapter 9 describes programs in operation.

Morrill, Weston H.; Oetting, Eugene R.; and Hurst, James C. "Dimensions of Counselor Functioning." *Personnel and Guidance Journal* 52, no. 6 (1974), pp. 354–359.

The article that introduced the cube concept as a basis for guidance programs. Examples of application are given in other sections of the same journal.

Rosenfeld, Anne H. *New Views on Older Lives.* Washington, D.C.: U.S. Government Printing Office, 1978.

A particularly useful reference for this chapter, as it describes a large number of programs. Chapter 4, on community services, is recommended.

Shaw, Merville C. *School Guidance Systems.* Boston: Houghton Mifflin, 1973.

A comprehensive and valuable reference for program building in the school setting. Chapter 4 is highly recommended for an overview of concepts. Other chapters describe various models in detail.

Shertzer, Bruce, and Stone, Shelley C. *Fundamentals of Guidance.* 4th ed. Boston: Houghton Mifflin, 1981.

Another classification of guidance models is given in Chapter 3. The authors base their classification on general aims, e.g., "social reconstruction."

Walz, Garry R., and Benjamin, Libby, eds. *New Imperatives for Guidance.* Ann Arbor, Mich.: ERIC Counseling and Personnel Services Clearinghouse, 1978.

Two articles discuss program building in the school setting: Campbell (pp. 30–62), and Mitchell (pp. 113–148). Both are very useful with this chapter, and both apply to other settings besides the school.

Zax, Melvin, and Specter, Gerald A. *An Introduction to Community Psychology.* New York: John Wiley and Sons, 1974.

A comprehensive reference on community programs; any chapter will be useful. Chapter 4, on restructuring the hospital, is a good starting place.

Chapter
8
Counseling Individuals and Groups

The most unique and professionally demanding function the counselor performs is counseling. Although it is by no means the only important function, working with individuals one to one or in small groups is the hallmark of the profession of those who carry the title "counselor." This chapter provides an overview of counseling, including roles, theoretical foundations, and techniques. Emphases vary according to settings and target groups, but the basic principles apply wherever the counselor works or whomever the counselees may be.

Definitions, Examples, and Trends

Counseling is by no means a static concept; the way it is defined and implemented is undergoing significant change. Debates over its limits continue. One frequently expressed concern is its degree of similarity to psychotherapy; another is the question how counseling and guidance differ. These issues and others reviewed in this section will help acquaint you with professional concerns that have significant implications for career planning. If career and life-style are to harmonize, it is important to learn about and seriously consider these aspects in the early planning stage.

Counseling and Psychotherapy

Similarities and differences between counseling and psychotherapy cause persistent concern. Some equate the two terms, but there are significant differences. The two most important involve the type of problem and level of adjustment of the counselee. Counseling is the process of helping relatively normal individuals develop, make decisions, and solve mild situational problems. Psychotherapy is assistance for individuals with deep-seated, long-term emotional problems that rate as severe and often debilitating. Psychotherapy is the typical work of the psychiatrist, the psychoanalyst, and the clinical psychologist. Still, the distinction is difficult to maintain; many writers use the terms synonymously, and it is true that quite often the psychiatrist is offering short-term help to relatively normal individuals and the counselor is providing a therapeutic experience for the counselee. Moreover, counselors draw on approaches and techniques from psychotherapy in working with counselees. But the difference is important both for day-to-day helping activities as well as for public relations. Many individuals find it easier to approach the counselor than a psychotherapist. Educational institutions are more likely to support counseling services than psychotherapy.

Perceptions of the Counselor's Role

Various people perceive the role of the counselor in different ways; these perceptions have a certain impact on the counseling-psychotherapy question. Regardless of their adjustment status, pupils seem to consider personal characteristics of helpers when requesting counseling (Larson and Rice 1967). The designated counselor is likely to be turned to in program planning; other types or problems are taken to different persons. Brough (1968) found no differences between ninth graders who requested counseling and those who did not. The evidence suggests that pupils prefer and use voluntary services. There is some indication that those who request counseling come from more affluent families and are more ambitious and success-oriented (Tseng and Thompson 1968). Socioeconomic status of pupils also affects their perceptions of counselors (Haettenschwiller 1969). Those of higher socioeconomic status, for example, have more expectation of respect from parents, teachers, and counselors. Pupils in general expect more empathy, respect, and concreteness from counselors than from parents; and girls anticipate more respect from parents, teachers, and counselors than boys.

Obviously, the counselor can expect pupils to bring many personal preconceptions and preferences to the counseling session (those from higher socioeconomic levels, for example, are likely to be more positive), and they have little understanding of the counseling process and their part in it.

Certain preferences form definite patterns. Counselees tend to choose counselors of the same race (Riccio and Barnes 1973); race, subculture, and sex of the counselor are all important to black students. High school seniors have a much clearer perception of who could be of help with problems of social adjustment and religious and racial prejudice than do freshmen. A common racial background does seem to facilitate the counselor's rapport in the first contact, but there is insufficient evidence to say that there is a compelling need for the counselor to belong to the same race as the counselee (see Chapter 9).

Counselees also have definite ideas about who they will turn to for what types of help. Rosen (1967) found that high school pupils consider school counselors fairly helpful with educational and vocational problems, but prefer not to take emotional problems to them. They prefer a directive type of counseling, but differences in personality and sex affect the choice of counselor. Pupils value appropriate and adequate information, understanding the purposes of counseling, interest, empathy, availability, and sensitivity to feelings and attitudes (Staudenmeier 1967). Males rate high the encouragement to speak; females consider listening very effective counseling behavior.

The counselor-psychotherapy issue appears to be a factor in pupils' minds when they are asked to refer individuals with various sorts of problems. Heilfron's study (1960) demonstrates pupils' tendency to refer the obviously maladjusted to the counselor but to take no action for those needing developmental help.

Administrators and faculty see the counselor's role quite differently than the counselor sees it (Riese and Stoner 1969; Hart and Prince 1970) (Chapter 3). One of the major differences involves providing personal emotional counseling. Principals feel that counselors should share many of the clerical and noncounseling duties in the school. Even so, principals and counselors agree on the importance of the same functions, but disagree on their relative standing (Sweeney 1966). Both give services to individual students first priority and place establishing and maintaining staff relationships second; counselors, however, rank community relationships third, while principals give that rank to promoting the school program. It does not appear that principals understand the work of the counselor (Boller 1973), and there appears to be a need for counselors to become more central to the school program (Haettenschwiller and Jabs 1969). Teachers and administrators apparently expect the counselor to be more active in classroom sessions and in summarizing and interpreting information for school use. Elementary teachers generally are positive about work with counselors but see the function as mainly remedial (Masih 1969).

Other information on perceptions of counselors has been discussed in Chapters 2, 3, and 4, on settings, and in Chapter 9, on special groups. It is clear that the counselor may not always be viewed as the approachable helper that he or she prefers to be. It is also apparent that all counselors should be concerned with communicating a realistic and accurate role description.

Counselors' Preferences and Conflicts

It is not surprising that counselors' attitudes and preferences have an effect on how their role is implemented. Counselors must, of course, be sensitive to the effects of their attitudes on the perceptions of counselees.

For example, counselors have ideal counselees from whom they expect greater progress; typically, these pupils are more like the counselor in personality, agree about the cause of the presenting problem, value counseling, and have better grades. Counselor biases about sex, age, race, and social class can prevent effective help. The better the counselor's understanding of the values and mores of minority and other special groups (e.g., the opposite sex, older persons), the more effective counseling is likely to be.

Counselors tend to value a personal-problem type of assistance, regardless of the needs of pupils. Warman's studies (1960) show that college counselors rate adjustment problems first, career problems second, and school-routine problems third. School counselors, however, rated career problems first in importance, school routine second, and adjustment third. These studies were done some time ago; it might be expected that upgrading the preparation for school counseling would result in preferences more like those of college counselors, and the literature on major intervention strategies seems to bear this supposition out. But as Leviton (1977) points out, pupils have other expectations; they want help with career and educational problems. This is one of the areas of concern to prospective counselors: What type of help would they feel comfortable in providing? Is this preference in line with needs of pupils?

Another critical question for the counselor is the congruence of personal values and those espoused by the institution. To what extent should the counselor adopt the values of the work setting? Rothney (1970) argues that counselors have a responsibility to conform to the standards of the employing institution and takes issue with the attitude that they can follow their own philosophical orientation and social views, regardless of impact on others. Many institutions are conservative, and the needs of contemporary individuals may not be met (Stubbins 1970). Moreover, the counselor experiences the conflict between the needs of the individual and the demands of the marketplace for salable skills (Brigante 1958). Wrenn (1970) brings up other ways that questions concerning values impinge on the counselor's work. Can counselors hold to their own values and yet enter into the world of other people? Can they show they care for counselees as individuals and yet get involved in controlling their lives? Can a counselor continue to be a warm, accepting, helping person, and yet carry out the numerous demanding tasks required of the professional practitioner?

Counselors in all settings may encounter a wide range of role options. Attempts to be all things to all people are futile; the counselor must establish a clear-cut, specific role (Kushel 1970). Suggestions involve new concepts as well as urging counselors to adopt a specific approach.

Another way of clarifying the role is to emphasize the counseling function. Brammer (1968) suggests that the counselor drop guidance activities and concentrate on psychological counseling (see Chapter 7). Felix (1968), however, characterizes the school worker's duties as primarily educational and argues for noncounseling guidance activities. Their controversy triggered many responses, pro and con (Easton and Resnikoff 1969; Hopkins 1969; Wyatt 1969; Dash 1969). A related question is the therapeutic v. the school-counseling model. Aubrey (1969) takes issue with the school use of therapy and recommends attention to the sociological factors in the school and strategies to change the educational setting over intensive treatment of individual pupils. This position, too, evoked many responses, which attests to its significance (Call 1970; Jones 1970; Keefe 1970).

Roles are intimately related to the program models described in Chapters 2–4, and the merits of counseling v. other interventions should be considered from the standpoint of utility. Individual counseling is one type of intervention. If others are needed, as the cube and generalist-specialist models suggest, then obviously the counselor's role must embrace a wide range of interventions. This expansion appears to be taking place as new treatment methods are developed. One model combines elements of formerly disparate roles; the major feature is the use of psychological principles as the base for a variety of approaches including counseling,

Proactive help reaches out to assist before the damage is done.

consulting, and teaching. Pine (1975) argues that this is the model needed to maintain counseling as a viable service in schools. Major emphasis is on giving school counseling away to teachers and others who work face to face with students, and helping them respond to pupils' feelings. The counselor is thus a consultant, a trainer, and a psychological educator whose function is to help pupils, parents, teachers, families, and members of the community make use of helping techniques.

Action orientation and outreach are major strategies by which the counselor may have an impact on the environment. Starting with a study of the effects of the school and community, more productive and positive environments are designed (Conyne 1975). Blocher (1974) describes this as the "ecological" approach, because it not only deals with the student potential but enhances it by improving their various environments — the school, community, and home. Building constructive learning environments is a high-priority task.

The term "change agent" is an older role concept recommended for counselors (Walz and Benjamin 1977, pp. 2–7; Warnath 1973b). As Cook (1972) points out, counselors have avoided the role, as it involves risk. But the role can be implemented both through serving as a student advocate and through helping to modify the organization to meet students' goals.

Outreach is another trend (Lipsman 1969). Relatively new techniques and strategies — e.g., peer counseling (Drum and Figger 1972), behavior modification (Toews 1969), building coping skills, and changing the social system (Lipsman 1969) — provide the tools the counselor needs. But opinions differ about suitability of such new ways of changing behavior as behavior modification (Lane 1970; Lifton 1969).

Peer facilitation or peer advising is gaining popularity in school, college, and community settings (see Chapters 3 and 4). Peers are used in school settings for helping other pupils with personal problems, with orientation to school, and the like. The extensive involvement of peers in higher-education student personnel work is described in Chapter 4. This type of student participation fits in quite well with the student development approach. Peers have been used for many years in community settings. They are particularly valuable when working with those with similar characteristics — age, handicap, socioeconomic status.

Peers are selected, prepared, and supervised by counselors. These counselor responsibilities are minimal compared to the considerable breadth given to helping services. This greatly helps the program to meet accountability requirements.

Career counseling and guidance have regained status in recent years because of career education and a new recognition that career counseling involves the total person rather than a superficial consideration of test scores and occupational information (Dolliver and Nelson 1975). Moreover, the report by Christopher Jencks (*Inequality: A Reassessment of the*

Effect of Family and Schooling in America, 1972) leads Menacker (1975) to suggest new developments in career counseling to expand and make more active the role of the counselor and to give added importance to the counselee's family and peers. Out-of-school variables are becoming more important (Giddan and Price 1975). This expanded concept of career guidance and counseling incorporates aspects of the role of change agent and elements of outreach, consulting, and action strategy.

The trend in evaluation, quite appropriately, is on counselee accomplishments rather than on counselor duties. All types of services are used to help the counselee reach goals mutually agreed on. The approach reflects the trend toward a clearer specification of what counseling is supposed to do and how well it accomplishes its objective.

Many of the emphases already described are similar to those of the 1973 Vail Conference on professional psychology (Ivey and Leppaluoto 1975). The recommendations of the conference, which supports developments already under way and introduces new ones, are likely to have a significant impact on school counseling. For example, the report emphasizes the need to espouse values and attitudes that enhance society; counselors need to work for a society responsive to people's needs, and greater attention is going to the practitioner (as opposed to the practitioner-scientist). A major emphasis is on an active role in which the counselor participates in institutional changes, provides services to large groups, and has an impact on local institutions and the community. These recommendations sharply contrast with the older focus on one-to-one, self-initiated help, and it has been suggested that the new concepts outlined at the conference would justify creating an Association for Human Development within the American Personnel and Guidance Association.

Points of View About Counseling

A counseling point of view is a set of principles that guide the counselor's work and is the basis for choosing techniques. Other terms can be used (e.g., theory, orientation, system, school, or approach). All mean the same thing, although "theory" implies to some experts something more comprehensive and rigorous than a counseling point of view.

Theories (points of view) are sometimes thought to be impractical ("Once I began work, I had to forget all that theory!"). The attitude is wrong; a good theory is the most practical part of the counselor's preparation. It provides the road map that shows where one is going and how to get there. It justifies the counselor's activities and provides a basis for predicting effects. To operate as a professional without a theory is dangerous and unethical.

Negative feelings about points of view may arise from resistance to the need to adopt a particular theory. But a counselor's rationale is highly individual and involves personal characteristics, elements of formal positions, and preferences (Ratigan 1967, p. 139; Shoben 1962). Very likely no single specific point of view given here will suit you "as is," and you may wish to combine parts of various approaches, using, for example, an approach like Ponzo's (1976). He divides the counseling process into stages (e.g., awareness of the problem) and adapts aspects of five of the approaches discussed here to facilitate counselee progress. But learning about approaches is a necessary first step in developing a personal style.

Regardless of points of view, effective counselors tend to be very much alike in the ways they help and relate to others (Combs and Soper 1963; Fiedler 1950; La Crosse and Barak 1976). While research has dealt more with therapeutic practice, it is reasonable to assume and there is evidence to support the position that the same is true for other counselors.

Depending on who is writing or talking, the number of counseling points of view ranges from three or four to twenty or thirty. Twelve that are of importance, directly or indirectly, to the counselor are arranged here on a continuum from counseling to psychotherapy. Starting at the counseling end the list is as follows: trait-factor, decision-making, behavioral, reality, Adlerian, rational-emotive, transactional analysis, client-centered, Gestalt, existential, psychoanalytic, and eclectic counseling.

The eclectic point of view constitutes a systematic and widely used approach, although agreement on this position is certainly not unanimous. There is also disagreement about calling a point of view "developmental" — the term is more frequently used with guidance. It is possible to group several approaches under more general headings; cognitive decision making, for example, would include the trait-factor, decision-making, developmental, and behavioral points of view. To help develop an awareness of the similarities and differences of the various approaches to helping, however, each will be considered separately.

The theories of learning and personal development discussed in Chapter 6 are the sources of much of what is done in counseling. The focus in this chapter is on how the counselor utilizes the theories in helping counselees to change.

Trait-Factor Counseling

In one variation or another this approach is widely used in educational, placement, and rehabilitation settings. One application, the mechanical process of "testing and telling," has come under fire, but it is nonetheless one of the major points of view covered in reviews, has a long and respectable history, and contains much of value for the school counselor.

The label "trait-factor" has always been to some degree a pejorative misnomer. A more suitable term would convey that the approach is scientific, systematic, instructional, largely cognitive, and leads to choice, also indicating the important role given to affect and values. It has been described as mechanical and factual, but Williamson (1965, p. 203) makes clear that the approach does include the personal and emotional aspects of helping. Major emphasis is put upon attaining the "good life," involving happiness through the productive use of potential for personal and social improvement.

The approach rests on the assumptions that individuals with adequate information can make logical, rational decisions; that the traits of individuals differ measurably; and that educational and occupational settings require differential levels of such traits as verbal intelligence or mechanical understanding.

Trait-factor counselors employ a sequence of five steps, starting with identifying the reason for counseling and ending with a check on the suitability of plans (Williamson 1950, pp. 101–126). The first step, analysis, involves collecting all sorts of data about the individual and may be done in part before the first interview. The interview itself, however, provides essential data about attitudes, motivations, conflicts, and goals.

The second step, synthesis, is a process of organizing data and inferring meaning, detecting patterns, and identifying strengths, potential, weaknesses, and problems. Success in this step depends upon the adequacy of the analysis phase.

Diagnosis follows — the problem is identified; causes are ferreted out, and a prognosis is made about the likelihood of success of problem-solving strategies. Diagnosis is a cooperative process in which the counselee takes an active part.

Counseling, the fourth step, follows next. It may emphasize teaching new ways of behaving, helping to utilize information in decision making, formulating steps to solve problems — it is the cooperative activity that leads to planning and learning an approach to problem solving.

Finally, there is the fifth step, the follow-up. As the name implies, it is a check on how well plans have worked out and whether or not additional assistance is needed.

While newer models of counseling emphasize affective elements and play down the use of diagnostic data (e.g., cumulative records), this point of view is useful to many counselees, particularly in educational and career planning. It clearly makes the counselor an "expert" (with respect to assessment, diagnostic interviewing, career and other information, and in techniques of cooperative planning).

Decision-Making Counseling

While practically all theories include this element, decision making derived from economic decision theory and psychological studies of the decision process amounts to a unique counseling approach, not only for educational and career assistance, but for the whole gamut of problems faced by the counselor. It is somewhat similar to the trait-factor approach because it incorporates a systematic decision-making process that provides a framework for the counselor's work.

Both group and individual counseling may be based on this approach; this point of view is adaptable to a great variety of situations (e.g., classroom-sized groups, orientation, packaged programs, and computer guidance systems). It uses the framework of a decision process such as Gelatt's model (1962) in which a strategy is used to help counselees solve problems, prepare to meet needs, and learn a process that will serve them in future situations. The actual techniques are the same as those used in other approaches — providing information, assembling data about abilities, reflection of feeling, inventorying of values, and use of the core facilitative conditions (see next section).

This approach, developed by Gelatt, Varenhorst, and Carey, is used in *Deciding* (1972). The group process begins by helping pupils identify values and then goes into locating and using information and identifying alternatives. Next, individuals are helped to examine how much risk they will accept. Finally, individuals review strategies for achieving goals. *Deciding* exemplifies a group application of a decision model.

Two new programs have been developed. One, for teenagers, older students, and adults, is *Decision and Outcomes* (Gelatt, Varenhorst, Carey, and Miller 1973); the other, for women, is *How to Decide* (Scholz, Prince, and Miller 1975). All three programs are somewhat along the lines of the decision model described by Gelatt (1962; 1967, pp. 101–114) and summarized above.

Other decision-making theories emphasizing different processes have been developed; each provides a framework for counseling (Tolbert 1974, pp. 68–69). Several provide rationales for computer programs that enable the counselee to move through the decision process step by step.

Behavioral Counseling

This point of view of counseling, clearly illustrating the application of learning principles to the helping relationship, has experienced tremendous growth in the past few years. It is covered in one form or another in most publications on the theories of counseling and psychotherapy; it has applications in settings ranging from the elementary school to community clinics. It is also the basis for a book and a series of eight films put out by the American Personnel and Guidance Association (Hosford and de Visser 1974). It is not the only approach portrayed on film, but the process is alone in being the subject of a book keyed to a series of explanatory films.

"Behavioral" is a term that can be applied to both counseling and psychotherapy and actually involves a wide variety of different but closely related approaches (Patterson 1973, pp. 83–84). Psychotherapeutic methods have been developed to work with all sorts of neuroses and psychoses (O'Leary and Wilson 1975). Counseling applications cover a wide range of activities such as conditioning (both classical and operant), modeling, and behavior modification. The behavioral approach has wide application in school situations and appears to be gaining acceptance in individual counseling, group work, and the classroom. Interestingly enough, college students expressed a preference for this type of counseling over others when given the choice after listening to tapes of various counseling approaches.

The basic assumption is that behavior is learned; thus, old behaviors can be unlearned and new behaviors can be mastered. Counselors employ various learning strategies to assist the counselee in mastering new and desired behavior. The goal of counseling is usually stated in specific terms so that progress may be assessed and methods for reaching it may be planned. The counselor then decides which strategy is likely to be the most effective. Hosford and de Visser (1974, p. 23) divide the process into six steps. First, the problem is identified. A counselor may use various types of learning techniques (e.g., reinforcement) to motivate the counselee to bring out needed information. The problem must be specified in behavioral terms and important reinforcers identified (p. 49).

Next, counseling goals are formulated; the counselee decides on a desired course of action. Goals must be in specific terms so that it will be possible to specify what is to be learned, under what conditions it will be demonstrated, and what it will achieve (p. 65).

The third step (pp. 80–81) is to identify the counselee's status with respect to the desired goal. This information helps in setting up a strategy and gives a base for estimating progress. For example, if the counselee wants to develop positive feelings toward peers and classmates, it would make quite a difference in the strategy if at the beginning of counseling the person were very hostile and withdrawn rather than moderately outgoing.

The next step is to select and carry out a counseling strategy for reaching the goal (pp. 96–97). Typical ones involve operant and classical conditioning, social modeling, or assertiveness training. There are others, but these are the major types.

Next, there is an evaluation of success in reaching the goal. Since it has been stated in specific terms including levels of performance, evaluation is relatively easy. The last and final step involves termination of counseling; if the goal has not been reached, however, the whole process may be repeated. There may even be a need to further identify the problem.

The behavioral point of view has strong supporters and equally strong critics. Detractors often assert that the behavioral therapist or counselor is a manipulator, not concerned with the quality of the therapeutic relationship, who takes responsibility away from the counselee. Supporters reply that the relationship is extremely important and that rapport is considered essential. They insist further that the counselee has a choice in setting goals; after all, it is the counselee who comes and requests help in achieving a desired objective and there is no compulsion to undergo behavior modification.

There are numerous examples of effective use of the approach. Career counseling is one (Woody 1968; Krumboltz and Baker 1973, pp. 235, 283). Successful results have been obtained with juvenile delinquents (Sarason 1968). Behavior modification is widely used in schools, for example, by reinforcing pupils for improved behavior (Vannote 1974). Groups using reinforcement techniques to improve study habits have been shown to be more successful than discussion groups (Harris and Trujillo 1975). Learning theory utilizing reinforcement and modeling can be used to teach disruptive children new productive skills to gain rewards from teachers and classmates (De Voe and Sherman 1975). Other programs have used behavior modification to effect positive change in individuals through positive reinforcement, a token economy, modeling, and systematic desensitization (Stolz, Wienckowski, and Brown 1975). Systematic desensitization as developed by Wolpe (Goldstein 1973, p. 227) is widely used. Anxiety is reduced by pairing its stimuli with relaxation. Many applications have been made in elementary school. In one example the counselor and teacher used a reinforcement schedule to strengthen positive behavior and reduce negative responses. After setting up a baseline, the procedure was tried and disruptive behavior was sharply reduced; positive behavior increased (Englehardt, Sulzer, and Alterkruse 1971).

Reality Therapy

The term "therapy" is typically used in this point of view, although it is not necessarily limited to individuals with emotional problems. It might, for example, be used with high school pupils both in groups and individual settings for a wide variety of behavior problems, personal difficulties, and decision-making tasks. Most use, however, has been with young (incarcerated) delinquents whose need to face reality is very apparent.

Reality therapy, an approach developed by William Glasser, is very much like behavioral counseling with two major differences — the individuals in therapy are held responsible for their behavior (Arbuckle 1974), and it is essential that the counselor form a strong emotional bond with the counselee — far beyond what is expected in behavioral, or even most relationship therapies. Learning theory is used, and the counselee is taught new and more productive and appropriate behavior (as determined by the therapist). For example, the young, incarcerated delinquent who gets in fights with fellow inmates and rebels against regulations will be told that such behaviors are irresponsible; consequences will be pointed out, and the therapist's ideas of appropriate behavior will be described. If the new behaviors are not learned, the consequences must be accepted. If they are mastered, however, rewards will be forthcoming.

This therapy is based on the idea that the most important human need is to attain a success identity. To achieve this identity, an individual must feel loved and of personal value. Each person can choose; responsible choices lead to the success identity. On the other hand, the individual can choose a failure identity by engaging in activities that do not lead to love and a sense of self-worth. The results are pain, disappointment, and feelings of rejection.

The fact is made clear that the individual has a choice, and can choose to flaunt the reality of the situation. But the approach also underscores personal responsibility for one's actions. The therapist decides which new behaviors will provide reward and thus be reinforcing. Usually the established goals are in keeping with the realities of society. The therapeutic process requires a close counselor-counselee working relationship that focuses on present behavior rather than an examination of the past. Assigning a value to the present behavior, counselees must decide whether they want to change. If so, a plan is developed for positive actions to attain the goal of a success identity. Commitment is necessary, and counselees must take responsibility for actions. The counselor neither accepts excuses nor punishes for failure to carry out commitments (Wubbolding 1975). But the climate is far from unfeeling; the counselor communicates caring, understanding, and warmth (Glasser and Zunin 1973, p. 298).

The approach has considerable merit for applications in a variety of situations. Successful programs to teach the method to counselors and teachers have been reported (Wubbolding 1975). Anxiety problems, marital conflicts, and perversions have been treated by this approach. In fact, Glasser and Zunin (1973, p. 308) recommend reality therapy for any problems faced by individuals or groups, even those national in scope.

Adlerian Psychotherapy

This approach is based on the work of Alfred Adler, at one time a colleague of Freud. The system, which takes a holistic view of persons, emphasizes the purposive, creative, self-determining social-being nature of individuals. At the time of Adler's split with Freud, the concepts of Adlerian psychology, or individual psychology, as it is also called, were considered to be quite radical, departing as they did from Freud's assumptions in many ways. Now, however, because of the work of Rudolph Dreikurs, Adlerian psychotherapy or counseling is enjoying wide acceptance and application.

The major assumptions of Adlerian counseling make this approach particularly appropriate for school, college, and agency settings today.

This is because there is an emphasis on the total individual in social interaction, with motives and goals being primarily social. Striving for
power and counteracting feelings of inferiority are seen to be main concerns of the individual. The individual has freedom to choose; choices may
be toward positive goals or negative ones. Reasons for choice may be in the
individual's awareness, or they may be hidden. To understand the individual we need to understand his or her life-style and the place occupied in
the social environment (Mosak and Driekurs 1973, pp. 39–43).

The helping process involves analyzing life-style, goals, and patterns
of dealing with others, helping the individual understand these factors,
and assisting him or her to build new constructive attitudes and behaviors.
The approach is particularly effective in group work, as the group situation
facilitates the gaining of insight and learning new social relations orientations. The approach is also admirably suited to consulting. Those dealing
directly with the individual can be helped to understand what he or she is
striving to do (e.g., causes of misbehavior), and help turn the individual
toward more constructive directions. Marriage and family counselors often
use similar theory and techniques. Other applications include correctional
settings. Eckstein (1980) describes the use of Adlerian techniques with
inmates who have difficulty in seeing consequences of behaviors and who
have been using inappropriate and destructive ways of gaining attention.

Rational-Emotive Therapy (RET)

This is another therapy type of treatment widely used in schools and
colleges. Often a counselor will say, "I used some RET to help the client
look at what he's telling himself." Applications to school counseling are
based on the assumption that the approach is essentially educational rather
than medical, suitable for treating relatively normal persons, and useful for
individuals experiencing problems, conflicts, and needs that are part of
growing to maturity (Protinsky 1976; Ellis 1975b).

This point of view is recommended for individuals and groups, from
elementary school age to older persons. The originator of RET sees it
as valuable for working with teachers and parents, as well as pupils
(Ellis 1975b).

Although some counselors consider the approach to be uncaring and
to ignore the individual's feelings, proponents argue that RET incorporates
techniques from other approaches to provide the facilitative core conditions. Clients are accepted and supported regardless of their negative feelings or resistance to the therapist (Ellis 1975). But the therapist does
at times push the individual to bring out and look at ideas that cause
problems.

"Problems" are defined quite simply as an individual's irrational ideas. It was thought earlier that since they are so universal, they are innate; the current position is that they arise from home, family, and social development (Ellis 1975b). The aim of the therapy is to rid the client of these irrational ideas.

The approach is based on the assumptions that emotions result from thinking. Rational thinking results in good feelings; irrational thinking causes pain and unhappiness (Patterson 1973, pp. 51–52). An *ABCDE* model may be used. *A* is the activating event; irrational thinking results in internal verbalization. For example, the pupil may say to himself, "I must have perfect grades to be good." This is an irrational idea, and therapy helps to bring it out.

B, the belief system, may contain both rational and irrational thoughts, but the one used by the individual is irrational. (It would be rational enough, of course, to be disappointed by failure, but not to consider oneself worthless!) *C* represents the painful emotions resulting from the irrational belief system. The *D* stage is the therapist's efforts (e.g., confronting, teaching, explaining) to get the individual to face the irrational self-talk and replace it with rational thinking (Protinsky 1976). For example, the therapist might urge the client to look at the sentence, "To be less than perfect means I'm worthless." The therapist might dispute the sentence, question why it is so, and ask from whom it was derived.

E, the final step, is the formulation of more effective and rational goals for the future. The client now has replaced the irrational thoughts in the belief system (e.g., can now say, "I failed that program and I'm disappointed, but I can do other things well.").

Transactional Analysis (TA)

This method of therapy has achieved phenomenal visibility in recent years. Next to encounter and sensitivity groups, it is probably one of the best-known psychological innovations. The expressions "games people play," and "I'm O.K. — You're O.K.," for example, have their origin in this theory.

TA is a group approach (Harris 1969) with its own vocabulary. The interaction of group members is an essential part of the process, but TA is therapy in a group rather than group therapy. It is based on interactions between persons, the roles they take in these interactions, and the needs they display. The transaction is an exchange between two people (an action and a reaction, or a statement and a reply). Each transaction is based on one of three roles: parent, adult, or child (Harris 1969, pp. 16, 36). The parent role embodies the "shoulds" and "oughts" and rules derived from early interaction with parents. The child reflects smallness, dependence, clumsiness, and helplessness. The adult is a computer (Harris 1969, p. 30) using data from the child, parent, and adult to determine the best response in the present situation. The concept of "strokes" is involved in either positive or negative responses from other people; everyone needs them. In fact, people "play games" to obtain strokes.

There are four positions in which a person may visualize himself (Harris 1969, p. 43). Each consists of classifying oneself and the other person as "O.K." or "not O.K." Each person has a life script that he or she plays out to demonstrate one of these roles. "I'm O.K. — You're O.K." is the most desirable of the four positions. The therapeutic process analyzes transactions. The objective is to base more and more transactions on the adult role.

The approach was developed by Eric Berne (G. Holland 1973, pp. 356–357) as a theory of personality development and group treatment. "Script analysis," an investigation of life dramas that persons play, is the means used to free them from irrational decisions based on fixed scripts. For example, some people may have to be liked by everyone in order to feel "O.K." The assumption is that by understanding their scripts and with the support of the group, people can cognitively choose to change their ways of behaving, and thus feel better about themselves.

The treatment was originally developed for psychiatric populations but has wide applicability. It has been employed to help college students in career planning by analyzing scripts and determining roles for realistic planning (Kurtz 1974). Teachers have been helped to understand the roles they are playing in order to develop more positive opinions of themselves (Hannaford 1974). It has been used with adolescents who are having difficulties with teachers, peers, and parents (Hipple and Muto 1974). Some critics accuse TA of promoting sex stereotypes; for example, qualities considered "feminine" in the TA context seem to resemble those of a child and include little of the decision-making qualities of the adult (Roney 1975). G. Holland (1973, p. 398), however, see effects as positive and the approach as useful in practically any situation where psychological principles may be applied.

Client-Centered Counseling

Only a few years ago the counseling profession was preoccupied with the great debate about the relative merits of directive versus nondirective counseling. The debate still surfaces in various disguised ways, but the terms have disappeared. Now we hear about other conflicts (e.g., humanism v. reinforcement). The nondirective approach of Rogers that appeared in the 1940s (Rogers 1942; Rogers and Wallen 1946), called "client-centered," probably has had a greater impact on counseling than any single other factor (including accountability, NDEA institutes, or any others). It is given a place of prominence in publications on counseling and therapy (Patterson 1969b, 1973; Grummon 1965, 1972; Meador and Rogers 1973). It is one of the major approaches you will encounter in preparation and work.

This counseling approach is based on a theory of personality that views the individual as in a process of becoming, growing, achieving worth and dignity, and seeking to actualize potential (Patterson 1969b, 1973; Meador and Rogers 1973). Maintenance and enhancement of the self are the overriding concerns in a person's life. The individual's own perceptions of his or her world, not someone else's, are reality.

The personality theory grew out of the therapy experience (Rogers 1951, pp. 481–483). Recordings of counselor-counselee interactions were analyzed, and patterns and themes were detected that gave support to the theory's explanation of behavior and the processes individuals use to solve problems.

As enhancement of the self is a basic process of growth and development, threats to it, such as lack of love or lack of positive regard, arouse defenses that tend to distort reality and arouse anxiety. Excessive threat causes a breakdown in defenses and results in emotional disturbances.

Therapy is aimed at helping the individual utilize growth potential in the drive toward self-actualization. The therapist supplies the necessary and sufficient conditions for positive change, positive regard, empathy, and genuineness (Patterson 1973, pp. 388–389). Reflection of feeling is the primary technique used, but the emphasis is on building a relationship that is accepting, safe, and understanding. Empathy is considered to be the most potent of all counselor qualities (Rogers 1975, p. 3). Because of the relationship, the counselee can identify and look at threat; adjust perceptions; and carry out self-exploration to understand values, needs, and beliefs. Self-exploration, usually negative at first, leads individuals to trust their own perceptions more fully, to become more actualized, and to make fuller use of potential.

Other types of assistance, such as providing information, are not part of the therapeutic process (Patterson 1969b, pp. 9–10, 21). Therapy, by definition, applies only to the process of interaction for self-exploration; by freeing potential, therapy enables the client to take positive action to find the information.

The counselor does not direct, manipulate, or control. Responsibility for what to discuss, goals to be reached, and decisions about the length of therapy rests with the counselee (Arbuckle 1974). A facilitative human relation is provided; positive growth results.

Rogers has recently been more involved in encounter-group work than in individual counseling. The approach serves quite well as a basis for group work, and his concepts of facilitative conditions have been utilized by Carkhuff, Truax, and others in building training and research models (Calia 1974).

How applicable is this approach to counseling in educational institutions? Opinions differ, but there has been an extensive adaptation of the basic attitudes, techniques, and particularly the facilitative conditions for counselor preparation and work. While the fairly lengthy process implied by this point of view may often not be possible with the day-to-day demands in the educational setting, adaptations are useful for counselors as they develop their own unique styles.

Gestalt Therapy

This approach is mainly used with groups rather than individuals, but can be applied in one-to-one settings. Even though the name implies help for emotional problems, the approach is experiencing wide use in schools, college and community settings (Raming and Frey 1974).

Because of the name, it may be assumed that it is based on Gestalt psychology, and to some extent it is (Emerson and Smith 1974, pp. 8–12). Both deal with the relative importance of figure and ground in perception, the impact of total configuration as opposed to separate parts, and effects of unfinished business. While Perls, the originator of the theory, acknowledges his debt to the academic schools of Gestalt psychology, he has not been claimed by the school (Emerson and Smith 1974, p. 12).

Gestalt therapy aims at promoting growth defined as openness to experience and willingness to interact with others (Harman 1975, p. 363). A problem results when there is a split between what individuals are and what they should be or feel they should be (Ward and Rouzer 1974, p. 20). Attempts to actualize the ideal picture of self by excessive control fail because of an unrealistic self-image (Ward and Rouzer 1974, p. 20). Therapy is designed to remove obstacles to growth by emphasizing the here and now in therapy and making it a period of actual emotional challenge rather than a safe, comfortable place.

The therapist uses several modes of helping the client to deal with the present. One is to make the client aware of the present (e.g., by pointing out nonverbal behavior). Fantasy may be used to explore situations from the perspective of "What would happen if . . . ?" (Harman 1975, p. 365). The empty chair is one of the best-known and most powerful techniques (Fagan, Lauver, Smith, Deloach, Katz, and Wood 1974, p. 33). Clients interact with the "occupant," who may represent part of their own personality or some significant person in their lives. The therapist helps clients understand the conflicts that emerge, with attention to nonverbal as well as verbal data.

To carry out the role of helper in this context, the therapist acts honestly and spontaneously, sometimes frustrating and challenging clients, and placing responsibility for change on them — for instance, by forcing them to find their own direction, to "own" responses, and to face denied or unpleasant experiences (Raming and Frey 1974, p. 182).

The approach is used with either individuals or groups, but the group approach may be considered as individual work done with others present (Harman and Franklin 1975, p. 49). For example, a major technique is concentrating on members in turn. The group setting offers a number of advantages; there are opportunities to try out roles for observation and interaction (Harman and Franklin 1975). In marathon groups, one-to-one techniques have been used (Foulds and Hannigan 1976). The number of persons involved depends on the needs of those seeking help (Kempler 1973, pp. 275–276).

Existential Counseling

As a philosophy or attitude about counseling this point of view has had considerable impact, but its theory and techniques are not greatly in evidence (Patterson 1973, p. 424). The relationship of intimacy — what Arbuckle calls "human to human sharing" (1974, p. 216) — is the essence. Beyond this the counselor may employ all sorts of techniques (e.g., reflecting, confronting, giving information).

A major facet of the approach with considerable appeal relates to freedom and responsibility (Brown and Herrnstein 1975). Individuals have some degree of free will. They choose to be what they are and are responsible for what they become (Patterson 1973, p. 431). Thus, counselors care about their counselees but do not attempt to interfere with their freedom and responsibility.

Another major emphasis is on the concept of "being-in-world" (Brown and Herrnstein 1975, p. 564; Kemp 1971, p. 10). A person's being extends beyond bodily boundaries and involves all personal concerns. Thus, the counselee is in the counselor's world, and the counselor exists in the counselee's world. The counselor is "with" the counselee; the process of becoming and evolving includes both persons.

Major goals are to help individuals achieve self-realization and to be authentic (reducing guilt over neglecting their potential); and to help them gain meaning for life and come to feel they are of value (subduing feelings of emptiness and nonbeing).

The relationship of oneness with the other person provides the setting in which these tasks can be accomplished. Beyond that, the counselor attempts to understand the counselee's world as the counselee experiences it, acts in an authentic manner, and communicates his understanding to the counselee (Tolbert 1972, p. 86). He may provide information, help in identifying alternatives, reflect, ask questions, and set up turning points for major changes in direction (Ratigan 1967, p. 122).

Existential therapy is actually a conglomeration of several points of view. All share the central concern of understanding individuals in their own world as they themselves see it. But there are different applications. As a variation of psychoanalytic therapy it is referred to as *daseinalyse* (being through analysis) and, as such, puts more emphasis on the present condition of the client in his perceived world.

Psychoanalytic Therapy

More than any of the other theories discussed, this is therapy for those with deep-seated, long-term emotional problems. A counselor is not a psychoanalyst; psychoanalysis is included here because it is well developed and offers a comprehensive personality and therapy theory, and because many techniques of Freud and his followers are used in some current counseling systems. Besides, many psychoanalytic concepts appear in literature, everyday conversations, and practically every facet of daily life.

As pointed out in Chapter 6, the personality and psychotherapy theory includes three structures, the ego, the id, and the superego. Psychic energy (libido) comes from the *id*, which is the source of instinctual energy and strives for immediate gratification. The *ego* is reality-oriented and decides how gratification demanded by the id can be obtained in the real world. It also has a certain reserve of energy that it uses, for example, to hold back primitive, pleasure-seeking id forces. The *superego*, which can be thought of as the conscience, is made up of values, attitudes, and moral precepts; its energy may side with the ego or with the id, though usually it sides with the former. These three terms are frequently used in everyday conversation with somewhat the same meaning.

Each stage of biological development has its own significance for personality development and therapy. In the first, the oral stage, the mouth is the primary source of gratification. Such adult personality characteristics as dependency stem from parental treatment at this stage. Later stages include the anal, phallic, latency, and finally the genital stage of adulthood. Fixation may cause the individual to remain at a particular stage, and may be due to parental overindulgence or denial. (But the characteristics associated with each level never completely disappear.)

The individual copes with the world by mechanisms such as repression and sublimation. The unconscious, encompassing repressed material and id demands of which the individual has never been fully aware, exert a powerful effect on personality and are the source of much behavior, particularly that which to the observer appears irrational.

Therapy is designed to bring out hidden motives, conflicts, and distortions of perceptions to allow individuals to gain control over their emotional lives. The process taps the unconscious by free association, dream analysis, and other techniques; clients can bring out material threatening and unacceptable to themselves. A transference relationship is developed in which clients react to the therapist in modes used in past relationships. Through interpretation of dreams, resistance, free association material, the transference relationship, and other data, clients are able to understand their defenses, conflicts, and anxieties, and integrate new insights in their emotional lives.

Eclectic Counseling

This often maligned approach to counseling mixes elements from many other points of view. Patterson's definition clarifies the confusion that has typically been associated with the term:

> Eclecticism differs from theoretical positions of schools or cults, in that, on the one hand, it is more comprehensive, attempting to integrate or synthesize the valid or demonstrated elements of these narrower or more restricted theories, and, on the other hand, it is a more open-ended, loose, or tentative theoretical position. (1973, p. 461)

Thorne (1973) takes basically the same position, particularly emphasizing the openness to revision and the importance of the unique features of the particular case in adapting counseling strategies. All writers agree that the critical aspects are to determine the causes of problems and to select the most appropriate helping strategies. The need for a *rationale* for selection of strategies cannot be overemphasized.

The eclectic approach is more widely subscribed to than is apparent, and has much to offer counselors because of its adaptability, utilization of new research and theory, and suitability for the new functions of the school counselor.

It is difficult to define eclecticism in a universally acceptable way and equally hard to define an eclectic counselor. Still, Tyler (1958, 1960, 1969) and Ratigan (1967, 1972) are certainly two counselors who can be identified as eclectic. Tyler's method of building a personal theory from social sciences, religion, and personal experience, in order to help a wide variety of clients implies that she agrees. Ponzo (1976) takes an eclectic position in a carefully developed statement of how he forges his helping theory. There are others; Patterson (1973, p. 462) reports that in the 25-year period from 1945 to 1970, the percentage of members of the APA's Division of Clinical Psychology who identified themselves as eclectic rose from zero to about 50 percent. A similar trend in school counselors' preferences can be inferred.

There is considerable value in the eclectic position, provided it is more than indiscriminate picking and choosing. Eclecticism promotes an openness to new research findings and new theorizing, in addition to being well suited to incorporating the insights arising from daily experience. An eclectic approach can make use of learning theory, career development theory, sociology, economics, and decision making; developmental tasks can be used for goal setting. A useful major emphasis can be placed on generalizing accomplishments in counseling to daily life (e.g., homework involving exploratory and tryout experiences), on the assumption that real growth must take place in the counselee's own daily environment (Tolbert 1959, pp. 156–178; 1972, pp. 95–107; 1974, pp. 75–76, 165–174, 192–199).

There are important counselor characteristics that cut across various approaches. Understanding these basic characteristics (e.g., caring, experiencing), the eclectic counselor varies them to fit the needs of different counselees (Brammer 1969). While providing a relationship that involves acceptance, understanding, and sincerity, the counselor intervenes with strategies that directly respond to counselee needs. Thus, information may be provided, assessment may be used, and tryout activities may be utilized. Typically, the initial counseling contacts are used to explore feelings and to identify problems and needs. Later, there is usually more emphasis on setting up objectives, deciding on alternatives, and planning reality-testing experiences.

Eclecticism is a different matter for the psychotherapist with an affluent clientele and the school counselor with a heterogeneous group to serve. The cases a psychotherapist takes on may run for months, but the school counselor may have five minutes in the hall between classes with the pupil who expresses irritation at a teacher, or be involved in long sessions with a troubled and angry potential dropout (Shoben 1969). Would concepts developed in long-term therapeutic relationships be useful to the counselor? The answer is yes, although obviously extensive adaptations must be made. In a sense, every counselor is an eclectic. "Freud was a Freudian and Rogers a Rogerian . . . " (Brammer 1969, p. 193) because of personal experiences and preferences. No one can exactly duplicate someone else's approach.

Theory Applications

A number of applications in both group and individual settings were pointed out in theory discussions. The question, however, of which approach to use by which counselor with which counselee, is one that has to be faced. One way to answer it is to adopt a particular theory and use it as a framework for working with all counselees. This method may serve very well if one can select his or her counselees and has adequate referral resources for those that are deemed unsuitable. It is, of course, possible that the counselor feels that the adopted approach is suitable for *all* counselees. This position is not recommended here, although many highly competent and professional counselors do use this approach. As Hutchins (1979) points out, each approach has its strong and persuasive advocates who can provide evidence of its effectiveness. What does the counselor do if his or her preferred way of working is to seek to match strategies and counselees?

Hutchins (1979) takes the position that no one approach is best for all persons in all situations. For a particular counselee problem situation, some strategies have a better chance of being effective than others. Identifying relevant aspects of behavior as thoughts, feelings, and actions, Hutchins suggests that an approach be selected to have the most impact on the primary focus of the intervention, that is, on either thinking, feeling, or acting. For example, if the primary counselor intervention is on "thinking," a rational-emotive approach might be used. Hutchins gives an example of the thinking focus by describing the case of a client who is concerned about overeating. The focus is first on thinking about eating (e.g., setting up specific mealtimes). Emphasis on feelings may follow (e.g., how the client feels about accomplishing the cognitive tasks). Actions may be emphasized next; the client eats balanced meals without intervening snacks.

Another view of the same problem — selecting an appropriative strategy or strategies — is presented by Frey and Raming (1979). They identify processes and goals of points of view of 14 well-known American counselors or psychotherapists (e.g., Rogers, Williamson). As the authors say, the work they have done "does not necessarily help with the value judgments one must make about where to go (the goals) and the method of getting there (the processes)" (p. 31). The relationships they have identified among theories, goals, and processes, however, give the counselor a way of thinking about the array of approaches available and provides guidelines for considering which one might be productive. Their work adds support to the position that the counselor should be skillful in a number of intervention methods and utilize those that appear to have the best chance of effecting positive change.

Selecting strategies to use also depends upon the values the counselor holds (see Chapter 6). While to some extent each of the theories reflects a value orientation, the *reasons* the counselor uses to choose one or another approach come from the philosophical views he or she has about the nature of man, what is good, and what is true. A comprehensive knowledge of theories gives the counselor a wide array of methods to select from to implement values in relation to the needs and problems of specific counselees. Values play a major role in the selection process.

Counseling Strategies and Techniques

Each of the theories already discussed provides a basis for a strategy, which in turn calls for the use of appropriate techniques. Strategies involve the process the counselor follows in working with the counselee. They are analogous to the road maps that serve as a guide to determining how you get to where you want to go. Techniques are the means of getting there. Thus, techniques may be used with any of the points of view, although some are more closely related to one approach than another.

An example of the relation of a technique to a counseling approach is reflection of feeling in client-centered counseling. It is a major technique in this approach, but many others also utilize it, too. Interpretation has more limited use; it is heavily used in psychoanalysis, for example, but would not be appropriate for client-centered counseling and similar approaches. Information about careers and other areas of choice is used in decision-making counseling, but would not be part of the therapeutic approaches such as Gestalt and TA. But many techniques cut across all or most approaches and are the counselor behaviors that help to implement theory.

Techniques may be classified in various ways. Typical methods include arranging them on a spectrum from directive to permissive or from cognitive to affective. Techniques are also classified on a spectrum from verbal to nonverbal. Additional dimensions can be used (e.g., interpretative to reflective), but most are similar to the first two. For example, interpretation is a relatively directive technique.

Examples of counselor responses illustrate differences. Suppose the counselee says: "I'm feeling so low that I don't want to talk today." How would you respond? The reply of a directive counselor, indicating how the counselee should proceed, might be: "What has happened today to get you down?" The counselor is structuring the counselee's response by indicating what to talk about. This response is also cognitive; the counselor does not actually respond directly to the feeling expressed.

A more permissive response would be: "Would you care to talk about it?" This reply, too, is more cognitive than affective, but it does not specify how the counselee should respond as clearly as the first one does.

A more affective and permissive response would be: "You're really hurting." Here the focus is on the feelings expressed by the counselee, and there is no indication of what the counselee should say next.

The directive to permissive classification is one of the most useful and interesting. At one end we have responses like questions and suggestions that represent control on the part of the counselor, who is directing what the counselee will do. Responses like "uh-huh" and others that acknowledge counselee responses are toward the permissive end; they do not affect the direction of the interview (unless, of course, they reinforce the counselee to keep going in the same direction). At the permissive extreme are responses that are based on what the counselee is thinking or, more particularly, feeling. The counselor reflects the counselee's expressed or implied feelings and goes along when the counselee proceeds; no direction is provided. A counseling approach that places most responsibility on the counselee makes extensive use of techniques on the permissive end of the continuum.

The classification from cognitive to affective is of somewhat the same type. A cognitive technique is more directive; an affective one is more permissive. The similarity is not total; the counselor may use affective responses in a very directive way (e.g., insisting that the counselee talk about a traumatic event). But cognitive responses tend to prompt a certain kind of counselee response (e.g., naming siblings, estimating grades), while affective ones shift responsibilities to the counselee for both direction of the interview and depth of feeling expressed.

Verbal and nonverbal techniques involve both counselor responses and the utilization of counselee behavior. For example, the counselor may smile, nod, lean forward, or look expectantly at the counselee. But the counselor may also direct attention to nonverbal responses of the counselee — for example, if the counselee clenches her hands while discussing her home situation, and the counselor comments that the topic evokes strong feelings.

Facilitative conditions such as empathy, positive regard, genuineness, concreteness, and immediacy represent techniques, even though these are pervasive conditions involving the counselor's pattern of relating. They are generated by specific as well as general counselor behaviors, are used in a number of counseling approaches, and can be assessed with some degree of reliability. These conditions have been found to be highly related to counselee growth and improvement, regardless of the counseling approach used.

These core facilitative conditions have been extensively studied, and scales have been developed to assess the degree to which counselors provide them (Carkhuff 1969, pp. 315–327). Empathy can range from no awareness of counselee feelings to sensitivity to both surface and deeper emotions. For example, if the counselee says, "How can a person deal with all these pressures!" the feeling expressed is one of being overwhelmed and being unable to cope with the situation. A no-empathy counselor response could be: "What pressures are you facing?" It may be important to identify the pressures. They will probably come out spontaneously later on anyway. But an empathic response such as, "It's almost too much for you," touches on the feelings expressed. It shows that the counselor is aware of the counselee's feelings and can communicate this awareness to the counselee.

The presence or absence of each of the other conditions can be determined by examples and guidelines given in Carkhuff (1969, pp. 315–328) and Egan (1975, Chs. 4, 5). Positive regard ranges from a low of no respect to a high level of deep respect for the individual as unique and valued. Counselor genuineness may be at a level where communications are completely unrelated to his or her inner emotions or to those that reflect the counselor's true feelings. Concreteness ranges from vague consideration of generalities and abstractions to dealing with specifics (e.g., the specific feelings of the child when parents were fighting). Immediacy may range from a low of counselor ignoring counselee comments about the counselor-counselee relationship to the counselor responding openly and directly to such counselee reactions.

The status of techniques has varied considerably over the years; the summary of the history of guidance in Chapter 5 gives the background for differing levels of interest. In the early development of the profession, they were considerably emphasized. Then the focus shifted to the counseling relationship, and techniques per se were downgraded. Now, however, there is a revival of interest brought about by new ways of teaching skills and results of research on effectiveness (Ivey 1974b). Microcounseling has been effective for building skills in specific techniques such as attending behavior, using open-ended questions, selective listening, and interpretation (Ivey 1974b; Ivey and Gluckstern 1974). Dyer and Vriend (1975) highlight techniques like questioning, giving information, and establishing connections. There seems to be substantial agreement that counseling techniques deserve serious consideration; that they help to deepen the relationship; and that counselors, regardless of preferences for approaches, need to master them.

Techniques reflect the counselor's philosophy and theory; they put into effect attitudes and beliefs about human nature and the helping process. A counselor can start with a preferred theory and decide on appropriate techniques for implementation (along the lines the theory sections of this chapter suggest) or work the other way around, starting from preferred techniques and searching for reasons for having chosen them so as to infer theory. For example, if the counselor uses reflection to help the counselee bring out and face feelings, the emphasis appears to be on a theory that gives importance to the counselee's perceptions of self.

Other Techniques and Approaches

There are some exotic techniques or approaches that have received considerable visibility in newspapers, magazines, and TV. Some hold considerable promise; others are of questionable value. Transcendental meditation is a method for self-improvement that received wide publicity in the early 1970s. Self-help programs abound (see Rosen 1976). Hypnosis is a technique that has been used in helping procedures (see Hilgard 1973). Biofeedback enables the individual to control bodily processes (see Schwartz 1973; Lazarus 1975). Primal therapy is aimed at enabling the individual to release the infantile pain that causes emotional problems (see Brown and Herrnstein 1975, pp. 620–622). There are others, and new ones are certain to emerge. Potential value to the counselor varies; it is good to have a working commitment to certain beliefs and from this basic orientation to maintain both an open mind and healthy skepticism.

Group Adaptations

The bases for these group approaches come from points of view of counseling and therapy, psychology of group action, and theories of personality. Many of the counseling approaches described earlier are used for group work (e.g., client-centered, Gestalt, decision making). The unique feature of group application is the interaction among members, the leader's role as facilitator, and the roles that members play in the social situation. Regardless of the type of group (with the exception of an information-giving format), the emphasis is on providing a growth-producing setting where members can learn to understand themselves, experience the reactions of others, and develop more effective life-styles.

Group counseling is growing rapidly in all settings. Often the purpose is to facilitate developmental tasks — establishing group relations with peers, improving communication, developing social skills, enhancing the self-concept, and many others. While the underlying rationale may differ from group to group, the emphasis is on a counseling type of relationship. The group is small enough to provide for intimacy and extensive participation. The leader is typically a participant-facilitator who enters into the activities, helps members express feelings, models techniques such as feedback, and in further ways works to generate a growth-producing climate.

Counseling groups tend to go through stages. In the initial period members get to know each other. Some trust may be established, but anxiety is high. As trust is developed, a group feeling emerges. Expression of feeling increases. In later stages, the group is characterized by intimacy, trust, and cohesiveness. Group counseling may run from eight to ten meetings but may continue longer.

Psychological education is a relatively new concept, bringing together a number of techniques and procedures in which the counselor takes the "initiative in deliberately teaching aspects of mental health to larger groups" (Ivey and Alschuler 1973b, p. 589). It draws heavily on psychology, and involves both cognitive and affective experiences; the counselor's role is therefore expanded considerably. It may involve such features as peer counseling (Carroll 1973, p. 357), moral education (Ivey and Alschuler 1973a, p. 593), values clarification (Simon 1973), or communications training (Gray and Tindall 1974). Developing teachers' skills is given high priority so as, in effect, to "give away school counseling" (Pine 1974, p. 94). The detailed description of one working program (Mosher and Sprinthall 1971, pp. 3–82) includes activities such as peer counseling, improvisational drama, and pupil participation in child development seminars. This approach, emphasizing long-term personal learning, strategic timing of activities, multiple techniques, and changes in the school itself (Ivey and Alschuler 1973*a*), has great potential for spreading the counselor's effect throughout the total institution.

Affective education deals with the emotional aspects of learning, such as feelings of competency, acceptance, and attitudes toward school (Stilwell 1976). Teachers utilize prepared programs in the classroom to facilitate affective responses. The counselor's role includes demonstrating techniques for the teacher to use and supplementing the program with group and individual counseling.

Encounter and sensitivity groups involve 10 to 15 members who wish to deepen experiencing, reduce defenses, and develop new behavior styles (Eddy and Lubin 1971). Sensitivity training provides for interactions to help members become more aware of themselves, and to experience interactions with others more accurately (Eddy and Lubin 1971). Encounter and sensitivity group therapy are designed to increase the quality of personal experience, improve interpersonal competency, and free potential; they do not attempt to reduce severe emotional conflict.

Assertiveness training, which is essentially a behavioral counseling application, is becoming popular, particularly with women. It is designed to help counselees overcome a submissive, withdrawn style of interacting with others and facilitate positive, expressive, outgoing behavior. The counselor or therapist offers encouragement and otherwise attempts to get the group members to engage in new patterns of behavior to achieve a more rewarding life-style (Rathus 1975). Typical activities could include coaching another group member to be assertive, using a planned episode to obtain new responses, or keeping a diary of both assertive and unassertive behaviors (Cotler 1975).

Several applications are particularly good illustrations of the versatility and utility of group approaches. One is in the area of marriage and family counseling; a number of innovative approaches have been developed to provide assistance for a variety of marital and family conflicts and needs. Career development is another application that is gaining in popularity. Others are in communications training, stress management and prevention, and values education. An overview of these specialties and some examples are given next.

Marriage and Family Counseling.   As Schreiber (1980, pp. 1–17) points out, marriage counseling as a separate profession has emerged only recently. Even more recently marriage counseling and family counseling have merged. In addition, the fields of premarital counseling, postmarital counseling, and sex therapy have emerged and are growing in popularity. While individual assistance may be provided, the emphasis is upon working with couples or families.

There are a number of sound approaches for marriage and family counseling, but there are also some recent ones that are faddish and without theoretical basis (Gurman 1979). The ones that provide the most soundly based approaches for couples in conflict are psychoanalytically oriented theory, social learning theory, and systems theory (Gurman 1979). The emphasis is on the family, or the couple, and their relationship. The term "conjoint" is used to indicate work with both husband and wife. In some cases, two counselors or therapists may be used in cotherapy to demonstrate constructive relationships and serve as a model of interactions. Marital problems are often treated from the perspective of family problems. Approaches may emphasize underlying dynamics, communications and intrafamily behavior, or the organization of the family (Levant 1980) This listing does not include all of the strategies used today but does illustrate some major points of view. Each is based on a rationale (usually one of the theories already discussed), and each includes a method of working with families.

Bauer (1979) describes an approach to family therapy based on Gestalt theory. Two techniques, the "empty chair" and the "experiment," are given as examples. In the first, the empty chair, the individual is able to reidentify an earlier-learned aspect of the way or relating to others. For example, a mother is able to re-own aggressive feeling toward her child — feelings that were experienced earlier toward a harsh father but disowned. In the experiment, family situations in which family boundaries or contacts are involved are used as the source of difficulty. If boundaries of members are too rigid, contact suffers. If they are too vague, there may be a lack of differentiation among family members. Thus, in the case of a child with a handicap, there may be an overinvolvement among family members. In the therapy situation, family members may experiment with new behaviors to lessen the excessive involvement.

The application of family systems therapy principles is described by Woodburn and Barnhill (1977). Utilizing systems principles such as wholeness of the system (family), equifinality (the same outcomes regardless of what is put in the system), and homeostasis, the therapist initiates an intervention that is designed to focus on one of the dimensions of the healthy family (e.g., a sense of belonging versus feelings of isolation).

Another approach, group counseling, is discussed by Kilgo (1975). Using both marriage and group counseling principles, Kilgo worked with a small number of couples for about 12 weeks, utilizing techniques such as role playing and sociometrics to assist them to solve problems and gain insight into how others perceive them.

Career Counseling. Group counseling for career development has grown phenomenally in recent years. In a process that combines group counseling and career development concepts, group members typically explore career attitudes, values, and competencies, provide feedback to each other, and learn decision-making skills. A 15-meeting career exploration course described by Gillingham and Lounsbury (1979) initially focused on self- and career awareness, skill inventorying, and occupational information collection. Following these activities, the second part of the process involved decision making, utilizing self-data and career data. In the final phase, members were helped to extend decisions into life planning.

Other Approaches.   Stress management is another example of the utilization of group procedures. Many of the counseling theories already discussed serve as bases for stress management assistance. Sparks and Ingram (1979) describe a brief workshop approach for teachers that would be useful in many other situations. Early steps include a review of workshop goals (reducing isolation, identifying sources of stress and satisfaction, and formulating a plan to reduce stress) and the recognition of blocks to self-understanding and problem solving that will likely occur in the workshop. Next, procedures are used to identify sources of success and of stress. These are followed by activities designed to help individuals learn how to manage stress. Next there is a sharing of effective practices with one another, and last, available resources for members (e.g., assertiveness training) are pointed out.

There are a number of other applications. Hennessy (1980), in the guest editor's introduction to a special issue of the *Personnel and Guidance Journal*, "Values and the Counselor," emphasizes the importance of counseling that focuses on values. Both group and individual strategies are covered.

This discussion does not represent all of the group approaches but includes many that counselors may use. It gives some idea of the tremendous range of possibilities and clearly illustrates why the counselor needs to be competent in group methods. New approaches are developing constantly. A sampling of applications recently listed by a college counseling program includes:

- *Women in transition.* For those experiencing major transition, e.g., re-entry into the labor force.
- *Couples enrichment groups.* For dating and married couples, to facilitate improved relationships.
- *Couples communications groups.* For couples, to achieve new patterns of interactions.
- *Student's problems with alcohol.*
- *Women's sexual enrichment.* Learning to be more open to sexual experiences and how to deal with guilt.
- *Gestalt-oriented growth groups.* To promote growth of the whole person.
- *Dating skills interaction groups.* To develop meaningful relations in dating.

- *Interpersonal growth groups.* To improve communication skills.
- *Male sexual and social roles.* For exploring the male role in society.
- *Assertiveness training groups.* To enhance self-awareness and effectiveness in personal relationships.

Another college program offered family communication groups, relaxation groups, gay groups, and groups for the overweight.

These programs illustrate how group procedures, involving both counseling and guidance techniques, are structured to meet needs of particular populations. While these groups are for the college level, the same needs-meeting approaches can be used in other settings.

New Approaches and New Technology

Very remarkable developments are taking place in counseling, with respect both to new ways of helping and to sophisticated uses of technology. Many of the new ways (e.g., psychological education) have been covered in the previous section; Chapter 10, which deals with providing information, includes further discussion of new technology, but specific contributions to group counseling merit recognition here.

New Approaches to Counseling and Guidance.   Standardized, field-tested kits for administration by counselors, teachers, and support personnel are a major new development. There are also self-administered guidance techniques for the counselee. Peers and other paraprofessionals carry out specific face-to-face helping activities with kits and free the counselor for services requiring full professional skills.

Two of the best-known programs are DUSO (Developing Understanding Self and Others) and VEG (Vocational Exploration Group), the latter put out by Studies for Urban Man, Inc., Vocational Exploration Group, Tempe, Arizona. DUSO is available for two levels: kindergarten and lower primary, and upper primary and grade 4. The materials can be used by the classroom teacher and involve children in actively dealing with developmental problems. Tapes, hand puppets, and similar materials are used (American Guidance Service, Circle Pines, Minnesota 55014).

The VEG is a sequence of career guidance activities and makes extensive use of group interaction designed to further counselees' self-knowledge and to help them relate knowledge to job demands and satisfactions. The program, which is available in both a short and a long version (two hours or about four hours), ends with an individual plan to be implemented after the group session is concluded. The program is particularly appropriate for the high school years, but has also been used with college students and adults.

There are numerous other programs, some taped with learning aids, some described in books (see Chapter 3). A well-known one is PET (Parent

Effective Training), which is the name both of a book (Gordon 1970) and of a course offered by persons with special training provided by Effectiveness Training Associates, Pasadena, California. Dinkmeyer and McKay's *Systematic Training for Effective Parenting* (STEP), distributed by the American Guidance Service, is another widely used program for helping parents develop positive relationships with children.

Three how-to-do-it life-skills books prepared by Robert Carkhuff (1973*a* and *b*, 1974) cover helping, problem solving, and program development. For counselees, the one on problem solving is particularly useful; it goes through the process step by step, from exploring all aspects of the problem to incorporating the entire problem-solving process in handling day-to-day situations.

Counselors can turn to many well-developed programs. The ones mentioned have been tested and evaluated in research studies and help the counselor considerably in implementing guidance practices in the school.

Summary Concepts

Counseling — individual and group — is the counselor's most important and professionally demanding function. It differs from psychotherapy, although the boundaries are difficult to establish with precision. Role perceptions indicate that others' expectations may not always be in line with counselor preferences. In working with individuals or groups, counselors select the theory or theories that offer the best chance of effecting change. There are guides to this selection, but no comprehensive and validated methods are available for the selection process. Counseling techniques provide ways to translate the theory into a helping process. There is a wide range of group counseling procedures — among them, marriage counseling, career development, stress management, values clarification, and assertiveness training. Technology and kits provide assistance to the counselor through the use of programmed systematic procedures.

Examples of Research on a Topic
Effects of Counseling: Individual and Group

The following studies provide varying types of evidence about the effectiveness of counseling. As you read them, formulate an opinion about effectiveness. How convincing are these data? What factors appear to be related to effectiveness?

Research on counseling and psychotherapy has covered a large number of designs, populations, and counseling styles. Summaries by Tyler (1969, pp. 217–237) and Meltzoff and Kornreich (1970) give an overview of the variety and indicate the difficulty of this type of work. (Fewer studies deal specifically with school counseling; more cover therapeutic types of help.) Results of these reviews are too extensive to summarize here, as they cover all facets of counseling, but several representative ones are described below to illustrate the nature of this type of research.

Several representative studies are those by Fiedler (1950), Combs and Soper (1963), Rogers (1954), and Carkhuff and Alexik (1967). They illustrate how efforts have been made to understand and improve the counseling process. In the Carkhuff and Alexik study, people playing the role of counselees used different levels of self-exploration with experienced counselors. Those counselors who had been functioning at high levels of the core conditions (empathy, respect, genuineness, and concreteness) tended to maintain their levels of effectiveness, but those who had been functioning at lower levels were negatively affected by counselees' lowering level of self-exploration and failed to regain their initial level of facilitation.

Fiedler's study (1950b), starting from the proposition that in all types of therapy (and counseling) the counselor-counselee relationship is considered to be of paramount importance, investigated the opinions of professionals representing several different points of view about the ideal therapeutic relationship. He asked nondirective, psychoanalytical, and eclectic therapists to sort statements describing the ideal therapeutic relationship (e.g., "The patient feels free to say what he likes") (p. 241). Correlations among therapists were significant at the .01 level. Typical ideal characteristics of the fourteen found are an empathic relationship, good patient-therapist relations, ability of the therapist to stay close to the patient's problem, and mutual trust.

A second study found that laypersons who had never been in therapy described the same type of ideal relationship, suggesting that it would be desirable in daily life.

Both studies revealed that expert counselors representing different approaches were more alike than experienced and inexperienced counselors representing the same point of view.

Combs and Soper (1963) studied the perceptual organization of twenty-nine counselors in training and found that those rated best by instructors differed from the less effective counselors on twelve perceptual dimensions at at least the .05 level. Some of the dimensions are the internal frame of reference (concerned with how others see things), friendliness (sees others as positive and nonthreatening), confidence of ability to cope with problems. As the raters in the study represented a single approach (client-centered), Combs and Soper raise the question whether different results would have been obtained with raters of other orientations, but refer to Fiedler's study to support the position that a recognition of the importance of a good relationship transcends schools of counseling and psychotherapy.

Truax (1963) reported a series of studies that gave evidence of the importance of high levels of accurate empathy, positive regard, and self-congruence in the helping relationship, and of the negative effects of low levels. A number of other studies also deal with therapist-offered conditions (referred to as techniques in this chapter). The study by Carkhuff and Alexik (1967) is an example. A coached client varied the level of self-exploration with counselors who had been providing either high or low levels of empathy, positive regard, congruence, and concreteness (emphasis on specific rather than vague and general feelings and experiences). The counselors who had been providing low levels of the helping conditions were less effective than the high-level counselors when manipulated by the client, i.e., when the client deliberately reduced the level of self-exploration.

The extensive study by Rogers and Dymond (1954) found that clients in client-centered therapy increase congruence between real and ideal selves, and demonstrated more mature behavior (Rogers 1954, pp. 416–423). The difficulty of research on human subjects involving a helping process is illustrated by criticisms of the design, e.g., not placing individuals who need immediate attention in the "wait control group" (Meltzoff and Kornreich 1970, p. 126).

The central question is whether or not counseling and psychotherapy work. Some reports have been negative (Eysenck 1952). But most careful research comparing spontaneous recovery rates and results achieved in controlled studies show that it does help (Brown and Herrnstein 1975, pp. 596–599; Meltzoff and Kornreich 1970, p. 177; Tyler 1969, pp. 236–237) in varying degrees in varying situations. What is less certain is exactly which factors increase improvement rates.

Group counseling has been used for educational, career, and personal-social problems. Results have not been uniformly positive, but overall the approach seems to be productive.

Baymor and Patterson (1960) compared the effectiveness of client-centered group counseling, individual counseling, and a one-session motivational-encouragement meeting for 32 underachieving eleventh graders. No significant improvements were found in study habits and grades, although pupils counseled individually and in groups taken together showed improvement at the .05 level on personal adjustment when compared with the one-session motivational group and the control group. The small number of subjects and the need to use pupils with vacant periods for groups may have reduced the probability of significant results.

Benson and Blocher (1967) studied the effects of group developmental counseling on low achievers in the tenth grade. Two groups of six pupils each met for eighteen 55-minute periods. The groups, led by the same counselor, moved over the course of the counseling from guidance informational activities to exploration of feelings. Results showed that grades and feelings of adequacy improved significantly (.05 level or better). Disciplinary referrals and dropping out were reduced to a degree that had practical significance for the school. The authors point out that this was a limited study, but it does suggest that group counseling may be a useful strategy for low achievers.

Hansen, Niland, and Zani (1969) investigated the effectiveness of model reinforcement with elementary school pupils who had low sociometric status. Fifty-four low-social-acceptance pupils and eighteen high-ranking ones participated. The eight meetings used in the study emphasized getting along with others and developing social maturity. Results (from p. 743) were as follows:

t-Values for Differences Between Counseling Treatments

Treatment	t
Model reinforcement v. reinforcement	2.16^a
Model reinforcement v. control	2.44^a
Reinforcement v. control	0.08

^{a} $P < .05$

Not only did group members with social models improve significantly in sociometric ratings, but a follow-up two months later showed that improvement had been maintained.

The study by Thoresen, Hosford, and Krumboltz (1970) investigated the effects of peer social models with eleventh graders. With information-seeking behavior as the criterion, pupils in low-, medium-, and high-success groups were exposed to videotapes showing a counselee at different levels of social, academic, and athletic success. Part of the tape showed the counselee developing a strategy for collecting information for future planning. For the four schools used, results varied, and no support was gained for the social-power hypothesis. In some cases, high-effective models did stimulate a significant amount of information-seeking behavior. Overall it appears that the reinforcing power of the counselor is an important variable.

Harris and Trujillo (1975) used self-management through behavior modification and group discussion techniques to help junior high school pupils improve study habits. Both treatment groups differed significantly from the control group, though not from each other. However, the self-management group reported better study habits (e.g., having a time and place to study).

What do the studies suggest about the effectiveness of individual and group counseling? If you were asked by a layperson to justify counseling services, how would you respond?

Experiential Activities

Two kinds of experiential activities are suggested. One type involves practicing techniques (items 1 and 2). The other brings you into contact with counselors in various settings (items 3 and 4). Each of these should provide assistance to you in understanding the nature of counseling and in identifying settings of interest.

1. Counselor Styles

Write out the roles that appear below and have members of a small group select one each without revealing the choice. Then go around the group with each member explaining in a minute or less how to help the pupil described below. At the conclusion ask members to describe their feelings about the helping procedure.

Roles:

1. Counselor X — A recordkeeper and program adviser. Stays in office and can quickly provide up-to-date data on students. Knows a great deal about the institution and is in good standing with the faculty.
2. Counselor Y — An individual therapist. Believes in one-to-one work emphasizing feelings. Has been very effective with difficult cases. Prefers to handle problems without conferring with others.
3. Counselor Z — Gives counseling away. Works with others. Provides direct individual and small-group help only if needed. Prefers to get others involved in the helping process. Sometimes difficult to find.

Counselee:

A high school freshman who is having a great deal of difficulty with school subjects. Parents are separated, and he lives with each for a period of time. Recently he has been skipping school, and there are rumors that he is using drugs. Both parents express concern, but say they don't have time to come to the school for a conference.

2. Group Interaction

In small groups (4 to 6 members) begin by having all members introduce themselves and suggest one way the group could help identify personal values. Then have the group appoint a leader, agree on one of the suggestions, and deal with it for a few minutes.

At the end of the group activity (about ten minutes) discuss the following questions:

- What was the major difficulty in choosing a topic?
- Who helped resolve the difficulty?
- Who was the synthesizer (helped to get those with different points of view together)? What did this person do to help the group?
- Who was the scapegoat (someone blamed for the group's difficulties)?
- Who was the facilitator (helped the group to move forward with its task)?
- Decide which of the following behaviors were present or absent in the group:

  1. General conversation.
  2. Advice.
  3. Expressions of feeling.
  4. "I" statements (about one's own thoughts and feelings).
  5. "You" statements (in which one member "interprets" the meanings of another).
  6. "Should" statements (in which one member suggests what the group ought to do).

Which of these factors helped and which hindered group progress?

3. Participation as a Counselee

Volunteer for counseling by a campus on community service. Either individual or group counseling may be elected, but participation in both types is desirable. (Some counselor education programs include this "non-patient" type of experience and have resources available.) If educational or community services are used, it is strongly recommended that the reason for counseling be explained to the counselor, that is, as an experience for a course. Case loads may make this use inadvisable.

4. Visit to a Counseling Service

Visit a counseling service to learn about the type of counseling provided. While observation of actual individual or group counseling will not be possible, there may be videotapes or films that can be viewed. Ask what approaches are used and what results are expected.

(*See also* Appendix E, "Counselor Responses," and Appendix D, "Three-Session Group Development Experience.")

Suggested Readings

Atkinson, Donald R.; Morton, George; and Sue, Derald Wing; eds. *Counseling American Minorities*. Dubuque, Iowa: William C. Brown and Company, 1979.

An excellent reference on the application of counseling theories and techniques to minority groups. The introductory chapters, 1 and 2 (pp. 3–27), are recommended as a start. The model for identity development, pages 190–200 should be valuable for developing helping strategies. Other readings of interest may be selected from sections on American Indians, Asian Americans, black Americans, and Latinos.

Barclay, James R. "The Revolution in Counseling: Some Editorial Comments." *Personnel and Guidance Journal* 58, no. 7 (1980), p. 457.

The introduction to a special issue on the behavioral approach to counseling. All articles add depth to one's understanding of this theoretical position. The one by Krumboltz, pages 463–472, is recommended as a start.

Benjamin, Libby, and Walz, Garry R., eds. *Counseling Exceptional People*. Ann Arbor, Mich.: ERIC Counseling and Personnel Services Clearinghouse, 1980.

A comprehensive, practical, and lucid reference on counseling with exceptional individuals. The reader will find excellent discussions of counseling with 5 types of handicapped individuals; the gifted; plus chapters on techniques, counseling, and consultation. Use the Table of Contents to locate chapters of interest.

Betz, Ellen. "The Counselor Role." In *Student Services,* edited by Ursula Delworth and Gary R. Hanson, pp. 175–190. San Francisco: Jossey-Bass, 1980.

A very useful discussion of the counselor's role in student personnel services. The value of counseling skills for other staff members is also covered.

Blimline, Carol A., ed. *Innovations in Counseling Services*. Washington, D.C.: International Association of Counseling Services (not dated).

A compilation of descriptions of innovative counseling services. While many articles are mainly descriptions of services, some present strategies and techniques; for example, Finley's discussion of a therapeutic group for blacks with emotional problems, pages 165–171.

Carroll, Marguerite R. "Introduction." *School Counselor* 20, no. 5 (1973), p. 333.

A special issue on psychological education containing five articles describing new approaches to implementing the counselor's role in the school.

Corsini, Raymond, ed. *Current Psychotherapies*. Itasca, Ill.: F. E. Peacock, 1973.

One of the major references on theories, covering 12 different points of view and providing illustrative case material. Reading may be selected according to preferences.

Ganikos, Mary L.; Grady, Kathleen A.; and Olson, Jane B. *Counseling the Aged.* Washington, D.C.: American Personnel and Guidance Association, 1979.

A comprehensive reference on counseling older persons. For this chapter, Module VII, "Counseling Older Adults: Suggested Approaches," pages 173–225, is recommended.

Harmon, Lenore W.; Birk, Janice M.; Fitzgerald, Laurine E.; and Tanney, Mary Faith, eds. *Counseling Women.* Monterey, Calif.: Brooks/Cole Publishing Company, 1978.

A collection of articles, primarily from the *Counseling Psychologist,* providing an in-depth treatment of all aspects of counseling women. The author recommends "Women in Groups" (pp. 34–58) by Whiteley as a start, followed by "Career Counseling for Women" (pp. 75–93), by Vetter.

Hennessy, Thomas C. "Introduction to the Special Issue, 'Values and the Counselors.'" *Personnel and Guidance Journal* 58, no. 9 (1980), pp. 557–558.

The guest editor's introduction to a special issue on both group and individual approaches to counseling regarding values and moral development. The article by Glaser and Kirschenbaum, pages 569–574 (with reactions by Leona Tyler, pages 574–575), is an excellent discussion of the use of values clarification. The Table of Contents may be consulted for other articles of interest.

Lee, James L., and Pulvino, Charles J., eds. *Group Counseling: Theory, Research and Practice.* Washington, D.C.: American Personnel and Guidance Assn., 1973.

A collection of outstanding articles on groups from journals of the American Personnel and Guidance Association. The school level is well represented.

Leopard, Judy Gaines, and Wachowiak, Dale. "Introduction to Coupling." *Personnel and Guidance Journal* 55, no. 9 (1977), p. 503.

The guest editor's introduction to a special issue on marriage counseling. In addition to marriage counseling models, other marital areas are covered (e.g., divorce counseling, social forces affecting marriage).

Patterson, C. H. "A Current View of Client-Centered or Relationship Theory." *Counseling Psychologist* 1, no. 2 (1969), pp. 2–25.

Patterson gives a lucid explanation of the client-centered point of view.

————. *Theories of Counseling and Psychotherapy.* 2nd ed. New York: Harper and Row, 1973.

Contains summaries of many of the counseling points of view discussed in this chapter. One of the major references on the subject. Select sections according to interests.

Thoresen, Carl E., and Coates, Thomas J. "What Does It Mean to Be a Behavior Therapist?" *Counseling Psychologist* 7, no. 3 (1978), pp. 3–21.

The lead article in a special issue on this theory of counseling. Valuable as a detailed and theoretical discussion of the behavioral approach. Other articles in the same issue discuss pros and cons of the approach.

Walz, Garry R., and Benjamin, Libby, eds. *New Imperatives for Guidance.* ERIC Counseling and Personnel Services Clearinghouse, 1978.

Several sections of this timely book are valuable for portraying the expanded role of the school counselor. Chapter 7, "The Counselor's New Challenge: Parent Education," is recommended.

Weinrach, Stephen G. "Reviews." *Personnel and Guidance Journal* 55, no. 9 (1977), pp. 556–559, and 55, no. 10 (1977), pp. 612–618.

Reviews of many of the best-known packaged group techniques, including some that are briefly mentioned in this chapter (PET, values clarification). Comments of evaluators, many of whom took part in group leader training, and responses of originators of the techniques are extremely helpful in understanding the purpose and effectiveness of those new approaches to group work.

Chapter
9

The Counselor and
Special Groups

One of the certainties in the counseling profession is that members will give more and more attention to groups that have unique needs. This is not to say that everything about these special groups is different from the general population — the commonalities are substantial. But these groups are encountering conditions, customs, and problems that call for an understanding of their unique situations. Innovative helping approaches are often required. Moreover, members of these groups have in the past been neglected, avoided, or simply ignored by counselors. Now a number of factors — some legal, some humanistic, some financial, and some arising from population characteristics — have made it clear that the neglect of these special groups is a thing of the past.

The special groups discussed here are: women, minorities, the disadvantaged, midlife and older persons, the handicapped, and the gifted. There are others, of course, but these appear to be the major groups with which counselors will be increasingly involved.

Special Groups:
What the Counselor Needs to Know

What would be of most value to you, the student beginning the counselor education program, to know about special groups? One way to answer this question is to try to put yourself in the place of a member of a special group. You would no doubt want counselors to be aware that your group exists. In addition, it seems highly probable that you would like for it to be considered important. These may appear to be modest expectations and so obvious that they hardly need to be mentioned. But experience suggests otherwise. Many individuals who are members of the groups identified here (some may be in this class) can likely attest to the fact that counselors have not seemed to be aware of their existence.

Second, you would want counselors to learn something about your group as a group — its personality characteristics, values, attitudes, goals — plus some factual data about numbers, socioeconomic status, and geographical locations. The focus is on general information that more or less applies to all members.

Next, you would like to be perceived as a unique individual as well as a group member. General characteristics are the backdrop against which to view each person, but each person is an individual rather than a faceless member of a crowd.

Then, it would seem that you would want counselors to learn about particular needs that are characteristic of most, if not all, of the members of your group. Needs are aspects of the general characteristics, but they are so important for counseling services that they deserve separate treatment. Needs do not in themselves adequately portray a group, but they do point to goals for counseling services.

Finally, you most probably would want counselors to be aware of your attitudes toward counseling services. Are they positive or negative? Do you use services? Do you perceive counselors as valuing individuals in your group?

Such information will not only facilitate your understanding of special groups but will also help you identify preferred work settings and populations. Obviously, only a limited amount of information can be presented in one chapter, but the brief treatments presented here can provide a start. Extended interactions with members of special groups and further reading will help immeasurably in building a base of understanding for effective work in the practical experiences that come later in the program.

Insofar as information is available, these three topics — general characteristics, needs, and reactions to counseling services — are covered in the sections that follow.

Women

General Characteristics

When women are identified as a "subgroup," the classification seems almost paradoxical. Women make up approximately one-half of the population and constitute about the same proportion of the labor force. Recent legislation has opened previously closed doors in work, education, and the military. In addition, women certainly do not represent a homogeneous group — ethnic, racial, and other differences could support much more detailed breakdowns. But there are certain attributes, largely the result of the socialization process, that make this a group of special concern for counselors; for example, inequality in job opportunities and remuneration, stereotyping, and others that are discussed here.

From what has already been said, it is apparent that changes are taking place in the status of women as far as tradition is concerned. As Westervelt (1973) points out, the "women's revolution . . . is a social convulsion of a magnitude hitherto unknown in human history" (p. 4). The times, however, may not be that turbulent for all women. Those with higher levels of education, about whom Westervelt is writing, are likely to be in closer touch with current social trends as well as more interested in enhancement of status. But when the popular media feature articles on the changing status of women — such as *Newsweek*'s extensive account of "The Superwoman Squeeze" (Langway, Lord, Reese, Simons, Maitland, Gelman, and Witman 1980), it is apparent that changes cover a wide spectrum of society. At the same time, state legislatures' votes on the Equal Rights Amendment (ERA) and the controversy at the 1980 major-party national political conventions suggest that differences of opinion exist about the directions and desirability of changes. But regardless of the status of large-scale movements, there are increasing signs of significant changes that add important details to an overall view of women today.

One such factor is legislative support for opening up opportunities in work, education, and recreation. Title IX of the Education Amendments Act of 1972 is only one of a series of legislative milestones that have paved the way for full participation of women in educational activities. Probably the most widely discussed impact is on school and college athletics, but this is only one aspect. As a group, women now have legal support for many opportunities that were heretofore subtly or openly denied them.

Legal sanctions, however, do not insure that all problems will disappear. Not only does society support stereotypes and myths about suitable roles, motivations, and abilities, but women themselves have internalized attitudes and often support the stereotypes unconsciously. The development of stereotypes has been studied extensively (Bingham 1975; Kincaid 1979; Wolleat 1979); it is clear that stereotyping begins very early in the child's life. Society's position is vividly illustrated by the heavy concentration of lower-level jobs, and lower pay, in women's traditional occupations. Many girls and women also choose to limit their own opportunities by imposing restrictions on themselves about selecting nontraditional careers (Bingham 1975, p. 34), by avoiding success (Esposito 1977), and by playing down achievement in typical male occupations (Fitzgerald and Crites 1980). Attitudes of women are changing, and there is no way to accurately estimate how many lean toward traditional roles, are in the middle, and are at the stage where they feel free to adopt a preferred role without being bound by tradition.

Women in the workplace make up more than half of the total number of all women. Almost half of married women with young children work outside the home. Sixty percent of the net increase in working wives comes from families where the husband's income is in the upper-middle to upper levels (Ryscavage 1979). Women are not part-time workers; more than half worked full time in 1978, and the number has been steadily increasing. In addition, the number of women who maintain families is also increasing, with almost half having incomes below the poverty levels (Bureau of Labor Statistics 1980). In spite of high participation levels, however, salaries, job levels, and promotions show the effects of discrimination (DeWitt 1980; "Women at Work: Still Fighting 'Stereotyped Roles'" 1979).

Women are participating in education and training to a greater degree than ever before, particularly in professional schools, even though educational institutions at times deliberately or inadvertently steer women away from nontraditional programs and hamper full use of talents. The number of women 25 years of age and older attending college has taken a sharp upturn — tenfold in the past two decades (Smallwood 1980). In 1978 two thirds of college students over 35 were women (Young 1980). Education is of increasing importance to women of *all* social levels for a number of reasons, but accessibility is a major one (Haymon, Pollard, and Bobby 1979).

Patterns of marriage and family life are changing, and these changes affect women in a number of ways. The decline in the full-time homemaker role and the increase in dual-career marriages have already been discussed. Divorce has increased — the ratio of divorces to marriage was 1 to 6 in 1940. In 1975 it was 1 to 2.

Cohabitation has become a pattern for an increasing number of persons. Often the ramifications — legal, economic, child custody — are not considered (Bernstein 1977). These factors may work against the woman because her expectations from the relationship may be different from the man's. Newcomb (1979) points to the evidence that suggests that more women than men expect that the relationship will lead to sexual exclusivity and marriage.

Needs

From the foregoing discussion, one could hardly help from concluding that career needs are central. To be able to compete with equality in the job market — to have equal job stability, pay, and promotional opportunities compared with men — are essential. In addition, to be free from prejudice, discrimination, and sexual harassment in education and work are certainly reasonable expectations. Just as is true for any group that has had partial equality (e.g., minorities), the job is the major path to true equality.

Women should, of course, have the opportunity to choose their own preferred life-style — career, marriage and homemaking, home and career, or single status. Not all women may want a career, but there are pressures in that direction now just as there were pressures in the homemaking direction in the past. The new shift means that the woman not only has to deal with society's expectations and customs but must also find a way to handle the effects of socialization that almost inevitably impose some constraints on choice.

There are other needs that have been identified earlier — protection from, and assistance in dealing with sex-related criminal acts and abuse, for example, the battered wife. Furthermore, older women, minority-group members, and the handicapped have additional problems and needs that go beyond those enumerated here.

Attitudes Toward Counseling Services

It would be helpful to have information about any unique perceptions that women have about the total range of counseling services — group, individual, large-scale programs, and so on. There is very little evidence, however, to suggest that women differ much from men on these perceptions. Even for the one-to-one relationship, the evidence for a same-sex or opposite-sex counselor is inconclusive (Tanney and Birk 1978, pp. 210–215). It seems reasonable to assume that women have generally positive reactions to counseling services, whatever the setting. This seems to be the case even though there is evidence of sexual bias, particularly in career-oriented assistance (Fitzgerald and Crites 1980). In fact, from elementary school on females tend to view helping services more positively than males and to make more extensive use of counseling and personnel resources.

Minorities

General Characteristics

There could be almost any number of minority groups when classifications are made according to social, economic, religious, and other characteristics as well as the ethnic and racial ones used here (Atkinson, Morten, and Sue 1979, p. viii). As a matter of fact, all of the special groups in this chapter, with the exception of women, are, in a sense, "minority" groups. For example, the midlife and older groups constitute age-determined minorities. This section, however, deals with the major racial and ethnic groups in the United States — those with whom the counselor is most likely to work.

The minorities discussed in this section are: blacks, Hispanics, Indians, and Asian Americans. A case could be made that there are other groups that should be included, but space limitations would make the discussion much too brief. Moreover, the groups chosen are those that, in my judgment, have the greatest need because of past neglect and are the least understood groups today.

In their book, *Counseling American Minorities*, Atkinson, Morten and Sue (1979, pp. 3–7) point out the differences between *race* and *ethnicity*, two terms that are sometimes used in a confusingly interchangeable way. Briefly, race refers to those identified by distinguishing physical characteristics. Ethnic identification is culturally defined, including, for example, citizens of a country. These definitions are adequate for present purposes; further explanations introduce more complexity than is needed. An ethnic group may include different races, and vice versa; the important point is the difference between the terms.)

There is a difference, too, between the terms *minority* and *disadvantaged*. The latter term refers to an individual or group that lacks something, (economic resources, occupational competencies, educational background, social skills). That question of lack is based on a comparison with some group. If a capable individual wants to enter college but has a very poor high school record, he or she could be said to be educationally disadvantaged. Thus, being a member of a minority group does not automatically make one disadvantaged. The term "culturally disadvantaged," as Atkinson, Morten, and Sue (1979, p. 5) point out, implies a deficiency, but it is actually a way of saying that the majority culture is better. Since each group has its own personally meaningful and complex culture, the use of the term *culturally disadvantaged* is not relevant.

A final word about the groups that are discussed. Individuals within them vary a great deal. As Clayton (1978) says:

> "Minority students" is a catch-all concept and should never be used when a more culturally definite term is needed. One actually counsels Spanish-speaking students whose families came from Mexico, Puerto Rico, Cuba, or Spain; Asian American students whose parents came from China, Japan, or Taiwan; Native American students whose parents came from the Plains, the Great Southwest, the East, the Southeast, and Black students whose parents came from Africa, South America, Latin America, or Urban Rural, Southern, or Northern United States." (pp. 268–269)

To these could be added others, such as Cambodians, Vietnamese, Haitians. Furthermore, the point that Clayton makes applies in any setting — school, college, and community. Understanding and appreciating special groups involves the more specific and cultural differences as well as the broad classifications. The use of the "melting-pot" concept of past years is fading, and differences are not only accepted but valued (Korchin 1980; Tidwell 1980).

Blacks

General Characteristics

Harper (1979, pp. 113–117) points out that for an understanding of blacks, one needs to know about their history, sociology, economics, and psychology. This background gives some understanding of the works of the black individual. Not only will it be possible to perceive current pressures, barriers, and needs, but this breadth of understanding will help to dispel stereotypes that are particularly negative for this special group. In the paragraphs that follow, some points related to these areas are summarized.

Picou (1975, pp. 407–409) suggests that it will help to understand what it means to be black in a predominately white society if one is aware of the way minority-group members look at life and how perceptions differ from those of the majority. For example, blacks define "humanism" as a value involving concern for warm and caring relationships between self and others, willingly relating to diversity, and deriving pleasure from service to others. Among whites there is also a desire to help the community through a career choice rather than promote one's own success as a main goal, but the definition given by whites tended to emphasize tolerance, even though it was of a superficial nature. At the same time, there is a lower expectation of success than accorded whites for expended efforts. These and other hypothesized characteristics are discussed by Picou in relation to how they impinge upon the research data-collection process using black respondents, but they are relevant for the counselor's work.

Various views have been advanced to explain attitudes and dynamics of change. The 1950s have been characterized as the period of the acquiescent individual. This label was, as Seymour and Bardo point out (1979, pp. 122–123) based less on research than on therapists' reports explaining lack of effectiveness with black clients. In the 1960s one of the dominant themes identifed by counselors who were, as Bryson and Bardo state, "interested in explaining away Blacks" (p. 125), was self-hate. These themes reflect the search for simple explanations of the times and do nothing to help others understand blacks. A more useful way of conceptualization is based on stages in the transformation process experienced by black Americans.

Picou (1975, pp. 410–412) summarizes research and theory that supports a five-stage sequence for blacks to move to a level of self-actualization. First, there is a rejection-of-race attitude, somewhat akin to the self-hate mentioned above. Then comes some experience that shatters the previous views of one's self and one's place in American culture. This experience leads to introspection about being black and to the third stage that is called "immersion-emersion" (p. 411). Paramount here is a total orientation to — and pride in being — black. Rage toward the white majority may be present. The next two stages involve movement through internalization of attitudes and to confidence, community concern, and constructive action steps. Individuals may be at any stage of this process and fixation at a stage can occur. When this occurs the individual may manifest primarily hostile attitudes.

These explanatory concepts, although somewhat tentative, help the counselor understand how the black counselee might perceive the social, economic, and political situations in this country. But it is more important to look at each individual and, as Clayton (1978, p. 274) says, understand his or her background, present status, and potentialities. One of the critical life-areas is career, and it is viewed here as a major aspect of life-style.

Attitudes about work and knowledge of opportunities play important roles in career programs. Self-confidence, for example, believing that one can succeed, appears to be related to better jobs and better earnings (Casey 1979, pp. 2–3). But many black individuals feel that they lack the ability to exert control, are less positive about themselves, and less able to cope with educational and occupational demands (Williams 1979) than whites. Black students tend to select from a limited range of occupations; they lack role models for many areas of work and may not consider many careers as reasonable possibilities. In addition, minority youths may view the school as not helpful and drop out because it is monetarily useless for them to continue — the additional education is not seen as helpful in job getting or job success. Johnson (1980) considers the disparity between being qualified and failing to gain employment because of discrimination as negating the effectiveness of career education and career guidance. But career and educational problems are essentially reflections of general barriers to development experienced in society (Davidson 1980).

Unemployment, underemployment, job insecurity, and job-finding discouragement are everyday conditions for disproportionate numbers. Forty percent or more of the black teenagers who seek jobs cannot find them. Compared with whites, black workers are more adversely affected by economic downturns and their status improves more slowly in an economic recovery period. In addition, many individuals have been discouraged and have stopped looking for work. It is estimated that about 700,000 minority youths are not in school, not at work, or not looking for work, and that another 300,000 young adults have also given up the search for a job (Davidson 1980).

Coupled with these problems is that of restricted variety in occupational choice. There is extensive underrepresentation of blacks in a number of career areas, such as the sciences and engineering (Smith 1980). In a number of the career areas chosen by blacks, opportunities are decreasing. Higher education, once considered to be the key to career success, is increasingly proving to be a dead-end street, for example, in education and the social sciences (Rule 1980). Moving into the greater variety of occupations is a pattern historically used by whites, but blacks have lagged behind in this process (Griffith 1980). The spread has been inhibited by a number of factors — the economy, discrimination, inferior quality of educational preparation, and lack of successful role models.

Needs

Probably the greatest needs are represented by the dual problems of discrimination in education and work and lack of effective assistance that would enable blacks to be aware of their legal rights and to learn about opportunities in work and education. These are the paramount ones, although from the foregoing discussion it may appear that a better understanding of blacks' perceptions of the world may be the most critical factor. Certainly it is true that widespread acceptance of the concept of cultural pluralism (e.g., recognition of the validity of black pride) would have an impact on job and educational opportunities. But opening up opportunities for economic progress and everyday informal educational and occupational contacts should dispel barriers in all life areas — social, cultural, political, and educational.

Attitudes Toward Counseling Services

Blacks as well as members of other minority groups tend to make less use of services in schools, colleges, and community agencies than do white, middle-class individuals. The composition of staffs may be a factor — individuals may see no one like themselves in the office or agency. In addition, the individual who has experienced failure or rejection in one institution, such as the school, may readily transfer negative attitudes to a guidance and counseling service. Thus, suspicion or even hostility may characterize the attitudes of some members of minority groups.

The type of help provided may be viewed as ineffective or inappropriate. Direct assistance may be desired rather than the typical verbal type of interaction emphasizing self-exploration. Friends and family may be preferred as helpers, whereas the professional counselor is thought to be for "crazy" people. The culture, language, and attitudes of the minority individual may not be understood by the counselor. The counselor may, in fact, be guided by stereotypes in dealing with the counselee and may communicate this attitude in subtle ways. Moreover, the quality of help may actually be poorer; blacks are more likely to be offered custodial care than psychotherapy (Korchin 1980), for instance.

Attitudes are changing; they are helped by an increase in the number and visibility of black professionals and the use of indigenous paraprofessionals. But the fact remains, however, that many blacks do not view counseling services, whatever the setting, as helping agencies that have their best interests at heart.

Hispanic Americans

General Characteristics

Latinos, a term for those of Spanish origin and descent — primarily from Cuba, Mexico, and Puerto Rico — make up the second-largest minority in the United States today. According to Atkinson, Morten, and Sue (1979, pp. 147–148), there are an estimated 12 million Latinos in the United States today, but the number could actually be as high as 20 million. By the year 2000 they may constitute a majority of the population of California.

Although Hispanic Americans share a number of characteristics such as language and the preference for urban living, subgroups differ markedly. For one thing, they tend to live in areas near their home countries. Chicanos are concentrated in Texas and other Southwest states; those from Cuba tend to settle in Florida, while many Puerto Ricans live in urban areas on the east coast. Numbers vary also. Ruiz and Padilla (1977), using statistics that are almost ten years old, give counts as follows: Chicanos, 5 million; Puerto Ricans, 1.5 million; Cubans, 600,000; Central and South Americans, 1.5 million; and other, 1.5 million. More recent estimates put the number of Mexican Americans alone at 7.2 million, a substantial increase in only a few years. Increases in other groups have taken place (e.g., the recent influx of Cubans) (Williams, Kasindorf, McGuire, Copeland, Donosky, and Hager 1979).

While many cultural characteristics are shared to varying degrees, there are distinct subcultures, each with its own pattern of beliefs and behaviors. Some of these derive from the original cultures from which they came, and some are related to the reasons for emigrating to the United States (Ruiz and Padilla 1977). For Chicanos, the homeland is close at hand, and is a constant reminder of the cultural heritage they are determined not to lose. Understanding Puerto Ricans involves an awareness of their individualistic nature and their involvement in extended-family relationships. It also must be recognized that there are two groups — those born on the island who have moved to the United States and those born in this country. Both groups have many common characteristics, but there are differences, such as those based on the traditional strong family influence and the dominant language (Christensen 1975). Individuals from Cuba share Latino characteristics, such as strong family ties and dominant male role, but may have differing attitudes about the past and present political developments in Cuba. While unique subcultural nuances need to be understood, there are traits and problems that cut across all groups.

Needs

Probably the most dominant needs of all Latinos are to be understood and be given the opportunity to make their own place in American society. It follows that they must be free from stereotyping and must have the opportunity to preserve their cultures. Work and educational opportunities are basic to progress. Atkinson, Morten, and Sue (1979, p. 147) point out the depressing statistics that must be taken into account — fewer than 40 percent have completed high school; the median family income is almost a third lower than the national figure; almost one fourth have incomes below the poverty level. Moreover, the quality and type of mental health care is inferior (Korchin 1980, Nuttall 1979). Although there is ample evidence of progress (e.g., in the Spanish section of Miami and in the Barrios of Los Angeles), much more is needed.

Attitudes Toward Counseling Services

In spite of their obvious problems and needs, Latinos utilize counseling services less than the general population in schools, colleges, and community agencies. Services are not seen as helpful or attuned to cultural uniqueness. Agency procedures, locations, and language often present barriers. Ruiz and Padilla (1977) question the assumptions that the extended family help, religion, and similar cultural support systems replace counseling services and attribute the lack of their use to specifics already mentioned, such as lack of bilingual counselors.

Native Americans

General Characteristics

The American Indian has been "fighting a defensive war for their right to freedom, their lands, their organizations, their traditions and beliefs, their way of life, and their very lives" (Atkinson, Morten, and Sue 1979, p. 31). This statement may sound like an exaggeration, but hard facts support it. Their number has decreased from 3 million to around 600,000. Infant mortality is three times the national average. The teenage suicide rate for Indians is many times that of whites. The number of young persons not completing high school is much greater than for the general population (Atkinson, Morten, and Sue 1979, p. 31). There is a pervasive lack of understanding of needs, cultural values, and aspirations by those providing services (Deloria 1979, pp. 33–34; Onstad 1971; Spang 1971). Occupational plans and opportunities are severely restricted (Spencer, Windham, and Peterson 1975, pp. 216–218).

Indians are probably the most stereotyped of all minority groups. Not only does this obscure actual characteristics, but it leads one to assume that they are a homogenous group. The diversity, however, is great (Deloria 1979, pp. 45–48; Youngman and Sadongei 1974). Thus, the counselor should learn as much as possible about the particular subculture if he or she is going to be an effective helper. There are general characteristics on which to build an understanding — sharing one's material goods, importance of respect for the individual, patience, independence (Lewis and Ho 1979, pp. 52–53). It is particularly important not to assume that one is an instant Indian expert. Deloria emphasizes this point by saying that "Our foremost plight is our transparency" (p. 33). Just by looking at Indians, the "expert" can tell what they want, what they are like, and what they need.

Needs

The needs of Indians resemble those of other minority groups in many ways, including understanding of and respect for cultural values and characteristics. Moreover, it is particularly important to realize that the Indian child is involved, to some degree, in conflict between two cultures. Communication is often a problem because of differences in language and cultural values. Education in general and counseling in particular need to give proper weight to the Indians' cultural needs and contributions (Spang 1971). Educational and work opportunities should be expanded; realistic career planning is one way to help ease economic and other problems.

Attitudes Toward Counseling Services

There seems to be a widespread suspicion and rejection of helping services. Lewis and Ho (1979, p. 51) attribute this rejection to helpers' lack of understanding of the culture, stereotyping, and the use of traditional techniques and strategies that do not fit the Indians' styles of interaction. A comment by an Indian student identifies much of the difficulty:

> I think we need Indian counselors on all levels of education. The non-Indian counselor perceives the Indian as other non-Indians have taught him. He has not experienced reservation life, and the values of his own culture prevent him from understanding us. (Onstad 1971, p. 103)

Asian Americans

General Characteristics

The term "Asian American" covers a number of groups, some of long standing in the United States and some who are relative newcomers. Chinese were the first to arrive in this country in large numbers. Later there were substantial numbers of Japanese. Recently there has been a sizable influx of Vietnamese, and even more recently some refugees from Cambodia have been admitted. (There are other Asian groups, but these are the major ones.)

Each of these cultures is unique; its background, values, and problems of coping need to be understood. It is important to be aware that large-scale immigration from China began in the 1840s to fill the demand for cheap labor on the west coast and that when there was an economic turndown, the new arrivals became the target of official and unofficial persecution. Hence the origin of the expression, "Not a Chinaman's chance" (Sue 1975a, p. 100). Later, in the 1890s, Japanese began to come to the United States in large numbers. General attitudes toward Orientals, plus the phenomenal success of the Japanese in agricultural occupations, helped to generate negative reactions. Various types of community hostility and legislative discrimination caused both of these two ethnic groups to build their own communities (Sue 1979, pp. 85–86).

Attitudes toward Japanese and Chinese as well as other minority groups typically reflect the relationship between the United States and the country from which the minority group came. Thus, during World War II over a hundred thousand Japanese Americans were moved to internment camps after the attack on Pearl Harbor. The Chinese, however, were viewed more favorably (Sue and Kitano 1979, p. 78). Since the 1940s there has been an increase in positive attitudes toward Chinese and Japanese.

Much of this improvement is based on the stereotype of the educated, competent, law-abiding, successful, affluent Oriental. While there is some truth in these assumptions, stereotypes always tend to obscure differences between ethnic groups and needs of the subcultures. For example, the higher-than-average family incomes of Chinese and Japanese families are the result, to some extent, of the fact that families usually have more than one wage earner (Sue 1977). Moreover, it may not be recognized that many are caught in a culture conflict that leads to an identity crisis and marginal psychological existence between two cultures. In some cases an anti-American "Yellow Power" attitude may crystallize (Sue 1975a, pp. 103–104). The term "banana" is used as a derogatory label for those who have become over Americanized — yellow on the outside and white on the inside (Sue 1979, p. 87).

More recent ethnic groups come from different subcultures and have different reasons for leaving their homelands. The Vietnamese are an example, although there are others such as Cambodian refugees. Starting in the mid-1970s, approximately one-third of a million Vietnamese have come to this country, and there is a continuous influx (Brower 1980). Not only are there marked cultural differences from United States patterns (to the Vietnamese, for example, looking directly at someone is a sign of disrespect), there are also significant differences between the early immigrants and the more recent ones. Many of those arriving in 1975–1976 were well educated and had worked with French and Americans. The later arrivals were much more heterogeneous. Many were from rural areas, but some were ethnic Chinese, which is a subculture within Vietnam (Brower 1980).

Needs

It is apparent for Asian Americans as for other minority groups that it is essential to be aware of historical events, values, cultural conflicts, and styles of interactions. These, as Sue (1975a, pp. 117–118) points out, have effects that cut across life-styles and affect achievement, personality, career goals, and emotional stability. In addition, it is particularly important to look beyond the stereotypes of financial success, high achievement, hard work, and conforming to see the problems and needs that exist, the unique characteristics of each subculture, and the dilemmas brought about by being caught between cultures.

Attitudes Toward Counseling Services

Cultural factors may make it difficult for some Asian Americans to admit the need for assistance because it may represent failure. Family members are often seen as more appropriate helpers. Moreover, the usual helping strategies involving open, self-disclosing verbal interaction may be contrary to acceptable ways of relating to others. The counselor may be perceived as lacking understanding or as intent on fitting the individual to the majority culture. In fact, particularly for more recent arrivals, the whole rationale for helping services may not be understood or accepted.

The Disadvantaged

General Characteristics

This group is composed of those who are so severely deprived that they are not able to compete successfully in society. In some ways this deprivation may be viewed as a handicap such as the physical and psychological ones taken up in later sections. However, here the concern is for deprivation that is economic and educational. Furthermore, minority status is not the same; while discrimination and prejudice may more frequently push minority individuals into a disadvantaged status, any individual, regardless of race or ethnic origin, can be disadvantaged. Thus, the term "culturally disadvantaged" has no useful meaning. As Atkinson, Morten, and Sue (1979, p. 5) point out, the use of the term suggests a *lack* of a culture. In the discussion of minorities in the preceding sections it has been emphasized over and over that these groups have rich and complex cultures; they are not deprived in a cultural sense.

While almost anyone may experience deprivation of some sort, the situation is usually not so acute as to practically preclude successful coping. To be unable to attend an expensive university is not economic deprivation; to have a poor background in mathematics is not educational deprivation. But to have had an inferior type of education or none at all, to lack funds for any kind of education or training, to be so unaware of work attitudes that one does not realize that it is necessary to be on time to a job are forms of economic and educational deprivation. The individual deprived in this way does not have the means, experience, attitudes, and basic communication skills to be successful in the kinds of tasks that must be accomplished in our society. This is a more rigorous definition than is sometimes used. For example, Lazes and Feldberg (1978) apply the definition in a general way to adults with special needs.

Needs

The disadvantaged can be defined at least to some extent in terms of career development needs. There are other factors, of course, but attitudes and skills related to coping in the world of work reflect the major dimensions of deprivation in vivid ways. Oetting and Miller's (1977) work adjustment hierarchy identifies the critical needs as: developing a work role identification, job readiness, and job getting. There are further steps, but these highlight the essential first-stage needs. Developing a work role identification involves a complex of attitudes in which the individual perceives the value of work, wants to work, can see himself or herself as a worker, is aware that work is an expectation of others, and visualizes rewards from work. Job readiness includes some understanding of personal attributes and needs and of work opportunities. Job-getting calls for knowledge of helping resources and possession of skills needed to do such things as take part in an employment interview. The same authors (Miller and Oetting 1977) further identify needs such as child care, transportation, and job skills. Work experience is also one of the most pressing problems. Lack of success experiences is characterized as a common denominator shared by disadvantaged youth ("Youth Unemployment: Guidance is a must," 1979).

Attitudes Toward Counseling Services

It might be expected that the disadvantaged would be apathetic or even negative about the efficacy of counseling services. Little or no use of, or confidence in, helping services are aspects of the meaning of the term "disadvantaged." Thus, in initial contacts between the disadvantaged and helping services these are often the individual's reactions. The use of indigenous paraprofessionals, the provisions of concrete aid, and the communication of understanding and caring can do much to bridge the gap. As with other minorities, stereotypes about the group lead to lack of understanding and failure to provide meaningful help. It is often assumed that the disadvantaged have no ambition, don't want to work, and cannot learn to stick to a task, but research does not support these stereotypical attitudes (*Vocational Counseling the Disadvantaged Students* 1980).

Midlife and Older

General Characteristics

These two categories, midlife and older, could each merit separate sections — they are new and significant areas of interest for counselors. Concern about the midlife period is of fairly recent origin and is due in part to studies of the life span, the increasing number of career changes in this period, and the awareness that midlife crises often required professional assistance. Widespread concern about the needs of older persons is also relatively new. Humanistic concerns plus the growing number of older persons have given this group high visibility insofar as helping services is concerned. These two groups, particularly the latter, will almost certainly claim more and more of the counselor's time in the years ahead.

As had been mentioned, the midlife period has recently been the subject of an increasing amount of research. Levinson, Darrow, Klein, Levinson and McKee (1976) characterize the widespread belief that there is a settling down and stable period after adolescence as a "cruel illusion." In the late 30s the individual may experience a sense of constraint or oppression in work, marriage, and other relationships that he is involved in and may search for affirmation of worth from society. This phase is followed by a transition period in which the disparity between goals and achievements is reviewed. The individual then moves to a stable structure for middle adult life. Other research has shown that events expected to be life crises for women — change of life, children leaving home — do not have a traumatic effect because they are anticipated. For men, retirement is handled the same way. But the unanticipated events, such as divorce, do have a strong negative effect. The difference has to do with events that upset the rhythm of life, that is, the expected life cycle (Neugarten 1976).

Role changes tend to occur; in the middle years alternations take place that result in increased affiliative needs of husbands and more assertive and independent modes for wives (Grunebaum 1979). These types of developmental changes provide bases for helping strategies.

The career development implications of characteristics of the midlife stage are particularly significant for counselors. Occupational changes are made. Reentry into education or training takes place. Murphy and Burck (1976) suggest that a stage of *renewal* should be added to the usual midlife career development tasks as a process that takes place from the mid-30s to the mid-40s. This addition augments the positive aspects of the period and helps lay the groundwork for a developmental emphasis in helping services.

Job changers' motives reflect characteristics of this stage. Individuals are often willing to take a cut in pay to achieve personal satisfaction — for example, the 49-year-old successful dentist who became a commercial fisherman, or the 31-year-old career counselor who changed careers to become a tour and travel manager (Dreyfus 1980). Today, there is a more widespread knowledge of occupational areas than in the past, and negative reactions about changing jobs is decreasing. These conditions plus more economic security than one typically has in the 30s help make career changing easier.

Women are reentering the job market or entering it for the first time with greater frequency than in past years. Minority women, too, are actively returning to the world of work; currently the percentage is greater than for white women (Haymon, Pollard, and Bobby 1979). For many women, reentry presents a novel and threatening event; various types of supportive services, such as group counseling and assertiveness training, are needed to smooth the transition.

Colleges, too, are experiencing an increase in the number of midlife persons doing both graduate and undergraduate work. Many institutions offer nontraditional programs for adults (von der Embse and Childs 1979). Older students do not perceive the value of student services in the same way younger ones do; one of the reasons for this difference is the way services are provided (Kasworm 1980). More attention needs to be given to structuring programs and services for midlife persons. It is clear that the years ahead will witness higher rates of participation in educational and training opportunities. Predictions have been made that there is a potential of 40 million persons in career transition; almost half are in the midlife range, and most of them want additional education or training (Arbeiter, Aslanian, Schmerbeck, and Brickell 1978, pp. 9–11). Other research gives support to the position that the desire for further education is triggered by significant events such as retirement, reentering the job market, being fired, or being promoted ("Crisis Triggers Learning" 1980).

The age at which persons are classified as *older* is generally set at 65 (Blake and Peterson 1979). In the middle 1970's, there were 22 million persons (more than 10 percent of the total population) in this category, and the growth rate is about one-half million per year. At this same time, those 60 years of age and older numbered over 30 million and made up about 15 percent of the population. The 75-plus age group was more than 8 million at this same time and constituted about 4 percent of the population (Blake and Peterson 1979, pp. 4–5). This last age group is the fastest-growing population segment (Benedict 1980).

Projections highlight the importance of this group. By the year 2030, those 65 and over will account for perhaps as much as one fifth of the population. These predictions call for assumptions about the birthrate and other factors (medical care). Whatever the number, it will bring drastic social and economic changes in the two-to-three decades ahead. Older persons will demand a larger share of services, and resources will have the political power to support their expectations. Already legislation to provide a variety of services is appearing, for example, the Older American Acts Amendments of 1978.

One of the most striking features of the older population is its heterogeneity. As Kieffer (1980) says, some are in poor health, and some are unable to work or uninterested in work. But more than 90 percent are mentally alert and could be successful in many types of productive activity. Moreover, the health and physical condition of older persons are improving. Not only will they live longer, but they will be interested in productive work and leisure for an increased number of years.

Retirement is one of the major events in the lives of older persons. Recent legislation, however, has moved back the mandatory age to 70 in all sectors and eliminated it as a requirement for federal employees (with a few specific exceptions) (Odell 1979, pp. 298–300). While many persons will choose to work, others will find it necessary because of inflation. Those on fixed retirement incomes are experiencing increasing difficulty in maintaining an adequate life-style. The problem is due in part to lack of retirement planning, which along with inflation leaves the individual or family with inadequate resources.

How older persons cope with problems of aging is illuminated by theory and research emphasizing the effects of social and environmental conditions or mental health. Negative labeling, lack of reference groups, and loss of familiar roles with no replacements lead to poor psychological functioning and social breakdown (Brine 1979, pp. 67–71). Many of the typical attitudes about older persons, and the types of care available, contribute to their problems and speed up the decline in physical and mental abilities.

Needs

The needs of older persons are comprehensive — psychological, sociological, economic, and physical. Minority and handicapped status often add to their difficulties. Physical, safety, and financial needs often head the list of concerns of older persons, but these are so intertwined with psychological problems that it is difficult to determine the most basic problem. For example, nursing home care may attend to basic physiological and safety needs but may be so impoverished psychologically that the older person rapidly sinks into the appearance of acute senility. An adequate support network, informal (friends and neighbors) and formal (community clubs and social agencies), is of critical importance. Preretirement planning assistance that takes attitudinal and financial factors both into consideration is important. Learning how to cope with increasing limitations and to make use of remaining capabilities is essential for older persons' well-being. Effective coping involves helpers, family members, and community persons who understand what it is like to deal with increasing limitations (e.g., sensory and physical decline).

As is the case with any special group, older persons need understanding, recognition of potential contributions, and an awareness of how they see the world. Too often the negative attitudes of others are accepted by older persons and are used as self-criticism and negative self-evaluation.

Attitudes Toward Counseling Services

Attitudes of counselors toward older persons, and older persons' perceptions of counselors, may involve bias and negative reactions. In the case of older persons, however, there does not seem to be substantial evidence that they are uniformly negative toward helping services. Some are reluctant to reveal personal information, to fill-in and sign forms requesting extensive information, or to accept help that is viewed as charity or that implies the presence of mental disorder. In some cases, personnel services such as those on community college and college campuses, are perceived as oriented toward the young and thus as not appropriate. Counselors and personnel workers are usually younger than potential service users in educational and community settings, but this factor does not in itself appear to be a barrier to effective work. The counselor's attitude toward older persons, the amount of care that is communicated, and the level of empathy seem to be more critical than age differences. The effects of stereotyping can be particularly harmful, as so many of the current attitudes about older persons are negative.

The Handicapped

General Characteristics

The decade of the 1970s, as Hohenshil and Humes (1979) indicate, has seen a remarkable upsurge of concern about the rights of handicapped persons of all ages. Equal opportunity is the guiding concept, replacing a more custodial emphasis on segregated settings for education and work.

Reasons for the current attitude go back only a few years. Corrigan (1978) believes that major new legislation (PL94-142) aimed at schools had its roots in the civil rights movement of the 1960s and goes far beyond the schools — it calls for social, political, and economic reforms as well. While support for vocational rehabilitation has been a long-standing policy, additional legislation in the 1970s (PL 93-112) provides the handicapped with equal rights in entering post-high-school training or education and insures that a handicap will not be used as a reason for denying employment. In addition, health-care and social welfare services are made accessible (Hohenshil and Humes 1979; Foster, Szoke, Kapisovsky, and Kriger 1977, pp. 361–378).

The scope of the problem is almost overwhelming. While statistics vary considerably, it is estimated that approximately 8 million children 19 years of age and under have handicaps and that only about half are served by schools. In addition (based on early 1970s data), it is estimated that approximately 11 million, or 9 percent, of all persons ages 16–64 have permanent work disabilities. Finally, for the same period, it has been estimated that there are approximately 25 million persons who are limited by chronic mental and/or physical conditions (Fagan and Wallace 1979). Overs (1975a, p. 179) presents data showing more than 5 percent of those in the labor force are too ill or handicapped to work.

The term *handicapped* is, to some extent, a misleading one from the counselor's point of view. A person may be disabled, but is handicapped according to the situation — social, educational, or occupational. Thus, a hearing-impaired individual might not be handicapped at all in performing a detailed analysis of data or fine assembly work — the disability might, in fact, facilitate concentration.

It is also important to realize not only that are there different categories of handicapped persons with quite different needs, capabilities, and learning styles, but also that there are degrees of handicaps within each category. For example, the mentally retarded and the hearing-impaired are unlike in potential, types of counseling needed, and goals. Then, within the latter category, the hearing-impaired may have from mild to profound loss with related degrees of impaired language development (Overs 1975a, pp. 177–178; Vernon and Ottinger 1980, pp. 113–115).

The categories in PL 94-142 give a good perspective of the types of handicaps that counselors will deal with in schools as well as other settings. Fagan and Wallace (1979) give helpful descriptions of the types covered:

1. *Hearing-Impaired* — this category includes the hard-of-hearing and the deaf.
2. *Deaf-Blind* — a combination of these two handicaps.
3. *Visually Handicapped* — this category includes individuals who are partially sighted as well as those who are blind.

4. *Speech-Impaired* — the individual has a speech disorder that interferes with learning and other activities to the extent that it causes maladjustment.

5. *Mentally Retarded* — below-average intellectual ability, accompanied by deficiencies in adaptative behavior. In terms of I.Q., the following classification may be used: 50–70, educable; 30–50, trainable; and below 30 profound retardation. Other evidence besides test scores is used for classification.

6. *Specific Learning Disability* — the individual has a disorder in one or more of the basic processes of learning and understanding language, for example, dyslexia, perceptual difficulties. This category does not include those with problems such as visual handicaps or educational deprivation.

7. *Seriously Emotionally Disturbed* — the individual who has a persistent and obvious emotional condition which adversely affects learning, interpersonal relationship, mood, and other aspects of daily life. The category does not include the socially maladjusted.

8. *Orthopedically Impaired* — this category includes those with severe orthopedic impairment of congenital, disease, or injury origin which has a negative effect on educational achievement.

9. *Other Health-Impaired* — this category includes any of a variety of medically diagnosed conditions that affect school progress, for example, a heart condition, asthma.

10. *Multihandicapped* — this condition includes combinations of handicaps other than deaf-blind that involve more extensive treatment than required for any of the specific handicaps involved and which causes severe educational problems.

It is apparent that some of these categories are more likely to be the concern of the school counselor than the college or community agency counselor (community agencies other than rehabilitation services). But it is likely that all counselors will encounter parents, employers, or others affected by the handicapped, if not the disabled individual.

PL 94–142 identifies special responsibilities of school counselors in working with the handicapped. These responsibilities include counseling with the handicapped pupils, consulting with teachers and parents, assisting with the identification and assessment of the handicapped, and helping with the preparation and monitoring of the Individual Educational Program (IEP) that must be prepared for each handicapped pupil (McDowell, Coven, and Eash 1979, Noble and Kampwirth 1979). The major thrust of this legislation is away from segregation of the handicapped and toward introducing them into the least-restrictive environment, often referred to as *mainstreaming*.

Attitudes of counselors and others toward the handicapped constitute one of the most difficult barriers to understanding and helping those with disabilities. Nathanson (1979) identifies seven "Counselor Syndromes" that vividly depict harmful attitudes (e.g., the "I feel sorry for you" that is communicated to the handicapped counselee). The guidelines in Foster, Szoke, Kapisovsky, and Kriger (1977, p. 3) spell out the empathic and facilitative attitudes that are essential — stressing the handicapped persons' uniqueness, their need for respect as persons, the importance of them doing things for themselves, their right to become what they can become, and their need to participate in life rather than being shut off from it.

Needs

Aside from special teaching and counseling methods that take into account ways of communicating and learning styles and the physical facilities designed for comfort and safety, handicapped individuals need to be understood and viewed in positive ways. Understanding calls for knowledge of the types of handicaps, the ways limitations can affect the individual's self-perceptions, and the potential that is present. Viewing in a positive way means more than *acceptance* — a somewhat condescending attitude — and involves valuing as a person, interacting with, and recognizing positive and negative attributes, just as is done with nonhandicapped individuals. At times, adaptations in education, work, and social activities need to be made so that the handicapped can readily participate, but when these necessary special provisions are made the handicapped person should be expected to do his or her part — e.g., produce on a job.

Attitudes Toward Counseling Services

The handicapped are such a heterogeneous group that it is not possible to describe attitudes that apply across the board. It has long been thought that those with a particular handicap (e.g., the blind) develop a better rapport with similarly handicapped counselors. The nature of some handicaps may be such that the counselee has a negative attitude toward others, as in some types of emotional disturbance. Actually, however, dependency may be a greater problem than negative or hostile attitudes.

Much of the success of the counselor in promoting good working relationships will depend upon attitudes toward the counselee and selection of appropriate strategies, such as those described by Blanco (1980), by other authors in the book by Benjamin and Walz (1980), and by Foster, Szoke, Kapisovsky, and Kriger (1977). The approaches or strategies described in these references are ones in which the particular type of handicapped person can readily participate and that lead to appropriate goals.

The Gifted and Talented

General Characteristics

Several years ago a national figure made the statement that the gifted and talented were the most neglected minority in American education. Zaffrann and Colangelo (1980, p. 166) say that is still very much the situation today even though there is renewed interest in their educational needs. Yet, up to now, interest has only infrequently been translated into effective practices. This situation exists even though 45 of the 50 states have programs for the gifted and talented (Mitchell 1980), and at least 4 states require individualized education programs (IEP) for the gifted similar to those mandated for the handicapped by PL 94-142 (Renzulli 1978). Even so, of the 2 million to 2.5 million gifted and talented children in the United States today, about 1 in 8 are being served (Bennetts 1980).

Lack of adequate definitions contribute to problems of meeting the needs of the gifted. A classification must be broader than one based solely on IQ scores. Not only are there a number of types of giftedness, but the use of the IQ is thought to be misleading and discriminatory (Alvino and Wieler 1979).

Giftedness in years past has usually been defined as the top 1 percent of the population in intellectual ability as measured by a standard intelligence test. Recently the concept has been broadened to include multiple types of talent. The widely accepted United States Office of Education (now Department of Education) definition illustrates this change in conceptualization:

> Gifted and talented children are those . . . who by virtue of outstanding abilities are capable of high performance. These . . . children . . . require differentiated educational programs and/or services beyond those normally provided by the regular school program in order to realize their [potential] contribution to self and society.
>
> Children capable of high performance include those who have demonstrated any of the following abilities of aptitudes, singly or in combination:
>
> (1) general intellectual ability, (2) specific academic aptitude, (3) creative or productive thinking, (4) leadership ability, (5) visual and performing arts aptitude, (6) psychomotor ability. (Renzulli 1978, p. 181)

A somewhat different definition, which further clarifies the significant dimensions of giftedness, is given by Perrone, Male, and Karshner:

> Talented individuals demonstrate superior or advanced development when compared to peers in one or more of six recognized "Talent

categories" including: convergent thinking and behavior; divergent/ creative thinking and behavior; goal-related thinking and behavior; social skills and behavior; physical skills and behavior; and affective thinking and behavior. (1979, p. 17)

This definition gives weight to the three critical ingredients of giftedness suggested by Renzulli (1978): above average ability, task commitment, and creativity. Studies of highly productive persons have shown over and over that there is more to exceptional productivity in work and education than high test scores and school marks. Dimensions such as task commitment are more important. In fact, "more creative/productive persons come from below the ninety-fifth percentile than above it . . . " (Renzulli 1978, p. 182).

Needs

The needs of the gifted and talented manifest themselves in different ways in the process of development. As they move through the grades they develop more independent behavior than peers; by the time they are in high school, they are usually self-directed enough to need less external direction and more opportunity to follow personal interests (Perrone,

Gifted children are sometimes overwhelmed by their potential.

Male, and Karshner 1979). Factors relating specifically to females involve interest in specific career fields as a basis for course choice, effects of significant others on choices, and the importance of early identification of talent. As Fox and Richmond (1979) point out, these are three areas of particular concern for counselors, mainly because of the early start of stereotypes.

Different learning styles and learning needs call for experiences to mesh with the gifted individual's personal approach to new tasks. Zaffrann and Colangelo (1980, pp. 167–170) describe two learning styles — acceleration and enrichment — and identify the personal characteristics, program needs, and counseling needs of each. For example, the *accelerated* gifted individual is among other things quick in comprehension, needs a flexible school program, and may be highly self-critical if "failure" in his or her terms is experienced.

While the gifted may be *expected* to take care of their own needs in decision making, social relations, and coping with expectations of others, they actually may have more than their share of difficulties in those areas. Giftedness can alienate teacher, peers, and sometimes even other family members (Bennetts 1980; Hoyt 1974, pp. 104–146; Perrone, Male, and Karshner 1979). The importance of a needs-based, systematic program for assistance to the gifted is underlined by Zaffrann and Colangelo (1980, pp. 171–173). Program building involves an initial step of answering questions about philosophy and assumptions about the gifted and their development.

Attitudes Toward Counseling Services

In some cases the gifted have been given limited attention by counselors who seem to make the assumption that those with superior ability can find their own way in educational and social areas. Sometimes, however, counselors may tend to overtly or subtly reinforce certain directions (e.g., college, the "hard" sciences). When these attitudes prevail, it would not be surprising if gifted individuals, seeking help with self-directed planning, see little value in counseling services. In general, however, the gifted and talented appear to be receptive to, and positive about, services and programs that are focused on their needs and provide the opportunity for new and stimulating experiences and study (Borman, Nash, and Colson 1978; Perrone, Male, and Karshner 1979).

Summary Concepts

Counselors in all settings are going to have increasingly greater involvement with a number of subgroups that have special needs and that have been more or less neglected in the past. The major categories are: women; minorities, including blacks, Hispanic Americans, native Americans, and Asian Americans; the disadvantaged; midlife and older persons; the handicapped; and the gifted. There are a number of others that could be included, but these are the ones with the most pressing concerns. Counselors should know general characteristics of these special groups but should also be aware that each member is a unique individual. In addition to reading, extensive face-to-face interaction is essential for gaining an understanding of subgroup members. Major problems of each of the groups typically involve stereotyping, usually negative, but sometimes unrealistically positive — for example, the gifted have no problems of choice; the middle years are a time of stability and consistent goals. An understanding of the general characteristics of each group helps the counselor in being sensitive to needs that call for a wide variety of services. To varying degrees, each group has built-in attitudes about counselors and counseling services; these attitudes can often have a negative effect on the counselor's efforts to provide needed assistance.

Examples of Research on a Topic
Attitudes of Minority Individuals Toward Counseling Services

Several studies on how black individuals perceive counseling services are summarized next to illustrate the type of research that has been done and to shed some light on attitudes of this group. As you read these summaries, think of steps that could be taken to improve perceptions and facilitate use of services.

Bryson and Bardo (1979, pp. 126–128) summarize a number of studies made prior to the mid-1970s that point to the conclusion that race is a factor in blacks' attitudes toward counseling — they prefer black counselors.

More recent studies have tended to support the conclusions about preferences for same-race counselors. Gilsdorf (1978) used photographs of Mexican American, black, and white counselors to assess preferences of community college students. Two types of problems were used as the basis for counselor choice — financial aid and personal relations. Blacks chose the black counselor to a significant degree. Looking at the other side of the question — counselor reactions to counselees — Fuller and Kern (1978) found that racial category affected counselor anxiety levels. White counselors facing hostile black clients were significantly more anxious than they were when dealing with the same emotion in white clients.

Gordon and Grantham (1979) studied counselor preferences of disadvantaged black, Puerto Rican, white, and other college students. There was a slight preference for same-race counselor, but the overriding factor in choice of a helper was similar social class background. The authors suggest that racial designation cannot be used as the criterion for counselor-client matching. Moreover, they suggest that counselor choice is based on more than one dimension.

Racial similarity was found to have an effect on counseling techniques. In the study by Fry, Kropf, and Coe (1980), both black and white counselor trainees reacted in counseling session simulations by demonstrating more expressiveness with black than white clients. In addition, racial similarity between client and counselor facilitated interaction and communication.

Underutilization of mental health clinics was found by Tucker (1979) to be attributed to a number of factors, including negative evaluation of services, lack of information, and preference for a same-race helper. Moreover, many perceived a stigma of "craziness" to be associated with mental health problems.

These are a limited number of studies, and caution should be observed in making generalizations to include all blacks. On the basis of these data, however, what would you do to help improve the attitude of blacks toward counseling services in the setting in which you plan to work?

Experiential Activities

Two of the most valuable types of experiential activities for this chapter involve (1) interaction with members of a special group and, (2) putting yourself in their place. Some general suggestions for each of these types are given next.

1. Simulation

The purpose of this activity is to see how it feels to be a member of one or more of the groups described in this chapter. Some class members are identified as subgroup members while others act in a stereotypical way toward them. Make signs designating the subgroup — disadvantaged, Asian American, handicapped and specify the handicap (e.g., blind, paraplegic); attach the signs to the backs of participants without letting them know who they represent. Ask all class members to interact for 10 or 15 minutes emphasizing *stereotypical attitudes* toward subgroups. Then process the activity. How did the subgroup members feel? How did the "regular" class members change their usual style of interacting because of the subgroup membership of other students? What do class members conclude about relating to subgroup members?

2. Simulation

Some activities involving handicaps or loss of capacities because of age can be done by the total class. For vision loss, attach colored plastic to lenses of glasses or strips on either side of the glasses to simulate tunnel vision. Hearing loss can be experienced by covering the ears. Gloves can be worn to experience loss of tactile ability. Each type of activity should involve students attempting a task that is difficult because of the restriction (e.g., with visual restrictions, read directions on the blackboard). After each activity, hold a discussion of how students felt while participating.

3. Interacting with Subgroup Members

Invite members of subgroups to meet with the class to discuss their feelings about stereotypes, helping services, and other topics of interest. (It may be possible to use class members who represent subgroups to share experience and attitudes; for example, a handicapped person.)

4. Visits to Subgroup Settings

Some of the subgroups discussed have organizations, centers, or projects that may be visited for interactions with group members (an ethnic club, a recreational center for older persons, a sheltered workshop for the handicapped, a program for the gifted at a local school). Visits to settings may be arranged. Extended volunteer service can sometimes be engaged in, for example, in a nursing home.

Suggested Readings

Atkinson, Donald R.; Morten, George; and Sue, Derald Wing, eds. *Counseling American Minorities,* Dubuque, Iowa: William C. Brown and Company, 1979.

    A very useful collection of articles on cross-cultural counseling covering four minority groups. The introduction (Chapters 1 and 2) and the concluding section (Chapters 15 and 16) on developmental models and future directions are excellent overviews of problems, trends, and rationales for counseling members of minority groups. Major sections cover American Indians, Asian Americans, black Americans, and Latinos and are extremely valuable for in-depth study.

Benjamin, Libby, and Walz, Garry R., eds. *Counseling Exceptional People.* Ann Arbor, Mich.: ERIC Counseling and Personnel Services Clearinghouse, 1980.

    A particularly useful reference for counselors in any setting to learn about six types of exceptional pupils. Characteristics of each type and suggested counseling approaches are covered. The types are: mentally retarded, learning-disabled, emotionally disturbed, hearing-impaired, visually handicapped, and gifted. In addition, sexual fulfillment of the handicapped, consultation, and intervention strategies for specific handicaps are discussed. The entire book is highly recommended.

Colangelo, Nicholas, and Zaffrann, Ronald T., eds. *New Voices in Counseling the Gifted.* Dubuque, Iowa: Kendall/Hunt Publishing Company, 1979.

A comprehensive reference on all aspects of working with the gifted, including special populations. Rothney's "Foreword" (pp. ix–xiii) is a good starting place for reading.

Foster, June C.; Szoke, Claire Olsen; Kapisovsky, Peggy M.; and Kriger, Leslie S. *Guidance, Counseling, and Support Services for High School Students with Physical Disabilities.* Cambridge, Mass.: Technical Education Research Centers, 1977.

An excellent, comprehensive reference covering disabilities, their effects on personality and behavior, methods of helping the handicapped, and state and national resources. (Supplements for specific states may also be obtained.) The most useful reading for this chapter is the overview of handicaps in Chapter 1. Chapter 3, on psychological effects of handicaps, is also recommended.

Ganikos, Mary L.; Grady, Kathleen A.; and Olson, Jane B. *Counseling the Aged.* Washington, D.C.: American Personnel and Guidance Association, 1979.

A particularly valuable and comprehensive reference on all aspects of helping older persons. Seven modules give in-depth discussion of characteristics; all are appropriate background reading. As a start, Module I is recommended. It covers demographic aspects; for example, size of population and geographic distribution.

Harmon, Lenore W.; Birk, Janice M.; Fitzgerald, Laurine E.; and Tanney, Mary Faith, eds. *Counseling Women.* Monterey, Calif.: Brooks/Cole Publishing Company, 1978.

An excellent series of articles — primarily from vol. 4, no. 1 (1973) and vol. 6 no. 2 (1976), of the *Counseling Psychologist* — highlights typical deficiencies in counseling women and identifying critical problems in their lives. The first article (by Westervelt, pages 1–33) is a good starting place, but almost any part of the book is useful for this chapter.

Hohenshil, Thomas H. "Counseling Handicapped Persons and Their Families." *Personnel and Guidance Journal* 58, no. 4 (1979), pp. 213–214.

This article is the guest editor's introduction to an excellent special journal issue on the handicapped. The most appropriate articles for this chapter are the first four, particularly the one by Fagan and Wallace (pp. 215–220).

Picou, J. Steven, and Campbell, Robert E., eds. *Career Behavior of Special Groups.* Columbus, Ohio: Charles E. Merrill, 1975.

While the focus is on career development, the articles in this book are excellent in-depth reading for this chapter. Special groups covered are blacks, Asian Americans, handicapped, American Indians, and women.

Sinick, Daniel. "Guest Editor's Introduction." *Personnel and Guidance Journal* 55, no. 3 (1976), pp. 100–101.

The introduction to a special issue on counseling over the life span. Articles cover both the middle years and pre- and postretirement. All are appropriate for this chapter. The Table of Contents can be used to identify those of particular interest.

————. *Counseling Older Persons: Careers, Retirement, Dying.* New York: Human Sciences Press, 1977.

An excellent reference by an outstanding authority on counseling with older persons. Highly recommended.

Walz, Garry R., and Benjamin, Libby, eds. *New Imperatives for Guidance.* Ann Arbor, Mich.: ERIC Counseling and Personnel Services Clearinghouse, 1978.

Two chapters are particularly useful reference material on special groups. Minority groups are surveyed in Chapter 8, and suggestions for counseling are given.

Chapter
10
The Counselor's Use of Information

Individuals need information for almost every kind of problem or decision: the effects of drugs, the physiological changes in adolescence, birth control, college requirements, relationships to others, understanding handicaps, prejudice, occupational opportunities, community resources, emergency shelters. The list could be expanded indefinitely. Usually the need can be anticipated, but at times the need amounts to an emergency.

Counselors by the nature of their helping role are looked upon as sources of information; this is as it should be. Counselors know the types of information available and how to obtain it and are sensitive to the needs of the individual. Counselors can judge what information may be helpful, and they can help the individual utilize it for problem-solving, decision-making, and development.

Any setting will involve counselors in providing information. The following examples are illustrative, but they hardly scratch the surface: birth control planning information in the community center; drug information in the crisis center; how to study in the college counseling center; financial aid and scholarship sources in the high school guidance office; exploratory occupational information in the middle school resource center; how to make friends in the elementary school guidance programs. The information for these and other uses is available in increasing quantity and quality. Even technology, in the form of computers, video cassettes, audio cassettes, microfiche, and films, is contributing to information preparation and dissemination.

Types of Information

To give you an overview of what is meant by information, the following listing is presented:

Occupations

- What one does in the occupation.
- Requirements for employment (including training, education, experience, and psychological and physical factors).
- Remuneration (including fringe benefits).
- The relation of school subjects to the occupation.
- How to locate jobs, how to apply, and how to participate in employment interviews.
- Trends in the occupation, particularly numbers of persons needed compared with the number being prepared.
- Opportunities for advancement.
- Relations among occupations and groupings of similar occupations.
- The life-styles that go with occupations (the social climate, the sociological characteristics of the work setting, the life and career patterns of workers).
- Local full-time and part-time opportunities.
- Legislation related to special groups.

Educational and Training Opportunities

- Data about programs, entrance requirements, costs, housing, and degrees or certificates.
- Relation of training and education to occupations.
- Information about financial assistance, e.g., scholarships, fellowships, loans, and part-time work.
- Characteristics of students in the institution.
- Climate of institutions, particularly colleges and universities (academic, professional, social).
- Information about value derived from various educational or training programs (cultural values, occupational preparation, etc.).
- Legislation related to special groups.

Personal-Social Information.   Needs here run the gamut from self-understanding, home and family relations, and peer relations to drugs, sex, values, maturity, and physical and psychological development. New needs are constantly emerging as previously taboo subjects like abortion and homosexuality are being discussed more frankly. An almost endless variety of materials, differing in format, medium, and content, is available to meet these needs. The limited number of examples identified in this chapter illustrate the sources the counselor can turn to.

The above list of topics is only a minimum about which the counselor should know. Furthermore, it does not reflect the range of media and sources used. Both of these aspects are discussed later in this chapter.

Procedures for Using Information

Information may be provided in individual counseling, group counseling, through an information center, and in a number of other ways, including large-group meetings, courses, units, field trips, and work experience. For each of these procedures, theory provides guidelines for when and how the information should be used.

Providing Information Through Individual Counseling

The essential conditions for effective communication of information are the counselee's own awareness of need and expressed desire to receive it. The counselor may make use of a variety of materials and techniques (Krumboltz and Baker 1973), including job simulation, the occupational file, the *Occupational Outlook Handbook,* or homework involving viewing a film or slide-sound program, or interviewing a worker. The important factor is that the counselee participate actively in the process and assume responsibility for carrying out exploratory activities (Herr and Cramer 1972, p. 224). Newer technology such as computers can facilitate the process of obtaining information. The counselor can, for example, refer the counselee to the computer terminal for exploration of career options in line with abilities and interests (see page 260). When the counselee returns to the interview situation, the counselor can focus on the personal meaning of the computer reports and assist the counselee to use the data in decision making.

The same principles apply to other types of information and other media. The counselee may be given a booklet to read on personal or social problems. Later on, reactions, questions, and personal applications can be discussed with the counselor.

Providing Information Through Groups

The group situation has the double advantage of economy and interaction, and is the ideal setting for providing information. Whether the method is simulation, films, talks, interviews, modeling, or some other procedure, all members can learn at the same time. The interaction among members enhances the meaning and personal relevance of information.

Groups are usually more than strictly information-giving sessions; they combine personal exploration with the dispensing of factual material within the framework of a developmental theory. Healy's developmental group procedure (1973) is an example. Five sessions are used to explore personal concerns; learn about potentially suitable occupations; assess personal potential; plan a course of action; and implement the plan. Interaction is used throughout the process to encourage and support exploration and planning. Evaluation of the model showed positive results in terms of increased confidence in making a choice and willingness to engage in planning (Healy 1974).

The group approach provides an effective, interesting, and economical way for the counselor to expand the essential information-giving function. The benefits of face-to-face contacts both with counselor and peers are realized, and the personal meaning of information is enhanced. Programs like VEG (Vocational Exploration Group) and Deciding exploit the advantages of learnings that accrue from interactions among counselees. Resource persons — e.g., local employers — can meet with groups to present material and discuss opportunities. Groups have been used effectively to increase awareness of career options in sixth-grade girls (S. Harris 1974). Pupils in small schools can meet in group sessions to process information obtained in community visits to employers; this procedure contributes to the school career education program and enhances positive school-community relations (Stillwell and Collison 1974). In one junior high school, the language arts curriculum was used to help pupils explore interest and abilities through simulation materials and studies of occupational clusters, and thus greatly facilitated career development (Winter and Schmidt 1974).

Groups can effectively take advantage of learning theory and technology in promoting the use of information. Several types of reinforcement in group sessions motivated high school and college counselees to seek out more career information than those who did not receive this kind of stimulation (Krumboltz and Schroeder 1965; Fisher, Reardon, and Burck 1976). Groups have been used to enhance the effects of computer guidance systems (Cassel and Mehail 1973; Mallory and Drake 1973). Other types have been used to motivate truants to return to school (Grala and McCauley 1976).

Many methods of providing information are aimed at classes rather than small groups, particularly in elementary school. Activities include drawing pictures of jobs and discussing them, reviewing educational preferences, and discussing workers pupils know (Jefferies and Spedding 1974). Sequential team-building projects such as communication exercises, taking on work roles, and engaging in small-group career projects have also been tried (Wubbolding and Osborne 1974). Career units using a multimedia approach to study related occupations (Washburn and

Schmaljohn 1975) and job placement for in-school helping positions (Elleson and Onmink 1976) are other new and innovative approaches. Sustained career development activities in junior high school have been shown to increase students' occupational knowledge (Perrone and Kyle 1975).

School-wide information programs have in some cases been incorporated in career education programs, though in many schools counselors have no significant role in this new educational model. Mesa, Arizona (McKinnon and Jones 1975), has a system that uses guidance units with all types of information for K–12, and counselors here have played an active part. The guidance program has become an integral part of the total career educational model. The Detroit Developmental Career Guidance Project, a K–12 program for disadvantaged youth (Leonard and Vriend 1975), brings school and community together in a cooperative program, which utilizes classroom activities by teachers and counselors and provides a wide range of informational activities (e.g., films, career games, field trips, and work experience). A unique feature of the program is the heavy involvement of parents. It is an excellent example of a well-planned system that utilizes both school and community resources.

The Life-Career Development System (Walz and Benjamin 1974) is an example of a program for high school and adult populations. Nine modules, each consisting of several sessions, help participants develop the understanding and competencies for a successful and rewarding life. Emphasis is on applying learning to one's personal situation and on practicing new skills. This program illustrates a new generation of carefully planned developmental experiences for which leaders need to participate in preliminary training programs.

The Information Center

Information centers providing career, educational, social, and personal data bring together all types of media and techniques, including community resources. Data sources range from individual booklets on single occupations to computer memory banks with information about hundreds of occupations. Community resources are listed in a card file of persons who will talk with pupils interested in their line of work or of establishments where pupils can observe jobs or get part-time exploratory work experience. A counselor or paraprofessional may give group or individual help. Outreach programs are often provided in the form of large-scale group procedures such as career days and career fairs. Pupils with special needs may be helped by group sessions (e.g., those designed to teach effective participation in employment interviews). Packaged techniques (such as vocational exploration groups) may be used for those who need help in making choices.

Establishing the service involves assigning responsibility, assessing need, designing the system, selecting materials, testing the system, instructing both pupils and counselors how to use it, and follow-up and evaluation. The public schools in Newton, Massachusetts, have developed a complete career information center, including a library, job placement facilities, and follow-up services (Campbell, Walz, Miller, and Kriger 1973, pp. 125, 127–128).

The concept of a center is gaining in popularity because of a number of factors. One important impetus is related to technology — the capability of rapid collection and interesting presentation of information. The tightened labor market is another, particularly as it affects special groups such as women, the handicapped, and minorities. Legislation is a third — for example, the career information delivery systems grants provided to states in response to the Comprehensive Employment and Training Act Amendments of 1978 (14 States . . . , 1980, p. 12). Job changing, reentry to the labor market, and the increase in adult education are additional factors. There are others, but these illustrate the groundswell of support that reaches far beyond the focus on the school, once the major location of such centers.

Information centers may exist independently or, more typically, as part of a broader guidance and counseling service. However, a comprehensive service designed for adults should, according to Darkenwald (1980), be free of allegiance to one institution — it should be community-based. This point is well taken; information centers should be located so that they are readily available to target groups without the strictures implied by institutional sponsorship. If, however, those served are in school or college, institutional sponsorship would be appropriate.

The emphasis of centers should be congruent with the developmental levels and needs of those who use them. In the elementary school, career and self-awareness are important. Prepackaged materials are helpful to the teacher, but a variety of additional materials is needed (Meerbach 1978, pp. 33–35). At the middle or junior high school level, the emphasis is on exploration, clarifying goals, and direct contact with the realities of the work world (Meerbach 1978, pp. 33–36; Stamm and Nissman 1979, pp. 62–64). At the high school level, the focus is on detailed information about occupations, training and educational opportunities, and other data needed for the transition from school to further preparation or work. While much attention is given to resources of a career nature, the center should be well stocked with aids to personal and social development.

The school information center has an important mission in supporting career education and other curricular activities. Pupils make use of the information directly in projects and activities. Assistance is provided to teachers through consultation, assembling of materials for teacher use, or by classroom presentations. Moreover, the center provides a link to the community by listing of resource persons, agencies, and employers who are interested in providing information. Pupils, aides, and community volunteers can augment the counselor staff, taking over many of the day-to-day tasks of building and maintaining the center.

As has been pointed out, the information center may be part of a larger counseling and guidance service. This is true particularly in college and community settings. The state employment service, basically a job placement agency, has an extensive collection of publications, program descriptions, and other resources. Other agencies set up for special groups may provide in-depth information related to the agency's function, for example, women's legal rights.

On the college campus, the information center has a career emphasis and is typically part of the placement service (Reardon, Zunker, and Dyal 1979). Some of the new computer technology (discussed later) is designed for this level. In addition to an extensive collection of all sorts of publications and media, many centers provide brief courses or workshops in such career-related areas as decision-making skills, resume preparation, and job interview skills. An interesting extension of service was provided by the Center for Career Development and Occupational Information at Texas A & M University (Borman, Nash, and Colson 1978) for gifted and talented high school seniors. Various types of information including printed materials, guest speakers, and simulations were used to help pupils identify interest areas. Next, pupils took part in a shadowing experience under the direction of a faculty member to learn more about areas of interest. This experience was followed by an on-site work period. This multifaceted approach to information illustrates what can be done for a special group with local resources.

Information centers need to make adaptions for handicapped students. The program reported by White, Reardon, Barker, and Carlson (1979) illustrates how materials for use in a career center were adapted for blind students. Some visual media were recorded in audio casettes. A library of 35 audio casettes, titled *Occupational Information for the Blind* and covering approximately 600 jobs being held by blind persons, was purchased. A self-administered interest inventory, the *Self Directed Search*, was programmed so that it could be completed by blind individuals. Materials were arranged so that a blind person coming to the center could successfully participate in self-managed career planning. These and other adaptations made by the center are excellent illustrations of what can be done to design a service that is compatible with needs and capabilities of special-group users.

Community-based information systems, typically part of an adult guidance program, provide a variety of media, programs, and services (Herr and Whitson 1979). Career planning workshops, seminars, computer systems, telephone hot lines, and mobile vans are among the methods used. Special groups such as minorities usually make extensive use of facilities.

Placement

Placement has had a checkered past (Campbell, Walz, Miller, and Kriger 1973, p. 202) but is emerging as an important school service, particularly in career education (see Chapter 2). The information service has a responsibility to help individuals learn about occupations, make decisions, and develop ways to implement them. It ties in with both educational and occupational placement. Exploratory work experience, an excellent way to obtain occupational information, involves placement; pupils planning to go to work after high school rate it the best method (Jacobson 1975, pp. 68–71). Placement is coming to be accepted as a school responsibility emphasizing community linkage, development of pupil competence in getting jobs, and follow-through to provide additional help if needed (Odell, Pritchard, and Sinick 1974).

At the higher-education level, placement has enjoyed more acceptance over the years. The placement office has traditionally been the center that recruiters visit to interview students ready to graduate. With the increasing emphasis on career development for all ages, many campus placement services have added programs of assistance for undergraduates; for example, freshmen may be offered courses or group sessions focusing on educational and occupational planning. The placement center is thus shifting to an emphasis that is more in line with theories of choice and development.

Placement in any setting includes, or should include, more than pointing the individual toward an educational, occupational, or leisure opportunity. Preparation is essential, particularly for getting a job, but competencies for effective approaches to many, if not all, new experiences in the areas of work, education, and leisure have to be learned. In educational or leisure searches, much of the attention needs to be given to identifying suitable opportunities and selecting those that come closest to meeting needs. For job hunting, specific skills that are helpful in the process have been identified and can be taught (Galassi and Galassi 1978; Wegmann 1979). There is a trend toward providing these skill-building programs in schools, colleges, and agencies — for example, preparing resumes, and practicing interview behavior.

Issues and Problems

A number of problems and issues surround the use of information in counseling services. Many have to do with bias or slanted presentation in information. Others are related to the actual methods of use, that is, the amount of monitoring provided by the counselor. A third issue involves the qualifications and role of the dispenser. A fourth involves the coordination of the use of various types of information (e.g., relating data about preparation to career requirements). Each of these issues or problems is discussed in the sections that follow.

Bias in Information

It is quite easy for information to contain material that is biased in terms of sex, race, ethnic origin, or other ways. Words such as "he" when referring to a particular occupation inject a sex bias. Illustrations frequently contain bias. Lauver, Gastellum, and Sheehey (1975) analyzed photographic illustrations in the *Occupational Outlook Handbook* in terms of sex, age, and ethnic origin of workers on different jobs. In one occupational category, scientific and technical workers, results are as follows:

Sex —
> female: 8   total: 40   percentage female: 20

Age —
> twenties: 2   thirties: 11   forties: 9   fifty and over: 6

Ethnic Origin —
> minority: 5   total: 32   percentage minority: 16

Minimum Educational Requirements —
> 8th grade and below: 0   above 8th grade: 31

The authors point out that the representation in illustrations does not match occupational distributions; women make up a much higher percentage of the work force. Illustrations are thought to exert a subtle force on the reader ("A picture is worth a thousand words").

Some take the position that this type of presentation does not show bias, and that it is an accurate portrayal of the real situation (Overs 1975). The question then, of course, arises: Should information reflect the status quo, or should it describe what should be? One point of view is that the person applying for a preparation program or a job ought to know the odds against him or her. Information should thus portray the current situation. Another position, which is supported here, is that information should present an unbiased view in keeping with legislation (e.g., Affirmative Action), public policy, and social goals. Information has an unknown but probably powerful effect on biases and stereotypes. It should certainly present the desirable situation as much as possible.

Another type of bias is sometimes present in information distributed by employers. Not surprisingly, it is designed to present the best possible portrayal of the employer's establishment or institution to attract the highest quality applicant. Users should be made aware of the intent and the slant of recruiting information.

Monitoring Use of Information

When the individual uses information, should there be a check on his or her interpretations and resulting decisions? This question is relevant for any type of information — personal, social, educational, occupational — but it is particularly important for occupational choices. For one thing, these choices usually lead to a large expenditure of time and financial resources. For another, there are so many types of information resources in the career area that *point* to choices. Thus, computer guidance systems usually "suggest" one or more occupational directions. But books, pamphlets, and films, while advising the user to consider his or her personal characteristics, can be used by the individual to make an unrealistic or personally unsuitable choice.

It could be said that choice is the individual's responsibility. The information user ought to have the freedom to accept, reject, incorporate, and decide as he or she wishes. It is suggested here, however, that there be some check on all use of information — at the least that individuals be *advised* to see a counselor. Many persons, of course, will find what they need and know how to use it; but others will misunderstand and misuse what they have read, heard, or viewed. Still others will be reluctant to ask questions even though they are well aware that they are confused. It is my position that making information available to others carries with it the responsibility for at least making an effort to insure its appropriate use.

Counselor Role

A third issue involves the most appropriate person to handle information. Should the counselor be responsible for this, or should it be handled by a specialist in information resources, either a professional or paraprofessional? (Regardless of who actually collects and manages the information resources, counselors use these resources in a number of ways.) The point of view here is that the counselor is the expert and should plan, organize, and supervise the information service. The actual work — obtaining and organizing information, helping users find materials, giving instructions for the use of equipment, and answering routine questions — should be done by a specialist prepared for these functions. Since the specialist will not be involved in counseling, the level of preparation could be quite different from that of the counselor. The major reason for this point of view is that the counselor's time should be reserved for counseling, consulting, and other similar tasks and thus should not be taken up with the mechanics of the information resources.

Relating Types of Information

Quite often in the helping process information about careers is not related to data about preparation, or counselees do not see the connection. In addition, human relations material is not considered along with planning for work. The three types of information appear to exist in isolation from each other. Some media avoid this separation — some computer systems (page 260) specify the personal qualifications and the preparation needed for each occupation considered.

The relationship of data would be based on the purposes of the data, preferably the following. Personal information helps the individual understand himself or herself and assists in selecting an occupation. (Personal information can have many other uses besides career planning, of course.) The occupation selected determines the type of education or training that is chosen. Cost, length of time for preparation, and qualifications need to be considered along with the occupational choice, but the occupation itself is the goal; preparation is the means for reaching it. At times, the relationship is reversed. Educational or training information is used to select a college or other type of institution without much, if any, thought being given to the end result — the career.

Information Media

To understand the counselor's task of supervising setting up and maintaining an information service, a rundown of some of the more widely used materials and technologies is helpful. Admittedly the area is complex; not only are resources extensive and of widely different types, but specific materials quickly go out of date; ongoing maintenance is needed. Local information such as that obtained directly from workers and employers is often the most useful. For example, it may be interesting to know that the need for carpenters nation-wide is increasing, but the individual who is considering this work in his community needs to know his chances for getting a job in local construction when voc-tech training and apprenticeship are completed. Both local and national information are integral to a complete information service.

Reference Works.   When the counselor initiates the building of an information center, a good first step is to obtain one or more indexes to help locate needed data. Three well-known reference works are *Vocational Guidance Quarterly, Inform,* and *Counselor's Information Service.* The first is the journal of the National Vocational Guidance Association (APGA, Two Skyline Place, 5203 Leesburg Pike, Falls Church, Va. 22041); it regularly contains a section on career literature and frequently includes a section on films. Both briefly describe and evaluate materials. *Counselor's Information Service*, a quarterly publication describing all sorts of information, may be obtained from B'nai B'rith Career and Counseling Services (1640 Rhode Island Avenue, N.W., Washington, D.C. 20036). *Inform* is issued ten times a year by the American Personnel and Guidance Association (address above) and provides sources of current career information and bibliographies on particular work areas such as science and public service.

A center typically includes books describing occupations. The best known is the *Occupational Outlook Handbook* (U.S. Department of Labor 1980) which covers several hundred occupations and 35 major industries; at $8, it is the best buy in the field. Another well-known set of books is the *Encyclopedia of Vocational Guidance* (3rd ed.; Garrett Park Press, Garrett Park, Md. 20766), covering data on 650 fields of work and related information. A new fourth edition of the *Dictionary of Occupational Titles* (U.S. Department of Labor 1977) to replace the widely used third edition published in 1965 provides valuable planning assistance to pupils and counselors. Occupational definitions and information about worker traits and occupational groups are provided. Two new publications related to the *DOT* and the *OOH* facilitate career exploration: *Guide for Occupational Exploration* (U.S. Department of Labor 1979) and *Exploring Careers* (U.S. Department of Labor 1980*a*). A separate publication of the new edition is specifically designed for work with high school pupils. There are many other books on occupations that can be used in the information service. The indexes provide an efficient way to locate them.

Much information is available in pamphlets and booklets, but such materials must be used with caution. Some are accurate and unbiased, but many of them, particularly free materials, are designed for recruiting purposes.

No one can begin to remember all the details pupils and parents request. But guides and directories to educational and training institutions make up an important part of the information service. Lists of publications may be found in Norris, Hatch, Engelkes, and Winborn (1979, pp. 169–179) and Tolbert (1980, pp. 158–160); current information about the most recent editions should be obtained from publishers. Users of the information service also need to know about opportunities for financial aid. This information is difficult to obtain, but college and training institution catalogues are of some help. The service should include the most recent catalogues and other publications of community and four-year colleges, universities, trade and technical schools, apprenticeship programs, and other types of information of potential interest to pupils.

The Informational File.   The basic information service resource is the occupational file. Even with computers and other technological aids, it is a standard aid. The counselor decides on the type of file and selects or institutes a plan for building and maintaining it. File folders are set up in some useful way (e.g., alphabetically). The most practical plan is to purchase a ready-made system such as those described in Hoppock (1976, pp. 55–62) or Norris, Hatch, Engelkes, and Winborn (1972, pp. 368–379). Files come complete with materials, and some publishers offer subscription services to keep files up to date.

Films, Filmstrips, and Related Materials.   The media have moved into the guidance field with a wide range of well-made and effective materials. Films, filmstrips, videotapes, and slide-sound programs cover the whole range of pupil needs — careers, education and training, social and personal questions. The American Personnel and Guidance Association's twelve-film series, WERC (Why Not Explore Rewarding Careers?), is an excellent example of information about careers that do not require a college degree. For preschoolers a sixteen-film series on career awareness, *The Kingdom That Could Be You,* helps develop a sense of the importance of work (Ralston 1974). The sound filmstrips prepared by Guidance Associates (757 Third Avenue, New York, N.Y. 10017) cover all areas and offer complete programs of series of sound filmstrips on topics such as drug abuse. Locally made films, slides, and audiotapes can be valuable supplements to the information service and have a special relevance for the particular school and community. For example, one counselor recorded a series of interviews with local workers for pupils to use in learning about community jobs.

Information Systems.   There are a number of what might be called "systems" for information, utilizing various media and equipped with instructions for use, that do not involve complex technology. The Guidance Associates drug program mentioned above is one example. Career Wheels, marketed by the American Personnel and Guidance Association, are relatively simple pupil-oriented devices for educational and occupational information; the pupil can dial information about occupations in five major areas, such as social science. The *Career Data Book* (Flanagan, Tiedeman, Willis, and McLaughlin 1973) gives profiles of aptitudes, abilities, interests, and other variables for a longitudinal study of high school pupils in various work groups (e.g., engineering, business). A second volume, *Using the Talent Profiles in Counseling* (Rossi, Bartlett, Campbell, Wise, McLaughlin 1975), explains how to use the profiles. A good way to learn about these programs and materials is to look through issues of *Vocational Guidance Quarterly* for brief reviews before contacting publishers. These materials are often expensive, and it is wise to request a preview before purchasing.

Informational techniques utilizing moderately complex technology are illustrated by the VIEW (Vital Information for Education and Work) system (Tolbert 1980, pp. 173–176). It consists of microfiche cards containing both national and local information about work and necessary preparation and a microfiche reader-printer that allows users to read and make personal copies of information. At a related level of complexity are programs in which the pupil operates a sound slide show using a special type of audiotape slide projector (Hansen 1970, pp. 88–97).

Information services often include simulation materials and games. *Job experience kits* (Krumboltz 1970) are an example. Following directions in the kit and working with materials provided, pupils, individually or in groups, learn about the work of, for example, a carpenter or accountant.

Computer guidance systems are the most sophisticated, complex, and expensive of all, but they offer the greatest potential for improving guidance. Picture the pupil sitting down at what appears to be a large typewriter keyboard with a screen like a TV beside it. Using the keyboard, the pupil asks about occupational areas that relate to interests and abilities. Suggested areas appear on the screen, along with comments about which ones look best. The pupil selects one or two and types questions about suitability. The screen shows comparisons and points out unrealistic goals, whether too high or too low. Detailed information about the work itself (e.g., opportunities for employment, remuneration) are available instantly. The pupil may spend only one or two hours at the computer terminal, but receives more information about occupations, educational opportunities, and how his or her personal qualities compare with those of workers in fields under consideration than a team of experts could have collected and provided in several days!

Computer guidance systems may be classified as "indirect inquiry systems," "direct inquiry systems without monitoring," and "direct inquiry systems with monitoring" (Harris 1972a, pp. 4–7). This classification does not include test reporting systems that compute scores and sometimes provide interpretive printouts. Systems have been developed in each of these categories, and are operational in schools and colleges.

The first category, involving *indirect inquiry*, usually operates on the basis of questions. Typically a system of this kind will store answers on a questionnaire, and hold them until enough data have been collected to return a report. For example, in college selection the pupil fills out a questionnaire about geographical preferences, grades, interests, test scores, and other data, and after an interval, receives a report on suitable colleges to apply to. Another example used in college placement centers is a system of matching seniors with employers.

In the second category, involving *direct inquiry without monitoring,* the pupil can obtain information directly from the computer; for example, by using a terminal keyboard to ask questions about occupations, educational institutions, and other areas. It is, as Harris says (1972a, p. 7), similar to using an automated library for instant information. The individual interacts with the computer, but it stores no personal data. Another example, the *Guidance Information System* (GIS), formerly known as the *Interactive*

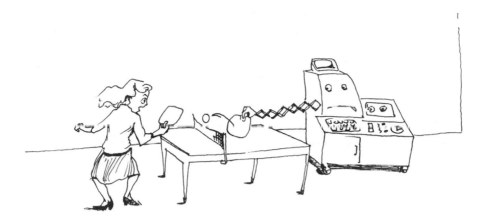

Computers can be programmed to provide almost any kind of service.

Learning System (ILS), is in use in over 1,400 career information centers in twenty-six states (Time Share n.d.). Now owned by Houghton Mifflin, this system provides occupational, educational, and financial-aid information and directs the user to other multimedia resources that are part of the total program.

The third category, involving *direct inquiry systems with monitoring,* is the most significant model for counselors. This is the type illustrated at the beginning of this section. The key features are: data banks with information about occupations and educational and training programs; data about the individual; data about interactions; and the capability to relate all of these. The computer, with the aid of a visual display, can answer questions about how the individual compares with those working in an occupation, evaluate decision-making ability, and suggest various options. It is somewhat like a "counseling" situation, although attempts to have computers actually counsel have not been successful (Super 1970, p. 4).

There are several systems of the third category serving pupils. SIGI (System of Interactive Guidance and Information) is in operation in a number of colleges (Katz 1980). CVIS (Computer Vocational Information System) is in operation at Willowbrook High School, Villa Park, Ill., and in approximately 375 other sites, serving junior high schools, secondary schools, and community colleges (Harris 1972b; Rabush 1976). ECES (Educational and Career Exploration System) is in operation in Genesee Intermediate School District, Genesee County, Mich. (Mallory 1972). This system has been incorporated in a counselor-computer plan for more effective help to pupils and has generated positive counselor attitudes toward computer capabilities (Mallory and Drake 1973, pp. 19–27). DISCOVER, a new system (Rayman, Bryson, Bowlsbey 1978; Harris-Bowlsbey 1978), forecasts a new generation of computer guidance systems. Some of the seven components, which range from self-concept clarification to implementing a career plan, require counselor, teacher, and community support; the system cannot stand alone. DISCOVER has been field-tested with pupils in grades 7–12 at all achievement levels and with college students. Results have shown it to be suitable for this entire range of subjects.

The computer guidance field is relatively new but is developing rapidly; for example, there are now low-cost mini-computers that can handle sophisticated programs. Harris predicts major new advances that will increase visual capability; offer users the opportunity to simulate occupational, educational, and personal experiences; enhance decision-making processes; and permit group interaction through computer terminals (1972a, pp. 10–11). Evaluation shows that operational systems are well accepted by users, do as well as counselors on certain tasks, increase vocational maturity, and are reasonable in cost (Harris 1974; Harris-Bowlsbey 1978, pp. 328–329).

Summary Concepts

Career, educational, and personal-social information together provide an essential base for counseling in all settings. Information may be provided directly in individual and group counseling. A number of group procedures can be of considerable help to counselors. The placement process is making increased use of information provided through group techniques, particularly in job hunting, to help individuals develop the skills needed for an effective search strategy. Information centers, often part of a more comprehensive counseling service in educational or community agencies, bring together a variety of media for easy use. There is evidence that centers meet a need; if they are effectively organized and staffed, extensive utilization will result. Issues and problems surrounding the use of information involves areas that are critical for effective helping. Bias in information is perhaps the most significant one, but other important ones involve roles and techniques for use. Information resources are increasing in sophistication and quality. Computers are the best example of newer resources to help counselors in the provision of current, appealing, comprehensive information.

Examples of Research on a Topic
The Impact of Information

Studies of the impact of information on users shed some light on methods and effects. Specific research is limited, however, because quite typically use of information is part of another procedure (individual counseling, group counseling, or career education). Thus, it is difficult to estimate effects of information only. Moreover, most studies are about effects of career information; much less is available about impacts of personal and social information.

With these limitations in mind, read the following summaries of studies and form your own conclusions about the impact on users.

Johnson, Korn, and Dunn (1975) employed three methods for presenting occupational information to 58 high school pupils, ages 15– 17, classified as reluctant learners. The three methods were printed word, audiotape, and slide-tape presentation; a control group received no treatment. A test was used to assess the amount of information learned, and preferences were obtained by a questionnaire. Differences among groups were significant at the .01 level, both for amount learned and preferences for methods. The slide-tape presentation was the most effective and the most widely preferred.

The authors point out the practicality of homemade information. Researching and producing the 32 slides and interviews took a total of 5.5 hours and cost less than $50. They suggest this approach for meeting the informational needs of special target groups.

Burlew (1980) compared the effects of three methods of helping 104 low-income black pupils from one high school develop positive perceptions of higher education. Individual counseling was provided for all pupils, but in addition one group had study skills counseling, a second had site visits to post-high-school institutions, and a third had group counseling. Each of the interventions was expected to have specific effects (e.g., study skills assistance would help pupils feel that they have more control over academic success). Site visits would help them become aware of educational opportunities. Results suggest that the three interventions were helpful, although in somewhat different ways than expected. Study skills assistance appears to be effective in raising the individual's expectancy of success in college and feelings of competency in completing applications. Site visits appear to be a good strategy to raise educational aspirations, but they also sharpen awareness of limited opportunity. Group counseling appeared to help participants become aware that others place importance on higher education. Additional research is needed, for example, to study the long-term effects of the interventions.

Harris and Wallin (1978) used three methods of presenting occupational information to seventh-grade pupils. The hypothesis tested was that those receiving the most information would consider a wider range of alternatives. The group treatments represented extremes in exposure to information. Group A members were asked to write on a sheet of paper the occupation they would like to enter after completing school. Group B members were first given a list of 48 occupations arranged by required levels of preparation and then asked to state a preference. Group C members were given the same list and also occupational descriptions containing nature of work, training needed, and potential earnings. Moreover, they were given time to study the data and collect additional information. Results showed that Group C pupils, those with the most information, considered a wider range of career alternatives. In addition, those with higher levels of mental ability tended to choose professional-level occupations regardless of the amount of information provided.

Day and Griffin (1980) studied the effects of the Magic Circle, a type of affective education curriculum for classroom use in the elementary school. Impacts on learning about selves, peers, and teachers; expression of feelings; and learning how to listen were assessed in grades 2, 4, and 6. From the comprehensive report of results, the following specific findings have been selected to show the impact of this approach. More than three-fourths of all grades liked the program. Second graders, however, were more positive than sixth graders. Fourth graders varied, sometimes resembling the more positive lower grade and at other times resembling the less enthusiastic higher grade. Almost nine out of ten in grades 2 and 4 felt that they had learned about themselves, but about seven out of ten in grade 6 felt this way. More than eight out of ten in all grades felt that they had learned about other pupils. The authors point out that the proficiency and enthusiasm of group leaders (teachers) likely affected results. Some cautions about the application of this technique to all pupils were also stated.

Evaluations of several computer guidance systems are summarized next. The use of the ECES (Educational and Career Exploration System) combined with counseling and a decision-making curriculum showed the following results:

- 79% of a group of eleventh graders felt that decision-making skills training and ECES gave them skills they could continue to use in career planning.
- 97% of another group, composed of tenth and eleventh graders, felt that decision-making skills training and ECES skills would continue to be helpful in their career planning.

Counselors rated students using ECES decision-making skills training significantly higher (<.01) in their preparedness for making career decisions than students who did not use ECES or did not have skills training (Mallory and Drake 1973, p. 22).

Katz (1980) reports on evaluation studies of SIGI (System of Interactive Guidance and Information), an interactive computer career guidance system. About 200 college students at six sites who had used SIGI, when compared with nonusers had, among other gains, a clearer understanding of values, more definite career plans, and greater confidence in their career decision-making ability.

Ryan, Drummond, and Shannon (1980) analyzed the impact of GIS (Guidance Information System), a computer guidance system, on its users. Six public secondary schools and six human service agencies were included in the field test, but results reported include only the schools. Those using the system reported the following:

- 75 percent said they learned a great deal about occupations.
- 41 percent said they were helped to confirm career plans.
- 40 percent said they were helped to clarify educational plans.
- 37 percent said they learned how to explore occupations.

The impact on counselors was demonstrated by more reading and study in the career area and more infusion of career education in the curriculum.

Two studies of career information centers shed some light on the impact of these resources. In one of the few such studies, Reardon, Domkowski, and Jackson (1980) describe the evaluation, by multiple methods, of a university career center. The impact aspect of the study covered effects on clients, faculty, and students-in-general. Clients gave the center high ratings on satisfaction with help provided. Impact on faculty awareness was relatively high; almost two-thirds of a sample knew about the service. Furthermore, those who were aware of the service were more in favor of bringing career development into classroom instruction than those faculty members who did not know about it. Slightly more than half of a sample of students knew about the service. An in-depth study of a small number of clients revealed that they were motivated to use the service because of a desire to analyze career choice factors in detail.

In 1972, Jacobson described information-center plans in four California schools; he emphasized the value of bringing sources of information together and the necessity of using paraprofessionals so that centers can be staffed at all times. He later evaluated information centers in California and found that they tend to fall in four levels: those just being organized; those providing information; those emphasizing career development; and those providing a full services program with professional staff and extensive integrated services (Jacobson 1975, pp. 5–7).

Pupil evaluations of each center's services include the following positive results (p. 75):

	Number of Visits to Career Center					
	None	1–2 Times	3–4 Times	5–6 Times	7 or More Times	F Lin Ratio
Receiving enough career guidance	2.20	2.66	3.01	3.35	3.57	80.63
Assistance in exploring careers	1.87	2.10	2.50	2.68	2.96	48.00

The results of only the two above items from the extensive data collected show (in the F test for linearity) that there is a significant increase in pupil satisfaction with guidance assistance the more the service is used. In addition, pupils in schools with no information centers give an average response of 2.25 to the first question ("Are you receiving enough career guidance?") — a rating of 2 means "not enough."

The complete findings show that career centers are needed in schools, that they should concentrate on encouraging pupils to make regular visits, and should help them learn how to utilize information and make decisions (Jacobson 1975, p. 115).

Experiential Activities

Three types of activities are helpful in learning about and using information resources. The examples given next illustrate specific activities, but you may think of others that would be more useful in your own situation.

1. Use an Information Resource

Computer systems, VIEW, and other types of technology may be available in the community or a local educational institution. Visit the service and request to use the resource. If a comprehensive information center is available, make a visit to examine files, books, directories, filmstrips, and other materials.

A related type of experience is to visit a place of employment or an educational institution to collect information about jobs and programs (e.g., interview a worker).

2. Small-Group Activities

In a small group ask members to think about an important career or educational decision the group members are making or expect to make in the future. Then have each person briefly present the decision and identify the three most important types of information needed to make it. The others note whether they agree or disagree with the stated priorities. After the presentation, have members give feedback to each other about agreement or disagreement with priorities.

In conclusion, discuss what members have learned about the utility and the relative importance of various types of information in decision making.

3. Providing Information

Interview an individual who expresses interest in obtaining information about work, education, or training. Then use one source discussed in this chapter to prepare a brief summary of information for the individual.

This experience can be used for obtaining information for your own career planning. You could collect information covering job descriptions, places of employment, job search strategies, and trends in areas of possible employment for personal use.

Utilize the same approach in providing information about personal-social or educational questions, such as the effects of various types of drugs.

Suggested Readings

Bowlsbey, Jo Ann Harris. "Careers by Special Delivery." In *New Imperatives for Guidance,* edited by Garry R. Walz and Libby Benjamin, pp. 327–374. Ann Arbor, Mich.: ERIC Counseling and Personnel Services Clearinghouse, 1978.

A brief, excellent review of all aspects of the use of computers in guidance. Very useful with this chapter.

Foster, June C.; Szoke, Claire Olsen; Kapisovsky, Peggy M.; and Kriger, Leslie S., *Guidance, Counseling and Support Services for High School Students with Physical Disabilities.* Cambridge, Mass.: Technical Education Research Centers, 1977.

Part II, pages 427–457, including supplements available for specific states, is an example of a comprehensive listing of resources for the handicapped. The section provides an excellent guide for building up a supply of information for the handicapped as well as identifying referral agencies and institutions.

Ganikos, Mary L.; Grady, Kathleen A.; and Olson, Jane B., eds. *Counseling the Aged.* Washington, D.C.: American Personnel and Guidance Association, 1979.

Module XI, pages 295–320, reviews the policies and legislation about which the counselor who works with older persons should know. Policies and legislation about special groups, in this case older persons, are essential components of the information service.

Herr, Edwin L., and Cramer, Stanley H. *Career Guidance Through the Life Span.* Boston: Little, Brown, 1979.

Chapter 13, on information, provides an interesting and useful way of looking at sources and identifies a large number of useful techniques and prepared kits.

Isaacson, Lee E. *Career Information in Counseling and Teaching.* 3rd ed. Boston: Allyn and Bacon, 1977.

A definitive text on career information and its use in guidance and counseling. Part 5, on occupational information materials and techniques, is particularly useful in connection with this chapter.

Jacobson, Thomas J. "Career Resource Centers." In *New Imperatives for Guidance,* edited by Garry R. Walz and Libby Benjamin, pp. 375–420. Ann Arbor, Mich.: ERIC Counseling and Personnel Services Clearinghouse, 1978.

A very helpful reference on the information center, covering history, purpose, managing, staffing, effects, and future prospects. Recommended.

Meerbach, John. *The Career Resource Center.* New York: Human Sciences Press, 1978.

An excellent reference devoted entirely to building and managing the information center.

Norris, Willa; Hatch, Raymond N.; Engelkes, James R.; and Winborn, Bob B. *The Career Information Service.* 4th ed. Chicago: Rand McNally, 1979.

A standard reference on information in counseling, guidance, and personnel work. Chapters 4, 5, and 6, on sources, expand on those given in this book. Chapters 7 and 8, on local information, are particularly useful.

Pietrofesa, John J., and Splete, Howard. *Career Development: Theory and Research.* New York: Grune and Stratton, 1975.

Chapter 8, on decision making, helpfully discusses how information can facilitate the guidance process. Other sections of the book deal with all the chief aspects of career development and provide a useful foundation in this area.

Shertzer, Bruce, and Stone, Shelley C. *Fundamentals of Guidance.* 4th ed. Boston: Houghton Mifflin, 1981.

Chapter 11, "The Informational Component," provides a comprehensive review of all aspects of information in counseling and guidance. Many of the techniques discussed are different from those covered in this chapter. Recommended for added depth.

Shippen, Samuel Joseph, and Wasil, Raymond A., eds. *Placement and Follow-Up.* Lexington, Mass.: Xerox Individualized Publishing, 1977.

A comprehensive reference on occupational placement. All phases are covered in a series of informative articles. The one by Buckingham emphasizing exploration (pp. 13–23) is a good starting place.

Tolbert, E. L. *Introduction to Counseling.* 2nd ed. New York: McGraw-Hill, 1972.

On pages 178–205, the author illustrates principles of using information in counseling with interview excerpts. The principles and procedures used are still relevant for individual work.

————. *Counseling for Career Development.* 2nd ed. Boston: Houghton Mifflin, 1980.

Chapter 5 reviews the information system, identifies types of information, and explains how they may be used. Chapter 6 describes local sources such as occupational surveys. The section on computer systems (pp. 161–173) is suggested for a brief overview of these sources.

Walz, Garry R.; Smith, Robert L.; and Benjamin, Libby, eds. *A Comprehensive View of Career Development.* Washington, D.C.: American Personnel and Guidance Association, 1974.

This contemporary review of promising trends and practices emphasizes career guidance, but also discusses various types of information systems.

Chapter

11

The Counselor's Use of Measurements

Anyone who reads the newspapers and news magazines and spends any time watching TV knows that testing is increasingly in the center of turmoil. Local minority groups protest the use of testing for promotion, placement in special programs, and graduation. There is legislation to require college admissions programs to provide users with copies of tests and answers. There are prohibitions against use of tests in some state school systems, charges of sex bias, complaints that tests are used to evaluate schools and being used for accountability. Tests are seen as an invasion of privacy. The list of controversies and problems seem to be growing. Recently the college admissions tests in one area had to be rescored because a pupil, after studying the copy that was returned to him, found an error in scoring.

But testing is obviously here to stay. Tests provide types of data that can be obtained in no other way; they facilitate choices and plans in career and other areas; and they provide administrators and agency directors with essential information for planning and decision making. Counselors in all settings need to know how to interpret and use tests. They also need to know the issues and problems surrounding tests and to have thought out their positions on these issues. Sooner or later, you will be confronted with problems involving the use of tests.

Purposes of Assessment, Evaluation, and Testing

In any setting, each of these three functions — assessment, evaluation, and testing — may be carried out. It is important for the counselor to be aware of their similarities and differences and to understand when and why each would be used.

Assessment is a broad concept involving testing and other methods to determine an individual's characteristics, qualities, or achievements. Assessment of mechanical ability, for example, might involve a test, an evaluation of work experiences, and proficiency in using materials. Testing utilizes a specific standardized technique to determine the individual levels of performance. A test of mechanical ability might determine the pupil's ability to answer fifty questions about mechanical principles. A test attempts to measure an individual's maximum performance. An inventory taps preferences, attitudes, or beliefs. Pupils might be asked whether they like to work with tools. There is no right or wrong answer; results show something about individual attitudes. Evaluation is quite similar to assessment — it is a broad term covering different techniques to determine the results of a program, or to build relatively complete personal descriptions. For example, you could administer a test to measure a specific mechanical aptitude, such as understanding how mechanical devices work. To assess mechanical ability, however, you would use as much data about the individual as possible — hobbies, work experience, school courses, and test results. You could *evaluate* the effectiveness of the counseling program.

Testing is the most complex and controversial of the three functions. A policy statement of the American Personnel and Guidance Association (APGA Policy Statement 1978, p. 5) sets forth purposes and cautions for human service agencies as follows:

a. Placement: If the purpose is selection or placement (selection is a simple in-out sort of placement), the test selector and interpreter must know about the programs or institutions in which the client may be placed and be able to judge the consequences of such placement or exclusion for the client.

b. *Prediction/Expectancies:* If the purpose is prediction, the persons deciding to test and/or interpret the results must understand the pitfalls of labeling, stereotyping and prejudging people. Ways to avoid these potentially invidious outcomes should be known.

c. *Description-Diagnosis:* If the purpose is diagnosis or description, the selector or interpreter should understand enough about the general domain being measured to be able to identify those aspects adequately measured and those not.

d. *Growth/Change Assessment:* If the purpose is to examine growth, the person designing the study and interpreting the results needs to know the many problems associated with such measurement:
   1. the unreliability of change measures;
   2. the pitfalls in using norms as reference points;
   3. the associated problems of articulation and comparability;
   4. the limitations of scoring scales, such as grade equivalents, that may not have the comparable meaning which they appear to have at different grade levels. (p. 5)

The categories of purposes give some indication of the types of tests and inventories available for use. A more specific listing is given next.

Types of Tests and Inventories

Six types of standardized measurements cover a wide range of psychological aspects of the individual. Some are designed for individual administration, but the most widely used are those suitable for group administration.

Mental Ability

Terms such as "mental ability," "intelligence," or "academic aptitude" refer to the ability mentally to manipulate verbal, quantitative, and other abstract symbols. Tests may be designed for individual or group administration (typically used in the school). Although their titles imply that these are tests of some sort of general ability to cope with intellectual challenges of life, items are typically related to school learning (e.g., vocabulary), and correlate with success in academic types of tasks. The Stanford-Binet and the Weschler scales — e.g., the WAIS (Weschler Adult Intelligence Scale) and the WISC (Weschler Intelligence Scale for Children) — are among the best-known individual intelligence tests. Widely used group tests are the California Test of Mental Maturity and the Otis Lennon Mental Ability Test. The exact nature of and proper means of measuring "intelligence" are among the most controversial issues in our field.

Achievement Tests

This type measures how much has been learned, how far skills have been developed, or what competencies have been acquired. A paper-and-pencil test may be used to measure learning in social studies, but a work sample demonstrating a skill also represents achievement. Test items are usually selected to represent the content of a course; thus, this is a major type of test used to demonstrate accountability. Results may be used diagnostically (to determine strengths and weaknesses in a subject area). Results of past achievement are among the best indicators of future progress; tests therefore can be used for prediction. There are a number of well-known achievement batteries, among them the California Achievement Tests for grades 1–14, the Stanford Achievement Tests for grades 1–12, the Sequential Tests of Educational Progress (STEP) for grades 4–14, and the College Board achievement series and Graduate Record advanced exams.

Aptitude Tests

These are designed to estimate potential for future performance. Intelligence and achievement tests can be used for this purpose, but the term is usually applied to tests of vocational aptitude. A battery of tests is often prepared so that a profile with comparable scores for different aptitudes can be made up for the individual. One of the best known is the General Aptitude Test Battery (GATB) used in state employment services. (A non-reading edition is also available.) Work evaluation, such as the Singer Vocational Evaluation System (Cohen and Drugo 1976), involves handling materials and tools and has begun to incorporate methods of evaluating work personality. One of the best-known aptitude test batteries is the DAT (Differential Aptitude Test), which gives nine scores, including a composite score of verbal and numerical abilities similar to typical mental ability tests. A career planning questionnaire for use in conjunction with the test is also available.

Personality Inventories

These questionnaires gather information on the examinee's preferences, attitudes, or problems. Results are stated by comparison with a given group (e.g., a sample of high school pupils). Some inventories are lists of problems that counselees check to portray their own situations. A limitation of such instruments is that results may be faked, but some have scales to detect efforts to present a favorable picture. Other instruments are projective — the individual responds to unstructured material such as ink-blots, ambiguous pictures, or incomplete sentences. Such stimuli evoke responses that reveal personality needs and organization; they require specific preparation to administer and interpret, are more difficult to fake, but more subjective in their interpretation. Widley used personality inventories are the Minnesota Multiphasic Personality Inventory (MMPI), the Edwards Personal Preference Schedule, and the Myers-Briggs Type Indicator. The best-known projective tests are the Rorschach and the Thematic Apperception Test (TAT).

Career Interest

Interest inventories are special kinds of personality tests designed to get at pupils' career preferences by asking questions about preferred jobs, hobbies, and other activities. Responses are compared with those of others (e.g., a general group, or people successful in a particular occupation) to determine high and low interest levels. Intraindividual comparisons are also made; results might show, for instance, that a counselee likes mechanical activity more than literary work. But interest inventories do more than measure occupational likes and dislikes and may often generate personality measurements (Holland 1973, p. 7). The major inventories in use today are the Strong-Campbell Interest Inventory (SCII) and the Kuder Preference Record, which has several forms that are scored in different ways.

Career Development Measurements

This type, actually very much like interest rather than a separate category, includes both tests and inventories and gets at the individual's attitudes toward work, knowledge of occupations, and ability to use information in decision making. Results indicate the individual's status with respect to career development (Westbrook 1974). This is a relatively new area of measurement, but instruments incorporate the same type of content as achievement tests and personality and career-interest inventories. Those in use today include the Career Development Inventory (CDI), the Career Maturity Inventory (CMI), and the Cognitive Test of Vocational Maturity (CTVM).

In addition to these major assessment devices and techniques, there are interesting variations the counselor should know about. The individual can use the self-administered guidance technique, Self-Directed Search (Holland and Nafziger 1975), to arrive at career choices. The assessment approach of the staffing conference can determine students' progress and difficulties (Kelly and Dowd 1975). The High School Characteristics Index (Tolsma, Menne, and Hopper 1976) measures pupils' perceptions of the climate of the institution (Walz and Miller 1969).

Nontest Assessment Techniques

In addition to the types of standardized instruments already described, there are a number of other techniques counselors can use to learn about counselees and facilitate the development of insight. Some of the best known are the following:

Anecdotal Records

These are brief statements of actual behavior recorded by a teacher or counselor. The factual description gives a picture of how the person actually behaves in various sorts of situations. Interpretations, if any, are kept separate from the behavior description.

Ratings and Other Observational Techniques

These procedures involve an observer's ratings of characteristics such as motivation, empathy, or attending behavior. The same techniques may be used for self-rating. Sociometrics is a type of rating in which the individual selects others for some activity or characteristic.

Autobiographical and Other Self-Reports

Unless the instructions are quite detailed, this approach includes some projection. Reports may briefly treat such topics "My most positive experience," or "What I would like to be," or they run to lengthy autobiographies of several pages. Probably because much time is needed for preparation and analyzing results, the technique is used infrequently. But it does offer a helpful glimpse of the individual's inner world.

Time Schedules

These are used in how-to-study instruction. A time schedule shows how a pupil spends time, and is often a necessary first step in planning a more effective and balanced time distribution.

Instruments such as the above provide relatively subjective data that are often very useful in helping the individual develop self-understanding. Although standardization may be lacking (except for ratings that have been tested for reliability and validity) and objective comparisons with reference groups is not possible, these are useful data-gathering methods for the helping service.

Issues in Testing

Testing has always had strong advocates and strong detractors (Cronbach 1975). Recently, however, and for several reasons, it has increasingly come under fire. Chief factors include charges of cultural and sexual bias, lack of accurate predictions, and misuse of test results.

Tests and Cultural Bias

Culturally, test items tend to favor the middle-class American group and to work against minorities, particularly the disadvantaged and blacks (Williams 1970). The suggestion has been made to impose a moratorium on testing until better tests are constructed. But Messick and Anderson (1970) uphold the value of testing to show the current status of an individual, regardless of previous deprivation. Eliminating tests would result in more subjective assessment methods (Ebel 1975). Attempts to construct culture-fair or culture-free tests have not been successful (Wesman 1968). Cultural factors do seem to affect knowledge of items, attitudes toward taking tests, and feelings of competence about test taking; some resulting inequalities may be reduced by exercise and practice and some by remedial work. Williams's research on a *culture-specific* test of mental ability illustrates an approach to constructing measuring instruments that take into account the unique personality characteristics and learning styles of members of a

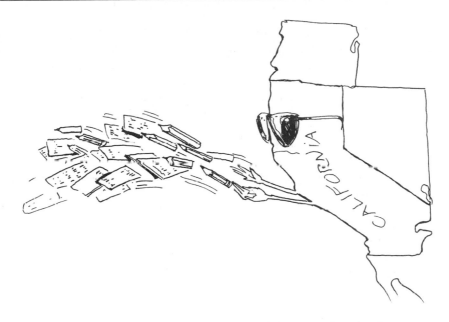

Some states are abolishing the use of mental ability tests in schools.

minority group (Wright and Isenstein 1977). So-called culture-fair or culture-free tests, however, have little or no validity for predicting academic success. Recent legal action has been directed at racial bias in tests. In California, the federal courts (Opton 1979) ruled that tests used to place children in classes for the educable mentally retarded are racially and culturally biased. There is now a permanent moratorium on the use of tests for this purpose in California. The decision, expected to lead to challenges in other courts, has far-reaching implications for the use of tests. For example, how are pupils to be evaluated for present level of competence or potential? How may comparisons with other pupils be made? In compliance with provisions of PL 94-142, how will those with learning difficulties be identified for special remedial work? It is *possible* that alternative methods used will be unreliable and subjected to the beliefs and attitudes of the evaluator? If tests are misused to the extent implied in legislation, it is also possible that any other types of evaluations will also be misused?

Tests and Sexual Bias

Sex bias in tests and inventories, particularly career-interest inventories, is another recent concern. Standards for interpretation and use of inventories (American Psychological Association, *Standards for Educational and Psychological Tests* 1974; National Vocational Guidance Association, *Career Development and Career Guidance* 1973) suggest ways to prevent bias in test use but have had limited effects (Tanney 1975). Relatively little sex bias has been found in general-interest inventories (Johansson 1975), but enough to call for such remedial action as establishing checklists for determining the amount of sex fairness and sex bias in career-interest inventories (Diamond 1975). Sex bias in computer guidance systems utilizing interest inventories has also been investigated (Harris-Bowlsbey 1975b). Little has been found, but suggestions have been made for future use, such as analyzing and making necessary revisions in the storage of occupational information. The issue of sex bias is not settled; some argue that it can be eliminated only at the cost of reduced usefulness of tests and inventories ("Standardized Tests: Sexy, Sexless, or Sexist?" 1975).

The 1980 APGA Policy Statement, "Responsibilities of Users of Standardized Tests" (APGA 1980), makes it clear that the user should be aware of comparison groups and take them into account when testing is done and results are interpreted. Under "purposes," the statement is made that the test user "determine limits to diagnosis, prediction or selection created by age, racial, sexual, ethnic or cultural characteristics of those to be tested" (p. 1). This principle clearly places the responsibility on the counselor to determine whether or not to use sex-based norms.

The Problem of Prediction

Another difficulty that must be faced is the problem of prediction, which requires that test results be compared with results of a specific relevant population. If, for example, a woman is considering an engineering program in college, test items have to take into account characteristics of the male-dominated field. But care must be taken to eliminate test items that do not relate directly to professional success. If workers in a given occupation tend to have a certain characteristic (with respect, for example, to race, sex, or socioeconomic level) that does not actually affect proficiency in essential tasks, a test showing high validity on this characteristic would be biased in favor of the status quo. Recently, controversy about the prediction problem has increased in response to the Nader/Nairn Report ("Nader Releases ETS Report, Hits Tests as Poor Predictors of Performance," 1980). The major point of the report is that the tests used by a major testing college and graduate school admissions testing service are of little value in predicting success. There are, of course, two sides to the issue. The testing service describes the predictive effectiveness in special publications and points out misconceptions in the Nader/Nairn Report (Educational Testing Service 1980a and 1980b). One aftershock effect of the report is the New York "truth-in-testing" law requiring that each college or graduate school applicant test-taker be later supplied with a copy of the test and a list of correct answers. The value of this legislation, too, is debatable, as Ravich (1979) and Brownstein and Nairn (1979) point out. On the negative side, the law will certainly increase the cost of testing. On the positive side, it will give all students a way to become familiar with tests without having to pay for expensive coaching classes.

The difference between achievement and aptitude tests poses further recurring problems. Since both measure the same thing — previous learning — deprivations of various sorts at school and home can result in low scores in both. Thus, aptitude tests, particularly those designed to measure academic aptitude, should not be considered, as they often are, to be measuring some unchanging psychological characteristic.

Much of the recent controversy over utility of tests in counseling was touched off by Goldman's statement (1972*b*) that tests and counseling made up a "marriage that had failed," and his contention that tests do not predict accurately enough to be helpful in counseling. Wesman (1972) and others take issue with this point of view and assert that tests supply needed information about counselees that is particularly useful in planning remedial help for the culturally deprived. Goldman himself has recommended developing new kinds of tests that would not only tell where a person stands but also provide ways to improve deficiencies (Goldman 1972*a*). Steps have been taken in this direction. For example, in the new system of multicultural pluralistic assessment (APA *Monitor* 1976, vol. 7, no. 5, p. 13), an individual's test scores are compared with those of others with similar social and cultural backgrounds.

Tests, regardless of predictive validity, do in any case provide vital information that may not be obtainable in any other way, or only at great difficulty and expense. It is true that tests make predictions only for groups (e.g., 50 percent of pupils with a given score will earn grades of C or better in college), not for specific individuals. Moreover, predictions usually have a large "error." On the basis of a test, a counselor might be able to tell a high school student: "Chances are two out of three that your college marks will fall between a C minus and a B plus." Quite a range! What is more, the counselor cannot be sure that the counselee will be competing with a group similar to the one on which validity and norms were originally computed. Other factors besides tested ability enter into the person's performance and contribute to its variability. Test scores used in prediction might account for only about 15 percent of the variability of predicted grades; even though this is not very much, it is still helpful, *provided* the concept is understood by both the counselor and the counselee. At present, there are not tests that are so efficient in prediction that a counselor could say: "Based on your score, you are certain to make an A average in college." It seems improbable that there ever will be. The modest contribution of a test, illustrated by the above example, is typical of today's instruments.

Misuse of Test Results

A fourth major criticism concerns misuse of tests and test results. Such problems usually arise because of a lack of understanding of tests on the part of counselors or teachers, the tendency to categorize individuals as if test scores were precise and unchangeable, and the failure to recognize factors (e.g., native language, cultural background) that cause tests to give results that are misinterpreted by the user. The main difficulty is that those who use test scores are inadequately prepared; the remedial strategy is to make sure they acquire a thorough understanding of the theory and construction of tests. One type of misuse has already been mentioned — the tendency to consider intelligence test scores as reflecting a fixed, unchanging attribute of the individual. A second type of misuse is to use scores as if they were precise measurements. For example, a college admissions program may set a specific score as required for acceptance. An individual who scores five points below the cut-off may be rejected although research on the test shows that results vary ten points below the cutoff point on repeated administrations. In other words, the rejected applicant might score above the cutoff point if the test were taken again. A third type of misuse stems from the selection of inappropriate comparison groups (norm groups). An individual might be quite low on the ability measured when compared with those in high schools that concentrate on college preparation for highly selective institutions; he might compare very well, however, with those in a school that is not so competitive-college oriented.

In spite of limitations, testing is here to stay. Tests are a widely accepted feature of our culture, and they are being improved. Counselors will continue to be involved in the selection, administration, and interpretation of instruments in colleges, schools, and agencies, and to work with individuals who face testing for admission to educational programs and jobs. Controversies will continue to arise on the subject of test bias, and the counselor will be called upon for an expert opinion. Tests provide the quickest and most inexpensive way to obtain a standardized sample of behavior for understanding the individual and for planning educational programs in line with status. They are essential for carrying out mandates of legislation such as Affirmative Action and PL 94-142. They are necessary in minimum competency programs in the schools and also for accountability. It is quite likely that the use of tests will increase in the years ahead, although it is clearly apparent the regulations about the employment of all types of measurements will continue to increase.

Settings for Testing

Tests and inventories are used in all of the settings covered in this book. Moreover, use contributes to the counseling and consulting functions and to the developmental focus of helping services. Tests can, for example, help in the early identification of pupils in need of remedial assistance or those who could profit from an accelerated program. In many instances the functions of counselors in schools, colleges, and community agencies (see Chapters 2, 3, and 4) involve the use of tests of various types. Some of these uses are discussed in paragraphs that follow.

School Testing Programs

Schools usually have an ongoing testing program, grades 1–12, to monitor achievement and mental ability; in the upper grades, career interest may be added. Programs differ considerably from school to school, but one common practice is to give mental ability and achievement tests every other year, using similar types to obtain comparable scores. Recently, accountability requirements have given rise to programs designed to measure pupils' status before and after the year's work.

The underlying rationale for school testing at the local level derives from the goals and objectives of the local school program. Tests are used to gather data that are otherwise difficult or impossible to obtain. Quite often, however, a testing program is established county-wide or even state-wide; while local objectives may be very well covered by such measurements, the school does not expressly select such tests on the basis of them.

School Counselor's Role

Although group testing has historically been an essential part of the counselor's role, current trends indicate that the counselor's participation in the testing program should be limited to helping with planning and coordination, instructing others in methods of administration and interpretation, and setting up ways to put data to use, that is, as a consultant (to share his expertise and concern for students) to others. Clerical tasks of the testing function have often fallen to the counselor, however, and the obtaining, distributing, and collecting involved have taken an inordinate amount of time, and it has been hard to get rid of these chores.

Usefulness of Tests to School Counselors

Counseling use of testing emphasizes direct help (e.g., helping an individual understand abilities before choosing a program). Instructional use estimates learning acquired and identifies areas needing special attention; this use is mainly a concern of the teaching staff. Used for administrative purposes, tests may provide information needed for setting up special classes, evaluating the status of pupil learning in the school, and allocating of resources; such use concerns the school administration and supervisory staff. The guidance function suffers if the counselor becomes too heavily involved in all these areas.

School-wide testing programs provide the counselor with helpful data. Results summarize pupil progress. Analysis of scores can be used in planning new teaching methods, courses, and objectives; the counselor participates in this process as a consultant. Second, the results, which are entered in the student's record, may be used directly in counseling and guidance.

Tests are also increasingly used in demonstrating accountability: Is the school accomplishing its objectives? Some programs represent a very serious misuse of tests. To evaluate the status and progress of a class or even a school without background information about differences among pupils is unwarranted, and it can only alienate teachers and others on the subject of tests. Tests that tap only a narrow part of course objectives can often give a biased report of learning that is taking place and thus can encourage teachers to concentrate on "teaching the test."

Today parents are coming into contact with tests more than ever before. Expanded test reports, accompanied by explanatory material that is supposed to make results easily understandable, are in many cases given to pupils to take home and discuss with parents. New legislation allows parents to inspect their children's school records (Worzbyt 1976; Wilhelm and Case 1975); these developments require school personnel who use tests, particularly counselors, to be knowledgeable about interpretation. The same legislation that opens up records to parents or guardians also requires their permission for administering certain types of tests to their children (Burgum and Anderson 1975, pp. 82–83). The counselor must exercise caution not only in administering and interpreting tests; other types of data in the cumulative record, such as comments and evaluations, may be used in libel suits if not handled with care. Adhering to the APGA's ethical guidelines for the use of tests (Ethical Standards, Appendix B, Section C, "Measurement and Evaluation") should lessen the likelihood of legal problems.

School assessment services often include college-admission testing, such as the College Board and American College Testing programs; typically, such tests are administered by an out-of-school agency, but the school receives the results for its records. The National Merit Scholarship Program and others like it test candidates for scholarships. The College Level Examination Program (CLEP) enables high school pupils to obtain credit for college course work. American College Testing (ACT) provides schools with a career guidance assessment package in addition to the well-known college admission test. The Career Planning Program for grades 8–11 assesses abilities, interests, and experiences and provides for exploration in six basic career clusters. This last type of prepared program, which combines well-designed measurements with strategies for planning and decision making, is particularly valuable for guidance and counseling.

Usefulness of Tests to Higher-Education Counselors

In addition to admission and advanced standing testing, higher-education counselors may utilize measurements, particularly interest and personality, in working with individuals and groups. Tests and inventories may be given to all entering students for orientation, counseling, and advising purposes, or to a special group for diagnostic or research purposes (e.g., in remedial programs). Various sorts of measurements provide ways to help reach student development objectives such as intellectual and identity development (King and Fields 1980). Colleges and university counseling or testing centers may administer tests for admission to graduate and professional programs. In some cases, licensure and certification examinations may be provided. Counselors are expected to be knowledgeable about measurement questions and problems and to be able to consult with other student personnel workers on the use of various sorts of measurements.

Tests and Community Agencies, Business, and Industry

Community agencies vary considerably in their use of measurements. Those providing career and educational planning services may make extensive use of tests. The state employment service's General Aptitude Test Battery (GATB) is an example. A community college's career clinic (Gelfman not dated, pp. 6–7), uses a specifically tailored test battery for each client as a regular step in its adult counseling program. Tests are less useful for older persons because of negative attitudes about measurements and because of the indications of abilities and interests that can be deduced from past experience; if they are used at all, the counselor should be sensitive and responsive to the concerns expressed by the test-takers (Wolff and Meyer 1979, pp. 177–178). The use of tests with the handicapped requires knowledge of the effect of the impairment on test performance and may entail special modifications in administration. Work samples (sample tasks from the job) and vocational evaluation (performance evaluation under standardized conditions) offer alternatives to standard paper-and-pencil group tests and inventories.

Whatever methods are used, the provisions of PL 94-142, as well as other legislation, must be taken into account. The test should be selected and administered to assess the aptitude or ability in question rather than reflect lack of sensory, manual, or speaking skills, unless these are being assessed (Foster, Szoke, Kapisovsky, and Kriger 1977, pp. 288–289, 307–312).

Tests and measurements are also used in private practice and in business and industrial settings. The private practitioner might use group and individual tests with clients to assess such factors as interests, personality characteristics, and intellectual ability; he or she may also provide testing services for educational institutions, governmental agencies, and business and industrial establishments. Business and industry frequently use measurements for such purposes as selection, placement, promotion, and assessment of employee satisfaction and morale. In-house counselors may do the testing, or it may be carried out by contract with a private counseling or consulting agency.

Using Assessment in Counseling

Criticisms stressing the inadequacies both of tests and of counselors have been leveled against the use of assessment in counseling (Goldman 1972b), but tests can and do help in planning and decision making, stimulating exploration, developing self-understanding, and establishing life goals in career, educational, and personal areas (Prediger 1980). Tests particularly selected for counseling and those that are given in the school testing program and go into the pupil's cumulative record can be employed in these ways (Kirk 1969). Such utilization requires an understanding of technical aspects of tests, and skills in helping pupils — individually or in groups — to use results.

Information about tests to be adopted or already in use is available in several forms. The technical report prepared by the test publisher is the best source of detailed technical data. Buros's *Mental Measurements Yearbooks* are the best single source of critical reviews and bibliographies of research studies. Reviews in journals such as *Measurement and Evaluation in Guidance* are also valuable. Test manuals (particularly their technical sections) can be used. The section on *Use* in the APA booklet on standards (American Psychological Association 1974) provides a helpful set of guidelines.

To make use of test evaluations and reviews, and to make personal analyses, the technical aspects of instruments need to be clearly understood. Reliability, validity, norms, and scores are essential concepts. Reliability indicates the stability of the test score. Validity shows how accurately the test measures what it is supposed to measure (e.g., success in school). There are other types of validity; it is important for the counselor to apply them in accordance with the use to which a particular test is put. Norm groups are another important factor; comparisons between individual pupils and groups should have bearing on the individuals' own choices or plans. The counselor therefore needs to be aware of the makeup of groups on which norms were established and of the difference between norm-referenced and criterion-referenced tests (Popham 1976; Hambleton and Novick 1972). (In norm-referenced tests, the individual's score is compared with scores of others. In criterion-referenced tests, the individual's scores are compared with a standard.) Scores, too, are complex; to interpret them, the counselor must understand how they are derived. Even the simplest types (e.g., percentiles, ratios) are likely to mystify a counselee. An example may help clarify their importance to the counselor. Suppose you have a test of forty questions measuring mechanical ability. Each question shows a picture of a tool, and the pupil is asked to check one of four choices indicating its use. If the test has been given to 1,000 high school seniors to establish score levels, these 1,000 pupils make up the norm group. If you give them the test twice and compare scores, you are assessing reliability (test-retest type). If you compare scores with grades in industrial arts, you are establishing a type of validity (predictive). Now, suppose you compare John Smith's score with the scores of the 1,000 pupils in the norm group, and he ranks near the top. You are using a norm-referenced approach to evaluate his performance. But if you decide that at least half the questions should be answered correctly to indicate success in industrial arts, you are not concerned with the scores of others but only with whether John scored high enough to complete his program successfully. You are now using a criterion-referenced approach.

Actual face-to-face interpretation of test data involves the application of counseling procedures. Much research has been done on how to use results with counselees (Sharf 1971), but there is not sufficient evidence to single any one approach out as the best. Kirk's strategy (1969), which includes the counselee in the test selection process, is highly recommended. Participation is as valuable in test selection as in other aspects of the counseling relationship; interpretation, in which the counselor and counselee explore reactions to results, is also a cooperative enterprise.

Test use in counseling has changed with the development of self-explanatory answer sheets or computer printouts with detailed discussions of the meaning of the scores (Sharf 1974). These printouts save the counselor a lot of time but do not replace the counselee's interaction with a counselor. Computer guidance systems, which provide somewhat the same type of data, may go further by furnishing the counselee with predictions based on test scores. Many school programs routinely provide comparisons of results from state, national, and local testing programs, thus providing large amounts of helpful information that can be used with counselees. The counselee needs help in using any of these data; the amount of assistance depends on the individual, but none of the results from test-data systems "stands alone."

The interpretation in counseling involves relating scores to an important life activity or concern. Prediger (1971) suggests comparisons to specific groups. This comparison facilitates exploratory behavior and helps the counselee reflect on how he or she would feel as a member of each group. The counselor has detailed information about the various groups and thus can plan with the counselee the steps to be taken to be successful in the chosen group. This approach brings together all sorts of data and helps the counselee form a well-rounded picture of choices and options.

Tests are improving; interpretive aids are better developed. As Prediger points out (for the career area), "Practitioners should expect even more from tests in the future. If test publishers do their part, counselors will no longer have to become psychometric experts to use career counseling tests properly. (After all, they don't have to know about the physics of light to use a filmstrip projector.) Tests will still need to be carefully evaluated (perhaps by an outside consultant) before they are adopted. Much of the time saved by front-line counselors, however, in learning all there is to know about the tests, in preparing for clinical interpretation of scores, and in conducting those interpretations, could be devoted to follow-through, to actively involving students in self/career exploration" (1980, p. 302).

Summary Concepts

Some types of measurements are used in virtually all settings in which counselors work; uses may be for placement, prediction, description, and for detecting indications of growth. Controversies surrounding the use of tests are increasing, and counselors are sure to encounter them in their work. While there have been many abuses in the use of tests, most problems center around the lack of competence of those who interpret results. Tests can perform some functions more efficiently than other techniques. Moreover, in spite of criticisms, new legislation and social programs require the types of data that tests provide. The counselor does not need to know all about measurement theory to use tests effectively but must have a basic understanding of what tests can and cannot do if he or she is to provide a sound and ethical service.

Examples of Research on a Topic
Using Test and Inventory Results in Counseling

Research on the use of measurement results in counseling should provide information about effective strategies. After you have read the following brief summaries, how would you answer these questions?

1. Are there effective ways to use measurement results in counseling?
2. What conditions appear to facilitate the presentation of measurement data?

Two related studies with college students, by Tuma and Gustad (1957) and Gustad and Tuma (1957), are examples of well-planned research on differential effects of counselors and methods on counselee learning. The first study compared: counselor-client similarity, three methods of test introduction, and four methods of test interpretation. The three methods of introducing tests were:

- Client-motivated.
- Counselor-originated (client selects tests).
- Counselor-directed (counselor assigns tests).

In the four methods of interpretation test scores were:

- Presented in general terms.
- Presented in specific terms (e.g., percentiles).
- Compared with clients' previously completed self-estimates on traits measured.
- Compared with clients' previously completed self-estimates, with client keeping the written comparison for further study.

The earlier study by Gustad and Tuma (1957) had shown no influence of different methods of test introduction and interpretation on client learning; this one revealed that if counselor and client had very similar personalities, clients learned more. Gustad and Tuma call for further research to assess the effects of different approaches to counseling and other variables (such as the counselor's sex) on client learning. (This research used only one counseling approach.)

Fernald and Markarewicz (1967) investigated the degree of accuracy with which college students could identify real v. fake descriptions of personal characteristics. Results showed subjects to be correct in most choices. Thus, the authors conclude that personal validations of test results by the counselee may be a helpful approach. These results obtained with college students may apply to the high school level.

Some studies have been done on secondary school pupils. Carey (1968), for example, used ninth and eleventh graders to compare the effects of oral v. written summaries of test results. Results showed that ninth graders who received written summaries along with counselors' oral interpretations learned more and were better satisfied; no differences were found for eleventh graders. Carey suggests several reasons for the differences at the ninth-grade level; testing was more recent, for example, and pupils were in a group guidance program at the time he conducted his study.

Miller and Cochran (1979) used three methods of reporting interest inventory results to high school junior and senior boys. One group viewed a slide-sound presentation. A second received results from a counselor. A third received both the slide-sound and the counselor presentations. A control group was given the inventory profile to read. All three experimental groups showed significant increases over the control group on factual information but did not differ among themselves. In addition, the three experimental groups showed more favorable attitudes — on coverage, clarity, and value of presentations — than the control group. The counselor-only group, however, rated coverage better than the other experimental groups.

How would you answer the two questions raised at the beginning of this section?

1. Are there effective ways to use measurement results in counseling?
2. What conditions appear to facilitate the presentation of measurement data?

Experiential Activities

Three types of activities are suggested to help learn about the counselor's use of measurements. These are: taking a test or inventory and having it interpreted; interviewing others to find out their attitudes about tests; and gathering data about an institution or agency's use of measurements. The following are suggested activities:

1. Taking a Test

Visit a counseling agency and request to be given one or more tests or inventories. (It is suggested that you tell the counselor the purpose of your request. A number of requests from a class may cost the service too much in time and money.) Participate in interpretation of results. An alternate activity could be to see if students in test and measurement courses need subjects for practice in administration and interpretation.

2. Surveying Attitudes about Tests

Ask a number of individuals to give their reactions about tests. How did they feel about taking tests? Were the directions and questions clear? Did they detect bias? Were the results used in a helpful way? Question members of special groups (those discussed in Chapter 9) for their attitudes.

3. Use of Tests and Measurements in a Program

Contact a setting of your choice and arrange to interview a counselor about the use of measurements. If the setting uses no measurements, ask about reasons for this position. For example, an agency that serves older persons may feel that measurements are not needed, that older persons perform poorly on tests, or that such instruments would create too much anxiety.

Suggested Readings

American Personnel and Guidance Association Policy Statement, "Responsibilities of Users of Standardized Tests." *Guidepost* 21, no. 5 (1978), pp. 5–8.

> An up-to-date, comprehensive, and clear statement for counselors on the use of measurements. Although it may be more suitable for the testing course, the statement has considerable value for use with this chapter.

American Psychological Association. *Standards for Educational and Psychological Tests.* Washington, D.C.: American Psychological Association, 1974.

> The major guide for technical aspects of tests and use of results. Pages 56–73, particularly "Interpretation of Scores" (pp. 68–73), are useful in the context of this chapter.

Association for Measurement and Evaluation in Guidance. "The Responsible Use of Tests: A Position Paper of AMEG, APGA, and NCME." *Measurement and Evaluation in Guidance* 5, no. 2 (1972), pp. 385–388.

> A statement by several concerned professional organizations on how to improve the use of tests and respond to increasing criticisms of testing.

Goldman, Leo. *Using Tests in Counseling.* 2nd ed. New York: Appleton-Century-Crofts, 1971.

> A comprehensive reference on the use of tests in counseling. Chapter 2, on the purposes of testing, is an excellent introduction to the subject.

Herr, Edwin L., and Cramer, Stanley H. *Career Guidance Through the Life Span.* Boston: Little, Brown, 1979.

> Chapter 14, while focusing on career guidance, covers principles and guidelines that are widely applicable. Detailed information on a number of tests and inventories is included. Particularly useful for a survey of the use of measurement in career guidance.

Miller, Frank W.; Fruehling, James A.; and Lewis, Gloria J. *Guidance Principles and Services.* 3rd ed. Columbus, Ohio: Charles E. Merrill, 1978.

> Chapter 8, on student appraisal services, contains extensive discussions of nontest procedures, tests and inventories, and school records. Particularly useful for the school counselor.

Miller, Theodore K., and Prince, Judith S. *The Future of Student Affairs.* San Francisco: Jossey-Bass, 1976.

> Chapter 3 describes the building of assessment procedures useful for the higher-education student development program. Various approaches for assessing student growth are described.

Pietrofesa, John J.; Bernstein, Bianca; Minor, Jo Anne; and Stanford, Susan. *Guidance: An Introduction.* Chicago: Rand McNally, 1980.

> Chapter 8, on the use of both test and nontest methods, is a recommended reading. The approach is completely different from that in this chapter, and it can be read with little or no duplication.

Shertzer, Bruce, and Stone, Shelley C. *Fundamentals of Guidance.* 4th ed. Boston: Houghton Mifflin, 1981.

> Chapters 9 and 10 cover tests and nontest appraisal methods. Comprehensive and timely, these sections provide valuable background to topics introduced in this chapter.

Stamm, Martin L., and Nissman, Blossom S. *Improving Middle School Guidance.* Boston: Allyn and Bacon, 1979.

   Chapter 7, on test and nontest procedures for pupil appraisal, covers principles, case examples, and nontest classroom activities to improve learning. An excellent reference for the middle school counselor.

Chapter

12

The Counseling Profession

A profession is a group of individuals who have common preparation, share many of the same attributes, and work toward agreed-upon goals. Membership provides benefits and entails responsibilities both for your individual work and for the profession. Anyone entering a profession should be fully aware of these benefits and responsibilities and begin to incorporate them in a career role. The growth, status, and benefits of the profession are largely functions of how individual members carry out responsibilities.

This chapter is about these benefits and responsibilities — what membership in the profession accords you and what responsibilities you are expected to assume. The right to practice, credentials for employment, status as a helping professional, membership in professional organizations, and contacts with others in similar work roles are important gains. Responsibilities include practice in accordance with ethical and legal standards, personal development, participation in organizations, sharing ideas and practices with colleagues, and accountability. These activities enhance the status of the profession, but responsibilities also include active participation in resolving issues and problems confronting the profession as a whole.

The major problems and issues discussed in this chapter center around credentialing. There are others, of course, such as communicating the counseling role to the public and building a support base in the community, but gaining the needed credentials for practice is the critical one. The crux of the issue is licensure. Without adequate provision for licensing, counselors will be denied many job opportunities. Their legal status will be weakened. Potential sources of income (e.g., payment by health insurance agencies) may be denied. The position of counselors vis-à-vis other helping professionals will be affected.

Counselors, therefore, have a responsibility to the profession to learn about and actively support efforts to secure appropriate credentialing. This chapter provides a background of information about issues and problems that will help you to participate effectively in activities to enhance the social, legal, and economic status of the profession.

The Meaning of a Profession

learn

The counselor needs to develop a sense of unique personal identity, and with it an awareness and appreciation of the meaning of a profession with all the specific guidelines, regulations, and policies that define the practice of the specialty. When one analyzes the definition of the term "professional," the importance of the aspects covered in this chapter is clear.

The major identifying characteristic of a profession is its knowledge base. Theory and research are organized to guide practice. Counseling, drawing on the disciplines of psychology, sociology, economics, and others, meets this criterion.

A second characteristic is a code of ethical practice. The counseling profession has for many years been concerned with ethical standards, and the American Personnel and Guidance Association has formulated a comprehensive and well-designed statement. It is up to the individual practitioner to observe standards voluntarily. Employers may use the APA and APGA's ethical standards as guidelines, but often look to the counselor when questions of improper conduct arise.

The control of preparation and practice are two further factors that help define a profession. Through establishing admissions standards for preparation programs and specifying what these programs should accomplish, the guidance profession does exercise some control. But the role of the profession is largely advisory; its recommendations have considerable influence but do not set the standards for all employers.

A fifth characteristic of professional identity is personal autonomy in the provision of service; the individual counselor exercises independent judgment, makes decisions, and provides help. Counselors may have considerable freedom in the way they practice their profession, but little control over allotment of time for specific activities. Even so, there is adequate autonomy for the counselor to utilize professional expertise.

A final professional characteristic involves the function of service to others. Counseling and guidance qualify as a profession by this criterion more fully than by any other. There is room for improvement in the applications of standards for preparation and practice; but professional status is justified in all crucial respects.

Preparation of Counselors

The American Personnel and Guidance Association through its Division, The Association for Counselor and Supervision, has done an impressive job over the years in formulating standards for the preparation of counselors and other personnel services specialists for all settings. The most recent statements cover entry-level preparation for counselors and personnel services specialists (ACES 1977) and advanced preparation for leadership positions (ACES 1978). The entry-level statement (see Appendix A) brings together existing statements in one unified and comprehensive report. It is significant enough to be included here as an appendix and is reviewed later in this section.

 ## Preparation Standards

The standards for entry programs provide for various models of preparation, which may include some undergraduate work. A minimum of one year of graduate study is essential, however. The advanced-level guidelines (for doctoral preparation) assume an entry-level program that meets the appropriate standards.

Preparation standards emphasize the commonalities of competencies needed in all settings, but also acknowledge the importance of unique goals that may exist for specific settings. Thus, it is suggested that those in special-interest areas prepare statements attending to those unique needs. A considerable amount of work along these lines has been done (e.g., a position paper on counselor preparation for career development and career education) (Hansen 1978). Others are mentioned later in this section.

The entry-level standards — the basic and comprehensive guidelines for all counselor preparation — include an introduction and four major sections. The introduction reflects many contemporary trends. First, it spells out the need for students to demonstrate competencies. Second, it assumes differential rates of student progress; some may take longer to acquire proficiency than others. Third, it considers various models that extend graduate preparation beyond a single year; one such program, for example, combines an undergraduate major in guidance with a year of graduate study.

The four major sections cover objectives; the program of studies and supervised experience; responsibilities concerning students in the program; and support for the counselor education program, administrative relations, and institutional resources.

The opening section, on objectives, sets the stage for the program. The major emphases are on explicit, cooperatively planned objectives evolving from input of those involved — counselor-educators, students, and practitioners. Objectives show sensitivity to needs, problems, and trends in schools and other settings; they are regularly revised and updated.

The program of studies calls for academic and practical work to enable students to move to increasing levels of competence and responsibility. There are opportunities for observation and involvement in guidance. Responsibility for working face to face with individuals and groups comes as competence is developed. Along with increasing competence in helping activities, the program fosters a spirit of inquiry, ethical sensitivity, and skill in self-evaluation. The practical-work component is given specific emphasis; in a one-year period, 60 hours should be spent in face-to-face individual or group work.

The third section deals with selection, retention, endorsement, and placement of students. It speaks to student rights, pointing out the need for making clear the criteria and procedures for admitting students, and retaining or separating them from the program. It also indicates the program's responsibility for endorsing and placing graduating students.

The final section covers institutional support for programs in guidance. Emphasis is on cooperative relationships with other college or university departments for courses, and with work settings for practical experience. It specifies a minimum full-time staff of three members and spells out the necessary professional qualifications for those working with students. These standards, which describe what the program should provide and define the professional competencies to be mastered, are of great significance to the beginning students.

Standards and Major Settings

The APGA standards require preparation to cover all settings of the profession; added emphasis on specialized work settings is to be provided through courses and practical work. For example, students preparing for elementary school counseling would concentrate particularly on courses and practical work designed for this educational level. Preparation for career guidance and participation in career education would feature added emphasis on these areas (Bradley 1973; Hoyt 1974, 1975a, 1975b). Moreover, a number of statements have been prepared (in addition to the career development position paper suggesting needed emphases. Herr (1980) gives a comprehensive list of competencies that the school counselor should acquire to participate in career education. In many programs the needed career development competencies are included in the regular counselor preparation program, but one department has established a separate track specifically for career development specialists (Reardon and Burck 1980).

Suggestions have been made for preparation emphases for the higher education and community counseling settings. Student development is the focus for counseling in the college and university (Pruitt 1979), with innovative preparation programs being organized to prepare practitioners who can handle the expanded range of functions that this model requires (Spooner 1979). Counselors in the community counseling area have been active in assessing the need for specific guidelines; most appear to feel that standards specifically for community agency counselors should be developed (Stadler and Stahl 1979). There is support for a preventive, system-change, proactive preparation model (Conyne 1980). Some work has been done by the American Mental Health Counselors Association in identifying specific competencies for community agency work.

It is highly desirable that each specialty establish preparation standards. Certification and accrediting guidelines (discussed later in this chapter) make this a critical task if graduates are to compete successfully in the job market.

In addition to settings-preparation standards, guidelines and recommendations have been suggested for work with special populations. Marriage and family counseling is an example. A program may be structured within the counselor education program in accordance with standards of the American Association for Marriage and Family Therapy, the official accrediting agency for this type of work (Piercy and Hovestadt 1980). Older persons are another example of a special population. An increasing number of programs provide courses in this area, although no specific set of standards is yet available (Sinick 1979). Emphases in practicums and internships can give the preparation the necessary focus (Fogelman 1979). Work with the handicapped is a third area. While standards for the preparation of rehabilitation counselors supplementing those of the American Personnel and Guidance Association have been developed (American Rehabilitation Counseling Association 1978, pp. 231–238) and modifications have been suggested to keep services in line with the needs and conditions of society (Ehrle 1979), all counselors have some responsibility for helping those with disabilities. While no formal preparation standards and guidelines have been prepared for the whole profession, a number of excellent proposals specifying needed competencies and preparation methods have been made available (Flugman, Goldman, and Katz 1979; Hosie 1979).

All that has been said about counselor preparation so far refers to graduate programs. Some institutions, however, offer an undergraduate major in guidance (Berg and Landreth 1980). Those graduating have obtained employment in helping positions in schools, community colleges, and community settings. Moreover, a number of program graduates have later entered graduate-level programs. Berg and Landreth point out that undergraduate preparation for guidance has important implications for the graduate program; students who have had the undergraduate courses may need additional or different experiences than those appropriate for the typical beginning student. The undergraduate major is a variation in preparation that opens up a new avenue for recruiting students for graduate-level study.

A major thrust of preparation programs is to provide extensive pre-service contacts with clients and settings. A particularly innovative approach to assuring realism is reported by Tolsma and Marks (1979). A counseling center, staffed by counseling students, was set up in a school to provide a full range of services to pupils, parents, and teachers. The students benefited from being in the work environment. Counselor education students not planning to enter school counseling were able to spend part of their time in other settings and to serve clients referred by other agencies. This approach not only helps students develop skills and competencies for counseling, consulting, and programming but also prepares them to move smoothly into a full-time counseling position; the break between preparation and work should be easily bridged.

Standards and Competency Areas

Current standards are oriented to competency, as are several contemporary preparation models. The system-based approach (Zifferblatt 1972) and HRD (Human Resources Development) (Carkhuff 1972), for example, emphasize specific competencies, systematic means of achieving them, and evaluation in terms of counselor effect on counselees. The ACES standards (Appendix A) emphasize that programs are to be evaluated in terms of competencies of each student. Such competencies would be illustrated by specific items such as supervised practice in working with groups. Zifferblatt discusses the systems approach, in which specific skills are learned (e.g., nonverbal communication), and students are recycled until they reach an acceptable level of competency (1972, p. 15). Another illustration exemplifies specific and measurable characteristics of many competency approaches in terms of the student's growing self-awareness:

> Given two hours with a group of fellow trainees, the trainee must be able to make five self-observation responses, the validity of which can be confirmed by a majority of group members. (Bernstein and LeComte 1976, p. 32)

It is clear that preparation standards for counselors in all settings emphasize competencies (see Appendix A). In the "Introduction" to the standards, this point is made in the following statement, taken from Appendix A, page 363: "The trend toward the development of competency based/performance based counselor education programs is likely to continue. However, whether or not a counselor education program is developed upon such a base, the standards reflect the concern that programs should give to the assessment of demonstrated competencies by students during various stages of their development."

A recent indication of the emphasis on competencies is the bulletin, *The Professional Counselor: Competencies, Performance Guidelines, and Assessment* (Dameron 1980). The contents of the manual illustrate the areas of competency the counselor should master (compare with Appendix A). Areas are:

learn

1. Personality characteristics of professional counselors (e.g., empathy, open-mindedness
2. Counseling competencies
   a. individual counseling
   b. school counseling (items specifically related to the school setting)
   c. playing therapy and family counseling
   d. group counseling
3. Consultation competencies
4. Coordination competencies
5. Career development competencies
6. Planning and development competencies
7. Measurement and evaluation competencies
8. Research competencies
9. Placement and follow-up competencies
10. Referral competencies

Each of these competency areas is stated in the form of a goal. The general goal is then put into competency statements. Performance guidelines are also given along with a rating scale. Table 12–1 illustrates the format. The competencies and guidelines provide an illustration of items in one type of competency-based program guide. The emphasis is on *competency* rather than on specific behavioral objectives.

The development of standards for preparation has provided assistance to departments that wish to improve the quality of their programs and has contributed to the accrediting process for counselor education programs. Until recently accreditation was done as part of the process of accrediting colleges of education by the National Council for Accreditation in Teacher Education (NCATE). The focus of this accreditation is on the preparation of school counselors, but a broader approach is needed because increasing numbers of students are preparing for other settings. This need is being met by the work of the Association for Counselor Education and Supervision (ACES). This division of the American Personnel and Guidance Association (APGA) has carried out a number of accrediting evaluations ("Four Schools Eyed by ACES Accreditation" 1980) (Stahl and Havens 1978). The preparation standards already described have been used. Quite recently, the APGA has taken steps to set up an accrediting

Table 12-1
COUNSELING COMPETENCIES

GOAL STATEMENT: The professional counselor develops and maintains effective counseling skills that help clients grow toward personal goals and strengthen their capacity to cope with life situations.

INDIVIDUAL COUNSELING

COMPETENCIES — The counselor is a skilled professional who is able to:	PERFORMANCE GUIDELINES — The professional counselor provides evidence of competence by demonstrating the ability to:		ASSESSMENT — Low Average High						
			1	2	3	4	5	NO	NE
1. Understand the basic principles of human growth, development, and learning and how they facilitate the learning and counseling process.	1.1 Understand and communicate with clients of different age levels and social maturity.	1.1							
	1.2 Use personal and unique data about clients to assess behavior.	1.2							
	1.3 Use environmental factors to determine content, procedures, and goals of counseling.	1.3							
2. Demonstrate a clear and concise understanding of the various counseling theories, techniques, and procedures.	2.1 Specify the basic assumptions and view of human nature associated with each of the major theories of counseling.	2.1							
	2.2 Explain the psychological and developmental stages of individual growth as postulated in the major theories of counseling.	2.2							

NO = No opportunity to assess
NE = Not essential for assessment

Source: Joseph D. Dameron, ed., *The Professional Counselor: Competencies, Performance Guidelines, and Assessment* (1980), p. 13, copyright, American Personnel and Guidance Association. Reprinted with permission.

procedure that meets the needs of the current situation in counselor education (Steele 1980). The process is complicated by the fact that a number of the counseling specialties mentioned earlier have their own accrediting agencies. In spite of these difficulties, however, accrediting of programs is important and will be expanded. One reason for this expansion is the close tie between preparation and licensure (Stahl and Havens 1978), which is emerging as a primary concern of our profession as it attempts to establish itself in the competitive mental health field.

Legal Status, Certification, and Licensing

These areas are among the most controversial and ambiguous in the counseling profession; they are of major concern to anyone planning to enter the field. Potential legal problems revolve around malpractice, right to privacy, serving as defendant in criminal action, encouraging an illegal act, or involvement in civil disobedience (Burgum and Anderson 1975). Certification poses fewer potential problems. Your program will probably meet requirements, but you should know not only the standards in your own state (which you will have the responsibility of meeting) but also those of any other state you may wish to move to. Licensure is of recent concern. Previously it was critical only for counselors in some nonschool settings, but it is now emerging as an issue for school counselors, too. Currently the employees of an educational institution are given sanctions to practice by virtue of their employment status; the institution authorizes their activity and assumes responsibility for performance. This may not be true in the future.

Recently there has been increased interest in a registry system for counselors. Such a system would provide both the public and employers of a national nature with a list of individuals who have been adjudged as competent practitioners by a duly authorized board ("Credentialing: Registry Questions Are Probed 1980) (Forster 1978). The system would take into account the variations in competencies needed in different settings and specialties and would be of substantial assistance in identifying who is qualified to fill a specific position or render a particular type of service. The two specialties that currently have a nation-wide registry are rehabilitation and mental health counselors. The rehabilitation counselors' registry, the Commission on Rehabilitation Counselor Certification, is the oldest and lists more than 10,000 individuals. The more recent registry, the National Academy of Certified Clinical Mental Health Counselors, published its first list in 1979 ("Credentialing: Registry Questions Are Probed" 1980). A registry for counselors would be a very important step for the profession and one that could provide substantial benefits to members.

Legal Status

An understanding of legal factors is essential both for day-to-day practice in conventional types of service and for anticipating problems that may arise with changing conditions. For example, a counselor may feel existing laws and regulations are harmful and ought to be challenged but must know the consequences of disregarding them and share this information with others who might need to know, particularly students. The processes one chooses to bring about changes are to some extent a function of one's political conviction (Drapela 1974; Adams 1973). Counselors are entitled to their own views, but there are harsh realities to consider when changes involve committing illegal acts.

Counseling today has no specific legal status. It has only recently come to be recognized as a formal part of school programs. Few court cases have dealt directly with school counseling, and even fewer statutes specify legal obligations and responsibilities. The status of counselors must be clarified in light of the few existing cases and statutes, and on the application of the law to people in general. Enough data are available to spell out some guidelines and to alert counselors to their responsibilities and limitations (Burgum and Anderson 1975, p. 7).

Increasing professionalization has generated rising concern about legal issues. Counseling today amounts to a service of therapeutic intervention in the counselees' lives. With the responsibility this implies, it is sometimes uncertain just how the counselor can offer most help to the counselee without violating civil and criminal law. As Burgum and Anderson point out, counselors have no general immunity from criminal law and are subject to civil law. Moreover, while statutes give some general guidelines, state and local laws vary enormously (Burgum and Anderson 1975, pp. 7, 12).

These are some of the questions a practicing counselor might encounter on a perfectly routine day: Can I assure the counselee of confidentiality? How about in group work? Can I be held liable for malpractice? Am I likely to become involved in a civil suit for carrying out my assigned responsibilities? Are there counseling activities that might lead to criminal charges?

Confidentiality and Civil Liability

Questions about confidentiality are the most frequent of all. Can counselors assure counselees of confidentiality? Except in a state that has privileged-communication statutes, the answer is no. Some states do have such statutes (Litwack 1975), but policies are hedged with restrictions. There is no general privileged communication for counselors, although Burgum and Anderson suggest the federal courts could extend it to them through interpretations of rules of evidence (1975, pp. 17–20).

Counselors should understand legal guidelines such as those that apply to civil liability and confidentiality

Regardless of national statutes, however, state and local precedents should be examined before assuring counselees of confidentiality. When the counselor has determined these legal limits, they should be explained to the counselee. In general, these principles are helpful (Nasman 1977, pp. 20–21):

1. If the counselee is a clear danger to self or others, the counselor cannot maintain confidentiality. Steps should be taken to protect others if they are in danger.
2. Generally the counselor respects the rights of others to confidentiality.
3. If a counselee is the victim of a crime, there is no privileged communication.
4. School counselors in most states do not have privileged communication. Where they do, laws may cover only certain types of information. (See Nasman 1977, pp. 53–80, for a summary of state laws and a model bill.)
5. For school use the term "privileged communication" can be defined as information shared with the counselor by the counselee,

which the counselor cannot release without the approval of the counselee.

6. An individual may subpoena personal case material in college files for use in other actions. In the Bates College case, for example (*Creel* v. *Brenann* 1968; Ware 1971), the court upheld the plaintiff's request to view information he thought was hampering his admission to other colleges. The more recent Buckley Amendment deals more completely with the question of access to records.

The counselor must also be concerned with the right to talk to others about the counselee without danger of legal action for libel and slander (Burgum and Anderson 1975, pp. 76–77). Usually if the counselor makes comments about pupils, sends reports to parents, and the like, believing the reports to be true, acting without malicious intent, and communicating only with individuals entitled to such information, legal action for libel and slander would not be successful.

Civil liability was an issue infrequently raised in past years, but it is a problem causing concern today. There is no sure way to judge what could be construed as counselor malpractice. If, however, the counselor follows the ethics and standards of the profession, malpractice liability would likely not be incurred, even if counseling has not been successful. A key requirement is that the counselor makes a referral when a problem becomes too difficult to handle. Group counseling involves the same responsibility, except that the probability of malpractice increases — there are more counselees to observe and understand. Some problems are more likely than others to raise the civil liability issue, particularly those involving sexual relations and abortion (a counselor who dispensed oral contraceptives, for example, would be guilty of practicing medicine without a license). According to Burgum and Anderson (1975, pp. 27–35), advice about abortions, including possible medical and psychological complications, are beyond the counselor's competency. Even so, counselors must deal with these problems every day.

The case of *Bogust* v. *Iverson* (Burgum and Anderson 1975, pp. 29–31) illustrates the extent of the counselor's liability. A counselor in Wisconsin worked with a girl, Jane Dunn, on career, educational, and personal problems for a period of six months. When he felt that she had made all the progress she could, he terminated the case. Six months later, she committed suicide. Her parents sued the counselor, but the court ruled that he was not liable for failure to inform parents of her condition, and in fact, his training did not make him competent to make a judgment about danger to herself. The six-month interval also weighed against placing liability on the counselor. If the counselee had become emotionally very upset at the termination of counseling, very likely the counselor would have been held liable.

Criminal Liability

With respect to libel, slander, and other areas of possible civil liability, the counselor has no special privilege. It is true that the counselor can talk or write about a counselee to those who are entitled to the information (e.g., parents, teachers, prospective employers) without liability for legal action. But giving information to those who are not entitled to it, or doing so with harmful intentions, could result in a defamation suit. The same principles apply to student records; the safest course of action is to include only factual information. Unverified damaging information may make one liable for a civil suit (Burgum and Anderson 1975, pp. 78–80, 85–87). Since parents can examine records, control release of information, and challenge the contents (Burcky and Childers 1976; Wilhelm and Case 1975; Worzbyt 1976), civil liability can easily be incurred. Professionally, though not legally, it is the counselor's responsibility to make sure that all school personnel understand the meaning and use of data (Worzbyt 1976).

Although it is unlikely, a counselor can, with the best of intentions, become a defendant in a criminal case. Burgum and Anderson list four possible types of charges (1975, p. 88):

- Accessory to a crime after the face.
- Encouraging an illegal abortion.
- Coconspirator in civil disobedience
- Contributing to the delinquency of a minor.

Reading their discussions of each of these situations (1975, pp. 69–70, 105, 113–115) will add depth to your understanding of guidelines for practice.

Burgum and Anderson also describe an illustrative case relating to criminal liability (1975, pp. 94–99) in which the school counselor, who had developed a good relationship with a boy in the custody of the juvenile court, inadvertently helped him avoid arrest. The boy, with two companions, robbed a service station and then, realizing the gravity of his actions, went to the counselor for help. The counselor convinced the boy that he should turn himself in, but it was late at night, and they agreed he would go to the police the following day. Meanwhile, however, the counselor committed a series of acts that could make him guilty of being an accessory to a felony. He denied to police that the boy was in his house. He gave the boy money, which was found in the youth's possession when he tried to skip town the next morning rather than reporting to the police. The counselor would have been well advised to report the matter to the boy's juvenile office, which would have been in his favor in a trial.

Another area of local concern to the counselor relates to the rights of pupils. The Gault case (Nasman 1977, pp. 8–10) brought about full guarantees of due process for minors. Counselors can help pupils by making them aware of their legal right to due process in education, free speech, and property ownership. Rights of the handicapped are emphasized by due process provisions of PL 94-142. As Nasman points out (1977, pp. 9–11), due process is not satisfied by establishing a standard procedure including such steps as informing the individual of charges and providing for a hearing, but rather it demands protection of pupils' rights under the Constitution, just as if they were adults involved in legal charges. Due process should fit the situation and protect the pupil from arbitrary, unfair, and autocratic rules and policies.

The Buckley Amendment, already mentioned, deserves special attention. This law restricts the use of information in personal records; enforcement involves the denial of federal funds if violations are allowed to occur (Nasman 1977, pp. 22–31). In the past, school records were not treated with respect for the individual's rights of privacy, nor have parents and pupils had access to most of the information contained in them (Russell Sage 1970). The Buckley Amendment (Burcky and Childers 1976) has given parents and pupils of legal age the right to inspect records, including letters, comments, and recommendations. (It is not a violation, however, to maintain a file of personal notes that does not fall under the access regulations of this law.) Besides opening up records to pupils and parents, the law restricts access of others to these data. In general, parents must give consent for information in records to be released. Nasman discusses the regulations in detail (1977, pp. 22–31). The complete law appears in the *APGA Ethical Standards Casebook* (Callis 1976, pp. 93–109).

Parts of the Buckley Amendment (the Family Rights and Privacy Act of 1974 and the Buckley Amendments to the Act) with specific applicability to counselors' use of student records are as follows:

> Each educational agency or institution except as may be provided by 99.12 [confidential information placed in the record prior to January 1, 1975] shall permit the parent of a student or an eligible student [usually 18 years of age] who is or has been in attendance at the agency or institution, to inspect and review the education records of the student.
>
> The parent of a student or an eligible student who believes the information contained in the education record of the student is inaccurate or misleading or violates the privacy or other rights of the student may request that the educational agency or institution which maintains the records amend them.

The legal status of counseling is being established through new laws, statutes, and court decisions. Relatively few cases directly affecting counseling have gone through the courts, but more can be expected as counseling achieves greater status and visibility as a helping service.

Certification

All states regulate the practice of school counseling through some type of certification. Certification is provided for rehabilitation counselors as an outgrowth of efforts by the American Rehabilitation Counseling Association (ARCA) and the National Rehabilitation Counseling Association (NRCA) (McAlees 1980, pp. 80–81). Similarly, a national system of certification is available for professional counselors from the American Mental Health Counselors Association (Messina 1980, pp. 103–104).

Program accreditation is related to certification of individuals; it gives students an important indication of the quality of a program (Dickey 1968) and enhances job-getting potential. Accreditation, however, is a program evaluation process and thus is quite different from the credentialing of individuals.

Licensure

This topic is relatively new for counselors, although psychologists have been active in formulating state licensure policies for at least two decades (Sweeney and Sturdevant 1974). School counselors have been concerned with certification and have only recently become aware of the potential importance for their work of developments in licensure (Cottingham 1975).

There are important differences between certification and licensure. Each provides a service to the users of counseling by indicating the adequacy of practitioners. Certification laws regulate the use of the title "counselor" and specify the amount and type of training required for practice. Licensing goes beyond regulating the use of the title and indicates the unique services and practices that fall in the domain of the profession (Sweeney and Sturdevant 1974a; Cottingham and Swanson 1976). The term "credentials" is often confused with certification. "Credentials" refers to the degree or other certificate the individual has been awarded; the term is also used to indicate competence for a job (e.g., an individual certified as a counselor has the "credentials" for the work).

Up to now, licensure has been a concern of counselors in community settings such as mental health agencies and private practice. But recent licensure laws have alerted counselors to the potential for state regulation of some or all of their work. In Ohio, for example, licensing laws on the practice of psychology have been interpreted to limit the use of tests by a counselor in off-duty hours. In the case, *City of Cleveland* v. *Cook* 1975, a counselor who was not a licensed psychologist was arrested for testing (the use of psychological tools). The court found in favor of the counselor defendant; Ohio counselors are contesting this interpretation of the law. The APGA Model Licensing Law specifies the points favored by the counseling profession "Licensure Committee Action Packet" 1979, pp. 22–29).

Both the American Psychological Association and the American Personnel and Guidance Association are actively promoting licensing laws. If counselors do not establish their own licensing criteria and procedures, others will do it for them. The American Personnel and Guidance Association aims to insure that counselors are represented on licensing boards and that licensing requirements are designed for counselors (Licensure Committee Action Packet: 1979, pp. 3–15).

The matter of third-party payments is an important one for counselors. For example, counselors performing a needed professional service to the individual should be able to receive payment from independent health-care providers. If counselors do not qualify for such payments, a large area of service is blocked out. As Asher (1980, pp. 134–135) points out, while many counselors have been employed in federally subsidized community mental health centers, if these and similar-type services eventually have to depend on health-insurer funds, counselors will not be employable, since they do not qualify for third-party payments. This has already happened in private agencies and institutions — counselors have been discharged. The Virginia counselors' licensure law, one of the few that has been passed, does not provide for these third-party payments.

Effective and well-designed licensure laws can enhance the counseling profession, protect the public, and open up new work opportunities; restrictive and unfair ones will interfere with the contributions of many potentially well qualified to offer others assistance. Sweeney and Sturdevant (1974a) and Cottingham (1975) recommend that counselors keep up with what is happening in licensure and support favorable alternatives. Their advice points out a responsibility of all members of the profession.

Ethics

As noted earlier, one mark of a profession is a code of ethics. It serves as a guide for providing services and enhances legality in carrying out these services. The counseling profession has a comprehensive, well-developed code, as well as special guidelines for work in schools.

Counselors have two major ethical statements and several other aids to use as guides. The first, "Ethical Standards" (APGA 1974) of the American Personnel and Guidance Association, is the result of several revisions of the first statement published in 1961 and is designed for counselors in any setting. A code of ethics for mental health counselors is also available (American Mental Health Counselors Association 1980–81, pp. 1, 3–4). The American Psychological Association's ethical standards (APA 1979) are useful as supplementary reading to help develop a broad perspective. Three casebooks, one by the American Personnel and Guidance Association (Callis 1976), a second by Stude and Goodyear (1975), and a third by the American Psychological Association (APA 1967) give examples of ethical problems and recommend solutions. Another publication of the American Psychological Association, *Ethical Principles in the Conduct of Research with Human Participants* (1973), is a standard reference for designing research studies.

The 1974 APGA ethical standards in Appendix includes a "Preamble" and six major sections: general; counselor-counselee relationships; measurement and evaluation; research and publication; consulting and private practice; and personnel administration. Each section gives general principles that apply to any situation the counselor may face.

The "Preamble" sets the stage for the areas that follow. The focus of the profession is on services to enhance the worth, dignity, potential, and uniqueness of each individual. The association thus serves the total society. The "Preamble" also recognizes that counselors practice in a variety of settings and that ethical standards must cover all settings.

"Section A: General," points out a number of guides for professional practice. All are of vital concern for counselors. The importance of continued professional growth and self-evaluation of effectiveness is one. Another particularly significant concern relates to employer relations. The counselor has a responsibility to the employing agency or institution as well as to the counselee. If the counselor's own professional principles are at variance with the employer's policies, he or she has the responsibility to seek a solution in line with ethical standards. Failing this, the counselor must seriously consider the advisability of terminating employment. A reading of the section is recommended at this time.

"Section B: Counseling-Relationship," deals with the most important aspect of the counselor's professional responsibility. The counselor's overriding concern is with the welfare of the counselee, including initiating, continuing, and ending the helping relationship. The guidelines for handling situations where there are clear indications of danger to the counselee or others are of particular importance for crisis situations. It would be well to go over these principles carefully at this time.

The main points of the section on measurement and evaluation are that the counselor should understand tests, be particularly cautious about their applicability for minority groups, and present or interpret results in keeping with test validity. The section on ethical standards for research and publishing identifies the welfare of the individual as the primary factor to be considered; the counselor should make every effort to avoid harmful effects of research and should take action to reduce or eliminate such effects if they occur.

The section on consulting and private practice deals more with the activities of the private consultant, although much of the counselor's work with teachers, administrators, and parents would be based on consultation principles. The section on personnel administration covers organizational and administrative responsibilities in the school counselor's work setting, particularly the need to establish mutually agreed-upon goals with administration for major aspects of the job (e.g., counseling relationships, confidentiality, work load, and accountability).

The final section deals with preparation standards and their importance to the beginning student.

The experiences at the end of this chapter are presented for discussion and solutions. Additional examples may be drawn from personal experience and from the casebooks already listed.

Organizations

Professional organizations provide counselors with support, facilitate professional development, bring together colleagues with similar interests, offer opportunities for active participation in leadership roles, and provide placement services. Counselors can help themselves by building a strong organization. Representatives of the profession are active at national, state, and local levels to promote favorable legislation and to obtain funds for improved services.

Participation can begin during preservice preparation. The American Personnel and Guidance Association, a federation of thirteen divisions, is the most important and best-known organization for counselors. The APGA offers student memberships at reduced rates, and students can attend APGA national conventions and take part in programs. (A history of the APGA appears in Chapter 5.)

Some divisions are particularly relevant for specific settings, while others cut across setting boundaries. In the first category, the American College Personnel Association (ACPA) emphasizes student personnel work and college-level counseling. The American School Counselor Association (ASCA) covers elementary, middle/junior, and senior high school counselors. The American Rehabilitation Counseling Association (ARCA) is made up primarily of those who work with the handicapped. Employment agency counselors are included in the National Employment Counselors Association (NECA). The Public Offender Counselor Association (POCA) is of particular interest to those working in penal institutions and other branches of the law enforcement system. The American Mental Health Counselors Association (AMHCA) includes among its members counselors working in community mental health agencies and other community settings. Those who are instructors in counselor education programs join the Association for Counselor Education and Supervision (ACES).

In addition, there are six divisions concerned with special populations or areas of interest. These are:

- National Vocational Guidance Association (NVGA).
- Association for Humanistic Education and Development (AHEAD).
- Association for Measurement and Evaluation in Guidance (AMEG).
- Association for Nonwhite Concerns in Personnel and Guidance (ANWC).
- Association for Religious and Value Issues in Counseling (ARVIC).
- Association for Specialists in Group Work (ASGW).

Descriptions of APGA divisions and major publications are contained in Appendix C. In addition, state branches of APGA provide opportunities for participation at state and local levels and regularly publish newsletters and other useful information.

Many useful materials are available from APGA. Program abstracts, published at the time of the national convention, give summaries of presentations. Educational aids ranging from brochures, reprint series, and books, to cassettes and films may be obtained at reasonable cost.

Students and counselors alike can participate in APGA by contributing to its many professional journals. Editors urge members who have something to say to submit material for publication (Carroll 1975; Sue 1975a). Journal staff members give helpful and detailed advice on how to prepare articles for publication, explain common faults that result in rejections, and describe the step-by-step process of editing and publishing a professional journal (Wall 1974; Alexander and Wall 1975). Articles that pass the editor are given blind reviews (i.e., the author's name is removed), and evaluators' comments are passed on to the author. At regular intervals each journal prints guidelines for authors specifying length, format, number of copies of manuscripts to be submitted, and other such basic information.

International Aspects

Learning about guidance in other countries can provide valuable concepts for counselors in the United States and help develop a new perspective on what we do (Goldman 1974). Bingham (1976) notes the tendency of American counselors to be uninformed about work in other countries. Comparative guidance as an area of study has gained only moderate visibility (Drapela 1975), although it offers the opportunity to broaden one's understanding of cultural diversity and can suggest new ideas and insights.

Counseling Emphases in Western Europe

To provide some flavor of the experience of studying guidance in other countries, the following paragraphs present some of my impressions of how foreign counseling services differ from ours. These observations do not apply to all countries, but mainly to the industrialized nations of Western Europe. (For a detailed report on helping services in the so-called developing and underdeveloped countries, see Drapela, *Guidance and Counseling Around the World* [1979] and issues of the *International Journal for the Advancement of Counseling*.)

Helping services tended to develop outside schools and to be more focused on transition periods in life. For example, considerable efforts are directed to the transition from high school to work. Services appear to have been an outgrowth of generally accepted needs in specific life periods. There are signs of emerging school-based programs, but these have followed out-of-program development.

Along with this general program development thrust, there has been more emphasis on manpower needs than is typical in this country. To some extent, this emphasis is a result of close working relationships among educational institutions, employers, and the community. This is not to say that counselors do only placement work, but there is an awareness of career opportunities that exist. Concern with economic resources appears to be one causitive factor. Moreover, when crisis unemployment problems arise, resources are concentrated on those problems. The feeling seems to be that the most efficient use of human resources is an imperative both for the individual and for the society. Along with this manpower emphasis there are sometimes specific jobs or percentages of jobs set aside for the handicapped, probably because of the large number of disabled persons the two world wars produced.

Parents appear to play a generally larger role than in the United States in assistance for school-age youth when counselors and schools are involved. In some cases, the parents make decisions for pupils; in others, parents are included in conferences, though the pupil's decisions are given some weight. In still others, school personnel make the decisions about the pupil's program. Parents, however, tend to be more influential than in this country, regardless of the power of schools and counselors.

Lifelong education and/or training is given considerable emphasis, with provisions for job leaves for additional study. Counseling services do not appear to be an integral part of these programs, but they are available in the community if needed.

The school and the home play major guidance roles in the lives of young people. Parents often make decisions about school programs of their children, or at least have a significant part to play in the choice process. In some countries all teachers serve as advisers and helpers in pupils' development processes — they provide what in England is called pastoral care.

Finally, counselors in other countries do not appear to build up high expectations for the mitigation of social, personal, occupational, or educational ills and problems. My impression is that the public's expectations are more realistic than they are in the United States, and thus there is less disillusionment when negative conditions are not alleviated. Consequently, programs are not discarded as quickly as they are in the United States.

The above observations are impressions I gained from reading about and observing programs in other countries. While each characteristic must be considered in light of social, economic, and political conditions of the particular country, a knowledge of the way other countries provide helping services gives us a new perspective on what we are doing and how practices may be improved.

Value of Learning about Counseling Abroad

Interest in international guidance has fluctuated over the years. One highlight was the appearance of Keller and Vitales' classic, *Vocational Guidance Throughout the World*, in 1937. Today we are witnessing a definite rise in concern about what others think of our practices and what colleagues in foreign countries are doing. The APGA International Education Committee has gained organizational support and publishes a regular newsletter. An organization of field representatives in this country and abroad has been set up by the committee to collect material about foreign programs and personalities, and to arrange tours. A textbook on guidance in other countries is in use in comparative guidance courses in several institutions (Drapela 1977). More recently, a landmark publication, *Guidance and Counseling Around the World*, has been edited by Drapela (1979).

We can gain valuable insights about ourselves by seeing our work through the eyes of foreign visitors (Goldman 1974). We are not particularly noted, at present, for our interest in the work of our foreign colleagues (Christie 1974), and are widely thought to be picking easy tasks that will show favorable results for purposes of accountability (Deen 1974). The need for various types of groups appears to some foreign observers to reflect the effects of a materialistic society (R. Harris 1974). We are criticized for our overenthusiasm for what is new and for anti-intellectualism (Ziv 1974). Watts's analysis (1973), containing his reactions after an extended stay in this country, points to the excessive amount of time given over to administrative tasks, principal concern for able and middle-class pupils, and an extremely therapeutically oriented approach. While not always complimentary, these perceptions help clarify our own thinking.

Despite a rather casual interest in what others in the profession are doing around the world, there have been a substantial number of programs at APGA conventions on guidance in such other parts of the world as the Middle East, the Philippines, and the Netherlands (Patouillet, Drapela, and Karayanni 1975; Ravelo 1975; Deen 1974). Wrenn's study (1976) of changing values in sixteen countries reveals that counseling changes in relation to changes in values and that, conditions permitting, counseling tends to become more humane. An analysis of career guidance in eight countries describes a number of models that have implications for domestic programs in such areas as community information and counseling services, relations with parents in occupational planning, and emphasis on flexible training programs (Tolbert 1976). A new journal, the *International Journal for the Advancement of Counselling*, was first published in 1978. Its aim is to promote an exchange of counseling information throughout the world. A recent issue included, among others, an article on a world view of rehabilitation counseling, educational and vocational guidance in Venezuela, and counseling in British schools. Articles also include reports on international conferences, studies of new strategies and techniques, and methods to stimulate guidance in developing countries.

Learning about guidance in other countries and getting involved in exchange of information is becoming easier. Besides the publications already mentioned, which give some background, foreign journals like the Canadian *School Guidance Worker* and the *British Journal of Guidance and Counselling* describe programs and practices. Recently the Canadian journal published a review of guidance in other countries. The International Association of Vocational and Educational Guidance holds biennial meetings and can provide addresses of persons in other countries to visit or correspond with (U.S. National Correspondent, IAEVG, 70 Frost Avenue, East Brunswick, N.J. 08816). The International Round Table for the Advancement of Counseling also brings together counselors from all over the world for biennial meetings (Livingston House, Livingston Road, London, E152LL).

APGA is active in building international communication. There is a Committee for International Education and a regular newsletter on activities, research, and foreign programs. The International Association of Counseling Services is an APGA affiliate.

The Counselor and Professional Development

In a provocative and insightful statement Walz and Benjamin (1978, p. 422) use the analogy of automobile racing to emphasize the importance of continuing professional development. In a race limited to 25 competitors, the 25th qualifier is described as "on the bubble" that is (likely to be bumped from the competition if a better qualifying time is posted). Counselors, they suggest, are "on the bubble." The strategy they suggest to compete successfully is renewal — to update knowledge and skills, to learn new approaches, and to develop new attitudes.

Renewal is the essence of continued professional development. The counselor's growth and development begins with a challenging preservice program that gives the prospective counselor a solid foundation in theory, techniques, organizational and programming skills, history, legal guidelines, and ethical standards. This is an important phase, but activities are highly structured. While the individual can do much on his or her own to enhance the preservice experience (e.g., by participation in meetings and workshops and by writing), the real test of self-motivated development comes after graduation.

The need for renewal is vividly apparent in day-to-day work. Walz and Benjamin (1978, pp. 423–425) identify four critical factors: (1) job survival, (2) ability to cope with increased role complexity, (3) ability to deal effectively with accountability, and (4) ability to be sensitive to social change. In our contemporary society, with its rapidly changing social and economic patterns, renewal is essential for professional credibility and survival (Dickinson 1978, p. 1).

Renewal programs may be on an individual basis or implemented in planned group activities. The key factor is a recognition that updating and/or new competencies are needed. One precipitating factor may be the sensing of the conditions identifying the beginnings of "burnout" (confusion about mission and role, lack of involvement with clients and colleagues) (Boy and Pine 1980; Romero and Pinkney 1980). Dickinson (1978, pp. 4–6) emphasizes the importance of making renewal a group activity involving systematic offerings for the institution or agency staff. Whatever structure is used, goals and evaluation are essential components.

My suggestions for continuing professional development, somewhat similar to the concept of renewal, include active participation in professional organizations, research, and writing. There is a wide enough range of activities in these areas to accommodate practically any style of involvement. The addition of planned renewal to meet specific needs provides a strategy to enable the counselor to accomplish the developmental goals that Boy and Pine (1980) identify (e.g., develop a sense of organizational involvement).

There are of course barriers to renewal and development. Any counselor can compile a list rather easily, but the comprehensive discussions in Dickinson (1978, pp. 7–16) and Walz and Benjamin (1978, pp. 440–448) are invaluable for bringing these barriers to awareness and finding ways to deal with them. For example, there is what Walz and Benjamin (1978, p. 448) call the "no-time" syndrome. One answer is that the organization should provide release time for renewal involvements.

Suggestions for, and examples of, renewal programs provide excellent guidelines for initiating the process in any setting. Dickinson's (1978) manual is a useful guide, covering all the essential steps and providing a wealth of useful forms. Both he and Walz and Benjamin describe operating programs that show what can be done. One particularly innovative plan is the Counseling and Personnel Services Clearinghouse "Counselor Renewal System" (CRS). The program covers many areas of major concern to counselors (e.g., change agentry, legal concerns, public relations) and is designed for use by an individual, by a trainer-facilitated group, or by self-led groups (Walz and Benjamin 1978, pp. 430–432).

An area of professional development that is becoming even more critical than in past years is what might be called the public relations, political action role. There is an element of renewal and increased professional identity derived from the endeavor of conveying to the public what counseling is and what it accomplishes. It is only one step further to put the information in a form that will have an impact on budgetmakers, legislators, and government agencies. Counselors need to keep up with legislation having an effect on counseling both to know what assistance it can provide and to be effective in influencing future legislative actions (Bagby 1978).

Continuing professional development is a multidimensional process involving participation in meetings, research, writing, actions to enhance the status and support base of the profession, and needs-based renewal. These are not separate processes; rather, they are an interrelated series of activities that help the counselor maintain a positive attitude and build an increasingly competent style in day-to-day work.

Summary Concepts

Counselors in whatever setting — school, college, community agency — share professional concerns. Each individual gains from the profession, and each also has obligations to it. The content and purpose of preparation standards should be understood; awareness is particularly important for the person beginning the counselor education program. Detailed standards are now available for entry-level programs; these standards serve as a guide for program building, evaluation, and accreditation. Accreditation is being carried out both by ACES and NCATE; the future will undoubtedly witness an expansion of the process. Students need to be aware of the accreditation status of their program. Counseling specialists should develop preparation standards. In several specialties, such as rehabilitation and mental health counseling, standards have been prepared and are being used in program accreditation. The legal and ethical guidelines for the profession make up a third area of concern. Ethical standards serve as a guide for day-to-day work. The counselor's legal position is enhanced if he or she has observed the profession's ethics, but the legal status of many aspects of practice, such as confidentiality, have not been established universally. It is incumbent on all counselors to be familiar with local, state, and national legal decisions and guidelines that affect their work.

A fourth area of concern involves credentialing — certification and licensure. Both processes currently have significant implications for employment and practice and may be expected to have an increasing impact in the future. Registry provides a means of acquainting the public with a listing of qualified professionals. A fifth area involves organizations; they exist for nearly all counseling specialties. Participation can begin during the preservice preparation program.

Two additional areas are worthy of concern but often do not attain the visibility of those already identified. One is professional development. It is becoming more and more apparent that keeping up with current developments, particularly through *renewal,* and communicating the effects of counseling to others are essential responsibilities for all counselors. It is also apparent, though to a much lesser degree, that counselors can profit from learning about the work of colleagues in other countries. An exchange of concepts and practices helps in identifying useful new approaches; in addition, counselors can gain a better understanding of their own approaches by comparing them with what others do in different social, cultural, political, and economic settings

Experiential Activities

Of the topics covered in this chapter, ethical and legal issues and problems provide the best opportunities for experiential treatment. One approach is to ask counselors in various settings about the ethical and legal problems they have faced and how they have handled these problems. It is also helpful to find out what bases they used for their decisions. As a final step, the decisions and choice of bases can be evaluated in terms of the material covered in this chapter and Appendix B, "Ethical Standards."

The second type of experiential activities uses selected ethical and legal problems found in various publications. The following are examples:

1. Applying Ethical Standards

Either individually or in small groups, evaluate the actions of the counselor with a plus if in accord with ethical principles and a minus if contrary to them.

Identify the ethical principle involved, using the standards in Appendix B.

1. A distressed student rushes into the counselor's office to report a clash with a teacher. The counselor allows the student's criticism of the teacher to be stated and "hears him out." He permits the student to explain the damage to his ego caused by the teacher and accepts the responsibility for helping the student work through the conflict situation.
2. Jim comes to the junior high school counselor to express criticism of a certain teacher. After Jim talks out his problem, the counselor feels that things could be best remedied by the counselor talking to the teacher. He asks permission from Jim, but Jim feels that he would be singled out if the counselor made this contact. The coun-

selor still thinks that talking to the teacher would be best and that Jim does not fully comprehend the situation; therefore, the counselor contacts the teacher. The teacher expresses surprise and some irritation that Jim has gone to a counselor. The counselor is unable to get any suggestions across to the teacher concerning her relationship with Jim. Subsequently the counselor sees Jim several times, but the boy expresses no interest in returning for any further discussions (Callis 1976, pp. 22–23).

Do not look at the paragraph below until after completion of the exercise.

The ethical principle involved is in section B.1 of Appendix B on the counselor-counselee relationship.

> The member's primary obligation is to respect the integrity and promote the welfare of the counselee(s), whether the counselee(s) is (are) assisted individually or in a group relationship. In a group setting, the member-leader is also responsible for protecting individuals from physical and/or psychological trauma resulting from interactions within the group.

The first description is in accord with this ethical principle; the second is not.

2. Ethical Issues in Referral

The following case description and discussion from Stude and Goodyear (1975, pp. 26–28) present a problem that calls for the counselor to make an ethical decision. Read over the case description, decide what you would do, and identify the ethical principles involved (see Appendix B). Then compare your decisions with those that follow. If you are working with a small group, have members give brief answers and compare them with the discussion on page 317.

> Situation: A counselor feels that one of his clients needs psychiatric treatment . . . (A psychiatric evaluation by a psychiatrist supports the counselor's feelings. Since the client is a minor, the counselor discusses the recommendations for psychiatric treatment with the parents.) The parents actively reject the recommendation and refuse to even consider the possibility of psychiatric treatment (Christianson 1972, p. 202).

- What are the issues involved?
- What ethical standard is involved?
- What would you do?

Ethical issue involved: One can expect this kind of problem when dealing with highly emotional situations such as referral for psychiatric treatment. [The] situation highlights two separate ethical issues. First, what are a counselor's obligations if a minor client's parents refuse to follow through on a recommended referral? Second, when a counselor realizes the client's problems are beyond his personal capabilities what ethical obligation does he have to continue to work with the client if the client's family refuses suggestions to seek more qualified professional assistance?

The APGA Code (see Appendix B) indicates that:

> If a member is unable to be of professional assistance to the counselee, the member avoids initiating the counseling relationship or the member terminates it. In either event, the member is obligated to refer the counselee to an appropriate specialist. . . . In the event the counselee declines the suggested referral, the member is not obligated to continue the relationship.

Discussion:

In applying these guidelines to the above situation, the following should be considered. Although the counselor's primary responsibility is to the client, *he must* realize his own professional limitations and capabilities. When situations arise that are beyond his abilities he has an obligation to make an appropriate referral. Consequently, the counselor was following acceptable ethical practice by providing for further evaluation of the client's problems and attempting to initiate a psychiatric referral.

However, the question that needs to be looked at is did the counselor approach the parents regarding the need for psychiatric treatment in the best possible manner? Did he request permission from the parents before obtaining the psychiatric evaluation? Since the client is a minor, the counselor should have obtained prior permission of the parents before arranging the psychiatric evaluation. If he did not obtain permission he may have already acted unethically. In the event the parents did agree to the psychiatric evaluation initially, why are they now rejecting efforts for further help?

Given the parent's active rejection of the recommendation, the counselor may want to schedule a joint conference of the parents, client, and psychiatrist. This would give the psychiatrist and counselor an opportunity to discuss with the parents the client's need and how therapy might benefit him. In the event that this suggestion is also rejected, the counselor should attempt to open better communication with the parents within a reasonable length of time and effort.

It should be made clear to the parents that if the counselor continues working with the client without referral, his actions may be detrimental to the client's well-being. Should the parents still refuse the recommendation, the counselor would be ethically obligated to terminate services. If the client, in his current condition, is detrimental to himself or others, the counselor may, within the guidelines and approval of his agency, refer the problem to appropriate authorities that have the power to intervene for the ultimate well-being of the client.

3. Legal Decisions

What are your answers to the following questions? Each is directed to a counselor, and each involves a legal principle.

In a small group, have each member give an answer, and take a few minutes to try to reach a consensus.

Questions:

1. "Mr. Snyder, if I tell you something, will you promise not to tell anyone?"
2. "Mrs. Goodyear, can you help me get an abortion so that my parents won't know?"
3. "Mr. Herrman, I'm Officer Gallant and I'd like to see Sam Powers for questioning."

Answers (do not read this section until completion of your group discussion):

1. Mr. Snyder can't promise not to tell *anyone,* but he should know and relate to the counselee the situations where he must tell someone.
2. Mrs. Goodyear can refer her counselee to someone who will provide abortion information, if it is legal in her state. Unless specifically required by policy, she would not have to notify the parents; but she should be aware that any routine record of the interview may be subject to discovery and disclosure.
3. Officer Gallant can see Sam if he insists, but Mr. Herrman or a school administrator should make immediate efforts to delay the interrogation until she or he can notify Sam's parents and give them an opportunity to be present or arrange for counsel.

4. The Limits of Confidentiality

Assume you are working with a student who threatened violence against an instructor and/or another pupil. You have the information, but the student will not give you permission to release it. What would you do? Could you be sued by the victim if violence actually took place?

Formulate your answer before reading the note below. If a small group is used, obtain responses from each member.

In the case of *Tarasoff* v. *Regents of the University of California,* the California Supreme Court ruled that the therapist should take steps to save human lives over all other considerations. In this case the therapist, who knew of a threat by Prosenjit Poddar, subsequently carried out, to kill Tatiana Tarasoff, was held liable for failing to warn and protect the victim (Whiteley and Whiteley 1977).

The principles given in these illustrations can be used when dealing with local ethical and legal problems. The same small-group discussion format is recommended.

Suggested Readings

Bolton, Brian, and Jacques, Marceline E., eds. *Rehabilitation Counseling.* Baltimore: University Park Press, 1978.

    Section V, pages 229–278, includes a number of articles on preparation of rehabilitation counselors. The "Statement of Policy" on preparation (pp. 231–238) is a good starting place for those who want to learn about this specialty.

Burgum, Thomas, and Anderson, Scott. *The Counselor and the Law.* Washington, D.C.: American Personnel and Guidance Association, 1975.

    A valuable reference during preparation and when legal problems and issues arise on the job. Chapter 1 gives an excellent overview of the legal status of the school counselor.

Callis, Robert. *Ethical Standards Casebook.* Washington, D.C.: American Personnel and Guidance Association, 1976.

    A revision of the widely used 1965 casebook, containing examples of appropriate and inappropriate counselor actions. An effective aid for learning to apply ethical standards. The Buckley Amendment is included as an appendix.

Canon, Harry J. "Developing Staff Potential." In *Student Services,* edited by Ursula Delworth and Gary R. Hanson, pp. 439–455. San Francisco: Jossey-Bass, 1980.

    The purposes of, and procedures for, staff development in student personnel services are discussed. The value of this process for enhancing the institution-wide impact of services is brought out.

Dameron, Joseph D., ed. *The Professional Counselor: Competencies, Performance Guidelines, and Assessment.* Falls Church, Va: American Personnel and Guidance Association, 1980.

    An excerpt from this publication, included in the text, shows how useful the book is for identifying and assessing counselor competencies.

Danish, Steven J., and Smyer, Michael A. "Unintended Consequences of Requiring a License to Help." *American Psychologist* 36, no. 1 (1981), pp. 13–21.

    Valuable reading for understanding the possible effects on licensure on professional practice.

Delworth, Ursula, and Hanson, Gary R. "Conclusion: Structure of the Profession and Recommended Curriculum." In *Student Services,* edited by Ursula Delworth and Gary R. Hanson, pp. 473–485. San Francisco: Jossey-Bass, 1980.

    A very helpful discussion of major aspects of the role of student personnel workers. Other sections of the chapter cover master's and doctoral levels of preparation programs.

Dickinson, James C. *Initiative for Professional Renewal: Selected Issues for the Counseling Practitioner.* Falls Church, Va.: American Personnel and Guidance Association, 1978.

    A well-designed how-to-do-it manual for setting up, running, and evaluating a renewal program. Chapter 1, on what renewal is and what it accomplishes, is a recommended reading.

Drapela, Victor J., ed. *Guidance and Counseling Around the World.* Washington, D.C.: University Press of America, 1979.

A broad and authoritative view of counseling services in other countries. Practically all regions are covered in the most comprehensive publication available today. Chapters 1 and 2 discuss the value of a comparative study of counseling.

Forster, Jerold. "What Shall We Do about Counseling?" *Personnel and Guidance Journal* 55, no. 10 (1977), pp. 572–576.

This is the lead article in a special-feature section on licensure and certification. All of the articles will add to the reader's understanding of the development of this critical issue.

Fretz, Bruce R., and Mills, David H. "Professional Certification in Counseling Psychology." *Counseling Psychologist* 9, no. 1 (1980), pp. 2–17.

A comprehensive examination of issues and problems in licensure. The focus of the article is on counseling psychologists, but many of the issues discussed are of major concern to counselors. Nine other articles in this issue also deal with credentialing.

Giroux, Roy F.; Biggs, Donald A.; Hoffman, Alan M.; and Pietrofesa, John J., eds. *College Student Development Revisited: Programs, Issues, and Practices.* Rev. ed. Falls Church, Va.: American Personnel and Guidance Association, 1979.

Chapter 6, pages 335–364, contains a number of valuable articles on the preparation of student development specialists for higher education. Pages 340–344 provide an excellent overview of needed competencies.

Herr, Edwin L. *Guidance and Counseling in the Schools: The Past, Present, and Future.* Falls Church, Va.: American Personnel and Guidance Association, 1979.

Part 3, on professional preparation and standards, sets forth a comprehensive, up-to-date account of issues and problems in school counselor preparation, certification, and renewal. Particularly useful for those interested in the school setting.

Lewis, Judith A., and Lewis, Michael D. *Community Counseling: A Human Services Approach.* New York: John Wiley and Sons, 1977.

Chapter 12 contains a discussion of the preparation of the community counselor, emphasizing new directions and strategies for different preparation settings. Excellent for helping to develop an understanding of competencies needed for community counseling.

"Licensure Committee Action Packet 1979." Falls Church, Va.: American Personnel and Guidance Association, 1979.

A thorough and informative review of all aspects of licensure, together with illustrative legislation, recommended policies, and an outline of licensure-support strategies. A very valuable resource.

Lindenberg, Steven P. "Attention Students: Be Advised . . ." *Personnel and Guidance Journal* 55, no. 1 (1976), pp. 34–36.

A thought-provoking look into the next decade, discussing possible developments in the licensure of school counselors.

Miller, Frank W.; Fruehling, James A.; and Lewis, Gloria J. *Guidance Principles and Services.* 3rd ed. Columbus, Ohio: Charles E. Merrill, 1978.

Miller, Fruehling, and Lewis' approach to professional issues (pp. 445–492) differs from the one in this book. Some topics not included here are covered (e.g., social workers, selection of school counselors). Useful for added depth.

Miller, Theodore K., and Carpenter, D. Stanley. "Professional Preparation for Today and Tomorrow." In *Student Development in Higher Education,* edited by Don C. Creamer, pp. 181–204. Cincinnati: American College Personnel Association, 1980.

   An interesting and insightful discussion of guidelines for professional preparation and continued development for student personnel workers.

Moore, Mary. "Counselor Training Meeting New Demands." *Personnel and Guidance Journal* 55, no. 6 (1977), pp. 359–362.

   A stimulating discussion of how the preparation of helpers can and should change to meet needs and give the profession increased viability.

Nasman, Daniel. *Legal Concerns for Counselors.* Washington, D.C.: American School Counselor Association, 1977.

   An excellent and lucid review of the legal aspects of the counselor's work. Includes several valuable appendixes, including information on the status of individual states on privileged-communication legislation.

Peterson, Donald R. "Is Psychology a Profession?" *American Psychologist* 31, no. 8 (1976), pp. 572–581.

   A discussion of the characteristics of a profession with significant implications for counselors.

Rappaport, Julian. *Community Psychology.* New York: Holt, Rinehart and Winston, 1977.

   For a comprehensive review of the community counseling setting, Chapter 11 is particularly helpful. The emphasis is on the role of the psychologist, but material will be helpful to the counselor. Pages 388–409 are recommended. (Early discussions, pages 372–388, are on the nonprofessional.)

Shertzer, Bruce, and Stone, Shelley C. *Fundamentals of Guidance.* 4th ed. Boston: Houghton Mifflin, 1981.

   Chapter 5 provides a comprehensive review of professional concerns of school counselors.

Stude, E. W., and Goodyear, Don L. *Ethics and the Counselor.* Fullerton: California Personnel and Guidance Association, 1975.

   A valuable aid to understanding the use of ethical standards in practice. After ethical problems are presented (see example in this chapter), relevant principles are identified and the issues involved are discussed. The book also contains a review of legal guidelines and several complete formulations of ethical standards.

Wall, Judy. "Getting into Print in *P & G*: How It's Done." *Personnel and Guidance Journal* 52, no. 9 (1974), pp. 594–602.

   This article removes the mystery from preparing and submitting an article for publication. A must for those starting out, and equally valuable for most of us who can use all the help we can get.

Walz, Garry R., and Benjamin, Libby. "Counselors on the Bubble." In *New Imperatives for Guidance,* edited by Garry R. Walz and Libby Benjamin, pp. 421–454. Ann Arbor, Mich.: ERIC Counseling and Personnel Services Clearinghouse, 1978.

   All about counselor renewal — why, how, examples, problems and obstacles. Highly recommended.

Warner, Richard W., Jr.; Brooks, David K., Jr.; and Thompson, Jean A., eds. *Coun-*

selor Licensure: Issues and Perspectives. Falls Church, Va.: American Personnel and Guidance Association, 1980.

A collection of articles that examine all aspects of the licensure issue. The Introduction, pages 1 – 5, gives an informative, brief overview of the development of the licensure movement in the counseling profession. Copies of the Alabama, Arkansas, and Virginia licensure laws are included.

Chapter
13
Accountability for Counselors

If counselors need to be reminded of the critical importance of accountability, they have only to look at recent budget cuts for all levels of social and educational institutions. Probably very few need a reminder, however. It will come as no surprise to read here that helping services are one target for those who wish to cut governmental costs. After all, what evidence is there that these services accomplish anything the public wants and is willing to pay for?

The crux of the problem is that all helping services — schools, colleges, and community agencies — obviously lack hard data to demonstrate that the effects of helping services are positive. A head count of numbers is not enough; nor are glittering generalities about how much a service meets a need. The same applies to detailed descriptions of counselors' qualifications, facilities, and equipment. The plea, "We're too busy helping people to use time for evaluation," will not make the difference either, as some counselors have discovered too late.

Solid, dependable data to show how individuals have been helped may not always be enough. Programs may be trimmed or dropped anyway. But the best chance for maintenance and expansion (even survival) of services comes from conclusive evidence about positive results. Community members are impressed by it; legislators are impressed by it; and the budgetmakers are impressed by it.

Accountability is important to counselors for reasons other than primarily financial. From a strictly humanistic point of view, we want to know if we are helping. What happens to counselees? Are we building false hopes in the public? Do we need to revise our approaches? Are we denying helping services to those needing them because we use time-consuming procedures when equally effective ones would take less time?

This chapter helps you understand accountability, its importance to you and to the counseling profession, and ways you can utilize the concept of your advantage. No part of this book is more important. No matter how effective services are, they cannot help anyone if they are closed down.

The Meaning of Accountability

Accountability is the ability to answer for performance — how well you are achieving relevant goals and objectives. It provides the answer to three questions:

1. What are you doing?
2. How much does it cost?
3. Does it work?

Accountability is not a new concept. Counselors have always been "accountable," that is, responsible for achieving results. In the past, however, there was a great deal of faith in the efficacy of services. Furthermore, services have grown in all settings with the increased professionalism of the counseling profession. Funding has likewise tended to grow, in keeping with the increase in the number of counselors and the expansion of services. It was not until the decades of the 1960s and 1970s that the term "accountability" burst on the national scene. The major arena was the schools, but the concept has permeated the provision of support of college and community counseling services.

Much of the visibility of accountability originated in federal policy in connection with an outpouring of financial support for new programs. At the same time, it was becoming part of the way of consumer thinking in this country. Barro (1970) identifies the educational factors as follows: emphasis on evaluation of school systems; the trend toward comparing educational output with costs; the need to provide education for the disadvantaged; and the trend toward making education responsive to local communities.

The use of accountability is very much a part of all educational and social service settings. Almost all include built-in evaluation procedures. But recent economic and political developments have elevated it to a place of major significance. Budget trimming, competition for funds, shifting services to the private sector, and "sunset legislation" (dropping a service if results are not demonstrated within a specific time period) are indications of current thinking. These attitudes very well may be portents of the future.

Points of View on Accountability

Counselors tend to see accountability in different ways. To some it implies a focus on specific types of cognitive learning; to others, a broad approach to human development. Still others view it as a method of organization, while in some cases it means reporting results to those who finance the program. There are also divergent opinions on the appropriateness of accountability within a helping enterprise.

The question of broad v. narrow applications is the major issue for counseling. It is easier to identify and measure specific behaviors (e.g., number of occupations one can describe, number of positive self-evaluations one checks) than it is to assess competencies such as adaptability to new situations or decision-making skills.

While accountability may be seen as a threat to professional autonomy, it can have significant benefits. Kaplan and Stoughton (1974, p. v) argue that identifying the target population and clarifying what is to be accomplished can bring helping services into the mainstream of the educational program. Krumboltz (1974) predicts increased support, improved public relations, enhanced professional status, and personal satisfaction. Accountability enables counselors to make a strong case for concentrating efforts on functions they are best prepared to carry out, and on targets that have the greatest need. Accountability has also provided the motivation for counselors and other educators to look for more effective ways to achieve results.

There is a strong current of positive thinking about the potential values of accountability to the counseling profession, the capability of

Accountability can help the counselor focus on the most important tasks.

guidance workers to provide valid data, and its place as a logical and needed feature of counseling. Accountability enables counselors to achieve responsible freedom and to prove their value within the total educational or agency setting. By pinpointing objectives and developing effective assessment procedures, the counselor can demonstrate the value of counseling services (Hays 1972). In times of critical scrutiny of all expenditures and priorities in helping services, accountability "may well save the day for guidance" (Humes 1972, p. 25).

There are those who see accountability as largely negative. Outside pressures may determine the goals and objectives of the service. Therefore, those that offer the best payoff may be adopted rather than those that are the most appropriate. The emphasis may be on short-term, specific, tangible results that do not relate to significant human achievements. Moreover, effects may be difficult to assess. How long will it take for a slight change in the individual's direction to be apparent? How is it possible to reflect convincingly the prevention of problems or the increased use of potential? In addition, it is anticipated that evaluation may often have a hidden agenda — it may be used to eliminate a service or dismiss employees.

Suggestions for Counselors

We can make three assumptions: (1) accountability in some form or other is here to stay; (2) the future of the counseling movement depends upon how effective professionals are in establishing workable accountability approaches and gathering evaluative data; and (3) it is possible to state guidance objectives so that they meet accountability requirements. The best strategy is to move as quickly and effectively as possible into the accountability mainstream.

The first step calls for learning about accountability. It helps to read in the references given and others, and to visit programs that have been developed or are in the process of being developed. Counselors also need to define their roles, first, for themselves, in keeping with standards and policies of professional organizations, and then for others — administrators, teachers, community persons, and legislators.

The steps that follow are essentially those outlined by Kaplan and Stoughton (1974, pp. 1–6) and used in most other accountability models. While this focus is on schools, principles apply to other settings.

1. *Goals.* The first is to develop a statement of goals representing the needs and desires of those involved in the school system — pupils, teachers, administrators, parents, and other community persons. It is not necessary to spell out all possible goals at the

outset; supplementary ones can be added as the program develops. The important point is that a number of important priority-ranked goals be established so that the development process can continue.

2. *Objectives.* The next step is to specify objectives for each goal in terms that make assessment possible. This is the most difficult task; it is necessary to describe what pupils will accomplish, how it will be assessed, and the level that represents success. Kaplan and Stoughton (1974, p. 3) recommend beginning with a relatively small number of objectives (e.g., five for each goal) and adding others later.

3. *Program Implementation.* Establishing the program and functions to achieve objectives is the next step. Quite often functions are mistakenly listed as objectives (e.g., "group counseling [a function] will be provided"). This stage utilizes capabilities in terms of staff, facilities, and other resources. If, for example, a counselor has a load of five hundred pupils, scheduling a conference with each one each term would consume most of the working hours. Keeping in mind the time required to reach objectives, staff and facilities should be used in the most effective ways possible.

4. *Evaluation.* Evaluation is carried out to determine whether or not the program has accomplished the results for which it is held accountable. The statements of objectives contain the guides needed for evaluation. Two purposes are served — to estimate how well the job is being done, and to identify areas that need to be improved. If evaluation is used to rate personnel for salary, promotion, or separation, it will produce resentment and anxiety and generate a host of ways to "play the game" and distort results. Methods must be devised to reward those who do outstanding work, but the emphasis of the evaluation is on helping individuals understand how well they are performing and what they can do to remedy deficiencies.

The use of evaluative data for feedback to improve the program merits special attention. Both costs and effectiveness data are used. For example, if test interpretation can be done just as efficiently in small groups as individually, the group method would be less expensive. If the group method were somewhat less effective, however, a comparison would have been made of relative benefits of the more costly method and compared with those of the less expensive one. This model is actually a version of the systems approach described in Chapter 7. It is quite apparent that this systems type of program building is well suited to the implementation of accountability.

Evaluation, Research, and Accountability

Accountability has forced the counseling profession to articulate clearly and fully the rationale for evaluation. The major purposes are: judging the effectiveness of programs; strengthening weak functions; revising elements; justifying continuation; obtaining financial support; and assembling information for public relations.

Program effectiveness is the key issue. It has always been the counselor's deep concern, but the pressure of day-to-day activities has left little time for a systematic assessment of results. Besides, until relatively recently, there was a general and uncritical trust in the value of helping services. But the question must be asked: Do counselors make a difference? From the ethical point of view, evaluation is an essential activity; if help is not effective, we must change our methods to make the most of the available resources.

Results must also be considered in terms of costs. Evaluation makes possible a comparison of costs and results, and can thus help suggest ways to achieve the same goals at a lower price. With the fierce competition for available funds, counseling services will have to marshal hard evidence to demonstrate the benefits it claims to deliver.

Adequate criteria — data by which to measure change — are essential in any evaluation plan. Pine (1975) identifies the criterion problem as the single most critical one in evaluation. It often gets only cursory or superficial treatment; criteria may be stated vaguely or not at all (Warner 1975). Solid criteria are tremendously difficult to define. Suppose, for example, that attitudes toward school or college are used as a criterion. What do we mean by attitudes toward the institution? How will they be demonstrated? How will we measure them? How will we know changes are due to the program? As the following illustration shows, "success" can be a problematic criterion: A withdrawn, compulsive individual becomes more outgoing and healthy as a result of counseling; achievement drops and assertive behavior increases; results of counseling appear negative by the criterion of academic achievement, but the individual is much improved from a mental health point of view (Pine 1975).

The trend in evaluation is to use techniques that provide counselors with up-to-the-minute information on the effectiveness of all aspects of a program. Pine (1975) recommends discrepancy evaluation; standards set up at the beginning of a program are used at each stage to assess performance in terms of design, installation, process, product, and cost. Discrepancies between the set standard and actual performance give the staff data on which to base needed adjustments. Brown (1978) describes new approaches to evaluation at the college level that provide data to help the administrator in decision making. While there is emphasis on process — how the program is working — effectiveness in terms of student changes is a major concern. Moreover, well-designed evaluation not only assesses effects on individuals served but provides input to enable the program to be a self-correcting system (Mitchell 1978, p. 125, 1979, p. 13).

Evaluation is the major strategy for meeting the demands of accountability. Varieties of innovative designs are available to handle almost any kinds of questions. Unfortunately, counselors tend to be better prepared to do research than evaluation. As pointed out in the next section, evaluation may utilize research techniques and instruments, but the two are quite different. Skill in evaluation does not automatically follow from skill in research.

Research Approaches

Research methods provide the counselor with a variety of techniques of evaluation ranging from simple to complex and from small scale to large scale. Standards for identifying needed data are also based on research principles. If we are to be held accountable for effects of counseling and guidance, we want to be certain that judgments are formed on the basis of dependable evidence.

The number of fundamental research strategies varies according to authorities. Shertzer and Stone (1981, pp. 466–471) identify three: survey, experimentation, and the single case. Pine's more extensive list (1975) gives nine:

1. Experimental
2. Tabulation
3. Follow-up
4. Expert opinion
5. Client opinion
6. External criteria (using a "yardstick" of effective practices as a basis for evaluation)
7. Opinion surveys (e.g., of teachers)
8. Descriptive approach
9. Case-study approach

The survey approach is quite similar to the public opinion poll; a representative sample is contacted for opinions, attitudes, and similar evaluative data. The needs survey is an example of this technique. Follow-up studies of former clients are one of the more widely used survey-type evaluations. The tabulations method (a type of survey) consists of counting facilities, personnel, and procedures and provides a quantitative evaluation. Standards for accreditation and program evaluation are usually of this type (Shertzer and Stone 1981, pp. 466–467; ACES 1967).

The descriptive approach resembles survey and tabulation methods;

for example, the organization of the program may be described, indicating who does what, when, and with what preparation. Usually little or no information is obtained that can attribute effects directly to activities.

In counseling, research most generally takes an experimental approach. Essentially, this involves administering a deliberate treatment to individuals and measuring its effects. Controls — individuals who do not receive treatment — should be used for comparison; conditions should be kept constant; and the test group should constitute a representative sample. The approach has its limitations. It restricts the counselor's daily work and gives results of effectiveness only after termination of the study; and it does not provide early input that can be used for improving programs (Pine 1975).

The case study as a research and evaluative approach has had varying degrees of status over the years. Recently, however, the N = 1 design has gained new popularity. It is the choice of the clinician (Spence 1973) and is particularly suitable when the counselor is trying to understand the causes of one's behavior (Miller and Warner 1975). The single-case type of evaluation can be made reliable and valid with the use of a base rate (describing typical behavior) and by checking inferences with the individual (Frey 1973).

The increasing evidence of the utility of research and the proliferation of innovative designs support a forecast of a more significant role for the research function in the future. For one thing, the process of using an accumulation of studies to validate a particular approach for working with individuals is being employed to provide evidence of the approach's effect. The analysis of this strategy for teaching methods by Walberg, Schiller, and Haertel (1979) suggests principles that could be used with counseling research. Changes in research methodology — for example, the variations of the intensive design, using one case and baseline data — are particularly well suited for counselors in schools and other settings (Huber 1980). In addition, there are a number of methods that are particularly useful for dealing with the significant problems and issues of counseling; for example, field studies or analysis of transactions (Goldman 1976).

New concepts and new approaches to research not only offer more useful ways to analyze significant counseling problems but also provide accountability data. The intensive design using one case can be used to estimate the progress of a counselee in reaching his or her personally significant goals.

Accountability: Small- to Large-Scale Methods and Examples

Much of what has been said implies that accountability is large scale — school-, college-, or agency-wide, district-wide, or even state-wide. It can take place on an individual basis, in which counselors evaluate their own work. On a slightly larger scale, it can involve one aspect of a program (e.g., how well the information service performs its function). The counselor's evaluation of each case is particularly helpful; it not only provides data on effectiveness but also serves as an approach to professional development.

Counselors' Personal Self-Evaluation

Counselors can evaluate the effectiveness of their own work by relatively simple and brief procedures (Tolbert 1972, pp. 376 380). Written records should be kept showing the problem, counselor actions, expected effects, and actual results as ascertained in a follow-up by interview, telephone, or letter. The procedure is somewhat like the systems approach. First, needs are identified. Second, objectives are established (the counselor and counselee decide what should be accomplished). Next, the helping activity is carried out with continuous feedback for revision and correction of plans. The results are compared with goals: further adjustments in helping are made if needed.

Values accrue to both counselor and counselee through this informal self-evaluation. The systematic checking of inferences with reality sharpens the counselor's ability to observe, synthesize, and hypothesize. The counselee benefits through a flexible mode of helping attuned to needs, an opportunity to return for more assistance, and the support of awareness that the counselor cares enough to see what happens.

Another approach consists of a survey to obtain needed data about questions such as how counselees see the counselor and sources of help they use (Weinrach 1975). An example is the survey of Heilfron (1960) to investigate pupils' perceptions of types of problems appropriate for counseling. This survey does not fulfill evaluation needs of the total guidance program, but does provide valuable input to help counselors improve the quality of their work.

A concept that can be incorporated in the counselor's personal evaluation has recently attracted considerable attention. The N = 1 research plan provides a framework (Frey 1973). The counselor uses bits of data, including base rates of behavior, to learn about the individual. As these are synthesized, an understanding of the person emerges. The longitudinal nature of the process makes it possible to gather data about the effects of counseling, to determine whether to continue the same treatment, or to vary the treatment. Moreover, a number of these studies that give similar results can provide substantial support for a principle.

The N = 1 (single-case) approach does not replace research involving groups, nor does it necessarily explain why behavior changes (Nordberg 1975). Other influences in the counselee's life may have made the difference. Moreover, it may be difficult to identify the specific actions or characteristics of the counselor that resulted in the effect.

Evaluation in Organization-Wide Accountability

Before discussing accountability programs, we will look at the essential aspects of the evaluation process. It will be helpful to review the models given in Chapter 7, which provide the framework and process for a school-wide accountability program. The systems approach (Miller and Grisdale 1975; Stufflebeam 1968), for example, begins with the determination of needs and continues until evaluation results are obtained. At the conclusion, the cost-effectiveness of each objective can be determined.

Four types of evaluation are included in the systems approach: context, input, process, and product (CIPP). Each of these involves an important type of evaluation and each provides data for planning the next step as well as improving previous steps (Jones, Tiedeman, Mitchell, Unruh, Helliwell, and Ganschow 1973, p. 2–3). Context evaluation indicates target population needs for formulating goals and objectives. For example, in your setting you might identify, in addition to the needs of the major population, the needs of several other groups such as minorities, the handicapped, and older persons. These needs constitute context evaluation.

The next type, input evaluation, assesses the personnel, facilities, existing programs, and other resources that may be used to achieve the goals and objectives of the program.

The third type, process evaluation, assesses the effects of implementing programs and determines how well parts are working. This stage may involve transactional evaluation to estimate effectiveness of communication during periods of stress and change. Formative evaluation is a similar process and measures success in getting the program into operation. For example, you may have decided on the basis of needs, objectives, and resources identified in the school that group career counseling should be provided to juniors and seniors. Process evaluation indicates success in setting up the group counseling program, but not the actual extent of help that these groups provide to pupils. Finally, product evaluation indicates results of the program, establishing, for example, whether pupils do make progress in school, establish good relations with others, or choose suitable occupations. This is the most significant type of evaluation for the purposes of accountability; results have more meaning to the public than any other type of data. Results are also more important to the clientele because they indicate how well needs are being met.

The first three types — context, input, process — are often included under the single term "process evaluation." Thus, evaluation may be described more simply as process and product. The latter type is the most critical for accountability.

One Approach for the Total Guidance Program

The Mesa, Arizona, Public School Career Education Accountability model is aimed at life goals and thus actually illustrates an approach for the total guidance program. Seven steps were carried out in building the program, from identifying target groups to setting up evaluative procedures. Counselors, with administrative support, with resources provided by special funding, and with the help of consultants, initiated the program with a needs assessment of all groups affected. Pupils, teachers, parents, community members, and employers were contacted. Questions and techniques for collecting needs information were prepared, and data were collected from representative samples in small-group meetings by cards sorted in four areas of pupil needs: intrapersonal, interpersonal, academic learning, and educational-vocational.

The next step was an assessment of the present guidance program resources. Counselors kept records of how time was spent and purposes of activities; results indicated priorities and provided data with which to compare needed and current emphases. When completed, this resources inventory described what was being done, who was doing it, how effective it was judged to be, and what facilities were available.

Following the collection of needs and resource data, a comparison was made to determine how well current practices matched need priorities. When discrepancies were found, goals were formulated to eliminate them. For example, the resources survey found that only about 5 percent of the counselors' time was spent in helping high school pupils get along better with others, although this was one of the top-priority needs given by pupils. The discrepancy was therefore the basis of a goal statement that set aside at least 20 percent of a counselor's time to deal with needs such as solving problems with parents, learning how to accept criticism, learning to be a better listener, and developing confidence and the ability to be at ease with others. All of these goals came under the general heading of learning how to get along with others.

The next step was to structure the guidance program; select target groups, materials, and procedures; and disseminate information about the program to pupils, parents, teachers, both to inform and obtain input.

After goals and objectives were formulated, translating them into a program was the next major task. Group sessions were used by counselors to identify ways to achieve goals. Useful materials and procedures already available were located and adopted. Small groups of counselors then undertook to plan for the accomplishment of each goal and its objectives. The general strategy adopted was counseling-learning units keyed to objectives. Flowcharts were developed for each goal, showing level of learning (comprehension, application, and analysis) and thus facilitating the most productive ordering of objectives. These preliminary steps provided the bases for constructing units.

Field-testing was done at elementary, junior high, and senior high school levels. An English course, "English and Careers," was used as the setting. Counselors taught units the first semester; teachers took over the second semester, during which period evaluations were carried out. The guidance center provided counselors to monitor progress, lead groups, and help individuals. The units enabled pupils to move at their own rates, and teachers and counselors served as resource persons and consultants, providing help, counseling, and materials.

Evaluation took place at all stages of program development. The formative evaluation included context evaluation for planning, input for structuring, and process for implementation. During implementation, it was possible to begin on product evaluation (i.e., the summative evaluation) to assess outcome. A variety of evaluative techniques were used to compare treatment and control groups, including criterion-referenced tests, pupil self-reports, and unobtrusive measurements (pupil requests for the next course). Very positive results were obtained for most of the evaluation, although in some areas (e.g., knowledge outcomes), it did not come up to expectations. Outcomes, particularly those indicating achievement below expectations, were used in formative evaluation to revise materials and procedures for the next program trial.

Future plans call for improving and expanding the program by bringing in additional departments, and enlarging the work observation, experience, and placement program to tie into career guidance.

Of course, not all evaluations follow the systems approach in its entirety. The several studies that follow are more representative of typical programs that are carefully designed to evaluate results and that may utilize some elements of a systems approach.

Other Approaches to Accountability Evaluation

Barrow (1980) describes a program-evaluation approach that followed-up program dropouts. Based on the assumptions that these data would expand the number of criteria for evaluation and would add unique and candid feedback, approximately 50 college students who dropped out of developmental programs were contacted by telephone. Nearly 30 of the group were actually interviewed with the caller using a structured data-gathering guide. Results were used to evaluate scheduling, format, and content of developmental activities. For example, the most frequently cited reason for dropping out was conflict with other activities. This conflict situation could be viewed as an expected problem on a college campus, or it could lead to a close scrutiny of time actually needed for the program to be effective. A long program could be divided into shorter, self-contained units. Other returns gave valuable leads about ways to improve the holding power of programs.

A community agency program, the Residential Youth Center, used a systematic evaluation program to assess its personal-growth impact on disadvantaged adolescents and their families (Zax and Specter 1974, pp. 249–256). The program had several unique features, such as setting up the service in the client's neighborhood and establishing goals through joint efforts of clients and staff. As many as 20 adolescents were housed in the center at any one time. Evaluation consisted of comparing residents with controls who did not participate in the program. Experimental and control groups were similar according to age and race, but residents were classified as the more difficult cases. On three criteria — occupational adjustment, attitude change, and commmunity adjustment — the experimental group greatly exceeded the control group at the conclusion of treatment. Prior to the program, the average number of arrests during a six-month period for the experimental group was 1.87 and 1.70 for the controls during the same period. During the six months after entering the program, the residents (experimental group) averaged .96 arrests, compared with 2.08 for the controls for a similar period.

State-level evaluations are also carried out and illustrate large-scale procedures. Wysong's evaluation package used in Ohio (1974) emphasizes assistance to pupils as the primary program objective. Secondary objectives are services to teachers, administrators, parents, and counselors so that they in turn can better assist pupils.

This well-developed program includes a self-study evaluative criteria that may be used by school staffs for self-evaluation, and a series of instruments for assessing pupil and teacher attitudes about guidance, knowledge of services, and utilization of helping activities. Additional materials describe the steps for preparing for the visit of the evaluation team. The procedure is cooperative and involves state guidance consultants, school staff, and the visiting team. A follow-up is conducted after a year by staff of the State Division of Guidance and Testing.

A study of the effects of the evaluation program by O'Connor (1973) showed that in the twenty schools studied nearly one third of the visting team's recommendations had been put into effect a year later. Another one third were in the process of being implemented, and the remaining third had not been acted upon. Lack of financial resources and time were the chief reasons for not making recommended changes. Schools reported that the evaluation had provided data that could be communicated to various publics, and the total evaluation procedure had helped the school staff develop a better understanding of guidance services and objectives.

An example of an extensive evaluation program involves the identification of exemplary career education programs for nation-wide dissemination as models to other school districts (Hamilton, Baker, and Mitchell

1979*a*; Hamilton and Mitchell 1979). Program evaluation focused on schools, but the procedures and methodology are appropriate in many other settings. A key element in the selection was the quality of the program evaluation component. A three-level screening procedure was used; of more than 250 programs submitted, only 10 passed all three levels. While the criteria used to assess the evaluation component of the programs are too extensive to report here, several items illustrate what program evaluation should include (Hamilton, Baker, and Mitchell 1979*a*):

1. "The evaluation design included a comparison group/standard of some kind." (p. 113)
2. "Does the activity do what it claims to be able to do?" (p. 114)
3. "Are the learning outcomes directly attributable to the activity and not to some other factor?" (p. 114)

These criteria, only a few of those used, clearly illustrate the care with which program evaluation should be designed.

Newer approaches to evaluation provide interesting and personnel-involving ways to demonstrate accountability. Brown (1978) describes three that have considerable potential for improving student affairs programs in the college setting — goal-free evaluation, responsive approach, and transactional evaluation. The first, goal-free evaluation, involves looking for the *actual* effects of the program rather than limiting evaluation to what the program purports to do. In the responsive approach, the evaluator looks at the program itself to determine how well it coincides with its description. The evaluation is primarily concerned with observing, interacting with, and responding to the program and its staff, and communicating conclusions to the administrator. The third type, transactional evaluation, involves the interpersonal barriers to change and development — how well the system works. The program itself is the focus of the evaluation. All of these approaches "place a high premium on people, process, and value" (p. 123) and therefore should be particularly palatable to counselors.

Many of the studies referred to in previous chapters are of an evaluative type. In some cases, the relation to accountability is clear — the studies provide evidence that the program is successfully doing what it is intended to do.

The Contribution of Technology to Accountability

The computer has made possible detailed analyses of evaluation data and continuous monitoring of effectiveness of programs. Needs data, allowing weighted responses and analysis by sex, grade levels, and other factors, require extensive manipulation that computers can easily handle. For example, the computer makes it possible to organize thousands of pupil responses about needs, rank them in order of priority, and summarize them by specific groups. Studies that would have been practically impossible because of clerical time and costs can be carried out with ease. Computers can "evaluate" pupils' decisions about educational programs and career and progress in programs. Most are capable of the three data-processing functions mentioned by Cramer, Herr, Morris, and Frantz (1970, p. 165): (1) storing large amounts of data for relatively simple analysis, e.g., test scores, school grades; (2) relatively more complex analyses of masses of data, e.g., correlating test scores with grades; and (3) highly complex analyses of smaller amounts of data, e.g., statistical analyses of experimental data. Computer guidance systems, however, are not usually programmed to provide formative and cumulative evaluations, but computer handling of data can be useful for evaluation. For example, pupil choices of programs can be compared with ratings of success.

The computer is being used more and more in research and evaluation. New technology will undoubtedly open new possibilities. Small hand-held computers, for example, can be programmed to do various sorts of data analyses. Project Talent (Flanagan 1973) has provided analyses of the impact of various factors on effectiveness of guidance programs; psychological profiles of a nation-wide sample of high school pupils graduating in 1960–63 (Flanagan, Tiedeman, Willis, and McLaughlin 1973; Rossi, Bartlett, Campbell, Wise, and McLaughlin 1975); and attitudes about education, work, personal and family life eleven years after school for more than 100,000 individuals (Wilson and Wise 1975). The PLAN system (Program of learning in Accordance with Needs) makes use of the computer to monitor pupils' progress and assists in planning individual learning programs (Flanagan 1977). Another large-scale research and evaluation study was done by Jencks (1972) on the effects of schooling. He used data from a number of other reports and found, among other things, that school achievement does not predict work performance very accurately (p. 192). The National Assessment Program (*NAEP Newsletter*, vol. 9, no. 4, pp. 1, 3–4), starting in 1964, is a large-scale national censuslike survey of the knowledge, skills, understandings, and attitudes of individuals at ages 9, 13, 17, and young adults between 26 and 35. The total sample is about 80,000. These types of evaluation studies greatly expand the data base for accountability planning and also illustrate techniques schools can use in their own accountability programs.

The use of mini-computers will almost certainly have a major impact on evaluation. Not only are more counselors learning this technology, but cost and convenience make these types of computers feasible for use by schools, colleges, and agencies.

After Evaluation:
Putting the Results to Work

In Chapter 7, program building was discussed, and suggestions for building programs were made. In a sense, the program-building process represents evaluation — needs, facilities, staff capabilities. Staff development and organizational development amount to putting results of evaluation to work. Using the results of the implemented-program evaluation, however, is the major contribution of evaluation; it is this use that can make the program accountable.

Two particularly important principles that serve as guides for putting results to work are given in *Standards for Evaluations of Educational Programs, Projects, and Materials* (Joint Committee on Standards for Educational Evaluation 1981).

Standard
Evaluations should be planned and conducted in ways that encourage follow-through by members of the audiences.

Overview
The impact of an evaluation refers to the influence it has on the decisions and actions of members of the audience. A beneficial impact is one that helps educators carry out their responsibilities and, in general, meet the educational needs of their students. The thrust of this standard is that evaluators should help their audiences use the evaluation findings in taking such beneficial actions as improving programs, projects, or materials; selecting more cost-beneficial products or approaches; or stopping wasteful, unproductive efforts.

Evaluators must not assume that improvements will occur automatically once the evaluation report is completed. Such improvements must be stimulated and guided, and evaluators can and should perform an important role in this process. In effect, they should play the role of a change agent, i.e., someone who plans, staffs, and conducts evaluation activities so as to ensure that the members of the audience will assess and make constructive use of the results of an evaluation. (p. 47)

Standard
The evaluation should be planned and conducted with anticipation of the different positions of various interest groups, so that their cooperation may be obtained, and so that possible attempts by any of these groups to curtail evaluation operations or to bias or misapply the results can be averted or counteracted.

Overview
An interest group is any group of individuals that seeks to influence policy in favor of some shared goal or concern. An evaluation has

political implications to the extent that it leads to decisions concerning reallocation of resources and influence. Evaluations are politically viable to the extent that their purposes can be achieved despite the pressures and actions applied by various interest groups.

If evaluators do not institute measures to ensure that their work is politically viable, they will often find that their efforts are either ineffectual or misapplied. They may have to abort evaluations when they discover their work is being manipulated beyond their control. Or they may discover too late that their work has been used by one group to gain an unfair advantage over another. And they may find that their efforts can be stopped or seriously impeded by a group that is threatened by an evaluation. On the positive side, evaluators who are sensitive to political pressures often will be able to make constructive use of diverse political forces in achieving the purposes of the evaluation. (p. 56)

These excerpts point out critical factors to consider in planning evaluations and implementing results. (The reference also contains additional guidelines for implementing the standards, pitfalls and what to avoid, an illustrative case, and an analysis of the case.) This comprehensive reference covers standards for all aspects of evaluation, from planning to final use. (It is applicable to evaluations in schools, colleges, and community settings.)

Making changes in school, college, and community programs is not an easy task. Consultation is the critical skill needed all through the evaluative process. Practical experience, maturity, sensitivity, and a tolerance for ambiguity enable evaluators to work effectively with staff and others and to gain respect and cooperation (Oetting and Hawkes 1974).

The ability to communicate effectively with the various publics who need to know results of current or future programs and who are instrumental in putting results into action is essential (Oetting and Hawkes 1974). For example, a report that would be understandable to other evaluators might not be suitable for parents, and a summary for presentation at a service club would not contain the detailed information needed by counselors.

A number of problems face the counselor in translating results into action. An overcommitment to the existing program may make it difficult to be objective (Warner 1975). It is possible for a new program to be so highly regarded that the institution decides to implement it even before there is an evaluation; in these circumstances an objective scrutiny cannot be afforded (Campbell 1969). Organization and management skills in relation to the particular institution are needed if results are to be incorporated in the program (Glaser and Taylor 1973). High-level research skills are required; errors can creep into interpretations when there is a need for immediate action, which often happens in social research and evaluation

(Wortman 1975). One of the most vivid illustrations of overenthusiastic acceptance is described by Glass (1968) in his article "Educational Piltdown Men." He gives examples of faulty research and evaluation that produced results eagerly snapped up by professionals and laypersons, just as readily as the discovery of Piltdown man was accepted as proof of Darwin's theory of evolution. This is a manifestation of the "wishful will to believe" when a miraculous solution is claimed.

The evaluator thus has a change-agent function, steering a course between overenthusiastic acceptance and rigid, ossified opposition. Moreover, involvement with the program must not result in attempts to oversell on the basis of faith, even though evaluative data do not warrant support.

Dustin's Five Principles of Change (1974) provide guidelines for the evaluator who seeks to implement results. They are:

1. *Outside pressure comes first.* Examples are plentiful — student unrest during the 1960s and 1970s, the demand for accountability, the career education movement. The evaluator needs to be aware of and utilize these forces.
2. *Change comes from the top down.* Administrative support is essential in every aspect of program development and evaluation. This principle is borne out by the evaluative reports summarized, and emphasizes the need for the evaluator to work closely with administration to effect change.
3. *Change takes place within the institution.* Those who will be responsible for carrying out changes should participate in evaluation. "Members most affected by a change should be brought into the change process" (Dustin 1974, p. 423).
4. *Change tends to be superficial.* This is particularly true when outside evaluators come for a short time, arrive at some sweeping conclusions, and leave. Surface changes may take place, but soon erode. New and expensive materials are bought or prepared, and end up stored in a closet. New techniques fade, and in-service preparation is neglected for new staff. If an evaluation is to have an impact, the evaluator needs to set up a system for continuous monitoring, establish school-based resource persons and coordinators, insure systematic preparation for new staff, and involve the regular staff.
5. *Extensive change may follow unsatisfactorily superficial change.* Pressure builds up with ineffective changes, and institutional directors eventually realize that extreme steps are needed to satisfy the public. Dustin suggests that the change agent's role at this stage is to build support through effective relationships, which enable the evaluator to introduce and support changes.

Summary Concepts

Accountability is a fact of life for counselors, regardless of where they work. Program support increasingly depends upon it. Counseling services have a positive impact, but hard supporting data are too infrequently collected. Evaluation provides the data needed to demonstrate accountability. Research is one major source of techniques useful in evaluation. Evaluation, however, is different from research; it requires specific skills and provides data for different purposes. A number of approaches to research are available for adaptations to evaluation. Accountability has generated strong attitudes, both pro and con. Counselors can make positive use of the concept and employ it to their advantage. Evaluation can contribute to accountability in a wide range of situations, from the individual's day-to-day work to large-scale state and national programs. The systems approach is a particularly effective way to organize for evaluation in the institution or agency. Newer approaches to evaluation tend to involve practitioners and administrators in an ongoing process of assessing effectiveness of services. Computer-technology greatly expands the capabilities of evaluation procedures by storing and manipulating huge amounts of data. Using evaluative data to improve programs utilizes consulting, organization development, and change-agent skills.

The real test of the utility of evaluation comes with implementation of results. What program elements are performing effectively and which ones need to be improved? Are new procedures and functions required to provide services more effectively? Should staff development be instituted to upgrade skills, improve coordination and communication, or build new competencies? The evaluation should enable the agency or institution staff to gain a clear picture of what it is accomplishing and what needs to be done. It also provides the data for reports to those key audiences on whom the continuance of the program depends.

Examples of Research on a Topic
Counselors' Attitudes about, and Understanding of, Accountability

Very few studies deal specifically with how counselors perceive and utilize evaluation for accountability. Many studies, of course, report evaluations that have been carried out, but do not assess counselors' attitudes about the process. The following four studies, however, do provide some evidence on attitudes and knowledge. After reading them, what do you think about the prospects for counselors to initiate and carry out well-designed and meaningful studies? Is there evidence that evaluation for accountability can and will be done effectively?

Buckner's study (1975) approached the question of accountability from the standpoint of counselors' awareness of the profession's position on responsibilities.

Respondents to a list of functions based on ASCA-ACES guidelines included 36 counselor education students, 37 secondary education pupils, 25 secondary school counselors, and 25 public school administrators, all from Utah.

Of a total of approximately 50 role and responsibility statements, there was disagreement of 20 percent or more between respondents on only 12 items. Other results showed that:

- Teachers, pupils, and administrators agree with the ASCA-ACES standards as much as practicing counselors (e.g., counselors did not seem to know their roles).
- Practicing counselors assume responsibility for enjoyable tasks but do not choose those that would make them controversial (e.g., counselors accepted routine, clerical tasks).
- Counselors do not inform administrators about unique skills and do not insist that they have the opportunity to use them (e.g., serving as a change agent, consulting, group counseling).
- Counselors appear to be unaware of professional responsibilities; in some cases administrators were better informed; (e.g., work with curriculum planning).

The American Institutes for Research (Hamilton, Baker, and Mitchell 1979a & b) review of evaluation studies, a large-scale, three-stage process, revealed the following: 257 evaluations of career education programs were identified for analysis. (It is fair to say that these were among the better evaluations done nation-wide. Moreover, career education was relatively well supported. Evaluation was typically emphasized in program planning.)

- *Level I Review.* Sixty-four reports passed. The criteria used were not very rigorous but did include evidence of effectiveness and a comparison group or standard of some kind.
- *Level II Review.* Twenty reports passed. Criteria for the Level II were more rigorous and included an extensive list of elements needed in a good evaluation study (Hamilton, Baker, and Mitchell 1979a).
- *Level III Review.* Ten reports passed this level. This screening emphasized the information needed for replicability as well as the overall quality of the report (Hamilton, Baker, and Mitchell 1979a).
- *Selection for Dissemination.* Seven of the reports were selected by the Joint Dissemination Review Panel for nationwide distribution of

outstanding programs. Program *effectiveness* was the sole criterion used by this panel.

Since the quality of research/evaluation studies is the foundation of accountability, it is important to be aware of how well these studies are designed and carried out. Some evidence is provided by Wandt's report of the evaluation of 125 articles from 41 educational and psychological journals, including *Personnel and Guidance Journal* and *Journal of Counseling Psychology.* A partial summary of results (1969, p. 5) appears in the table below.

While the studies evaluated are not specifically on the topic of accountability, the results indicate that the application of effective research methods often falls short of a desirable level. As an evaluation for accountability, some of the results could have been misleading.

One major problem in interpreting the significance of studies has to do with the chance to detect differences among programs if they actually exist. Suppose, for example, two counseling methods are compared, and one is actually more effective than the other. Does the statistical test detect this difference?

Haase (1974) analyzed sixty research reports published in *Counselor Education and Supervision* 1968–71, and arrived at the conclusion that in many cases differences would not have been likely to be detected even if

	Mean Ratings		
Characteristic	All Articles	81 Articles in Educational Journals	44 Articles in Related Professional Journals
Problem is significant	3.59[a]	3.31	4.09
Research design is appropriate to the solution of the problem	3.03	2.65	3.67
Method of sampling is appropriate	2.97	2.85	3.23
Conclusions are substantiated by the evidence presented	3.11	2.63	3.95

[a] 5 = excellent, 4 = good, 3 = mediocre, 2 = poor, 1 = horrible example.
"Related journals" included such publications as *Journal of Counseling Psychology* and *Journal of Educational Psychology.*
In addition to the above ratings, research evaluators in the study would have accepted only 19 of the total of 125 without revisions.

they existed. The results indicate that researchers need to design studies with particular attention to statistics used and sample size to avoid "stacking the statistical deck against themselves (p. 129)."

While this is a statistical concept that might not appear to be directly related to accountability, it has important implications for anyone evaluating the effectiveness of programs. Suppose, for example, you found that pupils were low in career maturity and you set up groups to help them improve in this area. At the end of the program you found that there was some improvement over baseline data but that it was not statistically significant.

You are about to drop the group program because it has not had the desired effects. Part of your job responsibility is to facilitate career development of pupils, so you look for other strategies.

But your statistical analysis may have failed to indicate results that were actually achieved. For example, if an expected improvement were in the medium range, and you had used statistical analysis in approximately the same way as employed in 40 percent of the studies analyzed, you would have had less than three chances in ten of finding a difference *even* though it existed. That is, even if your group procedures helped pupils improve career maturity, you would not have realized it in many cases.

In addition to answering the questions posed at the beginning of this section, compare your conclusions with Section II, p. 367, in the preparation standards, Appendix A; and Section D, pp. 385 in Appendix B. Also, use the section on "Research Competencies" in *The Professional Counselor: Competencies, Performance Guidelines, and Assessment* (Dameron 1980, pp. 64–69).

Experiential Activities

Two types of experiential activities are suggested. The first type is an investigation of evaluation and accountability programs in various settings. The second is simulation exercises in the classroom. You can no doubt think of others that will enhance your understanding of this area of counselor responsibility.

1. Investigating Evaluation and Accountability Programs

Make an appointment with the director in a counseling setting of your choice. Ask questions such as the following:

1. How is accountability defined?
2. How does the staff view accountability?
3. Does the agency or service demonstrate accountability? How?

If available, look over evaluation reports. What do they show about process and product evaluation?

Ask a counselor (or counselors) in a setting of your choice what his or her goals and objectives are. Also, inquire about data indicating how well these goals and objectives are achieved. Evaluate the responses in terms of the following:

1. Are the objectives reasonable? Practical?
2. Are they stated in terms that make evaluation possible?
3. Do the data provide support for the counselor's statements about effectiveness?

2. Simulations

Using a small group, ask each member this question: As a counselor in the setting of your choice, what are the three major things you would prefer to be accountable for? Ask group members to translate these things into objectives, means of achieving them, and criteria for evaluation. (Your salary and tenure will be based on end-of-year evidence of accomplishments.) At the conclusion, compare the ratio of affective to cognitive elements.

3. Implementing the Results of Evaluation

As a staff member in a setting of your choice, you have been carrying out an evaluation of the program. Results show that the present program has a number of shortcomings. Major ones are:

- It concentrates on a small fraction of the target group.
- Most of the counselors' time is taken up with administrative tasks.
- Counselors are spending most of their time in advice giving.

The director and many of the staff are very proud of the program and are pleased with the way it is operating. Besides, the current emphases are in line with the supervising board's policies.

- What will you do with your evaluation study?
- In a small group, have each member give a strategy.
- Role play a meeting with the director.

4. Accountability in Your Program

For the counselor education program in which you are enrolled, ask small groups to take roles of staff members and make accountability statements. What should the program accomplish and how should results be assessed? Compare your conclusions with what actually is done in the program. What, if anything, would you change in your program?

Suggested Readings

Buckner, Eugene T. "Accountable to Whom? The Counselor's Dilemma." *Measurement and Evaluation in Guidance* 8, no. 3 (1975), pp. 187–192.

This article, on which parts of this chapter are based, illustrates one reason why counselors are having problems with accountability.

Burck, Harman D.; Cottingham, Harold P.; and Reardon, Robert C. *Counseling and Accountability: Methods and Critique.* New York; Pergamon Press, 1973.

A useful discussion of aspects of research and evaluation with analyses of fourteen studies in counseling and guidance.

Cramer, Stanley H.; Herr, Edwin L.; Morris, Charles N.; and Frantz, Thomas T. *Research and the School Counselor.* Boston: Houghton Mifflin, 1970.

An excellent guide for research and evaluation of the types of research the counselor carries out most frequently.

Gelso, Charles J. "Research in Counseling: Methodological and Professional Issues." *Counseling Psychologist* 8, no. 3 (1979), pp. 7–36.

The feature article in a special issue on research. Other articles discuss the issues raised. Heavily theoretical and advanced, this article and the reaction statements that follow deal with concerns about research and evaluation for counselors regardless of settings.

Glass, Gene V. "Educational Piltdown Men." *Phi Delta Kappan* 50, no. 3 (1968), pp. 148–151.

A revealing look at what can happen if research and evaluation reports, especially ones that promise needed remedies, are accepted uncritically.

_____. "Primary, Secondary, and Meta-Analysis of Research." *Educational Researcher* 5 (1976), pp. 3–8.

A provocative proposal of ways to increase the value of large numbers of individual studies by a systematic evaluation and synthesis of results. It is interesting to compare this view with Goldman's.

Goldman, Leo, "A Revolution in Counseling Research." *Journal of Counseling Psychology* 23, no. 6 (1976), pp. 543–552.

The author discusses weaknesses and limitations of current research approaches and offers new strategies both to improve designs and to facilitate implementation of results.

_____. "Toward More Meaningful Research." *Personnel and Guidance Journal* 55, no. 6 (1977), pp. 363–368.

This article, very much like the one listed above (1976), reports the author's candid look at counseling research and concludes that new approaches are needed to help the practitioner and theory builder. Both of these articles have important implications for accountability.

Hays, Donald G., and Linn, Joan K. *Needs Assessment: Who Needs It?* Washington, D.C.: American School Counselor Association, 1977.

This monograph deals with needs assessment and illustrates how resulting data are translated into goals and objectives and used for program improvement. The easily understandable discussion and examples of programs make this a particularly valuable guide for the school counselor. Forms for local adaptation are included.

Joint Committee on Standards for Educational Evaluation. *Standards for Evaluations of Educational Programs, Projects, and Materials.* New York: McGraw-Hill, 1981.

A particularly timely and valuable reference for planning evaluation in any helping services setting. Every aspect of evaluation is covered.

Kerr, Robert A. "Evaluating the Services." In *Student Services,* edited by Ursula Delworth and Gary R. Hanson, pp. 421–438. San Francisco: Jossey-Bass, 1980.

Principles and examples of program evaluation in the college and university setting. A very helpful reading on evaluation in higher education.

Krumboltz, John D. "An Accountability Model for Counselors." *Personnel and Guidance Journal* 52, no. 10 (1974), pp. 639–642.

One of the most useful references for counselors on what accountability means, how it can be implemented, and how it can help identify cost-effectiveness of services.

Lasser, Barbara R. "An Outcomes Approach to Counseling Evaluation." *Measurement and Evaluation in Guidance* 8, no. 3 (1975), pp. 169–174.

A helpful discussion of the importance of goal setting and evaluation in counseling. The model is particularly useful for carrying out a self-appraisal of one's effectiveness and for changing techniques to achieve greater impact.

Miller, Frank W.; Fruehling, James A.; and Lewis, Gloria J. *Guidance Principles and Services.* 3rd ed. Columbus, Ohio: Charles E. Merrill, 1978.

Chapter 11, on research and evaluation, covers various types of research and evaluation, with emphasis on the school setting. Very useful for understanding the methods and purposes of the evaluation of school guidance programs.

Miller, Theodore K., and Prince, Judith S. *The Future of Student Affairs.* San Francisco: Jossey-Bass, 1976.

Program evaluation and accountability are discussed in Chapter 7. A recommended reading for those interested in colleges and universities.

Mitchell, Anita M. *Ways to Evaluate Types of Career Education Activities: A Handbook of Evaluation Models.* Paulo Alto, Calif.: American Institutes for Research in the Behavioral Sciences, 1978.

While the book is about the practitioner's evaluation of career education, the principles, models, and illustrations have applications to all settings. Well written in an informal, light, and appealing style, and illustrated with point-making cartoons. A review of the evaluation process.

————. *Counselor Program Effectiveness: Gathering, Using, and Reporting the Evidence.* Ann Arbor, Mich.: ERIC Counseling and Personnel Services Clearinghouse, 1979.

This brief publication (56 pages) is one of the most useful available for understanding why and how the counselor evaluates his or her work. The whole publication is highly recommended.

Rappaport, Julian. *Community Psychology.* New York: Holt, Rinehart and Winston, 1977.

The strategies and tactics of organizational change are discussed on pages 166–213. Although emphasis is on the community agency, the principles and guidelines are valuable to counselors in any setting for putting the results of evaluation to work.

Shertzer, Bruce, and Stone, Shelley C. *Fundamentals of Guidance.* 4th ed. Boston: Houghton Mifflin, 1981.

The chapter on evaluation, pages 457–485, gives a comprehensive review of research and evaluation approaches, problems, and use of results.

Sullivan, Howard J., and O'Hare, Robert W., eds. *Accountability in Pupil Personnel Services: A Process Guide for the Development of Objectives.* Fullerton: California Personnel and Guidance Association, 1971.

A comprehensive guide for building an accountable program, particularly useful for the many examples included.

Tolbert, E. L. *Research for Teachers and Counselors.* Minneapolis: Burgess Publishing Company, 1967.

A brief review of research approaches, with examples of action research and counselors' personnel applications of results.

Zax, Melvin, and Specter, Gerald A. *An Introduction to Community Psychology.* New York: John Wiley and Sons, 1974.

An excellent source of evaluative studies; many chapters have detailed summaries. Chapter 15 is on research, and pages 447–451 provide a very helpful discussion of issues and strategies in evaluation.

Chapter

14

The Future:
Issues, Trends,
and Prospects

Looking to the future is done not to predict *what* will happen, but to anticipate possibilities. Walz and Benjamin (1979) express the purpose well:

> A look to the future makes it clear that counseling as an organized profession will face many new, yet-unknown challenges and demands. In fact, the future will undoubtedly bring a variety of challenges and demands to all of our existing services and traditions. Only those professions which have given serious thought to alternative futures are likely to survive. It is in this spirit of encouraging our profession to think futuristically and to deal with what is important rather than just what is urgent, that we pose the following three major questions.
>
> We feel that these are questions we must be prepared to answer either explicitly or implicitly. By addressing them now, we will be in a better position to respond to them in the future. (p. 24)

The questions Walz and Benjamin then enumerate are central to the profession's ability to deal with future events, pressures, and demands:

1. "What is our primary mission?"
2. "What is excellence?"
3. "How can we insure self-renewal?" (pp. 24–27)

The answers Walz and Benjamin give to these questions not only lead to a broad concept of helping but also require well-thought-out accountability. Moreover, they require both an institutional and individual commitment to continued self-development.

Looking ahead, however, is not merely divining future options. It also involves shaping the future. A "Futuristic perspective can help them (counselors) to be a proactive force in shaping the future in preferable directions" (Walz and Leu, not dated, p. 13). Hays (1981, p. 2) supports this point of view by saying that "we can no longer take the future for granted — we must become aware of alternative futures and prepare to make decisions to build, to invent, the future we want" (p. 2).

This approach to the future — taking an active position in building a future by identifying alternatives and pushing forward with the most productive ones — is the theme of this chapter. The task is not easy. One way to begin is to look at what is needed in our society and relate what we can do to meet these needs. At the same time, there must be a consideration of social, economic, and political conditions that will affect the growth of services.

Need for Counseling Services

The conditions that support the need for counseling have been highlighted all through the preceding chapters. It is unlikely that any of them will fade away; recent events in social, economic, and political life show that problems and needs will become more complex and pressing.

The viability of counseling as a major helping service depends not only on the profusion of societal problems, complexities, and needs; it must be seen as an effective response. The many publics — students, parents, legislators, the community-at-large, and educators — must view counseling as a profession that provides a needed service, available from no other source. Two factors determine whether or not this will occur. The first is the sensitivity and perceptiveness of counselors in discerning the *real* problems and needs, particularly those of which the general public is only dimly aware. The second is the effectiveness in communicating goals and results to this same public.

Obviously, something positive has to happen in the lives of those who come in contact with guidance. Identifying needs and publicizing results will not alone accomplish the task of insuring the support of guidance services. But counseling already has the means to insure that it has a significant impact, and the dynamic nature of the profession, documented throughout this book, suggests that it will enlarge and improve on present approaches and techniques. There is already research available to support the position that counseling produces positive results, but more is needed. The situation is similar to that faced by psychotherapy; some data supporting positive results are available, but more can be provided if funds are available for additional evaluation (Foltz 1980).

Need can be inferred from a number of conditions and problem areas. Wrenn (1980), in making observations about counseling psychology in the year 2000, identifies several conditions, trends, and priorities that support a continuing need:

1. Cooperation among health-care providers — psychological and physical.
2. Specialization for help at life-stage crises.

3. Help for total life satisfaction.
4. Lifelong career planning.
5. Peers helping each other.
6. Helping that is free of sex bias.
7. Help for couples.
8. Services for the changing populations of schools and colleges.

Each of Wrenn's predictions implies not only a continuing need for counseling but an expansion over what now exists. There are other supporting predictions. Toffler (1980) speaks of the individual's search for meaning in his or her career, a search that involves assistance for understanding self and the world of work. Flanagan's (1978) research on improving the quality of life points to an array of conditions that further reinforce the importance of counseling services, such as the educational preferences of a large proportion of the population that include an expressed need for assistance in planning and decision making (Arbeiter, Aslanian, Schmerbeck, and Brickell 1978, pp. 2–3). In all life areas, questions and needs that call for counseling services are certain to be with us in the years to come.

Our Future and Implications for Guidance

Predictions are hazardous but necessary. The task is made easier by the postbicentennial climate of taking stock and looking to the future. A positive orientation toward the future is essential in the midst of the present confusions and dilemmas.

The bases for optimism are substantial. Resources are being depleted, but there are avenues available utilizing selective growth and alternative energy resources that can, if used fully and promptly, head off disaster. The nation's collective ingenuity can find new ways to cope with destructive trends. Scientific and social innovations and breakthroughs have served to improve the quality of life in past years and have the potential for equal or greater success in the future. We are only beginning to use our intellectual potential for progress on all fronts; education, especially, stands to gain enormously from new developments in both the cognitive and affective areas (Shane 1976). But we may need to experience a "socioquake" (Harman 1976, p. 135) — and thus arrive at new ways of viewing man in relation to the environment rather than patching up the old perceptions and practices.

With an assumption of constructive and positive changes, what are major directions for the next several decades? A review of even a handful of the significant themes requires a look at political, economic, social, and educational aspects (Shane 1976).

There is a continuity in the international political alignments among power blocs, even as new nations strive for status and recognition, and energy resources modify relations among countries. International politics will be based on power balances and energy resources, but there will be a greater recognition and acceptance of the concept of interdependence of nations. The related worldwide problems of growth, crowding, and inadequate resources will be faced; cooperative efforts will be made to slow down the population explosion, increase worldwide food production, and enhance the self-sufficiency of Third World countries.

Economic problems, primarily inflation, and unemployment, will continue to cause hardships for individuals, while increasing both the cost of services and the need for them. Cooperation among nations will be emphasized, while reduced energy resources and needs of undeveloped countries heighten economic problems in this country.

The trend of a rising median population age will continue, and the effects will be felt in every aspect of life. Not only will there be a shift in the emphasis of guidance and counseling, but retirement policies and benefits, education, housing, medical care, and the world of work will be dramatically affected.

Work and the work setting are changing in ways that will have profound effects in the years ahead. There will be an increased demand for job security as protection against the fluctuations in the economy. At the same time, however, more humane and stimulating working conditions will be sought. The workweek and workday will be shortened, and variations such as splitting jobs and self-selected work hours will be tested. The increasing age of the labor force and the steady trend for more female participation will affect the workplace in many ways not yet known to us.

Changes in education will range from introducing new financing plans to establishing programs for lifelong learning. As the proportion of school-age individuals decreases, the cost of public education rises, and the needs and political power of older persons become more visible, we may see a higher quality of schooling. It seems certain that there will be provisions for lifelong easy entry and exit in educational and training programs (Asimov 1976). New school models will merge education and life — family, community, and work — in ways that will make education more significant. Wirtz predicts that "some kind of provision for interspersing the earning and learning of a living, for interweaving employment and self-renewal, is going to have to be recognized as the essential condition for an effective career as worker, citizen, or human being" (1976, p. 129).

Other views of the future shed light on conditions with which counselors must cope. Hays (1981, pp. 12–18) describes five areas of concern:

1. *Global Problems:* Those concerns dealing with food, energy, national identity, and accord among nations.

2. *Economic Problems:* This category includes inflation, recession, employment, worker productivity, and attitudes toward work.
3. *Politics and Government Problems:* Under this heading come problems surrounding the relationship between the individual and the government, the politics of support for social services, and the counselor's participation in political activity.
4. *Science and Technology Problems:* This area includes problems relating to the impact of technology on individuals and the proper use of technology to improve the quality of life. Moreover, new developments such as genetic engineering, raise serious moral and ethical issues.
5. *Individual and Society Problems:* Under this type fall problems of human rights; the needs of special groups, such as minorities; emotional difficulties, and the conflicts and stresses brought about by the nature of our culture.

This brief itemization of points about the future only highlights areas of concern for counselors. Obviously, each area identified could be explored in much greater depth. Moreover, conditions change rapidly; even as this is written, events are taking shape that will have an effect on the future.

Effect of Future Conditions on Helping Services

If we translate the societal trends into guidelines for counseling and guidance, a general picture of increased pressure for services emerges. The need to make the most use possible of human and material resources leads to a greater concern for individual awareness of potential and opportunities. Material resources will be carefully used by those who are sensitive to the needs of others and are aware of the importance of sharing rather than thinking only of themselves.

The increasing interdependence among nations could enhance concern for problems that are common to different cultures and bring guidance workers in different countries closer together to pool strategies and techniques. Developing and underdeveloped countries can profit from learning about what is done in other areas if they have the opportunity to adapt principles and strategies for local use. It would be well to avoid an attitude that what is done in technologically advanced countries is best for others. A cooperative approach to unique needs of each culture would be a true implementation of the spirit of guidance.

Economic trends appear to guarantee that new life-styles will be adopted and that individuals will have to tap their personal resources to find satisfying and challenging ways to cope with changing conditions.

Many of the cutbacks that appear to be inevitable will very likely cause disruptions in established patterns of travel, recreation, and day-to-day living. New modes may actually be growth producing — there may, for example, be less dependence on commercial entertainment — but the changes may call for difficult adaptations.

The changing age of the population has obvious and important implications for helping services. Not only will there be a shift to include expanded services for those in their middle and later years, but new types of help will be needed (e.g., assisting midlife and older persons with educational and work planning) (Entine 1976; Quirk 1976).

The changing world of work offers some of the most direct implications for guidance and counseling of any aspect of life. Even though efforts are being made to adapt work to individuals and to develop new patterns of work hours and sharing jobs, the central problem of finding meaning and fulfillment will demand increased attention. Perhaps a combination of meaningful leisure activities and income-producing work will be needed. Whatever the eventual solutions, it seems that some kind of human development services both in the workplace and in the community will be needed.

The increasing need for accountability and making the most productive use of resources will make education give additional emphasis to helping all pupils understand and utilize their full potential. Questions are being raised about the assumed benefits of large schools ("School Consolidation: Is Bigger Always Better?" 1976; Chaffee 1976), and there is a shift emerging that emphasizes compulsory education, not just compulsory attendance (Ross 1976). These and other trends imply that help will be needed to make the school a place for learning and development attuned to the needs of the individual and the community.

The task of helping youth to find challenge, meaning, and stimulation in school programs, work, and productive community life is made even more demanding by the changing social and economic conditions. This is a school-community problem that demands the best efforts of practically everyone, but it is one in which guidance personnel have a unique opportunity for effective leadership and service.

Skills for the Future

A particularly helpful source of predictions about helping services in the years ahead is provided by surveys of leaders in the profession. Walz and Leu (not dated, pp. 2–14) summarize responses under the categories of skill development, program development, communication, and a futuristic perspective. The specifics covered under each of these areas are too numerous to mention, but a few of the more significant ones will be identified. (The complete section, which includes numerous verbatim comments of respondents, is recommended reading at this time.)

Needed skill development areas include those necessary for working with special groups, political activity, management, and the use of technology. Each of these skills enables the counselor to organize and expand services to meet existing and emerging needs. Moreover, increased proficiency along with the capability of identifying results of help will have a positive effect on the credentialing movement.

Program development skills are essential for making services available to those who need them and in a form that is appropriate. New models may be required. A major management skill is designing and carrying out of evaluation for accountability.

Communication skills are essential for building effective working relationships with colleagues in all settings (e.g., on the college campus). These skills are particularly critical for building wide support for helping services. Public relations should be emphasized in the community and also at the state and national levels.

Importance of a Futuristic Perspective

A futuristic perspective is essential if counselors are to be sensitive to changing times and will be able to have an impact on the way the profession develops. Futurism makes one aware that there are options and that it

A futuristic outlook can help the counselor to be a proactive force and thus shape social trends.

is unproductive and unwise to attempt to pin down exactly what the future holds.

Some more specific trends in the college and community settings seem to be signs of the future. Two of these involve the use of a career development model and organization development on the campus. Many career development concepts mesh well with the student development emphasis; there seems to be a definite trend to expand career development activities on the campus. Workshops, group counseling, and job-finding skills training are examples. The potential of organization development principles and strategies for help in achieving goals of student development is being recognized (Borland 1980, pp. 207–209). The contribution is particularly important as institutions of higher education cope with changes in student populations and reduced financial support for personnel as well as other services and functions. A number of other promising new concepts and strategies were identified in Chapter 3 (e.g., outreach, consultation, peer advising).

The use of counselors in community mental health services has introduced new concepts of helping and new roles in the community-wide setting. Lindenberg (1980, p. 1) says, "Mental Health Counselors will have the opportunity to lead the revolution of health care in the '80's. The counselor will move from being a rather benign after-thought in educational and other so-called traditional settings toward becoming an integral member of health care teams" (p. 1).

The traditional methods of delivery will not, in my opinion, be extinct in the year 2000, as Lindenberg predicts. However, the new strategies and concepts that he suggests — stress reduction, family counseling, contracted services for schools — do appear to be realities even now and hold to a promise of gaining more visibility in the future.

These changes and developments in providing services are accompanied by advances in professionalization and preparation of counselors. Counseling as a helping specialty is gaining increased visibility — the earlier review of settings underlines progress along this line. With this visibility, however, come new pressures and responsibilities. Sunbury and Cochran (1980) identify the areas in which actions need to be taken to meet these responsibilities:

1. Those in the profession need to demonstrate commitment through involvement with local, state, and national organizations.
2. Effective political and legal action to build public support and develop a solid legal base for counseling.
3. Continuing efforts for program accreditation.
4. Continuing improvement of counseling in terms of consumer needs and expectation.

These suggestions highlight the importance of licensure and renewal. The first, licensure, should pave the way for the establishment of status and working conditions that will give a firm base from which to operate. Renewal provides the most useful strategy available to keep competencies up-to-date and to provide the most helpful services possible.

There is a wide variety of new techniques, strategies, concepts, and developments to enable counselors to build a unique profession that is responsive to needs and that can demonstrate effectiveness. Using major features of present status and past developments, general statements can be made about options in the immediate and long-term future.

Counseling in the Immediate Future

Some trends appear to be clearly indicated by current developments. One of these is licensure. There almost certainly will be some type of widespread provisions for licensure, which will have an impact on school counselors. Effects will be felt more definitely by those in nonschool settings, however.

Accountability will be given more attention in all settings. Evidence of positive effects will be needed to insure the continued existence and support for programs. Moreover, counselors will be expected to expand services with little added financial support.

The counselor's role will be more clearly defined, partly because of accountability and partly because of the use of new strategies such as outreach and psychological education, which give the work a visible structure and purpose.

Increasing attention will be given to the needs of special groups (midlife and older persons, minorities, the handicapped, and women). Moreover, we will see at least the beginnings of the implementation of lifelong learning and school-community cooperative approaches. College career development and student personnel work with a broader conceptualization will be growth factors and major changes in the next five years.

Changes in public education will make the school a more dynamic and realistic learning environment. At the same time, the "basics" will be increasingly emphasized. All of these changes will offer counselors opportunities to serve in new ways and to build a solid position in education.

More processes and personnel will be utilized to expand the reach of services. Paraprofessionals are one example, particularly peer counselors. After their slow start in the past decade, computers will be used with increasing frequency.

As budgets are examined, and "tax revolts" emerge, questions will be raised about the necessity for counseling services. The predicted outcome, however, is that there will be an increase in the support for services because they offer ways to deal with the most pressing educational and community problems.

Helping Services in the Long-Term Future

In the next 15 to 20 years, the impact of the social, political, and economic trends discussed earlier in this chapter could have a more pronounced impact on counseling services than in the immediate future. Without ruling out alternative possibilities, it appears likely that several positive developments will have emerged. For one thing, credentialing problems will be resolved; licensure for counselors will be a reality. Helping strategies will be available to serve diverse populations. Accountability will no longer be as much of a threat as a way to help insure funding. There will be a wide understanding of, and support for, the counselor role. Technology will be employed to handle jobs such as detailed, clerical tasks, giving counselors time for professional functions such as counseling and consulting.

Lifelong education and school-community cooperation will be realities, and counselors will work with all ages in both school and community. There will be increases in the number of counselors needed; preparation standards will provide for differential staffing, with high levels of technical and human relations competency for those in supervisory positions. At the same time there will be increased attention to prevention of problems and the provision of easily available community-wide services. School counselors will be regarded as logical persons to coordinate school guidance and pupil personnel services and will provide leadership for community-wide coordination strategies. Colleges will perceive and implement the role of the student development specialist as a central part of their basic mission rather than as peripheral adjuncts to the academic program.

In the future we can expect to see an extensive system of program accreditation. Most likely all preparation programs will be accredited, and a national registry will be established. Counselors will participate in national health programs and will be eligible to receive third-party payments. Other developments critical to the status of the profession include a legal base for the practice of counseling and well-organized political action efforts. Legislators as well as the general public will have a much better understanding of what counseling is and what it does than is currently the case.

At all levels and in all settings there will be a research base for programs. Counselors will have the evidence to show convincingly that they do have an impact and can effect positive changes in individuals and institutions. There will be ample evidence to justify counselor positions in all settings. Renewal programs will be widely used for keeping up to date. Evaluation will be an essential component of every program.

The projections into the future that have been made are unabashedly optimistic. It would be easy to take a pessimistic stance and warn of cutbacks, restrictions to practice, and retrenchments. True, there are temporary setbacks and plateaus, but the long-range trend — the past seven or eight decades — has witnessed phenomenal growth in the profession. For that considerable part of this time span in which the author has been personally involved, progress has exceeded the expectations of even the most idealistic and uninhibited dreamer. But the progress made was not an accident. It was built by those who were futurists. The same thing can continue to happen.

Summary Concepts

It is important for members of a profession to look ahead and antici pate changes and developments. Will there be a continuing need for ser vices that the profession renders? This question can be answered in the affirmative; the needs and problems will be there. Counseling has already demonstrated responsiveness to these needs and problems. Economic, so cial, political, educational, and occupational trends have implications for counseling services. These implications point to an expansion of services to include lifelong assistance and a broadening to cover a variety of settings and groups. New techniques, strategies, and programs are being devel oped to attend to expanded needs. Moreover, the profession itself is chang ing; new roles, credentialing, program accreditation, and renewal are areas of particular significance. Looking to the immediate and long-term futures, optimistic predictions can be made about professionalization, fi nancial support, public understanding, expansion of services, development of new strategies, and demonstration of efficacy.

Suggested Readings

Brubaker, J. Craig. "Futures Consultation: Designing Desirable Futures." *Personnel and Guidance Journal* 56, no. 7 (1978), pp. 428–431.
    Innovative strategies to influence the future.
Burtnett, Francis E. *The School Counselor's Involvement in Career Education.* Falls Church, Va.: American Personnel and Guidance Association, 1980.
    A series of articles on an expanded role for counselors in career education, elementary through high school. A forward-looking report that is of particular value to those interested in the school setting.
Creamer, Don G., ed. *Student Development in Higher Education.* Cincinnati: Amer ican College Personnel Association, 1980.
    Part 3 contains articles emphasizing new directions. Any one of them will help the reader clarify current problems and identify trends. The one by Mable (pp. 230–238), on perspectives and needs-assessment strategies, is recom mended as a starting place.
Gibson, Robert L., and Mitchell, Marianne H. *Introduction to Guidance.* New York: Macmillan Publishing Company, 1981.

Pages 42–49 contain a brief, interesting discussion of the future of school guidance and counseling programs.

Harris, Philip R. "Guidance and Counseling in Year 2000." *Counselor Education and Supervision* 7, no. 3 (1968), pp. 262–266.

A perceptive look into the future, which suggests a number of developments similar to those discussed in this chapter.

Hays, Donald G. *Counseling and the Future: Concepts, Issues, and Strategies.* Ann Arbor, Mich.: ERIC Counseling and Personnel Services Clearinghouse, 1981.

A stimulating and well-prepared reference on the value of a futuristic perspective for counseling. Issues, needs, and counselor responses are covered. Exercises to sensitize counselors to a futuristic perspective are included.

Herr, Edwin L. *Guidance and Counseling in the Schools: The Past, Present, and Future.* Falls Church, Va.: American Personnel and Guidance Association, 1979.

A valuable reference for anyone interested in the school setting. Two sections are particularly appropriate — Part 4 on emerging directions and Part 5 on problems and recommended actions.

Hilton, Thomas L. *Confronting the Future: A Conceptual Framework for Secondary School Career Guidance.* New York: College Entrance Examination Board, 1979.

Particularly useful for a comprehensive analysis of how career guidance can contribute to secondary education. The "assumptions" on pages 1–8 identify pupil needs that call for well-developed career guidance services.

Lewis, Judith A., and Lewis, Michael D. *Community Counseling.* New York: John Wiley and Sons, 1977.

In Chapter 13, on the future of community counseling, the authors identify and respond to a series of critical questions about the future of work in the community setting. An excellent overview of issues and possible solutions.

Licensure Committee Action Packet 1979. Falls Church, Va.: American Personnel and Guidance Association, 1979.

The most recent collection of materials on licensure available from the APGA. (New editions will likely be available in the future.) Designed to be of assistance to those in the licensure movement, the packet is an excellent resource for learning about licensure. Pages 8–15 give a review of the topic.

Miller, Frank W.; Fruehling, James A.; and Lewis, Gloria J. *Guidance Principles and Services.* 3rd ed. Columbus, Ohio: Charles E. Merrill, 1978.

Perspectives, trends, and issues are reviewed in Chapter 13. A very useful reference in connection with this chapter, particularly the section on trends, pages 502–509.

Pietrofesa, John J.; Bernstein, Bianca; Minor, Jo Anne; and Stanford, Susan. *Guidance: An Introduction.* Chicago: Rand McNally, 1980.

Chapter 15, on issues and trends in school counseling and guidance, provides an in-depth analysis of areas of particular significance to professionals. Highly recommended.

Shertzer, Bruce, and Stone, Shelley C. *Fundamentals of Guidance.* 4th ed. Boston: Houghton Mifflin, 1981.

In Chapter 19, "Trends in Guidance," the authors predict future programs, preparation, and role. A valuable reading that projects an optimistic and realistic future.

Tyler, Leona E. "Counseling Girls and Women in the Year 2000." In *Counseling Girls and Women Over the Life Span,* edited by Edwin A. Whitfield and Alice Gustav, pp. 89–96. Washington, D.C.: National Vocational Guidance Association, 1972.

One of the leaders in the field gives an illuminating glimpse into the role of counseling women in the twenty-first century.

Walz, Garry R. "Swinging into the Future." *Personnel and Guidance Journal* 53, no. 9 (1975), pp. 712–716.

A provocative article about career guidance, touching on all aspects of life in the future and discussing implications for the counselor.

Walz, Garry R., and Benjamin, Libby. "Counselors on the Bubble." In *New Imperatives for Guidance,* edited by Garry R. Walz and Libby Benjamin, pp. 421–454. Ann Arbor, Mich.: ERIC Counseling and Personnel Services Clearinghouse, 1978.

The authors make a persuasive case for the value of renewal in the professional life of the counselor.

Walz, Garry R., and Benjamin, Libby. *A Futuristic Perspective for Counselors.* Ann Arbor, Mich.: ERIC Counseling and Personnel Services Clearinghouse, 1979.

An excellent reference on a futuristic perspective for counselors. This section on future-relevant counselor behaviors (pp. 14–17) is particularly stimulating.

Walz, Garry R., and Leu, Jane. *Futuristic Images of Guidance and Student Services.* Ann Arbor, Mich.: ERIC Counseling and Personnel Services Clearinghouse, not dated.

A report of the results of surveys of leaders' views of what needs to be done to prepare for the future. A comprehensive and stimulating reference.

Warner, Richard W., Jr.; Brooks, Jr., David K.; and Thompson, Jean A. *Counselor Licensure: Issues and Perspectives.* Falls Church, Va.: American Personnel and Guidance Association, 1980.

A comprehensive review of the licensure movement; includes copies of the Alabama, Arkansas, and Virginia licensure laws and an extensive bibliography of publications on certification, credentialing, and registry. Pages 1–5 contain a chronological history of licensure and related credentialing activities.

Whiteley, John M. "The Future of Counseling Psychology: Introduction." *Counseling Psychologist* 8, no. 4 (1980), p. 2.

The editor's introduction to a special issue on counseling psychology in the year 2000. Eighteen articles by leaders in the field give a broad perspective on forces that will affect counseling in the next two decades and predict how the profession may respond.

Wrenn, C. Gilbert. "Personal Perspectives — Past and Present." In *New Imperatives for Guidance,* edited by Garry R. Walz and Libby Benjamin, pp. 455–491. Ann Arbor, Mich.: ERIC Counseling and Personnel Services Clearinghouse, 1978.

A long view of the development of counseling services with emphasis on conditions that underline their continuing importance in our society. Particularly valuable for identifying the tasks that lie ahead.

Zaccaria, Joseph, and Bopp, Stephen G. *Approaches to Guidance in Contemporary Education.* 2nd ed. Cranston, R.I.: The Carroll Press, 1981.

Current status, trends, and directions are discussed on pages 288–302. The 23 points covered contain specific predictions that present a challenging picture of the future of the profession.

Appendix

A

Standards for the Preparation of Counselors and Other Personnel Services Specialists

Prepared by the Association
for Counselor Education and Supervision

Introduction

These Standards are intended as guidelines for the graduate preparation of counselors and other personnel services specialists. They should be beneficial to college and university staff who are involved in initiating programs of preparation or in evaluating existing programs. The Standards can also be helpful to state, regional and national accrediting agencies. While the Standards are designed to serve as guidelines for minimum preparation, they are flexible enough to allow for creative approaches to counselor education. The Standards do not include guidelines for the preparation of support personnel or professional personnel at the doctoral level.

These Standards recognize that:

The faculty has developed a written statement of philosophy for the counselor education program and that this statement has been accepted by the institution.

The trend toward the development of competency based/performance based counselor education programs is likely to continue. However, whether or not a counselor education program is developed upon such a base, the standards reflect the concern that all programs should give to the assessment of demonstrated competencies by students during various stages of their development.

Students take varying rates of time to demonstrate the competencies and professional maturation demanded in the complexities of counseling and personnel services work. While the standards recommend minimum hours of study in certain areas, these stated minimum hours should be interpreted in the context that some students will demonstrate the desired competency and professional maturation levels in a shorter time than indicated while others may take substantially longer.

The need of counselors and other personnel services specialists for self-renewal and in-service education beyond minimum preparation or certification will increase. Therefore, the counselor education program should provide enriching experiences for those who have already completed the minimum program.

Minimum study in counselor education will increasingly extend beyond the one year program of graduate preparation. Such programs might include (1) a combination of an undergraduate major in guidance and a year of graduate study in counselor education, (2) two years of graduate study in counselor education, or (3) other models which include a minimum of one year of graduate study.

All counselor education programs are not expected to prepare counselors and other personnel services specialists for all the work settings encompassed by the Standards. Institutions should offer preparation programs only in those areas where sufficient qualified full-time staff and other resources are available.

The Standards reflect current thinking concerning the preparation of counselors and other personnel services specialists and combine the three existing statements on counselor preparation previously adopted by the Association for Counselor Education and Supervision (ACES): "Standards for the Preparation of Secondary School Counselors — 1967"; "Standards for the Preparation of Elementary School Counselors," February, 1968; and "Guidelines for Graduate Programs in the Preparation of Student Personnel Workers in Higher Education — 1969."

In addition to acknowledging the similarity of preparation among the various specialists, the Standards also provide for different goals which may exist in various work settings. While this single document has been developed for the entire profession, the respective divisions of the American Personnel and Guidance Association and other professional groups are encouraged to develop jointly, with ACES, specific statements concerning the specialized needs of counselors and other personnel services specialists who work in different settings. In this respect, attention is called to Section II, B.2 of the Standards, "Environmental and Specialized Studies."

Leadership for the development of these Standards was assumed by the ACES Commission on Standards and Accreditation, working under the supervision of the Executive Council of ACES. The Standards were adopted by the membership of ACES in 1973.

Standards

Section I: Objectives

A. Objectives of the Program to Prepare Counselors and Other Personnel Services Specialists
1. *The faculty has developed program objectives.*
   a. Objectives reflect a knowledge of studies and recommendations of local, state, regional, and national lay and professional groups concerned with counseling and personal services needs of society.
   b. Objectives reflect the needs in society which are represented by different ethnic and cultural groups served by counselors and other personnel services specialists.
   c. Objectives are reviewed and revised continuously through student as well as faculty participation.
   d. Objectives are developed and reviewed with the assistance of personnel in cooperating agencies.
   e. Objectives are written in such a way that evaluation of a student can be based on demonstrated competencies as he progresses through the program.
2. *Objectives are implemented on a planned basis in all areas of the program including selection, retention and endorsement of students; curriculum; instructional methods; research activities; and administrative policies, procedures, and execution.*
3. *Personnel in cooperating agencies and faculty members with primary assignments in other disciplines are aware of and are encouraged to work toward the objectives of the counselor education program.*
4. *There is a planned procedure for a continuing evaluation of the outcomes of the program.*
   a. The program is evaluated in terms of demonstrated competencies of each student as he or she progresses through the program.
   b. Evaluation of the effectiveness of preparation is accomplished through evidence obtained from: (1) former students, (2) supervisors in agencies employing graduates of the program, and, (3) personnel in state and national licensing and accrediting agencies.

Section II: Curriculum — Program of Studies and Supervised Experiences

A. General Program Characteristics
 1. *The institution provides a graduate program in counselor education designed for the preparation of counselors and other personnel services specialists.*
  a. The opportunity for full-time study throughout the academic year is provided and actively encouraged.
  b. Flexibility is provided within the curriculum to allow for individual differences in competencies and understandings developed before entering the program.
  c. Descriptions of the various program options and requirements for graduate studies are published and distributed to prospective students.
  d. Concepts relating to differentiated staffing and preparation in counseling and personnel services are reflected in the program. The faculty is aware of lifetime opportunities for development and advancement in the field of counseling and personnel services. There is also an emphasis on the use of support personnel to free more professionally prepared personnel for the performance of higher level functions.
 2. *Continuing and/or in-service education offerings in counselor education meet all of the criteria in faculty qualifications, faculty load, physical facilities, faculty-student ratios, etc. as described in these Standards.*
 3. *There is evidence of high quality instruction in all aspects of the program.*
  a. Syllabi or other evidence of organized and coordinated instructional units of the curriculum are available.
  b. Resource materials are provided.
  c. Responsibilities are assigned to, or assumed by, faculty members only in those areas of the counselor education program for which they have demonstrated professional competency.
  d. Provisions are made for periodic evaluation by students and staff of all aspects of the program, i.e., course content, methods of instruction, and supervised experience, both on and off campus.
 4. *Planned sequences of educational experiences are provided.*
  a. Within the minimum counselor education program a sequence of basic and advanced graduate studies and other associated learning experiences is defined and provided.

    b. The program provides for the integration of didactic studies and supervised experiences.

    c. All prerequisite studies and other experiences are identified.

    d. Representatives of departments offering studies in related fields are regularly consulted regarding how related studies can be made more useful to counselor education majors.

    e. The faculty has identified performance indicators to determine whether the professional competencies to be developed by the sequence of educational experiences are achieved.

5. *A close relationship exists between the faculty of the counselor education program and the staff members in work settings.*

    a. The staff in the work settings is consulted in the design and implementation of all aspects of the program including practicum and internship experiences.

    b. The faculty of the preparation program is consulted in the design and implementation of in-service preparation of staff in work settings.

6. *Within the framework of the total program, there are opportunities for the student to develop understandings and skills beyond the minimum requirements of the program.*

    a. Elective courses and related experiences are available.

    b. Supervised individual study is available.

    c. Enrichment opportunities are provided and faculty encourage students to take part in them.

7. *The spirit of inquiry and the production and utilization of research data are encouraged among both faculty and students.*

    a. The statement of objectives of the program reflects an awareness of the role of research in the counseling and personnel services field.

    b. Instructional procedures make frequent use of, and reference to, research findings. Areas in which research is needed are identified.

8. *Opportunities for planned periodic self-evaluation and the development of greater self-understanding are provided for both students and faculty.*

    a. Self-analysis is encouraged through such activities as laboratory experiences, including audio and/or video tape recordings.

    b. Opportunities for improvement of interpersonal relationships are provided through small group activities.

    c. Counseling services for students are available and are provided by qualified persons other than counselor education faculty.

B. Program of Studies

1. *Common core: The common core is composed of general areas considered to be necessary in the preparation of all counselors and other personnel services specialists.*

   a. Human growth and development: Includes studies that provide a broad understanding of the nature and needs of individuals at all developmental levels. Emphasis is placed on psychological, sociological, and physiological approaches. Also included are such areas as human behavior (normal and abnormal), personality theory, and learning theory.

   b. Social and cultural foundations: Includes studies of change, ethnic groups, sub-cultures, changing roles of women, sexism, urban and rural societies, population patterns, cultural mores, use of leisure time, and differing life patterns. Such disciplines as the behavioral sciences, economics, and political science are involved.

   c. The helping relationship: Includes (a) philosophic bases of the helping relationship; (b) counseling theory, supervised practice, and application; (c) consultation theory, supervised practice, and application; and (d) an emphasis upon development of counselor and client (or consultee) self-awareness and self-understanding.

   d. Groups: Includes theory and types of groups, as well as descriptions of group practices, methods, dynamics, and facilitative skills. It also includes supervised practice.

   e. Life style and career development: Includes such areas as vocational choice theory, relationship between career choice and life style, sources of occupational and educational information, approaches to career decision-making processes, and career development exploration techniques.

   f. Appraisal of the individual: Includes the development of a framework for understanding the individual including methods of data gathering and interpretation, individual and group testing, case study approaches, and the study of individual differences. Ethnic, cultural, and sex factors are also considered.

   g. Research and evaluation: Includes such areas as statistics, research design, development of research and demonstration proposals. It also includes understanding legislation relating to the development of research, program development, and demonstration proposals, as well as the development and evaluation of program objectives.

   h. Professional orientation: Includes goals and objectives of professional organizations, codes of ethics, legal considerations, standards of preparation, certification, licensing, and role identity of counselors and other personnel services specialists.

2. *Environmental and Specialized Studies: The counselor education program includes those specialized studies necessary for practice in different work settings. There is evidence that the faculty, in planning and evaluating the counselor education curriculum, has taken into consideration statements made by other professional groups relating to role, function, and preparation.*

   a. Environmental studies: Includes the study of the environment in which the student is planning to practice. This includes history, philosophy, trends, purposes, ethics, legal aspects, standards, and roles within the institution or work setting where the student will practice.

   b. Specialized studies: Includes the specialized knowledge and skills needed to work effectively in the professional setting where the student plans to practice. For example, the student preparing to be an elementary school counselor may need to take, among other specialized courses, work in diagnosis of reading dysfunction; the student preparing to be a personnel services educator in higher education might need, among other specialized work, both course work and supervised experiences in student financial aid; or the student preparing to work in employment counseling may need additional information about employment trends as well as the sociology and psychology of work.

   The different professional associations jointly concerned with the preparation of counselors and other personnel services specialists are encouraged to develop statements concerning environmental and specialized studies, and make these statements available to the ACFS Commission on Standards and Accreditation and to the profession in general.

C. Supervised Experiences

1. *Appropriate supervised experiences provide for the integration and application of knowledge and skills gained in didactic study.*

   a. Students' supervised experiences are in settings which are compatible with their career goals.

   b. Supervised experiences include observation and direct work with individuals and groups within the appropriate work setting.

   c. Opportunities are provided for professional relationships with staff members in the work settings.

2. *Supervised experiences include laboratory, practicum, and internship.*

   a. Laboratory experiences, providing both observation and participation in specific activities, are offered throughout the preparatory program. This might include role-playing, listening to tapes, viewing video tape playbacks, testing, organizing and using personnel records, interviews with field practitioners, preparing and examining case studies, and using career information materials.

   b. Supervised counseling practicum experiences provide interaction with individuals and groups actually seeking services from counselors and other personnel services specialists. Some of these individuals and groups should come from the environments in which the counselor education student is preparing to work.

      (1) Specific counseling practica have sufficient duration and continuity to assure optimum professional development. The minimum recommended amount of actual contact with individuals and groups is 60 clock hours extending over a minimum nine-month period.

      (2) Supervision in consultation is also provided.

      (3) The supervisor's role is clearly identified and sufficient time for supervision is allocated. The recommended weekly minimum of supervision is one hour of individual supervision and one hour of supervision in a group for the duration of the practicum experiences. Supervisory responsibilities include critiquing of counseling, either observed or recorded on audio or video tape.

   c. Internship is a post-practicum experience that provides an actual on-the-job experience, and should be given central importance for each student.

      (1) The internship placement is selected on the basis of the student's career goals.

      (2) The internship includes all activities that a regularly employed staff member would be expected to perform. In the setting the intern is expected to behave as a professional and should be treated as one.

      (3) For those students who have no prior work experience in their particular setting, an intensified or expanded internship is provided.

      (4) The intern spends a minimum of 300 clock hours on the job. It is desirable that the internship be a paid experience.

(5) Supervision is performed by qualified staff in the field placement setting who have released time from other regular duties.

(6) The counselor education faculty provides these field supervisors opportunities for in-service education in counseling and personnel services supervision.

(7) There should be close cooperative working relationships between staff in field placement setting and the counselor education faculty.

3. *A qualified faculty and staff with adequate time allocated to supervision is provided for laboratory, practicum, and internship experiences.*

   a. Members of the on-campus faculty responsible for supervision include those who:

      (1) have earned doctoral degrees, preferably in counselor education, from accredited institutions.

      (2) have had experience and demonstrate competencies in counseling and other personnel services at the level appropriate for the students supervised.

   b. Doctoral students serving as supervisors of practicum experiences are themselves supervised by qualified faculty.

   c. The practicum and internship experiences are tutorial forms of instruction; therefore, the supervision of five students is considered equivalent to the teaching of one three semester-hour course. Such a ratio is considered maximum.

4. *Facilities, equipment, and materials are provided for supervised experiences in both on- and off-campus settings. (See also Section IV.)*

D. Program Development Outreach

1. *The counselor education faculty assists individual counselors and other personnel services specialists in off-campus agencies providing supervised experiences in the program of preparation.*

   a. The institution encourages agency personnel to seek the counselor education faculty's assistance in planning and conducting in-service education and in developing program improvement models.

   b. The counselor education faculty is provided a teaching-work load recognition for their part in in-service and program development activities in cooperating agencies.

   c. The counselor education faculty involves advanced graduate students in programs of in-service education and in program development planning and implementation at the agency level.

2. *The counselor education faculty provides on-campus assistance to agency personnel in resolving unique problems or difficulties.*
   a. The faculty encourages agency personnel to seek assistance through the use of such techniques as personal appointments, telephone access programs, information storage and retrieval, position papers, and various audio and/or visual media.
3. *The counselor education faculty integrates the experiences of the outreach activity into its counselor education program by adapting or modifying the counselor education program as may be appropriate. Outreach activities are viewed as a significant function in the preparation program.*

Section III: Responsibilities Concerning Students in the Program

A. Information
   1. *Information concerning major aspects of the counselor education program and the faculty is available in a variety of media for prospective students.*
      a. The academic areas in which the program offers preparation and the degrees offered are clearly stated.
      b. Counselor education faculty are available to discuss the program of preparation.
      c. Personnel in various counseling and related job settings have been designated as referral sources for discussion of their areas of interest with prospective students.
B. Selection
   1. *Applicants accepted meet the institution's standards for admission to graduate study.*
      a. There is evidence that staff in cooperating agencies have been consulted relative to admission policies and procedures.
      b. Students in the program reflect an effort, on the part of the faculty, to select individuals who represent a variety of sub-cultures and sub-groups within our society.
      c. A committee of faculty members makes the decisions concerning admission of applicants to the program based upon established criteria such as:
         (1) Potential effectiveness in close interpersonal relationships.
         (2) Aptitude for counseling and related human development responsibilities.

    (3) Commitment to a career in counseling and personnel work.

    (4) Potential for establishing facilitative relationships with people at various levels of development.

    (5) Openness to self-examination and commitment to self-growth.

C. Retention

    1. *A continuing evaluation through systematic review is made of students as they progress through the program.*

    2. *In situations where evaluations of a student indicates an inappropriateness for the counseling field, faculty members assist in facilitating change to an area more appropriate for the student.*

D. Endorsement

    1. *A statement of policy relating to the institution's procedure for formal endorsement has been adopted and approved by the faculty and administrative authorities.*

       a. Each candidate is informed of procedures of endorsement for certification, licensing, and employment.

       b. Insofar as possible, all faculty members acquainted with the student, including supervisors of practicum and internship experiences, should participate in the endorsement process.

    2. *Endorsement is given by the counselor education faculty only for the particular job setting for which the student has been prepared.*

    3. *Endorsement is given only on the basis of evidence of demonstrated proficiency. The candidate should have completed a substantial part of his graduate work in counselor education, including supervised counseling experience, at the endorsing institution.*

E. Placement

    1. *The institution has a placement service with policies and procedures consistent with recognized placement practices.*

       a. The faculty assist the student with the preparation of placement papers and the selection and securing of a suitable position.

       b. Placement services are available to graduates of the program throughout their professional careers.

       c. Opportunities are provided for students to participate in local, state, and federal examinations for employment opportunities.

F. Research and Evaluation

    1. *Policies and procedures relating to recruitment, selection, retention, and placement are continually studied through various research and evaluative methods.*

a. Regular follow-up studies are made of former students, including dropouts, students removed from the program, and graduates.
b. Evaluation is followed by appropriate revisions and improvements in the preparation program.

Section IV: Support for the Counselor Education Program, Administrative Relations, and Institutional Resources

1. *Administrative organization and procedures provide recognition and designated responsibilities for a counselor education program.*
   a. The program is a clearly identified part of the institution's graduate program.
      (1) There is preferably only one unit directly responsible for the preparation of counselors and other personnel services specialists.
      (2) If more than one unit in the institution is directly involved in the preparation of counselors and other personnel services specialists, there is evidence of close cooperation and coordination.
   b. Cooperative relationships exist between the counselor education program and other units of the institution related to the program.
      (1) Contributions of other units to the program are defined.
      (2) Channels of communication with faculty members in other units are identified and maintained.
   c. Use is made of a wide range of professional and community resources. Evidence of positive working relationships exists with agencies off the campus that have the potential for contributing to the preparation of counselors and other personnel services specialists. They may be potential employers of graduates of the program.
2. *The institution provides for the professional development of the counselor education faculty as well as students in the counselor education program.*
   a. Faculty are involved in professional activities on local, state, regional, and national levels.
   b. Faculty participate in voluntary professional service capacities.
   c. The institution provides encouragement and financial support for the faculty to participate in professional activities.
   d. Faculty engage in programs of research and contribute to literature of the field.

e. Students participate in the activities of professional organizations.

3. *The institution provides adequate faculty and supporting staff for all aspects of the counselor education program.*

   a. An individual is designated as the professional leader of the counselor education program.

     (1) This individual is an experienced counselor and possesses an earned doctorate in counselor education from an accredited institution.

     (2) This individual has full-time assignment to the counselor education program.

     (3) This individual is recognized for his leadership in the counseling profession.

     (4) This individual is qualified by preparation and experience to conduct and to supervise research activities.

4. *In addition to the designated leader there are at least two full-time faculty members with comparable qualifications.*

   a. Additional faculty are provided at the ratio of one full-time staff member for every ten full-time graduate students or their equivalent in part-time graduate students. This ratio should be reduced in institutions where a large percentage of the counselor education students are enrolled on a part-time basis and/or when program changes create the need for the faculty to spend more time in the evaluation of each student.

5. *The full-time teaching load of faculty members is consistent with that of other graduate units in the institution which require intensive supervision as an integral part of professional preparation.*

   a. The faculty load is modified in proportion to assigned responsibilities for graduate advisement and research supervision on a formula that is consistent with established graduate school policy in the institution.

   b. Time is provided within the total faculty work load for cooperative interdisciplinary activities with teaching faculty in related fields.

   c. The total work load of faculty members includes a recognition of time needed for professional research.

6. *Faculty in closely related disciplines are qualified in their respective areas and also are informed about the objectives of the counselor education program.*

7. *Off-campus agency personnel who supervise students are qualified through academic preparation and professional experience.*

   a. Such staff members have two or more years of appropriate professional experience.

   b. These staff members have at least two years of graduate work in counselor education or can demonstrate equivalent preparation.

8. *Graduate assistantships are provided to assist the faculty and to provide additional experiences for students in the program.*

   a. Regular procedures are established for the identification and assignment of qualified students to assistantships.

   b. A minimum of one half-time graduate student is assigned to the counselor education program for each 30 full-time equivalent students.

   c. Assignments are made in such a way as to enrich the professional learning experiences of the graduate assistants.

9. *Secretarial, clerical, and other supportive staff are provided in the counselor education program.*

   a. A minimum of one full-time secretary or equivalent is provided for the clerical work of the counselor education program.

   b. Additional clerical service is provided at the ratio of one full-time clerical assistant for the equivalent of every three faculty members.

   c. Responsibilities of secretarial, clerical and other supportive staff are defined and adequate supervision is provided.

10. *The institution provides facilities and a budget that insures continuous operation of all aspects of the counselor education program.*

   a. The institution provides a designated headquarters for the counselor education program.

     (1) The headquarters is located near the classroom and laboratory facilities used in the counselor education program.

     (2) The headquarters area includes a private office for each faculty member.

     (3) The headquarters area includes office space for secretarial, clerical, and other supportive staff.

     (4) The headquarters provides appropriate work space, equipment, and supplies for graduate assistants.

   b. Facilities for supervised experiences are provided in a coordinated laboratory setting on campus. Consideration is given to:

     (1) Facilities for individual counseling in rooms with assured privacy and adequate space for related equipment.

     (2) Facilities for small group work. The area provides for small group counseling, testing, staffing, meetings, and so forth.

     (3) Classroom and seminar meeting rooms.

     (4) Facilities appropriately equipped with the following:

(a) recording and listening devices, both portable and permanent

(b) one-way vision glass

(c) video-tape recording and playing devices, both portable and permanent

(5) Technical assistance for both operational and maintenance services.

(6) Acoustical treatment throughout the facility.

(7) Facilities that are conducive to modeling and demonstrating exemplary environments and practices in counseling and personnel services. The facilities should include a "model" counseling laboratory with related resource materials and audio-visual equipment. Included as resources in the "model" laboratory are:

(a) career occupational and educational information materials

(b) standardized tests and interpretation data

(c) a variety of media, equipment, and materials

(d) space for teaching and laboratory experiences

(8) Data processing assistance and equipment that are available for both teaching and research.

(9) Facilities that are located in close approximation to the counselor education faculty offices and away from centers of extreme noise and confusion.

c. Library facilities provide an appropriate supply of resource materials for study and research in counselor education.

(1) The facilities include basic resources, both books and periodicals, in areas in which the counselor education program provides preparation. Resources in related areas such as psychology, sociology, and economics are also available.

(2) Both current and historical materials are available.

(3) Library resources are available during evening and weekend hours.

(4) Inter-library loans, ERIC services, microfilm, and photocopy services are available.

(5) Multiple copies of frequently used publications are available.

11. *Research facilities are available to faculty and students in counselor education.*

a. Facilities include offices and laboratories equipped to provide opportunities for the collection, analysis, and synthesis of data.

  b. Consultant services are available from research specialists on
     the institution's faculty.
  c. Campus computer centers and other data-processing facilities
     are available.
  d. Appropriate settings, for research both off and on campus, are
     provided.
12. *The institution recognizes the individual needs of graduate students
    and provides services for personal as well as professional develop-
    ment.*
  a. Since full-time academic-year attendance is possible for most
     graduate students only if some form of financial assistance is
     available, efforts are made to develop financial assistance for
     students in the counselor education program.
     (1) The counselor education program is assigned a propor-
         tionate share of the institution's funds for student assis-
         tance.
     (2) Part-time work opportunities appropriate for students in
         the program are identified and efforts are made to secure
         assignments for those desiring such opportunities.
     (3) Loan resources are available to students in counselor edu-
         cation.
     (4) Prospective students are provided information about pos-
         sible sources of financial assistance.
  b. Personal counseling services are available to all counselor edu-
     cation students.
     (1) A counseling service is available from professionals other
         than the members of the counselor education faculty.
     (2) Procedures for referral are known by all faculty members.

Appendix

B

Ethical Standards

American Personnel and Guidance Association

(Approved by Executive Committee upon referral of the Board of Directors, January 17, 1981).

Preamble

The American Personnel and Guidance Association is an educational, scientific, and professional organization whose members are dedicated to the enhancement of the worth, dignity, potential, and uniqueness of each individual and thus to the service of society.

The Association recognizes that the role definitions and work settings of its members include a wide variety of academic disciplines, levels of academic preparation and agency services. This diversity reflects the breadth of the Association's interest and influence. It also poses challenging complexities in efforts to set standards for the performance of members, desired requisite preparation or practice, and supporting social, legal, and ethical controls.

The specification of ethical standards enables the Association to clarify to present and future members and to those served by members, the nature of ethical responsibilities held in common by its members.

The existence of such standards serves to stimulate greater concern by members for their own professional functioning and for the conduct of fellow professionals such as counselors, guidance and student personnel workers, and others in the helping professions. As the ethical code of the Association, this document establishes principles that define the ethical behavior of Association members.

Section A:
General

1. The member influences the development of the profession by continuous efforts to improve professional practices, teaching, services, and research. Professional growth is continuous throughout the member's career and is exemplified by the development of a philosophy that explains why and how a member functions in the helping relationship. Members must gather data on their effectiveness and be guided by the findings.

2. The member has a responsibility both to the individual who is served and to the institution within which the service is performed to maintain high standards of professional conduct. The member strives to maintain the highest levels of professional services offered to the individuals to be served. The member also strives to assist the agency, organization, or institution in providing the highest caliber of professional services. The acceptance of employment in an institution implies that the member is in agreement with the general policies and principles of the institution. Therefore the professional activities of the member are also in accord with the objectives of the institution. If, despite concerted efforts, the member cannot reach agreement with the employer as to acceptable standards of conduct that allow for changes in institutional policy conducive to the positive growth and development of clients, then terminating the affiliation should be seriously considered.

3. Ethical behavior among professional associates, both members and nonmembers, must be expected at all times. When information is possessed that raises doubt as to the ethical behavior of professional colleagues, whether Association members or not, the member must take action to attempt to rectify such a condition. Such action shall use the institution's channels first and then use procedures established by the state Branch, Division, or Association.

4. The member neither claims nor implies professional qualifications exceeding those possessed and is responsible for correcting any misrepresentations of these qualifications by others.

5. In establishing fees for professional counseling services, members must consider the financial status of clients and locality. In the event that the established fee structure is inappropriate for a client, assistance must be provided in finding comparable services of acceptable cost.

6. When members provide information to the public or to subordi-

nates, peers or supervisors, they have a responsibility to ensure that the content is general, unidentified client information that is accurate, unbiased, and consists of objective, factual data.

7. With regard to the delivery of professional services, members should accept only those positions for which they are professionally qualified.

8. In the counseling relationship the counselor is aware of the intimacy of the relationship and maintains respect for the client and avoids engaging in activities that seek to meet the counselor's personal needs at the expense of that client. Through awareness of the negative impact of both racial and sexual stereotyping and discrimination, the counselor guards the individual rights and personal dignity of the client in the counseling relationship.

Section B: Counseling Relationship

This section refers to practices and procedures of individual and/or group counseling relationships.

The member must recognize the need for client freedom of choice. Under those circumstances where this is not possible, the member must apprise clients of restrictions that may limit their freedom of choice.

1. The member's *primary* obligation is to respect the integrity and promote the welfare of the client(s), whether the client(s) is (are) assisted individually or in a group relationship. In a group setting, the member is also responsible for taking reasonable precautions to protect individuals from physical and/or psychological trauma resulting from interaction within the group.

2. The counseling relationship and information resulting therefrom be kept confidential, consistent with the obligations of the member as a professional person. In a group counseling setting, the counselor must set a norm of confidentiality regarding all group participants' disclosures.

3. If an individual is already in a counseling relationship with another professional person, the member does not enter into a counseling relationship without first contacting and receiving the approval of that other professional. If the member discovers that the client is in another counseling relationship after the counseling relationship begins, the member must gain the consent of the other professional or terminate the relationship, unless the client elects to terminate the other relationship.

4. When the client's condition indicates that there is clear and im-

minent danger to the client or others, the member must take reasonable personal action or inform responsible authorities. Consultation with other professionals must be used where possible. The assumption of responsibility for the client(s) behavior must be taken only after careful deliberation. The client must be involved in the resumption of responsibility as quickly as possible.

5. Records of the counseling relationship, including interview notes, test data, correspondence, tape recordings, and other documents, are to be considered professional information for use in counseling and they should not be considered a part of the records of the institution or agency in which the counselor is employed unless specified by state statute or regulation. Revelation to others of counseling material must occur only upon the expressed consent of the client.

6. Use of data derived from a counseling relationship for purposes of counselor training or research shall be confined to content that can be disguised to ensure full protection of the identity of the subject client.

7. The member must inform the client of the purposes, goals, techniques, rules of procedure and limitations that may affect the relationship at or before the time that the counseling relationship is entered.

8. The member must screen prospective group participants, especially when the emphasis is on self-understanding and growth through self-disclosure. The member must maintain an awareness of the group participants' compatibility throughout the life of the group.

9. The member may choose to consult with any other professionally competent person about a client. In choosing a consultant, the member must avoid placing the consultant in a conflict of interest situation that would preclude the consultant's being a proper party to the member's efforts to help the client.

10. If the member determines an inability to be of professional assistance to the client, the member must either avoid initiating the counseling relationship or immediately terminate that relationship. In either event, the member must suggest appropriate alternatives. (The member must be knowledgeable about referral resources so that a satisfactory referral can be initiated). In the event the client declines the suggested referral, the member is not obligated to continue the relationship.

11. When the member has other relationships, particularly of an administrative, supervisory and/or evaluative nature with an individual seeking counseling services, the member must not serve as

the counselor but should refer the individual to another professional. Only in instances where such an alternative is unavailable
and where the individual's situation warrants counseling intervention should the member enter into and/or maintain a counseling relationship. Dual relationships with clients that might im-
pair the member's objectivity and professional judgment (e.g., as
with close friends or relatives, sexual intimacies with any client)
must be avoided and/or the counseling relationship terminated
through referral to another competent professional.

12. All experimental methods of treatment must be clearly indicated
    to prospective recipients and safety precautions are to be
    adhered to by the member.

13. When the member is engaged in short-term group treatment/
    training programs (e.g., marathons and other encounter-type or
    growth groups), the member ensures that there is professional
    assistance available during and following the group experience.

14. Should the member be engaged in a work setting that calls for
    any variation from the above statements, the member is obli-
    gated to consult with other professionals whenever possible to
    consider justifiable alternatives.

Section C:
Measurement and Evaluation

The primary purpose of educational and psychological testing is to
provide descriptive measures that are objective and interpretable in either
comparative or absolute terms. The member must recognize the need to
interpret the statements that follow as applying to the whole range of
appraisal techniques including test and nontest data. Test results constitute only one of a variety of pertinent sources of information for personnel,
guidance, and counseling decisions.

1. The member must provide specific orientation or information to
   the examinee(s) prior to and following the test administration so
   that the results of testing may be placed in proper perspective
   with other relevant factors. In so doing, the member must recognize the effects of socioeconomic, ethnic and cultural factors on
   test scores. It is the member's professional responsibility to use
   additional unvalidated information carefully in modifying interpretation of the test results.

2. In selecting tests for use in a given situation or with a particular
   client, the member must consider carefully the specific validity,
   reliability, and appropriateness of the test(s). *General* validity,

reliability and the like may be questioned legally as well as ethically when tests are used for vocational and educational selection, placement, or counseling.

3. When making any statements to the public about tests and testing, the member must give accurate information and avoid false claims or misconceptions. Special efforts are often required to avoid unwarranted connotations of such terms as *IQ* and *grade equivalent scores.*

4. Different tests demand different levels of competence for administration, scoring, and interpretation. Members must recognize the limits of their competence and perform only those functions for which they are prepared.

5. Tests must be administered under the same conditions that were established in their standardization. When tests are not administered under standard conditions or when unusual behavior or irregularities occur during the testing session, those conditions must be noted and the results designated as invalid or of questionable validity. Unsupervised or inadequately supervised test-taking, such as the use of tests through the mails, is considered unethical. On the other hand, the use of instruments that are so designed or standardized to be self-administered and self-scored, such as interest inventories, is to be encouraged.

6. The meaningfulness of test results used in personnel, guidance, and counseling functions generally depends on the examinee's unfamiliarity with the specific items on the test. Any prior coaching or dissemination of the test materials can invalidate test results. Therefore, test security is one of the professional obligations of the member. Conditions that produce most favorable test results must be made known to the examinee.

7. The purpose of testing and the explicit use of the results must be made known to the examinee prior to testing. The counselor must ensure that instrument limitations are not exceeded and that periodic review and/or retesting are made to prevent client stereotyping.

8. The examinee's welfare and explicit prior understanding must be the criteria for determining the recipients of the test results. The member must see that specific interpretation accompanies any release of individual or group test data. The interpretation of test data must be related to the examinee's particular concerns.

9. The member must be cautious when interpreting the results of research instruments possessing insufficient technical data. The specific purposes for the use of such instruments must be stated explicitly to examinees.

10. The member must proceed with caution when attempting to

evaluate and interpret the performance of minority group members or other persons who are not represented in the norm group on which the instrument was standardized.

11. The member must guard against the appropriation, reproduction, or modifications of published tests or parts thereof without acknowledgment and permission from the previous publisher.

12. Regarding the preparation, publication and distribution of tests, reference should be made to:

    a. *Standards for Educational and Psychological Tests and Manuals*, revised edition, 1974, published by the American Psychological Association on behalf of itself, the American Educational Research Association and the National Council on Measurement in Education.

    b. The responsible use of tests: A position paper of AMEG, APGA, and NCME. *Measurement and Evaluation in Guidance*, 1972, 5, 385–388.

    c. "Responsibilities of Users of Standardized Tests," APGA, *Guidepost*, October 5, 1978, pp. 5–8.

Section D: Research and Publication

1. Guidelines on research with human subjects shall be adhered to, such as:

    a. *Ethical Principles in the Conduct of Research with Human Participants*, Washington, D.C.: American Psychological Association, Inc., 1973.

    b. Code of Federal Regulations, Title 45, Subtitle A, Part 46, as currently issued.

2. In planning any research activity dealing with human subjects, the member must be aware of and responsive to all pertinent ethical principles and ensure that the research problem, design, and execution are in full compliance with them.

3. Responsibility for ethical research practice lies with the principal researcher, while others involved in the research activities share ethical obligation and full responsibility for their own actions.

4. In research with human subjects, researchers are responsible for the subjects' welfare throughout the experiment and they must take all reasonable precautions to avoid causing injurious psychological, physical, or social effects on their subjects.

5. All research subjects must be informed of the purpose of the study except when withholding information or providing misin-

formation to them is essential to the investigation. In such research the member must be responsible for corrective action as soon as possible following completion of the research.

6. Participation in research must be voluntary. Involuntary participation is appropriate only when it can be demonstrated that participation will have no harmful effects on subjects and is essential to the investigation.

7. When reporting research results, explicit mention must be made of all variables and conditions known to the investigator that might affect the outcome of the investigation or the interpretation of the data.

8. The member must be responsible for conducting and reporting investigations in a manner that minimizes the possibility that results will be misleading.

9. The member has an obligation to make available sufficient original research data to qualified others who may wish to replicate the study.

10. When supplying data, aiding in the research of another person, reporting research results, or in making original data available, due care must be taken to disguise the identity of the subjects in the absence of specific authorization from such subjects to do otherwise.

11. When conducting and reporting research, the member must be familiar with, and give recognition to, previous work on the topic, as well as to observe all copyright laws and follow the principles of giving full credit to all to whom credit is due.

12. The member must give due credit through joint authorship, acknowledgment, footnote statements, or other appropriate means to those who have contributed significantly to the research and/or publication, in accordance with such contributions.

13. The member must communicate to other members the results of any research judged to be of professional or scientific value. Results reflecting unfavorably on institutions, programs, services, or vested interests must not be withheld for such reasons.

14. If members agree to cooperate with another individual in research and/or publication, they incur an obligation to cooperate as promised in terms of punctuality of performance and with full regard to the completeness and accuracy of the information required.

15. Ethical practice requires that authors not submit the same manuscript or one essentially similar in content, for simultaneous publication consideration by two or more journals. In addition, manuscripts published in whole or in substantial part, in another

journal or published work should not be submitted for publication without acknowledgment and permission from the previous publication.

Section E:
Consulting

Consultation refers to a voluntary relationship between a professional helper and help-needing individual, group or social unit in which the consultant is providing help to the client(s) in defining and solving a work-related problem or potential problem with a client or client system. (This definition is adapted from Kurpius, DeWayne. Consultation theory and process: An integrated model. *Personnel and Guidance Journal,* 1978, 56.

1. The member acting as consultant must have a high degree of self-awareness of his/her own values, knowledge, skills, limitations, and needs in entering a helping relationship that involves human and/or organizational change and that the focus of the relationship be on the issues to be resolved and not on the person(s) presenting the problem.

2. There must be understanding and agreement between member and client for the problem definition, change goals, and predicated consequences of interventions selected.

3. The member must be reasonably certain that she/he or the organization represented has the necessary competencies and resources for giving the kind of help that is needed now or may develop later and that appropriate referral resources are available to the consultant.

4. The consulting relationship must be one in which client adaptability and growth toward self-direction are encouraged and cultivated. The member must maintain this role consistently and not become a decision maker for the client or create a future dependency on the consultant.

5. When announcing consultant availability for services, the member conscientiously adheres to the Association's *Ethical Standards*.

6. The member must refuse a private fee or other remuneration for consultation with persons who are entitled to these services through the member's employing institution or agency. The policies of a particular agency may make explicit provisions for private practice with agency clients by members of its staff. In such instances, the clients must be apprised of other options open to them should they seek private counseling services.

Section F:
Private Practice

1. The member should assist the profession by facilitating the availability of counseling services in private as well as public settings.
2. In advertising services as a private practitioner, the member must advertise the services in such a manner so as to accurately inform the public as to services, expertise, profession, and techniques of counseling in a professional manner. A member who assumes an executive leadership role in the organization shall not permit his/her name to be used in professional notices during periods when not actively engaged in the private practice of counseling.

    The member may list the following: highest relevant degree, type and level of certification or license, type and/or description of services, and other relevant information. Such information must not contain false, inaccurate, misleading, partial, out-of-context, or deceptive material or statements.
3. Members may join in partnership/corporation with other members and/or other professionals provided that each member of the partnership or corporation makes clear the separate specialties by name in compliance with the regulations of the locality.
4. A member has an obligation to withdraw from a counseling relationship if it is believed that employment will result in violation of the *Ethical Standards*. If the mental or physical condition of the member renders it difficult to carry out an effective professional relationship or if the member is discharged by the client because the counseling relationship is no longer productive for the client, then the member is obligated to terminate the counseling relationship.
5. A member must adhere to the regulations for private practice of the locality where the services are offered.
6. It is unethical to use one's institutional affiliation to recruit clients for one's private practice.

Section G:
Personnel Administration

It is recognized that most members are employed in public or quasi-public institutions. The functioning of a member within an institution must contribute to the goals of the institution and vice versa if either is to accomplish their respective goals or objectives. It is therefore essential that the member and the institution function in ways to (a) make the institution's goals explicit and public; (b) make the member's contribution to institutional goals specific; and (c) foster mutual accountability for goal achievement.

To accomplish these objectives, it is recognized that the member and the employer must share responsibilities in the formulation and implementation of personnel policies.

1. Members must define and describe the parameters and levels of their professional competency.
2. Members must establish interpersonal relations and working agreements with supervisors and subordinates regarding counseling or clinical relationships, confidentiality, distinction between public and private material, maintenance, and dissemination of recorded information, work load and accountability. Working agreements in each instance must be specified and made known to those concerned.
3. Members must alert their employers to conditions that may be potentially disruptive or damaging.
4. Members must inform employers of conditions that may limit their effectiveness.
5. Members must submit regularly to professional review and evaluation.
6. Members must be responsible for inservice development of self and/or staff.
7. Members must inform their staff of goals and programs.
8. Members must provide personnel practices that guarantee and enhance the rights and welfare of each recipient of their service.
9. Members must select competent persons and assign responsibilities compatible with their skills and experiences.

Section H:
Preparation Standards

Members who are responsible for training others must be guided by the preparation standards of the Association and relevant Division(s). The member who functions in the capacity of trainer assumes unique ethical responsibilities that frequently go beyond that of the member who does not function in a training capacity. These ethical responsibilities are outlined as follows:

1. Members must orient students to program expectations, basic skills development, and employment prospects prior to admission to the program.

2. Members in charge of learning experiences must establish programs that integrate academic study and supervised practice.

3. Members must establish a program directed toward developing students' skills, knowledge, and self-understanding, stated whenever possible in competency or performance terms.

4. Members must identify the levels of competencies of their students in compliance with relevant Division standards. These competencies must accommodate the para-professional as well as the professional.

5. Members, through continual student evaluation and appraisal, must be aware of the personal limitations of the learner that might impede future performance. The instructor must not only assist the learner in securing remedial assistance but also screen from the program those individuals who are unable to provide competent services.

6. Members must provide a program that includes training in research commensurate with levels of role functioning. Paraprofessional and technician-level personnel must be trained as consumers of research. In addition, these personnel must learn how to evaluate their own and their program's effectiveness. Graduate training, especially at the doctoral level, would include preparation for original research by the member.

7. Members must make students aware of the ethical responsibilities and standards of the profession.

8. Preparatory programs must encourage students to value the ideals of service to individuals and to society. In this regard, direct financial remuneration or lack thereof must not influence the quality of service rendered. Monetary considerations must not be allowed to overshadow professional and humanitarian needs.

9. Members responsible for educational programs must be skilled as teachers and practitioners.

10. Members must present thoroughly varied theoretical positions so that students may make comparisons and have the opportunity to select a position.

11. Members must develop clear policies within their educational institutions regarding field placement and the roles of the student and the instructor in such placements.

12. Members must ensure that forms of learning focusing on self-understanding or growth are voluntary, or if required as part of the education program, are made known to prospective students prior to entering the program. When the education program offers a growth experience with an emphasis on self-disclosure or

other relatively intimate or personal involvement, the member must have no administrative, supervisory, or evaluating authority regarding the participant.

13. Members must conduct an educational program in keeping with the current relevant guidelines of the American Personnel and Guidance Association and its Divisions.

Appendix
C

National Divisions
of the American Personnel
and Guidance Association

APGA has 13 special interest divisions that members may join. Each division publishes a journal and many publish newsletters. The Divisions are described below:

Division 1:
American College Personnel Association (ACPA)

ACPA is the collective voice of the college student profession — teachers, counselors, deans, department heads, researchers. It meets the demands of individual students who seek help to make their college experience personally significant. Publication: The Journal of College Student Personnel.

Division 2:
Association for Counselor Education and Supervision (ACES)

ACES emphasizes the need for highly skilled guidance and personnel workers in efforts to improve counselor education and supervision at all levels of education, rehabilitation and employment settings. Publication: Counselor Education and Supervision; ACES Newsletter.

Division 3:
National Vocational Guidance Association (NVGA)

NVGA is concerned with the life-long use of people's knowledge, abilities and skills. NVGA seeks to gain recognition and status for the profession of counseling and to improve skills, systems and standards of service in counseling. Publications: The Vocational Guidance Quarterly; NVGA Newsletter.

Division 4:
Association for Humanistic Education and Development (AHEAD)

AHEAD seeks to provide a forum for the exchange of information about humanistically oriented educational practices and to promote changes in education which reflect the growing body of knowledge about human development and potential. Publication: The Humanist Educator.

Division 5:
American School Counselor Association (ASCA)

ASCA works to define and advance the role of the school counselor at all educational levels, elementary through post-secondary, and to achieve national recognition for this important function in education. Publications: The School Counselor; Elementary School Guidance and Counseling; ASCA Newsletter.

Division 6:
American Rehabilitation Counseling Association (ARCA)

The rehabilitation counselor works with physically, mentally or emotionally handicapped people. ARCA links the practitioner with a nationwide community of rehabilitation counselors. Publications: Rehabilitation Counseling Bulletin.

Division 7:
Association for Measurement and Evaluation in Guidance (AMEG)

AMEG members plan, administer and conduct testing programs; provide test scoring services; interpret and use test results; and develop evaluation instruments. They also teach college-level courses or conduct research in this area of interest. Publications: Measurement and Evaluation in Guidance; AMEG Newsnotes.

Division 8:
National Employment Counselors Association (NECA)

NECA offers professional leadership to people who counsel in an employment setting or to those employed in related areas of counselor education, research, administration or supervision in business and industry, colleges and universities and federal and state governments. Publication: Journal of Employment Counseling.

Division 9:
Association for Non-White Concerns In Personnel and Guidance (ANWC)

By seeking to eliminate prejudice and discrimination and by defending those human and civil rights which have been secured by law, ANWC is dedicated to the insurance of equality as regards the treatment, advancement, qualification and status of non-white individuals in personnel and guidance work. ANWC programs emphasized all charitable, scientific and educational activities which are designed to assist and further the interests of non-whites. Association members represent all personnel and guidance settings. Publications: Journal of Non-White Concerns in Personnel and Guidance, ANWC Newsletter.

Division 10:
Association for Religious and Value Issues in Counseling (ARVIC)

Through a common interest in promoting counseling and guidance services in parochial and nonpublic schools, ARVIC seeks to integrate values, theological and philosophical considerations and principles with current student-pupil personnel practices and to share this knowledge with colleagues in private and public education. Publication: Counseling and Values.

Division 11:
Association for Specialists in Group Work (ASGW)

This is the division of workers in education, mental health, physical health, offender rehabilitation, religion and the human potential movement who share a common interest in group work. ASGW seeks to assist and further the interests of children, youth and adults by seeking to provide effective services through the group medium to prevent problems; to promote maximum development and to remediate disabling behaviors. Publication: Journal for Specialists in Group Work.

Division 12:
Public Offender Counselor Association (POCA)

POCA is concerned with the delivery of effective counseling services to public offenders and is committed to provide leadership in developing public offender counseling as a profession. The division will work to improve the standards of service to offenders and to improve national awareness of public offender counseling through information activities. Membership is open to offender counselors and to other professionals interested in this field. A division publication is planned.

Division 13:
American Mental Health Counselors Association (AMHCA)

This division is for professionals in mental health centers, private practice, agency counseling and pastoral counseling. The interdisciplinary membership of AMHCA is dedicated to maintaining and improving the quality of mental health in the nation. Publication: AMHCA News (Bimonthly Newsletter) AMHCA Journal.

These three sessions are designed to help students in personal development by assisting them to get in touch with feelings, communicate with others, understand how they affect others, and better understand themselves. The major purpose, however, is to illustrate group techniques. The exercises described are typical of those used in schools, colleges, and other guidance settings.

General Comments

Use groups of seven to nine students; this size will enable extensive participation. Larger groups, including a class size of twenty to thirty, could be used, but the effect of the experience will be considerably less, and it will be difficult to involve everyone in the activities. In any size group, members sit in as small a circle as possible, with no back rows.

The three sessions should take about four to six hours to complete. Each meeting should consume about one to two hours, depending on the size of the group, extent of involvement in exercises, and the number of exercises used.

There is considerable structure used, because three meetings will allow only limited time for the development of a group feeling among members, and because the major purpose is to illustrate techniques. Following each activity it may be productive for the group to comment on its personal value and possible uses.

The leader's role is to describe the purposes of the meetings, actively participate in each of the exercises, support members' efforts to participate, and serve as a model for group members.

Initiating the Group

Explain that these three meetings are designed to assist students in their development as helping persons (e.g., to understand themselves better, to communicate with others, and to deal more effectively with others). Also point out that students will become aware of how participants in a group experience feel about their involvement, and will learn about group activities designed to facilitate personal development.

First Meeting: Getting Acquainted

Introductions

(Approximate time, 15 minutes). After an explanation of the purpose of the three-session experience, divide the group into pairs and ask them to spend about 10 minutes getting to know each other. Suggest that they think up questions to use, but include positive experiences each has had, something about themselves that others may not know, and the greatest influence on their lives. The emphasis of the get-acquainted discussion is affective rather than cognitive, but work experience, travel, educational experiences, and family data could be included.

After the interviews have been completed, ask each student to introduce the other member of the pair. It might be helpful to model the introduction by first doing one yourself, using the approach of "what interested me most about . . . ." Another approach is to structure introductions as if they are for a celebrity (i.e., "The person I am introducing is famous for . . . ").

Relating Names and Faces

(approximate time, 20 minutes). The introductions should help students to know each other, but information, at least for some members, will soon be forgotten unless it is used in some way. This exercise is designed to help students remember what has been discussed and to facilitate interaction in the group.

Members print block letters on a card to identify three things about themselves, pin the card on, and walk about silently, reading each other's cards. Then the cards are removed, and stacked face down in the middle of the circle. In turn, each member draws one, reads the three things, identifies the individual, and states a reason for the identification. (If one's own card is selected, slide it under the bottom of the pile.) At the end of each report the actual author identifies himself or herself.

Trusting Each Other

(approximate time, 15 minutes). Either of two exercises can be used to help members trust others in the group. In the first, members stand in a close circle, with each member taking a turn standing straight and rigid in the middle with eyes closed and arms at sides. The member in the middle falls toward the circle and is passed around and across the circle by others. Use only a brief period for each member. At the conclusion, ask participants to describe feelings during the experience.

A second version is to have members pair up, and take turns leading each other around the room, with the one being led either blindfolded or with eyes closed. After all individuals have had a turn, return to the circle and describe the feeling about the experience. Rate the person trusted on a scale of 1 to 5, with 1 being terrified and 5 being absolutely trusting.

Learning Names

(optional; approximate time, 20 minutes). In this exercise, emphasis is on learning names by using the first letter of the first name or nickname of each class member to make up words. (Allow only dictionary words.) In pairs members make up words without further checking the names of members, and then report to the group. Other members may challenge the letters used, and the reporters must state the names used. If incorrect names were used, the reporting team gains no points.

The winner is the pair that uses all of the correct letters in the fewest number of words.

Second Meeting: Improving Communication

The purpose of this meeting is to help participants listen to what others are communicating and to comprehend how one appears to others. Because group members will likely be at different levels of competence in these skills, activities are designed to be suitable for a wide range of persons.

Telling about Oneself

(approximate time, 20 minutes). The purpose of this activity is to help members communicate significant aspects of themselves to others. Each members needs a large sheet of paper and a crayon or marker. The sheet of paper is divided into four sections, and each member draws a symbol in the appropriate section for the following.

1. Upper left — how I feel right now.
2. Lower left — the person I admire the most.
3. Upper right — something I would like to change about myself.
4. Lower right — the best thing that could happen to me.

After they complete the drawings, ask each member to share the meanings of the symbols. Others ask questions and respond with their own feelings about the portrayals.

This exercise helps the individual communicate with others by a two-stage approach: (1) a symbol is presented; (2) verbal, self-disclosing comments are made.

Communicating Reactions to Others

(approximate time, 25 minutes). This activity involves receiving and responding to positive statements from others.

The leader first explains and models positive statements and feedback. For example, the leader may say to a member, "Jan, I see you as a person who knows what's important to you." In saying this, the speaker looks directly at the person, and uses the person's name. The recipient then responds by saying, "When you say that, Ron, it makes me feel good." It is important for the respondent to look at the speaker, to use the speaker's name, and to say how the comment makes him or her feel. (It may be necessary to practice this response until students learn how to use it relatively easily.)

Next, go around the circle with each member making a positive statement to one other person. The recipient responds by indicating feelings about the comment. (If necessary, model a comment that reflects something unique about the individual and a response that illustrates a personal reaction.) Although the exercise may seem repetitious, students are usually very much interested in comments from others and need practice to learn the type of response described.

This exercise is designed to help students learn how to give and receive positive statements and to respond in a way to reveal personal feelings.

Non-Verbal Communication

(approximate time, 20 minutes). Divide the group into sub-groups of three persons each. Ask one member to serve as observer, and the other two to talk for about five or six minutes about why they are in the counselor education program. The observer is to take note of all non-verbal behavior. At the conclusion, ask each observer to report non-verbal behavior that helped the conversation. What specifically was done to communicate interest and understanding? (At this stage in the group experience it may be best to emphasize only positive factors.) If necessary, ask questions such as: Was there eye contact? Did participants lean toward each other? Were expressions friendly (e.g., smiles)? Did participants nod or use other movements to show reactions?

Next, ask the total group to agree on three behaviors that facilitate communication. Then change roles and repeat the discussion — observer process, asking for observers; and discussants' comments at the end of each round.

The purpose of this activity is to help students understand the effects of their non-verbal behavior on communication and to experience a group technique involving this type of communication.

Third Meeting: The Use of Several Group Techniques

During this meeting, group techniques such as values clarification, assertiveness training, and unstructured group discussions are included. All three could be used, or the group could cover one or two in greater depth.

Values Clarification

(approximate time, 30 minutes). There are a wide variety of values clarification activities involving the selection of certain types of persons for survival when not all can be saved. In making choices, participants reveal values. Individuals can be identified in a number of ways (e.g., by college majors, occupations, or personal qualities). A suggested procedure is for each group to name three occupations for each of the following characteristics:

1. The highest income level.
2. The highest prestige.
3. The highest service to others.
4. The most unpleasant tasks.

After the twelve occupations have been agreed on, say that there has been a nuclear attack and it is necessary to take shelter in ten minutes. There is only one shelter available and it will hold no more than six persons for the time that they must remain inside. Which six of the twelve would the group select? After the group has selected (typically by vote) the six and given reasons for choices, discuss the values on which choices were made.

The purpose of this exercise is to help students identify personal values about who is essential in an emergency situation. (A question may arise about the morality of choosing who will survive and who will not. If that happens, emphasize that if all were taken in the shelter, oxygen and other resources would be exhausted and no one would be saved.)

Another approach would be to tell the group that you are going to auction a number of "factors" that they may wish to own. Each member will have $1,000 to purchase the factors that are the most important to them. The money can be spent in any way that the buyer chooses, but the amount given is all that is available to spend. Bids may be only in $50 increments, so that the auction of each item will not take too long. Only one type of factor would be used in each value auction (e.g., occupational).

Typical factors are illustrated in the table on page 403.

The items may be written on the board, listed on a ditto sheet, or printed on cards. Each is offered in turn for bidding, and the highest bidder wins.

At the conclusion, a discussion of what the exercise revealed about values may be productive. Ask questions to help participants think about their motives for bidding and reactions to the experience (such as Which factors were in greatest demand? Did anyone not get what they wanted?).

Assertiveness Training

(approximate time, 25 minutes). Assertive behavior is the type in which one expresses oneself in a positive, productive, and uninhibited manner in keeping with one's feelings. Assertive behavior is not hostile or overbearing; it can often be carried out in a friendly manner. For this exercise the emphasis is on one type of assertive response: saying no to a person who is trying to impose on the speaker.

In groups of three persons, one makes the request, the second is the recipient, the third judges the degree of assertiveness expressed. Judges are asked to rate the degree of assertiveness on the basis of the following behaviors:

1. Eye contact (should be maintained).
2. Posture.
3. Tone of voice (not too loud or too soft).
4. Expression.

Describe the following situation (or use one of your own that better fits the group):

> Another student that you do not particularly like and who has a rather aggressive manner wants to borrow your tape recorder for a few days. You do not absolutely need it, but it will inconvenience you to lend it because of some taping you would like to do. You also know that this particular person has a habit of not returning borrowed items.

Occupational	Educational	Personal
1. Being my own boss	1. Top marks	1. Popularity
2. Interesting work	2. Interesting subjects	2. Contentment with what I have
3. Short working hours	3. Assurance of receiving a degree	3. Being interested in others
4. Interesting colleagues	4. A good social life	4. Having no anxieties
5. Helping others	5. Excellence on standardized tests	5. Success in whatever I do
6. High income	6. Short class day	6. Self-confidence
7. Working in collaboration with others	7. Independent work	7. Leadership ability
8. Working alone	8. Stimulating teachers	8. Social skills
9. Little supervision	9. High reading skills	9. Recognition as an expert
10. Directing others	10. Much class interaction	10. Recognition as an effective helper
11. Early retirement	11. Lectures that cover all needed material	11. Satisfaction with accomplishments
12. Frequent vacations	12. Interesting classmates	12. Time to be alone
13. Meeting a social need	13. Frequent holidays	13. Time to be involved with others
14. Constructing an impressive technological product	14. Personal responsibility for learning	14. The opportunity to follow my own interests
15. Making general plans for projects	15. Specific requirements to ensure learning	15. Assertiveness
16. Carrying out specific details of plans	16. Highly competitive academic institution	16. Courage
17. Extensive responsibility	17. A program that focuses on personal development	17. Physical strength
18. Little responsibility	18. Evaluation based on effort	18. A physique of my own choosing (e.g., shorter, taller)
19. National recognition	19. A program in which some fail	19. Good health
20. Regular hours	20. A program in which there are no failures	20. Wealth

Begin with the borrower speaking (it will be helpful for the instructor to model both the request and the response). After one request, the judges comment on the four factors already given. The request and response are given again, with additional judges' evaluation. After several practices, roles are rotated so that each person has an opportunity to play each part. (Because the group is not one that requested help in developing assertive behavior, the assertive responses may not be difficult to make. To add reality to the experience, the instructor may need to use situations in which it is much more difficult to demonstrate assertive behavior. Students may be asked to name situations in which they find it difficult to state the way they feel in a positive and constructive manner.)

Following practice in small groups, assemble the total group and ask pairs to role-play an assertive response. All members of the group should give feedback. The situation should be one that the responder identifies as being difficult (e.g., asking an instructor to reconsider a grade that the student feels is too low). After completion of the practice, discuss feelings during exchanges and students' attitudes about the likelihood of generalizing assertive behavior to other situations.

The purposes of this exercise are to help students learn about this type of group experience, to provide some practice in assertive behavior, and to use an exercise that could be included in assertiveness training.

Unstructured Group Interaction

(approximate time, 30 minutes). This type of group procedure typically would not be used in only one segment of an ongoing group experience. Instead it would represent a mode for the total series of meetings. One brief period, however, will illustrate some of the techniques employed, and give some awareness of how it feels to participate in a group of this type. If several exercises have already been completed, members should know each other well enough to participate at a moderately effective level. (Because of the exercises used up to this point, students may continue to expect a great deal of structure. Explain that this procedure does not involve specific directions and is different from those in which planned activities are carried out.)

Begin by saying that this part of the meeting will involve spontaneous discussion and participants can use the time any way they like. They are asked, however, to try to keep comments focused on what is happening in the group, how they are feeling at the present time, and the meanings of others' comments.

The instructor could begin by modelling a response (e.g., "I get the feeling that some of you are not quite sure how to proceed," or "You're wondering how a group like this can be of value to people"). Quite often members will begin to tell about an experience or an event, or bring up political, social, or other problems. The leader may bring the focus back into the present by asking, "How do you feel about that now?"

Because this activity is designed to promote face-to-face affective interaction in an unstructured situation, not a great deal of progress can be expected in one short meeting. The major purpose of the experience is to introduce students to this type of group approach. Additional meetings could be held if desired, with the same emphasis (i.e., a focus on what is happening in the group and how members feel about it).

In the following counseling dialogue, the counselor is helping John Jones, a high school junior, with planning. The pupil lacks interest in school, is achieving poorly, and is confused about the future. He has come to the counselor partly because his social studies teacher has urged him to do so and partly because his parents have insisted on it. All the counselor knows is that John wants to discuss "a problem."

As you read through the text decide on the type of response the counselor makes and indicate your choice with the following symbols:

QS — Questions to stimulate the counselee to face issues and concerns.
Q — Questions for information.
G — General conversation.
L — Listening to show attention.
R — Reflection of feeling.
PI — Providing information.
S — Structuring (describing the purposes of counseling and suggesting ways to proceed).

Also, rate each response on a scale of directive to permissive, with 1 being permissive and 3 being directive. Classifications and ratings are given at the end of this section.

First Counseling Session

1. _____ *Counselor* (talking on telephone): You're John Jones. OK. Come on in. I'll be with you in a minute. [John sits in a chair furthest from the counselor and looks at the ceiling and out of the window.]

2. _____ *Counselor* (hanging up the telephone): I haven't seen you

407

since registration, wasn't it. . . . How are things going? Any particular questions . . . things you'd like to go over now?

John: Nothing much . . . grades, I guess mainly. The teacher . . . my social studies teacher, Mr. V. Tow, said I should see you . . . I don't know about what.

3. _____ *Counselor* (listens): Ummmmmmmm. . . .

John: And my parents, well, they're sort of up tight because I don't seem to be doing so great. Not the grades they want. . . .

4. _____ *Counselor:* Everybody's after you about . . . it's mostly their idea for you to see me?

John: Yeah. I don't see there's any big problem. Just a couple of grades.

5. _____ *Counselor:* You're not bothered. You're saying you're OK.

John: Well, OK? Yeah. Sure!

[Some more talk about no need to be there.]

6. _____ *Counselor:* What do you think you'll do for the rest of the year?

John: I'm thinking about dropping out, as soon as I'm 18, this spring, and getting a job. [somewhat belligerently] Learn something *on* the *job.* I don't see much value in most of this stuff . . . to me . . . all these subjects. I'm not going to college!

7. _____ *Counselor:* Uh huh. Drop out? But what'll you do? What kind of job were . . . are you thinking of?

John: Oh, I don't know. I know a lot of places. Well, I have a couple of places I know about. . . . I don't know. That's the main reason I came here. I guess I don't know too much about jobs . . . where you start. There are not many around I hear. I just thought I'd start looking. Just go all around to some places. . . . Maybe you know of some places that have openings?

8. _____ *Counselor:* I'd like to help. Maybe I can. But it seems to me that there could be . . . you could run into a couple of problems. One, there just aren't as many right now, as, say, there were last year. Two, you're not prepared for any specific one, and stay there. Unless you want to carry packages in the supermarket, or something like that all your life.

John: Yeah? . . . But you can learn on the job. I don't know. I know a lot of people who never finished school and they're big executives and own their own businesses, and riding around in big cars.

9. _____ *Counselor:* It might be helpful to use a plan to go about looking at possibilities. I'm going to suggest how we proceed, a way to look at goals, what we need to know, etc. And how to get it. This isn't telling you what to do. That's your decision. But how does that sound — using a plan to go about what we're doing?

John: OK, I guess. I don't know where to begin. You tell me.

10. _____ *Counselor:* Well . . . let's look at what we're trying to do here. How do you see it?

John: Do here? Well. Decide . . . what I ought to do. Stay in school. See what kinds of jobs I can get if I quit. How can I get a job?

11. _____ *Counselor:* Yeah. Sounds good. Decisions about that. And the information we need in something like that. For example, let's start off with home. How do your parents feel about dropping out versus staying in? How much influence are they going to exert?

John: Yeah. Probably a lot. They have an opinion about it. I guess they're actually a pretty big factor. Well, they want to be. But they're not telling me everything I'm going to do. I got to live my own life!

12. _____ *Counselor:* You seem to feel your parents are going to tell you.

[Further exploration of parents' attitudes, and the goals of counseling.]

13. _____ *Counselor:* Looks like we may need something about the "facts" if you drop out. What do you see as the most important things to be considered?

John: Facts? I don't know. What do you mean "facts"?

14. _____ *Counselor:* What should you consider when you're thinking about this choice? For example, if you do, could you live at home? What expenses would you have?

John: I don't know about that. I haven't thought too much about it. Except that I wouldn't be very welcome about the house. I can hear them now. "So you've quit, huh?"

15. _____ *Counselor:* OK. Let's take that as one of the things to consider on this choice. We also ought to figure in here somewhere your living expenses. It has a bearing on what kind of job . . . how much you would have to make. Do you want to look into that?

John: OK. . . . Ummmmm . . . I guess so.

16. _____ *Counselor:* You don't seem to feel that . . . well . . . that's worth looking into.

John: Sure. I got to consider it. I get sort of discouraged, though, when I start thinking about that.

17. _____ *Counselor:* Discouraged . . . ?

John: Yeah. You know. Sort of takes all the fun out of it. But you got to live, I know.

18. _____ *Counselor:* OK. . . . Along the same line, the question comes up about the kinds of jobs you might expect to get. Where could you start? Openings? How do you think we could go about that?

John: I don't know except to go around and ask people. I thought maybe you could help me with that. Where to go. What or who has jobs.

[As the interview continues, the counselor and counselee develop plans to obtain information.]

19. _____ *Counselor:* There's other information that we need here, don't you think? Grades, subjects you've liked and disliked, test scores, interests, other information about you. How do you feel about the future? What do you want out of life? We can go into these things here. I can get some of the information.

John: OK. I guess that's OK. Ummmm . . . I don't do too well on tests. And grades haven't been too good. [pause] I remember, there was one of those tests. . . . About jobs. It said I should be a forest ranger or a mechanic. Something else too. An accountant? That was last year. We all took it. What a lot of junk!

20. _____ *Counselor:* Didn't make much sense to you?

John: No. It didn't! That was weird. I don't know how it showed that. I don't want to do any of those things!

CLASSIFICATIONS AND RATINGS OF COUNSELOR'S RESPONSES

	Classification	Rating (Permissive to Directive)
1.	G	3
2.	Q	2
3.	L	1
4.	R	1
5.	R	1
6.	QS	3
7.	QS	3
8.	PI	3
9.	S	3
10.	S	3
11.	S	3
12.	R	1
13.	QS	3
14.	PI	3
15.	QS	3
16.	R	1
17.	R	1
18.	QS	3
19.	QS	1
20.	R	1

Bibliography

Abel, Janice. 1980. "Academic Advising: Goals and a Delivery System." *Journal of College Student Personnel* 21, no. 2, pp. 151–155.

Abert, James G. 1974. "Wanted: Experiments in Reducing the Cost of Education." *Phi Delta Kappan* 55, no. 7, pp. 444–445.

"Accreditation Criteria." 1979. *APA Monitor* 10, no. 4, pp. 14–17.

ACES 1978. "ACES Guidelines for Doctoral Preparation in Counselor Education," *Counselor Education and Supervision*, 17, no. 3, 163–166.

ACES 1977. "Standards for the Preparation of Counselors and Other Personnel Service Specialists," *Personnel and Guidance Journal*, 55, no 10, pp. 596–601.

Adams, Harold J. 1973. "The Progressive Heritage of Guidance: A View from the Left." *Personnel and Guidance Journal* 51, no. 8, pp. 531–538.

Agne, Russell M., and Nash, Robert J. 1973. "School Counselors: The Conscience of Career Education." *School Counselor* 21, no. 2, pp. 90–101.

Alexander, Jaclyn J., and Wall, Judy. 1975. "Righting the Wrongs of Writing: Copy Editors Speak Out." *Personnel and Guidance Journal* 53, no. 10, pp. 768–773.

Alexander, William M.; Williams, Emmett L.; Compton, Mary; Hines, Vynce A.; Prescott, Dan; and Kealy, Ronald. 1969. *The Emergent Middle School.* 2nd ed. New York: Holt, Rinehart and Winston.

Alford, Albert L. 1977. "The Education Amendments of 1976." *American Education* 13, no. 1, pp. 6–11.

Alvino, James, and Wieler, Jerome. 1979. "How Standardized Testing Fails to Identify the Gifted and What Teachers Can Do About It." *Phi Delta Kappan* 61, no. 2, pp. 106–109.

American Mental Health Counselors Association. 1980–81. Special Edition. "Code of Ethics for Certified Mental Health Counselors." *AMHCA News*, p. 4.

American Personnel and Guidance Association. 1974. "Ethical Standards." *Guidepost* 17, 4 July, pp. 4–5.

———. 1978. Policy Statement. "Responsibilities of Users of Standardized Tests." *Guidepost* 21, no. 5, pp. 5–8.

———. 1980. *Responsibilities of Users of Standardized Tests.* Falls Church, Va.: American Personnel and Guidance Association.

American Psychological Association. 1967. *Casebook on Ethical Standards of Psychologists.* Washington, D.C.: American Psychological Association.

———. 1973. *Ethical Principles in Conduct of Research with Human Participants.* Washington, D.C.: American Psychological Association.

———. 1974. *Standards for Educational and Psychological Tests.* Washington, D.C.: American Psychological Association.

———. 1976. "A New Method of Testing Children." *APA Monitor* 7, no. 5, p. 13.

———. 1979. "Latest Changes in the Ethics Code." *APA Monitor* 10, no. 11, pp. 16–17.

American Rehabilitation Counseling Association. "A Statement of Policy on the Professional Preparation of Rehabilitation Counselors." In *Rehabilitation Counseling,* edited by Brian Bolton and Madeline E. Jaques, pp. 231–238. Baltimore: University Park Press.

American School Counselor Association. 1976. "ASCA Position Paper." *School Counselor* 23, no. 4, pp. 281–288.

———. 1977. "The Role of the Secondary School Counselor." *School Counselor* 24, no. 4, pp. 228–234.

———. 1978*a*. "The Unique Role of the Elementary School Counselor." *Elementary School Guidance and Counseling* 12, no. 3, pp. 200–202.

———. 1978*b*. "The Unique Role of the Middle/Junior High School Counselor." *Elementary School Guidance and Counseling* 12, no. 3, pp. 203–205.

———. 1979*a*. "ASCA Position Statement on Peer Counseling." *School Counselor* 26, no. 4, pp. 273–275.

———. 1979*b*. "Developmental Guidance." *School Counselor* 26, no. 4, pp. 270–272.

American School Counselor Association and American Rehabilitation Counseling Association. 1979. "The Necessary Cooperation: Rehabilitation and School Counselors Must Work Together." *The School Counselor,* 27, no. 1, pp. 69–70.

APGA 1967. "Standards for the Preparation of Secondary School Counselors 1967." *Personnel and Guidance Journal,* 46, no. 1, pp. 96–106.

Arbuckle, Dugald S. 1974. "The Practice of the Theories of Counseling." *Counselor Education and Supervision* 13, no. 3, pp. 214–222.

Arbeiter, Solomon; Aslanian, Carol B.; Schmerbeck, Frances A.; and Brickell, Henry M. 1978. *40 Million Americans in Career Transition.* New York: College Entrance Examination Board.

Ard, Robert F., and Hyder, Lecter L., Jr. 1978. "Career Planning Objectives of College Students and Activities Perceived as Instrumental in Their Achievement." *Journal of College Student Personnel* 19, no. 1, pp. 48–54.

Asher, Janet K. 1980. "The Coming Exclusion of Counselors from the Mental Health Care System." In *Counselor Licensure: Issues and Perspectives,* edited by Richard W. Warner, Jr.; David K. Brooks, Jr.; and Jean A. Thompson, pp. 129–136. Falls Church; Va.: American Personnel and Guidance Association.

Asimov, Isaac. 1976. "His Own Particular Drummer." *Phi Delta Kappan* 58, no. 1, pp. 99–103.

Asser, Eliot S. 1978. "Social Class and Help-Seeking Behavior." *American Journal of Community Psychology* 6, no. 5, pp. 465–475.

Association for Counselor Education and Supervision. 1967. *Manual for Self-Study by a Counselor Education Staff.* Washington, D.C.: American Personnel and Guidance Association.

———. 1977. "Standards for the Preparation of Counselors and Other Personnel Services Specialists." *Personnel and Guidance Journal* 55, no. 10, pp. 596–601.

———. 1978. "ACES Guidelines for Doctoral Preparation in Counselor Education." *Counselor Education and Supervision* 17, no. 3, pp. 163–166.

Atkinson, Donald R.; Morten, George; and Sue, Derald Wing. 1979. *Counseling American Minorities.* Dubuque, Iowa: William C. Brown and Company.

Aubrey, Roger F. 1969. "Misapplication of Therapy Models to School Counseling." *Personnel and Guidance Journal* 48, no. 4, pp. 273–278.

———. 1977. "Historical Developments of Guidance and Counseling and Implications for the Future." *Personnel and Guidance Journal* 55, 6, pp. 288–295.

Bagby, James M. 1978. "Influencing the Legislative Process: An Overview." In *Solving the Legislative Puzzle,* edited by Harry N. Drier and Edwin L. Herr, pp. 59–64. Falls Church, Va.: American Personnel and Guidance Association.

Banikiotes, Paul G. 1977. "The Training of Counseling Psychologists." *Counseling Psychologist* 7, no. 2, pp. 23–26.

Bard, E. Ronald. 1977. "The Counselor and the Foster Child." *Elementary School Guidance and Counseling* 11, no. 3, pp. 215–222.

Barnes, Melvin W. 1974. "Junior High School: Yesterday and Tomorrow." In *The American Intermediate School,* edited by Max E. Brough and Russell L. Hamm, pp. 147–158. Danville, Ill.: Interstate Printers and Publishers.

Barro, Stephen M. 1970. "An Approach to Developing Accountability Measures in the Public Schools." *Phi Delta Kappan* 52, no. 4, pp. 196–205.

Barrow, John C. 1980. "Follow-Up of Dropouts from Developmental Programs: A Supplemental Program Evaluation Approach." *Personnel and Guidance Journal* 59, no. 3, pp. 186–189.

Barry, Ruth, and Wolf, Beverly. 1957. *Modern Issues in Guidance-Personnel Work.* New York: Bureau of Publications, Teachers College, Columbia University.

Bauer, Rudolph. 1979. "Gestalt Approach to Family Therapy." *American Journal of Family Therapy* 7, no. 3, pp. 41–45.

Baymor, F. R., and Patterson, C. H. 1960. "A Comparison of Three Methods of Assisting Underachieving High School Students." *Journal of Counseling Psychology* 7, no. 2, pp. 83–89.

Beale, Andrew V., and Bost, William A. 1979. "Selecting School Counselors: The Guidance Supervisor's Perspective." *School Counselor* 26, no. 5, pp. 307–310.

Beck, Carlton E. 1963. *Philosophical Foundations of Guidance.* Englewood Cliffs, N.J.: Prentice-Hall.

Benedict, Robert. 1980. "Forword," *Journal of Employment Counseling* 17, no. 1, pp. 2–3.

Benjamin, Libby, and Walz, Garry R., eds. 1980. *Counseling Exceptional People.* Ann Arbor, Mich.: ERIC Counseling and Personnel Services Clearinghouse.

Bennetts, Leslie. 1980. "Organizing to Overcome the Pain of Being Different." *New York Times.* 13, April, p. 20E.

Benson, Arland N., and Blocher, Donald H. 1975. "The Change Process Applied to Career Development Programs." *Personnel and Guidance Journal* 53, no. 9, pp. 656–661.

Benson, Ronald L., and Blocher, Donald H. 1967. "Evaluation of Developmental Counseling with Low Achievers in a High School Setting." *School Counselor* 14, pp. 215–220.

Bentel, David J. 1980. "Recognizing and Counseling the Troubled Employee Who DRINKS." *Career Planning and Adult Development Newsletter* 2, no. 7, pp. 1–3.

Berg, Robert C., and Landreth, Garry L. 1980. "Understanding Guidance Majors. Where Are They Now? A Five-Year Follow-up." *Counselor Education and Supervision* 19, no. 3, pp. 177–181.

Bernstein, Barton E. 1977. "Legal Problems of Cohabitation." *Family Coordinator* 26, no. 4, pp. 361–366.

Bernstein, Bianca L., and LeComte, Conrad. 1976. "An Integrative Competency-Based Counselor Education Model." *Counselor Education and Supervision* 16, no. 1, pp. 26–36.

Biggs, Donald A. 1963. "An Historic Philosophy of Guidance." *Counselor Education and Supervision* 2, no. 4, pp. 201–203.

Bingham, William C. 1975. "Building Bridges to Career Satisfaction." In *Facilitating Career Development for Women,* edited by Elaine House and Mildred E. Katzell, pp. 29–45. Washington, D.C.: American Personnel and Guidance Association.

———. 1976. "Comparative Guidance: A Call for Action." *Vocational Guidance Quarterly* 24, no. 4, pp. 360–365.

Bishop, John B. 1979. "Combining Counseling and Career Services: Conflicts and Choices." *Personnel and Guidance Journal* 57, no. 10, pp. 550–553.

Blaesser, Willard W. 1978. "Organization Change and Student Development." *Journal of College Student Personnel* 19, no. 2, pp. 109–118.

Blake, Richard. 1975*a*. "Counseling the Elderly: An Emerging Area for Counselor Education." *Counselor Education and Supervision* 15, no. 2, pp. 156–157.

———. 1975*b*. "Counseling in Gerontology." *Personnel and Guidance Journal* 53, no. 10, pp. 733–737.

Blake, Richard, and Peterson, David. 1979. "Demographic Aspects of Aging: Implications for Counseling." In *Counseling the Aged,* edited by Mary L. Ganikos, Kathleen A. Grady, and Jane B. Olson, pp. 31–128. Washington, D.C.: American Personnel and Guidance Association.

Blanco, Ralph F. 1980. "Prescriptive Interventions for Exceptional Children." In *Counseling Exceptional People,* edited by Libby Benjamin and Garry P. Walz, pp. 215–242. Ann Arbor, Mich.: ERIC Counseling and Personnel Services Clearinghouse.

Blocher, Donald H. 1974. "Toward an Ecology of Student Development." *Personnel and Guidance Journal* 52, no. 6, pp. 360–365.

———. 1977. "The Counselor's Impact on Learning Environments." *Personnel and Guidance Journal* 55, no. 6, pp. 352–355.

Blocher, Donald H., and Rapoza, Rita S. 1972. "A Systematic Eclectic Model for Counseling-Consulting." *Elementary School Guidance and Counseling* 7, no. 2, pp. 106–112.

Bloom, Bernard L., and Parad, Howard J. 1978. "The Psychologist in the Community Mental Health Center: An Analysis of Activities and Training Needs." *American Journal of Community Psychology* 6, no. 4, pp. 371–379.

Bluhm, Harry P., and Anderson, H. Reese. "Intervention in Elementary Guidance: One State's Approach." *Elementary School Guidance and Counseling* 10, no. 3, pp. 165–170.

Boller, Jon D. 1973. "Counselor Educators and Administrators: What Do They Want from Each Other?" *Counselor Education and Supervision* 13, no. 1, pp. 2–7.

Borland, David T. 1980. "Organization Development: A Professional Imperative." In *Student Development in Higher Education,* edited by Don G. Creamer, pp. 205–227. Cincinnati: American College Personnel Association.

Borman, Christopher; Nash, William; and Colson, Sharon. 1978. "Career Guidance for Gifted and Talented Students." *Vocational Guidance Quarterly* 27, no. 1, pp. 73–76.

Borow, Henry. 1964. "Milestones of Notable Events in the History of Vocational Guidance." In *Man in a World at Work,* edited by Henry Borow, pp. 45–64. Boston: Houghton Mifflin.

Boy, Angelo V., and Pine, Gerald J. 1980. "Avoiding Counselor Burnout Through Role Renewal." *Personnel and Guidance Journal* 59, no. 3, pp. 161–163.

Bradley, Richard W. 1973. "Following ACES Standards on Preparation of Secondary School Counselors in Career Guidance." *Counselor Education and Supervision* 13, no. 1, pp. 30–35.

Brammer, Lawrence M. 1968. "The Counselor Is a Psychologist." *Personnel and Guidance Journal* 47, no. 1, pp. 4–8.

————. 1969. "Eclecticism Revisited." *Personnel and Guidance Journal* 48, no. 3, pp. 192–197.

Breasure, Joyce M. 1980. "The Other Corner." *AMHCA News* 3, no. 6, p. 2.

Brewer, John M. 1942. *History of Vocational Guidance.* New York: Harper and Brothers.

Brigante, Thomas R. 1958. "Fromm's Marketing Orientation on the Values of the Counselor." *Journal of Counseling Psychology* 5, no. 2, pp. 83–88.

Brine, James M. 1979. "Psycho-Social Aspects of Aging: An Overview." In *Counseling the Aged,* edited by Mary L. Ganikos, Kathleen Grady, and Jane B. Olson, pp. 65–81. Washington, D.C.: American Personnel and Guidance Association.

Briskin, Alan S., and Anderson, Donna M. 1973. "Students as Contingency Managers." *Elementary School Guidance and Counseling* 7, no. 4, pp. 262–268.

Brodsky, Annette M. 1979. "Female Offenders." *Counseling Psychologist* 8, no. 1, pp. 43–44.

Brodzinski, Frederick R. 1979. "Trends and Projections on Student Affairs." *ACPA Developments* 6, no. 3, pp. 8, 12.

————. 1980. "The Changing Role of the Chief Student Personnel Administrator." *Journal of College Student Personnel* 21, no. 1, pp. 3–8.

Brough, James R. 1968. "A Comparison of Self-Referral Counselees and Non-Counseled Junior High School Students." *Personnel and Guidance Journal* 47, no. 4, pp. 329–332.

Brough, Max E., and Hamm, Russell L., eds. 1974. *The American Intermediate School.* Danville, Ill.: Interstate Printers and Publishers.

Brower, Imogene C. 1980. "Counseling Vietnamese." *Personnel and Guidance Journal* 58, no. 10, pp. 646–652.

Brown, Robert D. 1978. "Implications of New Evaluation Strategies for Accountability in Student Affairs." *Journal of College Student Personnel* 19, no. 2, pp. 123–126.

Brown, Roger, and Herrnstein, Richard J. 1975. *Psychology.* Boston: Little, Brown.

Brownstein, Ronald, and Nairn, Allen. 1979. "Are Truth-in-Testing Laws a Fraud? No!" *Phi Delta Kappan* 61, no. 3, pp. 189–191.

Bryson, Seymore, and Bardo, Harold. 1979. "Race and the Counseling Process." In *Counseling American Minorities,* edited by Donald R. Atkinson, George Morten, and Derald Wing Sue, pp. 122–132. Dubuque, Iowa: William C. Brown and Company.

Buckner, Donald R. 1977. "Restructuring Residence Hall Programming: Residence Hall Educators with a Curricuium." *Journal of College Student Personnel* 18, no. 5, pp. 389–392.

Buckner, Eugene T. 1975. "Accountable to Whom? The Counselor's Dilemma." *Measurement and Evaluation in Guidance* 8, no. 3, pp. 176–180.

Burcky, William D., and Childers, John H., Jr. 1976. "Buckley Amendment: Focus of a Professional Dilemma." *School Counselor* 23, no. 3, pp. 162–164.

Bureau of Labor Statistics. 1980. "Employment in Perspective: Working Women." Report 584. Washington, D.C.: U.S. Department of Labor.

Burgum, Thomas, and Anderson, Scott. 1975. *The Counselor and the Law.* Washington, D.C.: American Personnel and Guidance Association.

Burlew, Kathleen Hoard. 1980. "A Theoretical Approach to Developing Counseling Strategies for Black High School Students." *Journal of Non-White Concerns* 9, no. 1, pp. 34–48.

Calia, Vincent F. 1974. "Systematic Human Relations Training: Appraisal and Status." *Counselor Education and Supervision* 14, no. 2, pp. 85–94.

Call, O. Dean. 1970. "Make Counselor Education Relevant." *Personnel and Guidance Journal* 48, no. 10, pp. 797–798.

Callis, Robert. 1976. *Ethical Standards Casebook.* 2nd ed. Washington, D.C.: American Personnel and Guidance Association.

Campbell, David P. 1965. *The Results of Counseling: Twenty-Five Years Later.* Philadelphia: W. B. Saunders.

Campbell, Donald T. 1969. "Reforms as Experiments." *American Psychologist* 24, no. 4, pp. 409–419.

Campbell, Robert E.; Walz, Garry R.; Miller, Juliet V.; and Kriger, Sara F. 1973. *Career Guidance.* Columbus, Ohio: Charles E. Merrill.

Canon, Harry J. 1976. "A Developmental Model for Divisions of Student Affairs." *Journal of College Student Personnel* 17, no. 3, pp. 178–180.

Capuzzi, Dave. 1981. "From the Editor's Desk." *School Counselor* 28, no. 3, pp. 158–159.

Capuzzi, Dave, and Hensley, Anne. 1979. "Rape — Relationships and Recovery." *Personnel and Guidance Journal* 58, no. 2, pp. 133–138.

Career Counseling for Adults: An Overview of the Home-and-Community-Based Career Education Project. 1975. Washington, D.C.: U.S. Government Printing Office.

Career Education. 1971. Washington, D.C.: U.S. Government Printing Office.

Carey, Albert. 1968. "Test Interpretation: Verbal versus Written Summaries." *School Counselor* 16, no. 2, pp. 120–124.

Carkhuff, Robert R. 1969. *Helping and Human Relations.* vol. 2. New York: Holt, Rinehart and Winston.

———. 1972. "New Directions in Training for the Helping Professions: Toward

Technology for Human and Community Resource Development." *Counseling Psychology* 3, no. 3, part 1, pp. 12–30.

_____. 1973*a*. *The Art of Helping*. Amherst, Mass.: Human Resource Development Press.

_____. 1973*b*. *The Art of Problem-Solving*. Amherst, Mass.: Human Resource Development Press.

_____. 1974. *How to Help Yourself*. Amherst, Mass.: Human Resource Development Press.

Carkhuff, Robert R., and Alexik, Mae. 1967. "Effect of Client Depth of Self-Exploration upon High-and-Low Functioning Counselors." *Journal of Counseling Psychology* 14, no. 4, pp. 350–355.

Carlson, Jon; Cavins, David A.; and Dinkmeyer, Don. 1969. "Guidance for All Through Support Personnel." *School Counselor* 16, no. 5, pp. 360–366.

Carlson, Jon, and Pietrofesa, John J. 1971. "A Tri-Level Guidance Structure: An Answer to Our Apparent Ineffectiveness." *Elementary School Guidance and Counseling* 5, no. 3, pp. 190–195.

Carrington, Dan; Cleveland, Art; and Ketterman, Clark. 1978. "Collaborative Consultation in the Secondary School." *Personnel and Guidance Journal* 56, no. 6, pp. 355–358.

Carroll, Marguerite R. 1973. "The Regeneration of Guidance." *School Counselor* 20, no. 5, pp. 355–360.

_____. 1975. "What Every Editor Knows (and Everyone Else Should Know)." *School Counselor* 23, no. 2, pp. 76–77.

Casey, Florence M. *Work Experience and Work Attitudes*. Washington, D.C.: U.S. Government Printing Office.

Cassel, Russell N., and Mehail, Terry. 1973. "The Milwaukee Computerized Vocational Guidance System (VOCGUID)." *Vocational Guidance Quarterly* 21, no. 3, pp. 206–213.

Chaffee, John Jr. 1976. "This We Propose . . ." In *New Dimensions for Educating Youth*, edited by John Chaffee, Jr., and James P. Clark, pp. 1–2. Reston, Va.: National Association of Secondary School Principals.

Chaney, A. Clare Buie; and Hurst, James C. 1980. "The Applicability and Benefits of a Community Mental Health Outreach Model for Campus Ombudsman Programs." *Journal of College Student Personnel* 21, no. 3, pp. 215–222.

Chaney, Reece; Linkenhoker, Dan; and Horne, Arthur. 1977. "The Counselor and Children of Imprisoned Parents." *Elementary School Guidance and Counseling* 11, no. 3, pp. 177–184.

Cheikin, Martin L. 1979. "The Counselor in the Hospice: A New Role." *Personnel and Guidance Journal* 58, no. 3, pp. 186–189.

Christensen, Edward W. 1975. "Counseling Puerto Ricans: Some Cultural Considerations." *Personnel and Guidance Journal* 53, no. 5, pp. 349–356.

Christie, Charles A. 1974. "From Canada . . ." *Personnel and Guidance Journal* 53, no. 1, pp. 43–44.

Clapsaddle, David K. 1973. "Career Development and Teacher Inservice Preparation." *Elementary School Guidance and Counseling* 8, no. 2, pp. 92–97.

Clark-Stedman, Mary, and Wolleat, Patricia L. 1979. "A Nonsexist Group-Counseling Intervention: Moving Toward Androgyny." *School Counselor* 27, no. 2, pp. 110–118.

Clayton, Robert L. 1978. "At the Root of Counseling Minorities: A Need for Cross-Cultural Programming." In *New Imperatives for Guidance,* edited by Garry R. Walz and Libby Benjamin, pp. 264–290. Ann Arbor, Mich.: ERIC Counseling and Personnel Services Clearinghouse.

Cohen, Charles, and Drugo, John. 1976. "Test Re-Test Reliability of the Singer Vocational Evaluation System." *Vocational Guidance Quarterly* 24, no. 3, pp. 267–270.

Cole, Claire G. 1979. "A Model for a Middle School Guidance Program." *Elementary School Guidance and Counseling* 13, no. 4, pp. 292–298.

Collingwood, Thomas R.; Williams, Hadley; and Douds, Alex. 1976. "An *HRD* Approach to Police Diversion for Juvenile Offenders." *Personnel and Guidance Journal* 54, no. 8, pp. 435–437.

Combs, Arthur W., and Soper, Daniel W. 1963. "The Perceptual Organization of Effective Counselors." *Journal of Counseling Psychology* 10, no. 3, pp. 222–226.

Commission on Professional Development. 1974. "Student Personnel Services in Higher Education." *Journal of College Student Personnel* 15, no. 1, pp. 74–78.

Committee on Health Insurance and Office of Professional Affairs. 1979. *Psychology as a Health Care Profession.* Washington, D.C.: American Psychological Association.

Compton, Mary F. 1974. "The Middle School: Alternative to the Status Quo." In *The American Intermediate School,* edited by Max E. Brough and Russell L. Hamm, pp. 196–199. Danville, Ill.: Interstate Printers and Publishers.

Conant, James Bryant. 1969. *The American High School Today.* New York: McGraw-Hill.

———. *Slums and Suburbs.* 1961. New York: McGraw-Hill.

Conyne, Robert K. 1980. "The 'Community' in Community Counseling: Results of a National Survey." *Counselor Education and Supervision* 20, no. 1, pp. 22–28.

Conyne, Robert. 1975. "Environmental Assessment: Mapping for Counselor Action," *Personnel and Guidance Journal,* 54, no. 3, pp. 151–154.

Conyne, Robert K.; Banning, James H.; Clack, R. James; Corrazzini, Joan G.; Huebner, Lois A.; Keating, Lou Ann; and Wrenn, Robert L. 1979. "The Campus Environment as Client: A New Direction for College Counselors." *Personnel and Guidance Journal* 20, no. 5, pp. 437–442.

Cook, David R. 1972. "The Change Agent Counselor: A Conceptual Context." *School Counselor* 20, no. 1, pp. 9–15.

Cooker, Philip G. 1973. "Vocational Values of Children in Grades Four, Five, and Six." *Elementary School Guidance and Counseling* 8, no. 2, pp. 112–118.

Corrigan, Dean C. 1978. "Political and Moral Contexts That Produced P.L. 94-142." *Journal of Teacher Education* 29, no. 6, pp. 10–14.

Cotler, Sherwin B. 1975. "Assertion Training: A Road Leading Where?" *Counseling Psychologist* 5, no. 4, pp. 20–29.

Cottingham, Harold F. 1969. "Conceptualizing the Guidance Function in the Elementary School." *Elementary School Guidance and Counseling* 4, no. 2, pp. 112–119.

———. 1975. "School Counselors Face the Question of Licensing." *School Counselor* 22, no. 4, pp. 255–258.

Cottingham, Harold F., and Swanson, Carl D. 1976. "Recent Licensure Developments: Implications for Counselor Education." *Counselor Education and Supervision* 16, no. 2, pp. 84–87.

Cramer, Stanley H. 1974. "Planned Utilization and Change of Environments." In *Vocational Guidance and Human Development,* edited by Edwin L. Herr, pp. 399–418. Boston: Houghton Mifflin.

Cramer, Stanley H.; Herr, Edwin L.; Morris, Charles N.; and Frantz, Thomas T. 1970. *Research and the School Counselor.* Boston: Houghton Mifflin.

Cramer, Stanley H.; Wise, Pamela Sharrett; and Colburn, E. David. 1977. "An Evaluation of a Treatment to Expand the Career Perceptions of Junior High School Girls." *School Counselor* 25, no. 2, pp. 124–129.

Creaser, James W., and Carsello, Carmen. 1979. "Isolating Factors Related to Paraprofessional Effectiveness." *Journal of Counseling Psychology* 26, no. 3, pp. 259–262.

"Credentialing: Registry Questions Are Probed." 1980. *Guidepost* 22, no. 17, pp. 1, 8.

Cremin, Lawrence A. 1965. "The Progressive Heritage of the Guidance Movement." In *Guidance, An Examination,* edited by Ralph L. Mosher, Richard F. Carle, and Chris D. Kehas, pp. 3–12. New York: Harcourt, Brace, and World, Inc. "Crisis Triggers Learning." 1980. *Guidepost* 22, no. 13, p. 4.

Cristiani, Therese S., and Cristiani, Michael F. 1970. "The Application of Counseling Skills in the Business and Industrial Setting." *Personnel and Guidance Journal* 58, no. 3, pp. 166–169.

Crites, John O. 1969. *Vocational Psychology.* New York: McGraw-Hill.

Cronbach, Lee J. 1975. "Five Decades of Public Controversy Over Mental Testing." *American Psychologist,* 30, no. 1, pp. 1–14.

Crookston, Burnes B. 1975. "Human Development: Actualizing People in Actualizing Organizations." *Journal of College Student Personnel* 16, no. 5, pp. 368–375.

Cross, K. Patricia. 1980. "Our Changing Students and Their Impact on Colleges: Prospects for a True Learning Society." *Phi Delta Kappan* 61, no. 9, pp. 627–630.

Cross, William C., and Maldonado, Bonnie. 1971. "The Counselor, the Mexican-American and the Stereotype." *Elementary School Guidance and Counseling* 6, no. 1, pp. 27–31.

Dameron, Joseph D., ed. 1980. *The Professional Counselor: Competencies, Performance Guidelines, and Assessment.* Falls Church, Va.: American Personnel and Guidance Association.

Danish, Steven J.; D'Augelli, Anthony R.; and Brock, Gregory W. 1976. "An Evaluation of Helping Skills Training: Effects on Helpers' Verbal Responses." *Journal of Counseling Psychology* 23, no. 3, pp. 259–266.

Darkenald, Gordon G. 1980. "Educational and Career Guidance Systems for Adults: Delivery System Alternatives." *Vocational Guidance Quarterly* 28, no. 3, pp. 200–207.

Dash, Edward F. 1969. "Comment." *Personnel and Guidance Journal* 47, no. 6, pp. 599–601.

Davidson, Julia P. 1980. "Urban Black Youth and Career Development." *Journal of Non-White Concerns* 8, no. 3, pp. 119–140.

Day, Robert W., and Griffin, Robert E. 1980. "Children's Attitudes Towards the Magic Circle." *Elementary School Guidance and Counseling* 15, no. 2, pp. 136–146.

Deen, Nathan. 1974. "From the Netherlands . . ." *Personnel and Guidance Journal* 53, no. 1, pp. 45–46.

DeEsch, Jesse B. 1979. "Group Counseling with Disruptive Students." *Journal for Specialists in Group Work* 4, no. 3, pp. 117–122.

Deffenbacher, Jerry L., and Kemper, Calvin C. 1974. "Counseling Test-Anxious Sixth Graders." *Elementary School Guidance and Counseling* 9, no. 1, pp. 22–29.

Delaney, Jo Ann; Seidman, Edward; and Willis, Grant. 1978. "Crisis Intervention and the Prevention of Institutionalization: An Interrupted Time Series Analysis." *American Journal of Community Psychology* 6, no. 1, pp. 33–45.

Deloria V. 1979. "Indians Today, the Real and Unreal." In *Counseling American Minorities*, edited by Donald R. Atkinson, George Morton, and Derald Wing Sue, pp. 33–50. Dubuque, Iowa: William C. Brown and Company.

Dent, Marie W. 1974. "Consulting with Teachers via the Guidance Team." *Personnel and Guidance Journal* 52, no. 10, pp. 685–688.

DeVoe, Marianne, and Sherman, Thomas M. 1975. "Microtechnology: A Tool for Elementary School Counselors." *Elementary School Guidance and Counseling* 10, no. 2, pp. 110–115.

DeWitt, Karen. 1980. "Groups Seek to End Wage Lag of Women." *New York Times*, 4 May, p. 28.

Diamond, Esther E., ed. 1975. *Issues of Sex Bias and Sex Fairness in Careers Interest Measurement*. Washington, D.C.: U.S. Department of Health, Education, and Welfare, pp. xxiii–xxix.

Dickey, Frank G. 1968. "What Is Accrediting and Why Is It Important for Professional Organizations?" *Counselor Education and Supervision* 7, no. 3, pp. 194–199.

Dickinson, James C. 1978. *Initiative for Professional Renewal, Selected Issues for the Counseling Practitioner*. Falls Church, Va.: American Personnel and Guidance Association.

Dinkmeyer, Don. 1973. "Elementary School Counseling: Prospects and Potentials." *Personnel and Guidance Journal*, 52, no. 3, pp. 171–174.

———. 1971. "Developmental Counseling: Rationale and Relationship." *School Counselor* 18, no. 4, pp. 246–252.

———. 1973. *Elementary School Guidance and Counseling* 6, no. 2, pp. 81–85.

Dinkmeyer, Don, and McKay, Gary D. 1974. "Leading Effective Parent Study Groups." *Elementary School Guidance and Counseling* 9, no. 2, pp. 108–115.

———. 1976. *Sytematic Training for Effective Parenting*. Circle Pines, Minn.: American Guidance Service.

Dolliver, Robert H., and Nelson, Richard E. 1975. "Assumptions Regarding Vocational Counseling." *Vocational Guidance Quarterly* 24, no. 1, pp. 12–19.

Domke, Jane A.; Winkelpleck, Judy M.; and Westefeld, John. 1980. "Consultation and Outreach: Implementation at a University Counseling Center." *Journal of College Student Personnel* 21, no. 3, pp. 211–214.

Drapela, Victor J. 1974. "Counselors, Not Political Agitators." *Personnel and Guidance Journal* 52, no. 7, pp. 449–453.

———. 1975. "Comparative Guidance Through International Study." *Personnel and Guidance Journal* 52, no. 7, pp. 438–453.

———. 1977. "APGA International Education Committee." *Report*. 2 April.

_____. 1979. *Guidance and Counseling Around the World*. Washington, D.C.: University Press of America.

Dreyfus, Patricia A. 1980. "A Fresh Start in Mid-Life." *Money*. May, pp. 84–86, 88, 90, 92.

Drum, Davis J., and Figger, Howard E. 1972. *Outreach in Counseling: Applying the Growth and Prevention Model in Schools and Colleges*. New York: Intext Educational Publishers.

Dustin, Richard. 1974. "Training for Institutional Change." *Personnel and Guidance Journal* 52, no. 6, pp. 422–427.

Dye, Larry L., and Sansouci, James P. 1974. "Toward a New Era in Corrections." *Personnel and Guidance Journal* 53, no. 2, pp. 130–135.

Dyer, Wayne W., and Vriend, John. 1975. *Counseling Techniques That Work! Applications to Individual and Group Counseling*. Washington, D.C.: APGA Press.

Easton, Robert, and Resnikoff, Arthur. 1969. "Who Decided What?" *Personnel and Guidance Journal* 47, no. 6, pp. 597–598.

"EBCE: A Design for Career Education." 1975. *Curriculum Report* 4, no. 3, pp. 1–11.

Ebel, Robert L. 1975. "Educational Tests: Valid? Biased? Useful?" *Phi Delta Kappan* 57, no. 2, pp. 83–88.

Eckstein, Daniel G. 1980. "Adlerian Contributions to Correctional Counseling." *Journal of Offender Counseling* 1, no. 1, pp. 3–12.

Eddy, William B., and Lubin, Bernard. 1971. "Laboratory Training and Encounter Groups." *Personnel and Guidance Journal* 49, no. 8, pp. 625–635.

Edington, Everett D. 1976. "Evaluation of Methods of Using Resource People in Helping Kindergarten Students Become Aware of the World of Work." *Journal of Vocational Behavior* 8, no. 2, pp. 125–131.

"Editorial". 1973. *The School Guidance Worker*. 29, no. 1, pp. 2–3.

Editors of British Journal of Guidance and Counseling. 1973. "Editorial." *British Journal of Guidance and Counseling* 1, no. 1, p. 2.

Educational Testing Service. 1980a. *Test Scores and Family Income*. Princeton, N.J.: Educational Testing Service.

_____. 1980b. *Test Use and Validity*. Princeton, N.J.: Educational Testing Service.

Edwards, Patsy B., and Bloland, Paul A. 1980. "Leisure Counseling and Consultation." *Personnel and Guidance Journal* 58, no. 6, p. 435.

Egan, Gerard. 1975. *The Skilled Helper*. Monterey, Calif.: Brooks/Cole Publishing Company.

Ehrle, Raymond A. 1979. "Rehabilitation Counselors on the Threshold of the 1980's." *Counselor Education and Supervision* 18, no. 3, pp. 174–180.

Elleson, Vera J., and Onmink, Allen G. 1976. "Jobs Inc.–Inschool Career Education/Experience." *Elementary School Guidance and Counseling* 10, no. 4, pp. 290–292.

Ellis, Albert. 1975a. "A Commentary." *Personnel and Guidance Journal* 54, no. 2, pp. 92–93.

_____. 1975b. "Rational-Emotive Therapy and the School Counselor." *School Counselor* 22, no. 4, pp. 236–242.

Emerson, Patricia, and Smith, Edward W. L. 1974. "Contributions of Gestalt Psychology to Gestalt Therapy." *Counseling Psychologist* 4, no. 4, pp. 8–12.

Englehardt, Leah; Sulzer, Beth; and Alterkruse, Michael. 1971. "The Counselor as a

Consultant in Eliminating Out-of-Seat Behavior." *Elementary School Guidance and Counseling* 5, no. 3, pp. 196–204.

Entine, Alan D. 1976. "Mid-Life Counseling: Prognosis and Potential." *Personnel and Guidance Journal* 55, no. 3, pp. 112–114.

Esposito, Ronald P. 1977. "The Relationship Between the Motive to Avoid Success and Vocational Choice." *Journal of Vocational Behavior* 10, no. 3, pp. 347–357.

Eysenck, H. J. 1952. "The Effects of Psychotherapy: An Evaluation." *Journal of Consulting Psychology* 16, pp. 316–324.

Fagan, Joan; Lauver, David; Smith, Sally; Deloach, Stan; Katz, Michael; and Wood, Elaine. 1974. "Critical Incident in the Empty Chair." *Counseling Psychologist* 4, no. 4, pp. 33–42.

Fagan, Thomas, and Wallace, Anne. 1979. "Who Are the Handicapped?" *Personnel and Guidance Journal* 58, no. 4, pp. 215–220.

Fantaci, Anthony. 1973. "A Challenge Decade for Employment Counselors." *Personnel and Guidance Journal* 52, no. 3, pp. 161–166.

Faust, Verne. 1968. *History of Elementary School Counseling.* Boston: Houghton Mifflin.

Felix, Joseph L. 1968. "Who Decided That?" *Personnel and Guidance Journal* 47, pp. 9–11.

Fernald, Peter S., and Makarewicz, Joan F. 1967. "Use of Personal Validation." *Journal of Counseling Psychology* 14, no. 6, pp. 568–569.

Fiedler, F. E. 1950*a*. "A Comparison of the Therapeutic Relationships in Psychoanalytic, Non-Directive, and Adlerian Therapy." *Journal of Consulting Psychology* 14, pp. 436–445.

———. 1950*b*. "The Concept of an Ideal Therapeutic Relationship." *Journal of Consulting Psychology* 14, pp. 239–245.

Fisher, Thomas J.; Reardon, Robert C.; and Burck, Harman D. 1976. "Increasing Information-Seeking Behavior with a Model-Reinforced Videotape." *Journal of Counseling Psychology* 23, no. 3, pp. 234–238.

Fitzgerald, Louise F., and Crites, John O. 1980. "Toward a Career Psychology of Women: What Do We Know? What Do We Need to Know?" *Journal of Counseling Psychology* 27, no. 1, pp. 44–62.

Flanagan, John C. 1973. "The First Fifteen Years of Project Talent; Implications for Career Guidance," *Vocational Guidance Quarterly,* 22, no. 1, pp. 8–14.

———. 1977. "The PLAN System for Individualizing Education." *National Council on Measurement in Education,* vol. 2, pp. 1–8.

———. 1978. "A Research Approach to Improving Our Quality of Life." *American Psychologist* 33, no. 2, pp. 138–147.

Flanagan, John C.; Tiedeman, David V.; Wills, Mary B.; and McLaughlin, Donald H. 1973. *The Career Data Book.* Palo Alto, Calif.: American Institutes for Research.

Flugman, Bert; Goldman, Leo; and Katz, David. 1979. "Training Counselors for Special Education." *Personnel and Guidance Journal* 58, no. 4, pp. 284–287.

Fogelman, Charles J. 1979. "Practice and Internships for Student Counselors of the Aging." In *Counseling the Aged,* edited by Mary L. Ganikos, Kathleen Grady, and Jane B. Olson, pp. 279–294. Falls Church, Va.: American Personnel and Guidance Association.

Foltz, Donald, 1980. "OTA Report says 'Hard Facts' Possible on Psychotherapy," *APA Monitor*, 11, no. 12, pp. 6–7.

Foreman, Milton E. 1977. "The Changing Scene in Higher Education and the Identity of Counseling Psychology." *Counseling Psychologist* 7, no. 2, pp. 45–48.

Forrer, Stephen E. 1975. "Battered Children and Counselor Responsibility." *School Counselor* 22, no. 3, pp. 161–165.

Forster, Jerald. 1978. "Counselor Credentialing Revisited." *Personnel and Guidance Journal* 56, no. 10, pp. 593–598.

Foster, June C.; Szoke, Claire Olsen; Kapisovsky, Peggy M.; and Kriger, Leslie S. 1977. *Guidance, Counseling and Support Services for High School Students with Physical Disabilities.* Cambridge, Mass.: Technical Education Research Centers.

Foulds, Melvin L., and Hannigan, Patricia S. 1976. "Effects of Gestalt Marathon Workshops on Measured Self-Actualization: A Replication and Follow-Up Study." *Journal of Counseling Psychology* 23, no. 1, pp. 6–65.

"Four Schools Eyed by ACES Accreditation." 1980. *Guidepost* 22, no. 12, pp. 1, 12.

"14 States to Implement Career Information Systems." 1980. *Guidepost* 22, no. 13, p. 12.

Fox, Lynn H., and Richmond, Lee J. 1979. "Gifted Females: Are We Meeting Their Counseling Needs?" *Personnel and Guidance Journal* 57, no. 5, pp. 256–260.

Frazier, Fred, and Matthes, William S. 1975. "Parent Education: A Comparison of Adlerian and Behavioral Approaches." *Elementary School Guidance and Counseling* 10, no. 1, pp. 31–38.

Freiberg, Patricia, and Birdwell, Margaret W. 1978. "An Intervention Model for Rape and Unwanted Pregnancy." In *Counseling Women*, edited by Lenore W. Harman, Janice M. Birk, Laurine E. Fitzgerald, and Mary Faith Tanney, pp. 261–269. Monterey, Calif.: Brooks/Cole Publishing Company.

Frey, David H. 1973. "Being Systematic When You Have But One Subject: Ideographic Method, N = 1, and All That." *Measurement and Evaluation in Education* 6, no. 1, pp. 35–43.

Frey, David H., and Raming, Henry E. 1979. "A Taxonomy of Counseling Goals and Methods." *Personnel and Guidance Journal* 58, no. 1, pp. 26–33.

Froland, Charles; Brodsky, Gerry; Olson, Madeline; and Stewart, Linda. 1979. "Social Support and Social Adjustment: Implications for Mental Health Professionals." *Community Mental Health Journal* 15, no. 2, pp. 82–93.

Fry, P. S.; Kropf, G.; and Coe, K. J. 1980. "Effects of Counselor and Client Racial Similarity on the Counselor's Response Patterns and Skills." *Journal of Counseling Psychology* 27, no. 2, pp. 130–137.

Fuller, Chester, and Kern, Roy. 1978. "The Effects of Hostile Clients on the Opposite-Race Counselor." *Journal of Non-White Concerns* 6, no. 4, pp. 169–174.

Galassi, John P., and Galassi, Merna Dee. 1978. "Preparing Individuals for Job Interviews: Suggestions from More than 60 Years of Research." *Personnel and Guidance Journal* 57, no. 4, pp. 188–192.

Gamsky, Neal R. 1970. "A Follow-Up Study of Pupil Personnel Services." *Journal of the International Association of Pupil Personnel Workers* 15, no. 3, pp. 130–134.

Gamsky, Neal R., and Oleshamsky, Marc. 1980. "Do We Really Have a Commitment to Student Development Programs?" *Journal of College Student Personnel* 21, no. 4, pp. 328–334.

Ganikos, Mary L.; Grady, Kathleen A.; and Olson, Jane B., eds. 1979. *Counseling the Aged.* Washington, D.C.: American Personnel and Guidance Association.

Gatz, Margaret; Siegler, Ilene C.; and Dibner, Susan Schmidt. 1979. "Individual and Community: Normative Conflicts in the Development of a New Therapeutic Community for Older Persons." *International Journal of Aging and Human Development* 10, no. 3, pp. 249–263.

Geiwitz, James. 1976. *Looking at Ourselves.* Boston: Little, Brown.

Gelatt, H. B. 1962. "Decision-Making: A Conceptual Frame of Reference for Counseling." *Journal of Counseling Psychology,* 9, no. 3, pp. 240–245.

Gelatt, H. B. 1967. "Information and Decision Theories Applied to College Choice and Planning." In *Preparing School Counselors in Educational Guidance,* pp. 101–114. New York: College Entrance Examination Board.

Gelatt, H. B.; Varenhorst, Barbara; and Carey, Richard. 1972. *Deciding.* New York: College Entrance Examination Board.

Gelatt, H. B.; Varenhorst, Barbara; Carey, Richard; and Miller, Gordon P. 1973. *Decisions and Outcomes.* New York: College Entrance Examination Board.

Gelfman, Arnold J. not dated. "The Career Clinic: Testing and Counseling for the University." In *Innovations in Counseling Services,* edited by Carol A. Blimline, pp. 3–10. Falls Church, Va.: International Association of Counseling Services.

Gelso, Charles J.; Birk, Janice M.; Utz, Patrick W. and Silver, Anne E. 1977. "A Multigroup Evaluation of the Models and Functions of University Counseling Centers," *Journal of Counseling Psychology,* 24, no. 4, pp. 338–348.

George, Paul S. 1979. *What Is a Middle School—Really.* Gainesville: Univ. of Florida.

Getz, Hilda G., and Miles, Johnnie H. 1978. "Women and Peers as Counselors: A Look at Client Preferences." *Journal of College Student Personnel* 19, no. 1, pp. 37–41.

Giddan, Norman S., and Price, Mary K. 1975. "Whither Counseling?" *School Counselor* 22, no. 3, pp. 154–160.

Giddan, Robert L.; Mitchell, Marianne H.; and Higgins, Robert E. 1973. *The Development and Management of School Guidance Programs.* Dubuque, Iowa.: William C. Brown and Company.

Gillingham, William H., and Lounsbury, Jerald E. 1979. "A Description and Evaluation of a Career Exploration Course." *Journal of College Student Personnel* 20, no. 6, pp. 525–529.

Gilsdorf, Dale L., 1978. "Counselor Preference of Mexican American, Black, White Community College Students, *"Journal of Non-White Concerns,"* 6, no. 4, pp. 162–168.

Ginzberg, Eli. 1971. *Career Guidance.* New York: McGraw-Hill.

Glaser, Edward M., and Taylor, Samuel H. 1973. "Factors Affecting the Success of Applied Research." *American Psychologist* 28, no. 2, pp. 140–146.

Glass, Gene. 1968. "Educational Piltdown Men." *Phi Delta Kappan* 50, no. 3, pp. 148–151.

Glasser, William, and Zunin, Leonard M. 1973. "Reality Therapy." In *Current Psychotherapies,* edited by Raymond Corsini, pp. 287–315. Itasca, Ill.: F. E. Peacock Pubs., Inc.

Gnepp, Jackie; Keating, Daniel P.; and Masters, John C. 1980. "A Peer System for Academic Advising." *Journal of College Student Personnel* 21, no. 4, pp. 370–372.

Goethals, George W., and Klos, Dennis S. 1976. *Experiencing Youth.* Boston: Little, Brown.

Goldman, Leo. 1972*a*. "It's Time to Put Up or Shut Up." *Measurement and Evaluation in Guidance* 5, no. 3, pp. 420–423.

_____. 1972*b*. "Tests and Counseling: The Marriage That Failed." *Measurement and Evaluation in Guidance* 4, no. 4, pp. 213–220.

_____. 1974. "Guidance U.S.A.: Views from Abroad." *Personnel and Guidance Journal* 53, no. 1, p. 40.

_____. 1976. "A Revolution in Counseling Research." *Journal of Counseling Psychology* 23, no. 6, pp. 543–552.

Goldman, Leo; Carroll, Marguerite R. (Peg); Forsyth, Louise B.; Muro, James; and Graff, Franklyn A. 1978. "How Are We Doing in School Guidance? The Moody Colloquium." *School Counselor* 25, no. 5, pp. 307–325.

Goldstein, Alan. 1973. "Behavior Therapy." In *Current Psychotherapies,* edited by Raymond Corsini, pp. 207–250. Itasca, Ill.: F. E. Peacock.

Gordon, Myra, and Grantham, Robert J. 1979. "Helper Preference in Disadvantaged Students." *Journal of Counseling Psychology* 26, no. 4, pp. 337–343.

Gordon, Thomas. 1970. *P.E.T.: Parent Effectiveness Training.* New York: Peter H Wyden.

Gordon, Virginia. 1980. "Training Academic Advisers: Content and Method." *Journal of College Student Personnel* 21, no. 4, pp. 334–340.

Gould, Roger. 1975. "Adult Life Stages: Growth Toward Self-Tolerance." *Psychology Today* 8, no. 9, pp. 74–78.

Gourash, Nancy. 1978. "Help-Seeking: A Review of the Literature." *American Journal of Community Psychology* 16, no. 5, pp. 413–423.

Grala, Christopher, and McCauley, Clark. 1976. "Counseling Truants Back to School: Motivation Combined with a Program for Action." *Journal of Counseling Psychology* 23, no. 2, pp. 166–169.

Gray, H. Dean, and Tindall, Judith. 1974. "Communications Training Study: A Model for Training Junior High School Peer Counselors." *School Counselor* 22, no. 2, pp. 107–112.

Gray-Toft, Pamela. 1980. "Effectiveness of a Counseling Support Program for Hospice Nurses." *Journal of Counseling Psychology* 27, no. 4, pp. 346–354.

Griffith, Albert R. 1980. "A Survey of Career Development in Corporations." *Personnel and Guidance Journal* 58, no. 8, pp. 537–543.

Griggs, Shirley A., and Gale, Patricia. 1977. "The Abused Child: Focus for Counselors." *Elementary School Guidance and Counseling* 11, no. 3, pp. 187–194.

Grubb, W. Norton, and Lazerson, Marvin. 1975. "Rally 'Round the Workplace: Continuities and Fallacies in Career Education." *Harvard Educational Review* 45, no. 4, pp. 451–474.

Grummon, Donald L., "Client-Centered Theory", 1965. In Buford Stefflre (Ed.) *Theories of Counseling,* New York; McGraw-Hill Book Co., pp. 30–90.

_____. 1972. "Client-Centered Theory", in Buford Stefflre and W. Harold Grant (Eds.), *Theories of Counseling* (2nd Ed.). New York; McGraw-Hill Book Co., pp. 73–135.

Grunebaum, Henry. 1979. "Middle Age and Marriage: Affiliative Men and Assertive Women." *American Journal of Family Therapy* 17, no. 3, pp. 46–50.

Gubser, M. M., 1974. "Performance-Based Counseling: Accountability or Liability", *School Counselor*, 21, no. 4, pp. 296–302.

Gurman, Alan S. 1979. "Dimensions of Marital Therapy: A Comparative Analysis." *Journal of Marital and Family Therapy* 5, no. 1, pp. 51–18.

Gustad, John W., and Tuma, Abdul H. 1957. "The Effects of Different Methods of Test Introduction and Interpretation on Client Learning in Counseling." *Journal of Counseling Psychology* 4, no. 4, pp. 313–317.

Guzzetta, Robert A., 1976. "Acquisition and Transfer of Empathy by Parents of Early Adolescents Through Structured Learning Training," *Journal of Counseling Psychology*, 23, No. 5, pp. 449–453.

Gysbers, Norman C. 1978. "Career Guidance at the Crossroads." In *New Imperatives for Guidance,* edited by Garry R. Walz and Libby Benjamin, pp. 2–29. Ann Arbor, Mich.: ERIC Counseling and Personnel Services Clearinghouse.

Haase, Richard F. 1974. "Power Analysis of Research in Counselor Education." *Counselor Education and Supervision* 14, no. 2, pp. 124–132.

Haettenschwiller, Dustan L., 1969. "Style of Role Enactment Expected of Parent, Teacher, and Counselor," *Personnel and Guidance Journal,* 47, no. 10, pp. 963–969.

Haettenschwiller, Dustin L. and Jabs, William. 1969. "The Counselor and the Instructional Program," *The School Counselor,* 17, no. 2, pp. 118–125.

Hambleton, R. K., and Novick, M. R. 1972. *Toward an Integration of Theory and Method for Criterion-Referenced Tests.* Iowa City, Iowa: The American College Testing Program.

Hamilton, Andrew. 1975. "Career Education: Working Model." *American Education,* 11, no. 10, pp. 22–25.

Hamilton, Jack A.; Baker, Octave V., and Mitchell, Anita M. 1979a. "Identifying Well-Evaluated Activities in Career Education." *Measurement and Evaluation in Guidance* 12, no. 2, pp. 112–120.

Hamilton, Jack A. and Mitchell, Anita M. 1979. "Identifying and Approving Career Education Activities for National Dissemination." *The Vocational Guidance Quarterly,* 28, no. 1, pp. 71–81.

Hammond, Janice M. 1979. "Children of Divorce: Implications for Counselors." *School Counselor* 27, no. 1, pp. 7–14.

Hannaford, Mary Joe. 1974. "A TA Approach to Teacher Group Counseling." *Elementary School Guidance and Counseling* 9, no. 1, pp. 6–13.

Hansen, James D.; Niland, Thomas M.; and Zani, Leonard P. 1969. "Model Reinforcement in Group Counseling with Elementary School Children." *Personnel and Guidance Journal* 47, no. 8, pp. 741–744.

Hansen, John H., and Hearn, Arthur C. 1971. *The Middle School Program.* Chicago: Rand McNally.

Hansen, Lorraine Sundal. 1970. *Career Guidance Practices in School and Community.* Washington, D.C.: National Vocational Guidance Association.

Hansen, L. Sunny. 1978. "ACES Position Paper: Counselor Preparation for Career Development/Career Education." *Counselor Education and Supervision* 17, no. 3, pp. 168–179.

Hansen, L. Sunny, and Keierleber, Dennis L. 1978. "Born Free: A Collaborative

Consultation Model for Career Development and Sex-Role Stereotyping."
Personnel and Guidance Journal 56, no. 7, pp. 395–399.

Harman, Robert L. 1975. "A Gestalt Point of View on Facilitating Growth in Counseling." *Personnel and Guidance Journal* 53, no. 5, pp. 363–366.

Harman, Robert L., and Franklin, Richard W. 1975. "Gestalt Interactional Groups." *Personnel and Guidance Journal* 54, no. 1, pp. 49–54.

Harman, Willis W. 1976. " 'Seis-ing' of the Social Revolution." *Phi Delta Kappan* 58, no. 1, pp. 131–136.

Harper, Frederick D. 1979. "What Counselors Must Know about the Social Sciences of Black Americans." In *Counseling American Minorities,* edited by Donald R. Atkinson, George Morton, and Derald Wing Sue, pp. 113–121. Dubuque, Iowa: William C. Brown and Company.

Harris, Jo Ann. 1972a. *Computer Assisted Guidance Systems.* Washington, D.C.: National Vocational Guidance Association.

———. 1972b "Willowbank Computerized Vocational Information System." In *Career Education and the Technology of Career Development,* pp. 152–155. Palo Alto, Calif.: American Institutes for Research.

———. 1974. "The Computer: Guidance Tool of the Future." *Journal of Counseling Psychology* 21, no. 4, pp. 331–339.

Harris, Mary B., and Trujillo, Amaryllis E. 1975. "Improving Study Habits of Junior High School Students Through Self-Management versus Group Discussion." *Journal of Counseling Psychology* 22, no. 6, pp. 513–517.

Harris, Roy. 1974. "From England . . ." *Personnel and Guidance Journal* 53, no. 1, pp. 47–49.

Harris, Sandra R. 1974. "Sex Typing in Girls' Career Choices: A Challenge to Counselors." *Vocational Guidance Quarterly* 23, no. 2, pp. 128–133.

Harris, Thomas A. 1969. *I'm O.K.—You're O.K.* New York: Harper and Row.

Harris, Thomas L., and Jean S. Wallin. 1978. "Influencing Career Choices of Seventh Grade Students." *Vocational Guidance Quarterly* 27, no. 1, pp. 50–54.

Harris-Bowlsbey, Jo Ann, 1975a "A Model of Career Guidance," in *Models of Career Education Programs,* Columbus, Ohio: The Center for Vocational Education, pp. 15–25.

———. 1975b. "Sex Bias and Computer-Based Guidance Systems." In *Issues of Sex Bias and Sex Fairness in Career Interest Measurement,* edited by Esther E. Diamond, pp. 177–200. Washington, D.C.: U.S. Department of Health, Education, and Welfare.

———. 1978. "Careers by Special Delivery." In *New Imperatives for Guidance,* edited by Garry R. Walz and Libby Benjamin, pp. 328–374. Ann Arbor, Mich.: ERIC Counseling and Personnel Services Clearinghouse.

Hart, Darrell H., and Donald J. Prince. 1970. "Role Conflicts for School Counselors: Training versus Job Demands." *Personnel and Guidance Journal* 48, no. 5, pp. 374–380.

Harvey, Thomas R. 1976. "Student Development and the Future of Higher Education: A Force Analysis." *Journal of College Student Personnel* 17, no. 2, pp. 90–95.

Havighurst, Robert J. 1972. *Developmental Tasks and Education.* 3rd ed. New York: David McKay.

Haymon, Francene; Pollard, Diane E.; and Bobby, Annette M. 1979. "Reentering the Job Market for Minority Women." *Journal of Non-White Concerns* 8, no. 1, pp. 31–51.

Hays, Donald G. 1972. "Counselors — What Are You Worth?" *School Counselor* 19, no. 5, pp. 309–312.

———. 1981. *Counseling and the Future: Concepts, Issues, and Strategies.* Ann Arbor, Mich.: ERIC Counseling and Personnel Services Clearinghouse.

Healy, Charles C. 1973. "Toward a Replicable Method of Group Career Counseling." *Vocational Guidance Quarterly* 21, no. 3, pp. 214–221.

———. 1974. "Evaluation of a Replicable Group Career Counseling Procedure." *Vocational Guidance Quarterly* 23, no. 1, pp. 34–40.

Hecht, Murray. 1977. "A Cooperative Approach Toward Children from Alcoholic Families." *Elementary School Guidance and Counseling* 11, no. 3, pp. 197–203.

Heddesheimer, Janet C. 1975. *Managing Elementary School Guidance Programs.* Boston: Houghton Mifflin.

Heilfron, Marilyn. 1960. "The Function of Counseling as Perceived by High School Students." *Personnel and Guidance Journal* 39, no. 2, pp. 133–136.

Heitzmann, Dennis. 1979. "The Forgotten Facilitators: Humans Relations Training for Support Personnel." *Personnel and Guidance Journal* 57, no. 10, pp. 543–544.

Hendry, Andrew M. 1977. "Student Services in Five Alberta Colleges: A Measure of Quality." *Journal of College Student Personnel* 18, no. 5, pp. 376–381.

Hennessy, Thomas C. 1980. "Introduction to the Special Issue, 'Values and the Counselor.'" *Personnel and Guidance Journal* 58, no. 9, pp. 557–558.

Heppner, Mary J. 1978. "Counseling the Battered Wife: Myths, Facts, and Decisions." *Personnel and Guidance Journal* 56, no. 9, pp. 522–525.

Herbert, Wray. 1979. "Congress and White House at Odds Over Mental Health Systems Packages." *APA Monitor* 10, no. 12, pp. 1, 13.

Herr, Edwin L. 1974. "Manpower Policies, Vocational Guidance and Career Development." In *Vocational Guidance and Human Development,* edited by Edwin L. Herr, pp. 32–62. Boston: Houghton Mifflin.

———. 1979. *Guidance and Counseling in Schools: The Past, Present, and Future.* Falls Church, Va.: American Personnel and Guidance Association.

———. 1980. "Preparing the School Counselor to Function in Career Education." In *The School Counselor's Involvement in Career Education,* edited by Francis E. Burtnett, pp. 49–71A. Falls Church, Va.: American Personnel and Guidance Association.

Herr, Edwin L., and Cramer, Stanley H. 1972. *Vocational Guidance and Career Development in the Schools: Toward a Systems Approach.* Boston: Houghton Mifflin.

———. 1979. *Career Guidance Through the Life Span.* Boston: Little, Brown.

Herr, Edwin L., and Whitson, Karin Stork. 1979. "Career Guidance of Urban Adults: Some Perspectives on Needs and Action." *Vocational Guidance Quarterly* 28, no. 2, pp. 111–120.

Hilgard, Ernest R. 1973. "The Domain of Hypnosis." *American Psychologist* 28, no. 11, pp. 972–982.

Hill, George E. 1968. "Standards for the Preparation of Secondary School Counselors." *Counselor Education and Supervision* 7, no. 3, pp. 179–186.

———. 1974. *Management and Improvement of Guidance.* 2nd ed. Englewood Cliffs, N.J.: Prentice-Hall.

Hillman, Bill W., and Shields, Frank L. 1975. "The Encouragement Procedures in Guidance: Its Effect on School Achievement and Attending Behavior." *School Counselor* 22, no. 3, pp. 166–173.

Hiltzheimer, Nancy B., and Gumaer, Jim. 1979. "Behavior Management and Classroom Guidance in an Inner-City School." *Elementary School Guidance and Counseling* 13, no. 4, pp. 272–278.

Hipple, John L., and Muto, Lee. 1974. "The TA Group for Adolescents." *Personnel and Guidance Journal* 52, no. 10, pp. 675–681.

Hohenshil, Thomas H. 1979. "Counseling Handicapped Persons and their Families." *Personnel and Guidance Journal,* 58, no. 4, pp. 213–214.

Hohenshil, Thomas H., and Humes II, Charles W. 1979. "Roles of Counseling in Ensuring the Rights of the Handicapped." *Personnel and Guidance Journal* 58, no. 4, pp. 221–227.

Holland, Glen A. 1973. "Transactional Analysis." In *Current Psychotherapies,* edited by Raymond Corsini, pp. 353–399. Itasca, Ill.: F. E. Peacock.

Holland, John L. 1973. *Making Vocational Choices:* Englewood Cliffs, N.J. Prentice-Hall.

Holland, John L., and Nafziger, Dean H. 1975. "A Note on the Validity of Self-Directed Search." *Measurement and Evaluation in Guidance* 7, no. 4, pp. 259–262.

Hopkins, Robert F. 1969. "Comment." *Personnel and Guidance Journal* 47, no. 6, pp. 598–599.

Hoppock, Robert. 1976. *Occupational Information.* 4th ed. New York: McGraw-Hill.

Hornbuckle, Phyllis A.; Mahoney, John; and Borgard, John H. 1979. "A Structural Analysis of Student Perceptions of Faculty Advising." *Journal of College Student Personnel* 20, no. 4, pp. 296–300.

Hosford, Ray E., and de Visser, Louis A. J. M. 1974. *Behavioral Approaches to Counseling: An Introduction.* Washington, D. C.: American Personnel and Guidance Association.

Hosford, Ray E. and Ryan, T. Antionette, 1970. "Systems Design in the Development of Counseling and Guidance Programs," *Personnel and Guidance Journal,* 49, no. 4, pp. 221–230.

Hosie, Thomas W. 1974. "Preparing Counselors to Meet the Needs of the Handicapped." *Personnel and Guidance Journal* 58, no. 4, pp. 271–275.

Howard, Alvin W., and Stoumbis, George C. 1970. *The Junior High School and the Middle School: Issues and Practices.* Scranton, Pa.: Intext Educational Publishers.

Hoyt, Kenneth B. 1974. "Professional Preparation for Vocational Guidance." In *Vocational Guidance and Human Development,* edited by Edwin L. Herr, pp. 502–527. Boston: Houghton Mifflin.

———. 1975a. "Career Education: Challenges for Counselors." *Vocational Guidance Quarterly* 23 no. 4, pp. 303–310.

———. 1975b. "Career Education and Counselor Education." *Counselor Education and Supervision* 15, no. 1, pp. 6–11.

Huber, Charles H. 1980. "Research and the School Counselor." *School Counselor* 27, no. 3, pp. 210–216.

Humes, Charles W., Jr. 1972. "Accountability: A Boon to Guidance." *Personnel and Guidance Journal* 51, no. 1, pp. 21–26.

Huse, Edgar F. 1975. *Organization Development and Change.* New York: West Publishing Company.

———. 1978. "Organization Development." *Personnel and Guidance Journal* 56, no. 7, pp. 403–406.

Hutchins, David E. 1979. "Systematic Counseling: The T-F-A Model for Counselor Intervention." *Personnel and Guidance Journal* 57, no. 10, pp. 529–531.

"In Pre-Retirement Planning, Enthusiasm is Counseling Key." 1979. *Guidepost* 21, no. 13, p. 6.

Inniss, James. 1977. "Counseling the Culturally Disrupted Child." *Elementary School Guidance and Counseling* 11, no. 3, pp. 229–235.

Ivey, Allen E. 1974a. "Adapting Systems to People." *Personnel and Guidance Journal* 53, no. 2, pp. 137–139.

———. 1974b. "Micro Counseling and Media Therapy: State of the Art." *Counselor Education and Supervision* 13, no. 3, pp. 172–183.

Ivey, Allen E., and Alschuler, Alfred S. 1973a. "An Introduction to the Field." *Personnel and Guidance Journal* 51, no. 9, pp. 591–597.

———. 1973b. "Psychological Education Is . . ." *Personnel and Guidance Journal* 51, no. 9, pp. 588–589.

Ivey, Allen E., and Gluckstern, Norma B. 1974. *Basic Attending Skills, Leader Manual.* North Amherst, Mass.: Microtraining Associates.

Ivey, Allen E., and Leppaluoto, Jean R. 1975. "Changes Ahead! Implications of the Vail Conference." *Personnel and Guidance Journal* 53, no. 10, pp. 747–752.

Jacobson, Thomas J. 1972. "Career Guidance Centers." *Personnel and Guidance Journal* 50, no. 7, pp. 599–604.

———. 1975. "A Study of Career Centers in the State of California, Final Report." La Mesa, Calif.: Pupil Personnel Services, Grossmont Union High School District.

Jacobson, Thomas J., and Mitchell, Anita M. 1975. *Master Plan for Career Guidance and Counseling.* Grossmont, Calif.: Grossmont Union High School District.

Jasmine, Frank. 1974. "Diversions as an Alternative to Incarceration." *Personnel and Guidance Journal* 53, no. 2, pp. 140–141.

Jefferies, Doris, and Spedding, Sally. 1974. "Education and the World of Work." *Elementary School Guidance and Counseling* 9, no. 1, pp. 49–51.

Jencks, Christopher. 1972. *Inequality: A Reassessment of the Effect of the Family and Schooling in America.* New York: Basic Books.

Jersild, Arthur T.; Telford, Charles W.; and Sawrey, James M. 1975. *Child Psychology.* 7th ed. Englewood Cliffs, N.J.: Prentice-Hall.

Johansson, Charles B. 1975. "Technical Aspects: Problems of Scale Development, Norms, Item Differences by Sex, and the Rate of Change in Occupational and Group Characteristics." In *Issues of Sex Bias and Sex Fairness in Career Interest Measurement,* edited by Esther E. Diamond, pp. 65–88. Washington, D.C.: U.S. Department of Health, Education, and Welfare.

Johnson, Craig W., and Pinkney, James W. 1980. "Outreach: Counseling Service Impacts on Faculty Advising of Students." *Journal of College Student Personnel* 21, no. 1, pp. 80–84.

Johnson, Mauritz, Jr.; Busacker, William E.; and Bowman, Fred Q., Jr. 1961. *Junior High School Guidance.* New York: Harper and Brothers.

Johnson, Roosevelt. 1980. "School Models for Career Education/Development," *Journal of Non-White Concerns,* 8, no. 3, pp. 104–118.

Johnson, William F.; Korn, Thomas A.; and Dunn, Dennis J. 1975. "Comparing Three Methods of Presenting Occupational Information." *Vocational Guidance Quarterly* 24, no. 1, pp. 62–66.

Joint Committee on Standards for Educational Evaluation. 1981. *Standards for Evaluations of Educational Programs, Projects, and Materials.* New York: McGraw-Hill.

Jonassen, Ellen O., and Stripling, Robert O. 1977. "Priorities for Community College Student Personnel Services During the Next Decade." *Journal of College Student Personnel* 18, no. 2, pp. 83–86.

Jones, G. Brian; Tiedeman, David V.; Mitchell, Anita M.; Unruh, Waldemar R.; Helliwell, Carolyn B.; and Ganschow, Laurie H. 1973. *Planning, Structuring, and Evaluating Practical Career Guidance for Integration by Non-College-Bound Youths.* Palo Alto, Calif.: American Institutes for Research.

Jones, Wendell H. 1970. "Counselors in a Double-Bind." *Personnel and Guidance Journal* 48, no. 8, p. 606.

Kahnweiler, Jennifer Boretz, and Kahnweiler, William M. 1980. "A Dual Career Family Workshop for College Undergraduates." *Vocational Guidance Quarterly* 28, no. 3, pp. 225–230.

Kaiser, Herbert E., and Sillin, Percy C. 1977. "Guidance Effectiveness in the Elementary School." *Elementary School Guidance and Counseling* 12, no. 1, pp. 61–64.

Kaplan, Louis, and Stoughton, Robert W. 1974. *Pupil Personnel Services Guidelines for Introducing and Developing a Program for Accountability.* Princeton, N.J.: National Association of Pupil Personnel Administrators.

Kasworm, Carol E. 1980. "Student Services for the Older Undergraduate Student." *Journal of College Student Personnel* 21, no. 2, pp. 163–169.

Katz, Martin R. 1980. "SIGI: An Interactive Aid to Career Decision Making." *Journal of College Student Personnel* 21, no. 1, pp. 34–40.

Keefe, Joseph A. 1970. "The School Counselor as an Organizational Type." *Personnel and Guidance Journal* 48, no. 10, pp. 798–799.

Kearney, Annette G., and Clayton, Robert L. 1973. "Career Education and Blacks: Trick or Treat?" *School Counselor* 21, no. 2, pp. 102–108.

Keller, F. J., and Viteles, M. S. 1937. *Vocational Guidance Throughout the World.* New York. Norton.

Kelly, F. Donald, and Dowd, E. Thomas. 1975. "The Staffing Conference: An Approach to Student Evaluation." *Counselor Education and Supervision* 15, no. 2, pp. 135–139.

Kemp, C. Gratton. 1971. "Existential Counseling." *Counseling Psychologist* 2, no. 3, pp. 2–30.

Kempler, Walter. 1973. "Gestalt Therapy." In *Current Psychotherapies,* edited by Raymond Corsini, pp. 251–286. Itasca, Ill.: F. E. Peacock.

Kieffer, Jarold A. 1980. "Counselors and the Older Worker: An Overview." *Journal of Employment Counseling* 17, no. 1, pp. 8–16.

Kilgo, Reese Danley. 1975. "Counseling Couples in Groups: Rationale and Methodology." *Family Coordinator* 24, no. 3, pp. 337–342.

Kincaid, Marylou Butler. 1979. "Traditional-Age College Women." *Counseling Psychologist* 8, no. 1, pp. 23–24.

Kincaid, Marylou, and Kincaid, John. 1971. "Counseling for Peace." *Personnel and Guidance Journal* 49, no. 9, pp. 727–735.

Kindred, Leslie W., ed. 1968. *The Intermediate Schools.* Englewood Cliffs, N.J.: Prentice-Hall.

King, Patricia M., and Fields, A. Leo. 1980. "A Framework for Student Development: From Student Development Goals to Educational Opportunity Practice." *Journal of College Student Personnel* 21, no. 6, pp. 541–548.

Kirk, Barbara A. 1969. "'Counselee Participation' in Test Selection." *Counseling Psychologist* 1, no. 2, pp. 78–83.

Kladnik, Sallie. 1979. "A Survey of Career Development Programs in Bay Area Corporations." *Career Planning and Adult Development Newsletter* 1, no. 6, pp. 1–2.

Klopfer, Carol Lee. 1977. "The Effects of Information on Counseling Expectancies and Willingness: A Study of High School Youth." Doctoral dissertation, College of Education, University of Florida.

Knowdell, Richard L. 1980. "Employee Counseling in Industry." *Career Planning and Adult Development Newsletter* 2, no. 6, pp. 1–2.

Kohut, Sylvester, Jr. 1976. *The Middle School: A Bridge Between Elementary and Secondary Schools.* Washington, D.C.: National Education Association.

Korchin, Sheldon J. 1980. "Clinical Psychology and Minority Problems." *American Psychologist* 35, no. 3, pp. 262–269.

Kroll, Arthur M. 1976. "Career Education's Impact on Employability and Unemployment: Expectations and Realities." *Vocational Guidance Quarterly* 24, no. 3, pp. 209–218.

Krumboltz, John D. 1970. "Job Experience Kits." *Personnel and Guidance Journal* 49, no. 3, p. 233.

———. 1974. "An Accountability Model for Counselors." *Personnel and Guidance Journal* 52, no. 10, pp. 639–646.

Krumboltz, John D., and Baker, Ronald D. 1973. "Behavioral Counseling for Vocational Decision." In *Career Guidance for a New Age,* edited by Henry Borow, pp. 235–283. Boston: Houghton Mifflin.

Krumboltz, John D., and Schroeder, Wade W. 1965. "Promoting Career Planning Through Reinforcement." *Personnel and Guidance Journal* 44, no. 1, pp. 19–26.

Kulka, Richard A.; Veroff, Joseph; and Douvan, Elizabeth. 1979. "Social Class and the Use of Professional Help for Personal Problems: 1957 and 1976." *Journal of Health and Social Behavior* 20, no. 1.

Kurtz, Robert R. 1974. "Using a Transactional Analysis Format in Vocational Group Counseling." *Journal of College Student Personnel* 15, no. 6, pp. 447–451.

Kushel, Gerald. 1970. "The Counselor's Image and the Chameleon." *School Counselor* 17, no. 4, pp. 286–291.

Kuzniar, Joseph. 1973. "Teacher Consultation: A Case Study." *Personnel and Guidance Journal* 52, no. 2, pp. 108–111.

La Crosse, Michael B., and Barak, Azy. 1976. "Differential Perception of Counselor Behavior." *Journal of Counseling Psychology* 23, no. 2, pp. 170–172.

Lane, David. 1970. "A Sterile Feud." *Personnel and Guidance Journal* 48, no. 6, p. 421.

Langway, Lynn; Lord, Mary; Reese, Michael; Simons, Pamela Ellis; Maitland, Terrence; Gelman, Eric; and Witman, Lisa. 1980. "The Superwoman Squeeze." *Newsweek.* 19 May, pp. 72–74, 76, 78–79.

Larson, William E., and Rice, Roger E. 1967. "The Differential Perception of the School Counselor by Deviant and Non-Deviant Students." *School Counselor* 15, no. 1, pp. 26–31.

Lauver, Philip J.; Gastellum, Richard M.; and Sheehey, Marilyn. 1975. "Bias on OOH Illustrations?" *Vocational Guidance Quarterly* 23, no. 4, pp. 335–340.

Lazarus, Richard S. 1975. "A Cognitively Oriented Psychologist Looks at Bio-Feedback." *American Psychologist* 30, no. 5, pp. 553–561.

Lazes, Roberta S., and Feldberg, Mildred V. 1978. "Community Counseling in an Adult Education Setting." *Personnel and Guidance Journal* 57, no. 1, pp. 60–61.

Lee, Robert E., and Klopfer, Carol. 1978. "Counselors and Juvenile Delinquents: Toward a Comprehensive Treatment Approach." *Personnel and Guidance Journal* 57, no. 4, pp. 194–197.

Leonard, George E.; Sather, Greg; Sheggrud, Darryl B.; and Handel, Linda. 1973. "Career Guidance in the Elementary School." *Elementary School Guidance and Counseling* 7, no. 4, pp. 287–291.

Leonard, George E.; and Splete, Howard H. 1975. "Career Guidance in the Elementary School." *Elementary School Guidance and Counseling* 10, no. 1, pp. 50–56.

Leonard, George E.; Vriend, Thelma J. 1975. "Update: The Developmental Career Guidance Project." *Personnel and Guidance Journal* 53, no. 9, pp. 668–671.

Leung, Paul, and Fargle, Donnelle. 1980. "Counseling with the Elderly Living in Public Housing." *Personnel and Guidance Journal* 58, no. 6, pp. 442–445.

Levant, Ronald F. 1980. "A Classification of the Fields of Family Therapy: A Review of Prior Attempts and a New Paradigmatic Model." *American Journal of Family Therapy* 8, no. 1, pp. 3–16.

Levinson, Daniel J. 1977. "The Mid-Life Transition: A Period in Adult Psychosocial Development." *Psychiatry* 40, no. 2, pp. 99–112.

Levinson, Daniel J.; Darrow, Charlotte M.; Klein, Edward B.; Levinson, Maria H.; and McKee, Braxton. 1976. "Periods in the Adult Development of Men: Ages 18 to 45." *Counseling Psychologist* 6, no. 1, pp. 21–25.

Leviton, Harvey S. 1977. "Consumer Feedback on a Secondary School Guidance Program." *Personnel and Guidance Journal* 55, no. 5, pp. 242–244.

Lewis, Judith A., and Lewis, Michael D. 1977. *Community Counseling: A Human Services Approach.* New York: John Wiley and Sons.

Lewis, Judy. 1972. "Introduction." *Personnel and Guidance Journal* 51, no. 2, p. 85.

Lewis, Michael D., and Lewis, Judith A. 1970. "The Counselor and Civil Liberties." *Personnel and Guidance Journal* 49, no. 1, pp. 9–13.

Lewis, Ronald G., and Ho, Man Keong. 1979. "Social Work with Native Americans." In *Counseling American Minorities,* edited by Donald R. Atkinson, George Morton, and Derald Wing Sue, pp. 51–58. Dubuque, Iowa: William C. Brown and Company.

"Licensure Committee Action Packet." 1979. Mimeographed. Falls Church, Va.: American Personnel and Guidance Association.

Lifton, Walter M. 1969. "Making Mirror Images." *Personnel and Guidance Journal* 48, no. 2, pp. 133–134.

Lindenberg, Steven P. 1980. "Musings: Accountability; Logic; and Reason." *AMHCA News* 4, no. 1, p. 1.

Lipsett, Laurence. 1980. "A Career Counselor in Industry." *Vocational Guidance Quarterly* 28, no. 3, pp. 269–273.

Lipsman, Clair K. 1969. "Revolution and Prophecy: Community Involvement for Counselors." *Personnel and Guidance Journal* 48, no. 2, pp. 97–100.

Litwack, Lawrence. 1975. "Testimonial Privileged Communication: A Problem Re-examined." *School Counselor* 22, no. 3, pp. 194–196.

——. 1978. "Counseling Services in Community Colleges." *Journal of College Student Personnel* 19, no. 4, pp. 359–361.

Lombana, Judy. 1977. *Perspectives on Secondary Guidance.* Tallahassee, Fla.: Department of Education.

Lombana, Judy H. 1980. "Guidance of Handicapped Students: Counselor In-Service Needs." *Counselor Education and Supervision* 19, no. 4, pp. 269–275.

Long, James D. 1971. "School Phobia and the Elementary Counselor." *Elementary School Guidance and Counseling* 5, no. 4, pp. 289–294.

Lopez, Martina A. 1980. "Social-Skills Training with Institutionalized Elderly: Effects of Precounseling Structuring and Overlearning of Skill Acquisition and Transfer." *Journal of Counseling Psychology* 27, no. 3, pp. 286–292.

Lounsbury, John H. 1974. "How the Junior High School Came to Be." In *The American Intermediate School,* edited by Max E. Brough and Russell L. Hamm, pp. 5–8. Danville, Ill.: Interstate Printers and Publishers.

Lounsbury, John H., and Douglass, Harl R. 1974. "Recent Trends in Junior High School Practice, 1954–1964." In *The American Intermediate School,* edited by Max E. Brough and Russell L. Hamm, pp. 168–178. Danville, Ill.: Interstate Printers and Publishers.

Lovenheim, Barbara. 1979. "More Care Given Employees' Psyches." *New York Times.* 1 April, pp. 3, 5.

McAlees, Daniel C. 1980. "Toward a New Professionalism: Certification and Accreditation." In *Counselor Licensure: Issues and Perspectives,* edited by Richard W. Warner, Jr., David K. Brooks, Jr., and Jean A. Thompson, pp. 80–83. Falls Church, Va.: American Personnel and Guidance Association.

McBeath, Marcia. 1980. "Consulting with Teachers in Two Areas: Grief and Mourning: Relaxation Techniques." *Personnel and Guidance Journal* 58, no. 7, pp. 473–476.

McCann, Barbara Goldman. 1975. "Peer Counseling: An Approach to Psychological Education." *Elementary School Guidance and Counseling* 9, no. 3, pp. 180–187.

McDowell, William A.; Coven, Arnold B.; and Eash, Violette C. 1979. "The Handicapped: Special Needs and Strategies for Counseling." *Personnel and Guidance Journal* vol. 58, no. 7, pp. 228–232.

McGlasson, Maurice. 1973. *The Middle School: Whence? What? Whither?* Bloomington, Ind.: Phi Delta Kappa Educational Foundation.

McKee, James B. 1969. *Introduction to Sociology.* New York: Holt, Rinehart and Winston.

McKinnon, Byron E., and Jones, G. Brian. 1975. "Field Testing a Comprehensive Career Guidance Program, K–12." *Personnel and Guidance Journal* 53, no. 9, pp. 663–667.

Mable, Phyllis; Terry, Marilyn J.; and Duvall, William H. 1977. "A Model of Student Development Through Community Responsibility." *Journal of College Student Personnel* 18, no. 1, pp. 50–56.

Macaluso, Lila. 1976. "Case Analysis: Consultation and Counseling." *Elementary School Guidance and Counseling* 10, no. 3, pp. 218–220.

Maser, Arthur L. 1971. "Counselor Function in Secondary Schools," *School Counselor*, 18, no. 5, pp. 367–372.

Magnarella, Paul J. 1979. "The Continuing Evaluation of a Living-Learning Center." *Journal of College Student Personnel* 20, no. 1, pp. 4–8.

Mallory, Al. 1972. "IBM Educational and Career Exploration System (ECES)." In *Career Education and Technology for Career Development*, pp. 156–158. Palo Alto, Calif.: American Institutes for Research.

Mallory, Alva E., and Drake, Jeffrey W. 1973. *Final Report of the Educational and Career Exploration System (ECES) for 1972–73*. Flint, Mich.: Genesee Intermediate School District.

Marland, Sidney P., Jr. 1972. "Career Education Now." *Vocational Guidance Quarterly* 20, no. 3, pp. 188–192.

Marland, Sidney P., Jr.; Lichtenwald, Harold; and Burke, Ralph. 1975. "Career Education, Texas Style! The Skyline Center in Dallas." *Phi Delta Kappan* 56, no. 9, pp. 616 635.

Masih, Lait K. 1969. "Elementary School Teachers View Elementary Counseling." *School Counselor* 17, no. 2, pp. 105–107.

May, Eugene P. 1977. "Counseling Psychologists in General Medical and Surgical Hospitals." *Counseling Psychologist* 7, no. 2, pp. 82–85.

May, Ronald J., and Rademacher, Betty Green. 1980. "The Use of Paraprofessionals as Environmental Assessors in Student Affairs Agencies." *Journal of College Student Personnel* 21, no. 4, pp. 368–369.

Meador, Betty D., and Rogers, Carl R. 1973. "Client-Centered Therapy." In *Current Psychotherapies*, edited by Raymond Corsini, pp. 119–166. Itasca, Ill.: F. E. Peacock.

Meerbach, John. 1978. *The Career Resource Center*. New York: Human Sciences Press.

Meltzoff, Julian, and Kornreich, Melvin. 1970. *Research in Psychotherapy*. New York: Atherton.

"Mental Health Counselors: Fact Sheet." 1980. *AMHCA News* 4, no. 1, p. 4.

Menacker, Julius. 1975. "Inequality: Implications for Career Guidance," *Vocational Guidance Quarterly*, 23, no. 3, pp. 243–249.

Mesa Public Schools, *Toward Accountability*, Mesa, Arizona, Board of Education (Not Dated).

Messick, Damuel, and Anderson, Scarvia. 1970. "Educational Testing, Individual Development, and Social Responsibility." *Counseling Psychologist* 2, no. 2, pp. 80–88.

Messina, James J. 1980. "Why Establish a Certification System for Professional Counselors? A Rationale." In *Counselor Licensure: Issues and Perspectives*, edited by Richard W. Warner, Jr., David K. Brooks, Jr., and Jean A. Thompson, pp. 103–116. Falls Church, Va.: American Personnel and Guidance Association.

Meyer, Adolphe E. 1965. *An Educational History of the Western World*. New York: McGraw-Hill.

Miller, C. Dean, and Oetting, Gene. 1977. "Barriers to Employment and the Disadvantaged." *Personnel and Guidance Journal* 56, no. 2, pp. 89–93.

Miller, Carroll H. 1961. *Foundations of Guidance.* New York: Harper and Brothers.

————. 1964. "Vocational Guidance in the Perspective of Cultural Change." In *Man in a World at Work,* edited by Henry Borow, pp. 3–23. Boston: Houghton Mifflin.

————. 1973. "Historical and Recent Perspectives on Work and Vocational Guidance." In *Career Guidance for a New Age,* edited by Henry Borow, pp. 3–39. Boston: Houghton Mifflin.

Miller, Delbert C., and Form, William H. 1951. *Industrial Sociology.* New York: Harper and Brothers.

Miller, Donald H. 1974. *Community Mental Health.* Lexington, Mass.: Lexington Books.

Miller, Edith, and Warner, Richard W., Jr. 1975. "Single Subject Research and Evaluation." *Personnel and Guidance Journal* 54, no. 3, pp. 130–133.

Miller, Francis T.; Mazade, Noel A.; Muller, Sally; and Andrulis, Dennis. 1978. "Trends in Community Mental Health Programming." *American Journal of Community Psychology* 6, no. 2, pp. 194–195.

Miller, Juliet V., and Grisdale, George A. 1975. "Guidance Program Evaluation: What's Out There." *Measurement and Evaluation in Guidance* 8, no. 3, pp. 145–154.

Miller, Mark J., and Cochran, John R. 1979. "Comparison of the Effectiveness of Four Methods of Reporting Interest Inventory Results." *Journal of Counseling Psychology* 26, no. 3, pp. 263–266.

Miller, Theodore K., and Richardson, Robert L. 1978. "Professional Association Identification and Perceptions of the Student's Developmental Environment." *Journal of College Student Personnel* 19, no. 4, pp. 336–342.

Miller, Theresa M. 1979. "A Study of Counseling Services in Two-Year Colleges." *Journal of College Student Personnel* 20, no. 1, pp. 9–14.

Mitchell, Anita M. 1978. "The Design, Development, and Evaluation of Systematic Guidance Programs." In *New Imperatives for Guidance,* edited by Garry R. Walz and Libby Benjamin, pp. 113–148. Ann Arbor, Mich.: ERIC Counseling and Personnel Services Clearinghouse.

————. 1979. *Counselor Program Effectiveness: Gathering, Using, and Reporting Evidence.* Ann Arbor, Mich.: ERIC Counseling and Personnel Services Clearinghouse.

Mitchell, Anita M., and Saum, James A., eds. 1972. *A Master Plan for Pupil Services.* Fullerton: California Personnel and Guidance Association.

Mitchell, Bruce M. 1980. "What's Happening to Gifted Education in the United States Today?" *Phi Delta Kappan* 61, no. 8, pp. 563–564.

Mitchell, DeWayne W., and Crowell, Phyllis J. 1973. "Modifying Inappropriate Behavior in an Elementary Art Class." *Elementary School Guidance and Counseling* 8, no. 1, pp. 34–42.

Mosak, Harold H., and Driekurs, Rudolf. 1973. "Adlerian Psychology." In *Current Psychotherapies,* edited by Raymond Corsini, pp. 35–84. Itasca, Ill.: F. E. Peacock.

Mosher, Ralph L., and Sprinthall, Norman A. 1971. "Psychological Education: A Means to Promote Personal Development During Adolescence." *Counseling Psychologist* 2, no. 4, pp. 3–82.

Motsch, Peggy. 1980. "Peer Social Modeling: A Tool for Assisting Girls with Career Exploration." *Vocational Guidance Quarterly* 28, no. 3, pp. 231–240.

Murphy, Patrick P., and Burck, Harman D. 1976. "Career Development of Men at Mid-Life." *Journal of Vocational Behavior* 9, no. 3, pp. 337–343.

Murray, Donald, and Schmuck, Richard. 1972. "The Counselor-Consultant as a Specialist in Organization Development." *Elementary School Guidance and Counseling* 7, no. 2, pp. 99–104.

Myrick, Robert D., and Wilkinson, Gary. 1976. "The Occupational Specialist: A Study of Guidance Support Personnel." *Vocational Guidance Quarterly* 24, no. 3, pp. 244–249.

"Nader Releases ETS Report, Hits Tests as Poor Predictors of Performance." 1980. *APA Monitor* 11, no. 2, pp. 1, 7.

Nash, Robert J.; Saurman, Kenneth P.; and Sousa, George M. 1976. "A Humanistic Direction for Student Personnel — Student Development Educators." *Journal of College Student Personnel* 17, no. 3, pp. 243–251.

Nasman, Daniel H. 1977. *Legal Concerns for Counselors.* Washington, D.C.: American School Counselor Association.

Nathanson, Robert. 1979. "Counseling Persons with Disabilities: Are the Feelings, Thoughts, and Behaviors of Helping Professionals Helpful?" *Personnel and Guidance Journal* 58, no. 4, pp. 233–237.

National Vocational Guidance Association. 1971. *Guidelines for the Preparation and Evaluation of Career Information Media.* Washington, D.C.: American Personnel and Guidance Association.

———. 1973. "Career Development and Career Guidance." *NVGA Newsletter* 13, no. 1, pp. 5–8.

Necessary, Clara. 1979. "School Counselor Finds New Job Challenge." *Guidepost* 22, no. 4, p. 4.

Neugarten, Bernice L. 1976. "Adaptations and the Life Cycle." *Counseling Psychologist* 6, no. 1, pp. 16–20.

Newcomb, Paul R. 1979. "Cohabitation in America: An Assessment of Consequences." *Journal of Marriage and the Family* 41, no. 3, pp. 597–603.

Noble, Vincente M., and Kampwirth, Thomas J. 1979. "PL-94-142 and Counselor Activities." *Elementary School Guidance and Counseling* 13, no. 3, pp. 164–169.

Nolan, Edwin J., and Paradise, Louis V. 1979. "An Overview of Community College Counseling." *Journal of College Student Personnel* 20, no. 5, pp. 398–402.

Nordberg, Robert B. 1975. "Limitations of the Baseline Technique." *Personnel and Guidance Journal* 53, no. 7, p. 488.

Norris, Willa; Hatch, Raymond N.; Engelkes, James R.; and Winborn, Bob B. 1979. *The Career Information Service.* 4th ed. Chicago: Rand McNally.

Nuttall, Ena Vazquez. 1979. "The Support System and Coping Patterns of the Female Puerto Rican Single Parent." *Journal of Non-White Concerns* 7, no. 3, pp. 128–137.

O'Connor, James Robert. 1973. "Guidance Program Evaluation in 1970–71. A Follow-Up of Its Effectiveness and Value in Ohio Schools." Doctoral Dissertation, Ohio State University, Columbus, Ohio.

Odell, Charles E. 1979. "Aging — Relevant Issues, Policies, and Legislation: What the Counselor Should Know." In *Counseling the Aged,* edited by Mary L. Ganikos, Kathleen A. Grady, and Jane B. Olson, pp. 295–320. Washington, D.C.: American Personnel and Guidance Association.

Odell, Charles E.; Pritchard, David H.; Sinick, Daniel. 1974. "Whose Job Is Job Placement?" *Vocational Guidance Quarterly* 23, no. 2, pp. 138–145.

Odell, Louise M. 1973. "Secondary School Counseling: Past, Present, and Future." *Personnel and Guidance Journal* 52, no. 3, pp. 151–155.

Oetting, Eugene R., and Hawkes, James. 1974. "Training Professionals for Evaluative Research." *Personnel and Guidance Journal* 52, no. 6, pp. 434–438.

Oetting, Gene, and Miller, C. Dean. 1977. "Work and the Disadvantaged: The Work Adjustment Hierarchy." *Personnel and Guidance Journal* 56, no. 1, pp. 29–31, 34–45.

O'Leary, K. Daniel, and Wilson, G. Terence. 1975. *Behavior Therapy.* Englewood Cliffs, N.J.: Prentice-Hall.

Omvig, Clayton P.; Tulloch, Rodney W.; and Thomas, Edward G. 1975. "The Effect of Career Education on Career Maturity." *Journal of Vocational Behavior* 7, no. 2, pp. 265–273.

Onstad, Gwen. 1971. "A Talk with Some Native Americans." *Personnel and Guidance Journal* 50, no. 2, pp. 103–108.

Opton, Edward, Jr. 1979. "A Psychologist Takes a Closer Look at the Recent Landmark LARRY P. Opinion." *APA Monitor* 10, no. 12, pp. 1, 4.

Osipow, Samuel H. 1977. "Occupational Mental Health: Another Role for Counseling Psychologists." *Counseling Psychologist* 8, no. 1, pp. 65–70.

Otte, Fred L., and Sharpe, Debra L. 1979. "The Effects of Career Exploration on Self-Esteem, Achievement Motivation, and Occupational Knowledge." *Vocational Guidance Quarterly* 28, no. 1, pp. 63–70.

Overs, Robert P. 1975a. Career Behavior of the Physically and Mentally Handicapped." In *Career Behavior of Special Groups,* edited by J. Steven Picou and Robert E. Campbell, pp. 177–198. Columbus, Ohio: Charles E. Merrill.

––––––. 1975b. "Comment on 'Bias in OOH Illustrations.'" *Vocational Guidance Quarterly* 23, no. 4, pp. 340–341.

Page, Richard C., and Shearer, Robert A. 1980. "Some Curriculum Ideas for Training Public Offender Counselors." *Counselor Education and Supervision* 19, no. 4, pp. 293–300.

Palmo, Artis J., and Kuzniar, Joseph. 1972. "Modification of Behavior Through Group Counseling and Consultation." *Elementary School Guidance and Counseling* 6, no. 4, pp. 258–262.

Panther, Edward W. 1972. "Counselors and Legislators: A Case History." *Personnel and Guidance Journal* 50, no. 8, pp. 667–671.

Papalia, Anthony S., and Moore, S. Jerry. 1979. "Applying Educational Counseling Skills in Industry: A Role Expansion Model for Counselors." *Journal of College Student Personnel* 20, no. 1, pp. 23–27.

Parker, Clyde A. 1974. "Student Development: What Does it Mean?" *Journal of College Student Personnel* 15, no. 4, pp. 248–256.

Parker, Clyde A., and Jane Lawson. 1978. "From Theory to Practice to Theory: Consulting with College Faculty." *Personnel and Guidance Journal* 56, no. 7, pp. 424–427.

Parker, Clyde A., and Morrill, Weston. 1974. "Student Alternatives." *Journal of College Student Personnel* 15, no. 3, pp. 163–167.

Passons, William R. 1976. "Community Mental Health Consultants in Schools." *School Counselor* 23, no. 4, pp. 275–280.

Paterson, Donald G. 1938. "The Genesis of Modern Guidance." *Educational Record* 19, pp. 36–46.

Patouillet, Raymond; Drapela, Victor J.; and Karayanni, Mousa. 1975. "International Perspective on Vocational Guidance." *1975 Convention Summaries, Abstracts, and Research Reports.* Washington, D.C.: American Personnel and Guidance Association, pp. 43–44.

Patterson, C. H. 1969a. "The Counselor in the Elementary School." *Personnel and Guidance Journal* 47, no. 10, pp. 979–987.

_____. 1969b. "A Current View of Client-Centered or Relationship Therapy." *Counseling Psychologist* 1, no. 2, pp. 2–25.

_____. 1973. *Theories of Counseling and Psychotherapy.* 2nd ed. New York: Harper and Row.

Penney, James F. 1969. "Student Personnel Work: A Profession Stillborn." *Personnel and Guidance Journal* 47, no. 10, pp. 958–962.

Perovich, George M., and Mierzwa, John A. 1980. "Group Facilitation of Vocational Maturity and Self-Esteem in College Students." *Journal of College Student Personnel* 21, no. 3, pp. 206–211.

Perrone, Philip A., and Kyle, Gene W. 1975. "Evaluating the Effectiveness of a Grade 7–9 Career Development Program." *Vocational Guidance Quarterly* 23, no. 4, pp. 317–323.

Perrone, Philip A.; Male, Robert A.; and Karshner, Warner W. 1979. "Career Development Needs of Talented Students: A Perspective for Counselors." *School Counselor* 27, no. 1, pp. 16–23.

Peterson, James A., and Park, Dick. 1975. "Values in Career Education: Some Pitfalls." *Phi Delta Kappan* 56, no. 9, pp. 621–623.

Picou, J. Steven. 1975. "The Black Respondent and Career Behavior Research." In *Career Behavior of Special Groups,* edited by J. Steven Picou and Robert E. Campbell, pp. 404–423. Columbus, Ohio: Charles E. Merrill.

Piercy, Fred P., and Hovestadt, Alan J. 1980. "Marriage and Family Therapy within Counselor Education." *Counselor Education and Supervision* 20, no. 1, pp. 68–74.

Pierson, George A. 1965. *An Evaluation of Counselor Education in Regular Sessions Institutes.* Washington, D.C.: U.S. Government Printing Office.

Pine, Gerald J. 1974. "Let's Give Away School Counseling." *School Counselor* 22, no. 2, pp. 94–99.

_____. 1975. "Evaluating School Counseling Programs: Retrospect and Prospect." *Measurement and Evaluation in Guidance* 8, no. 3, pp. 136–144.

Pinsky, Sheldon, and Marks, Douglas. 1980. "Perceptions of Student Personnel Services at a Major Land Grant University." *Journal of College Student Personnel* 21, no. 2, pp. 99–105.

Placement Services. 1977. Ann Arbor, Mich.: Prakken Publications.

Ponzo, Zander. 1976. "Integrating Techniques from Five Counseling Theories." *Personnel and Guidance Journal* 54, no. 8, pp. 414–419.

Popham, W. James. 1976. "Normative Data for Criterion-Referenced Tests?" *Phi Delta Kappan* 57, no. 9, p. 594.

Pound, Ronald E., and Roberts, R. Jack. 1978. "Self-Management: Helping Children Learn to Control Attending Behavior." *School Counselor* 25, no. 3, pp. 199–202.

Prediger, Dale J. 1971. *Converting Test Data to Counseling Information.* Iowa City: The American College Testing Program.

———. 1980. "The Marriage Between Tests and Career Counseling: An Intimate Report." *Vocational Guidance Quarterly* 28, no. 4, pp. 297–305.

Protinsky, Howard, Jr. 1976. "Rational Counseling with Adolescents." *School Counselor* 23, no. 4, pp. 240–246.

Pruitt, Anne S. 1979. "Preparation of Student Development Specialists During the 1980's." *Counselor Education and Supervision* 18, no. 3, pp. 190–198.

Quirk, Daniel A. 1976. "Life-Span Opportunities for the Older Adult." *Personnel and Guidance Journal* 55, no. 3, pp. 140–142.

Rabush, Carol M. 1976. "CVIS Catalogue." Mimeographed. Westminster, Md.: Western Maryland College.

Ralston, Lee. 1974. "Using TV to Promote Career Awareness Among Preschoolers." *Vocational Guidance Quarterly* 21, no. 3, pp. 73–76.

Raming, Henry E., and Frey, David H. 1974. "A Taxonomic Approach to the Gestalt Theory of Perls." *Journal of Counseling Psychology* 21, no. 3, pp. 179–184.

Randolph, Daniel Lee. 1978. "The Counseling-Community Psychologist in the CMHC: Employer Perceptions." *Counselor Education and Supervision* 17, no. 4, pp. 244–253.

Randolph, Daniel Lee, and Saba, Robert G. 1973. "Changing Behavior through Modeling and Consultation." *Elementary School Guidance and Counseling* 8, no. 2, pp. 98–106.

Raney, Barbara. 1975. "Helping Students Understand the World of Work." *Florida Vocational Journal* 1, no. 1, pp. 14–17.

Rappaport, Julian. 1977. *Community Psychology.* New York: Holt, Rinehart and Winston.

Rathus, Spencer. 1975. "Principles and Practices of Assertive Training: An Eclectic Overview." *Counseling Psychologist* 5, no. 4, pp. 9–20.

Ratigan, William. 1967. "School Counseling Relation of Theory to Practice." In *School Counseling 1967,* edited by Alfred Stiller, pp. 93–130. Washington, D.C.: American School Counselor Association.

———. 1972. "Counseling Theory and Practice in the Schools," in Buford Stefflre and W. Harold Grant (Eds.) *Theories of Counseling* (2nd ed) New York: McGraw-Hill Book Co.

Ravelo, Antonio D. 1975. "A Process Model for Counseling in a Developing Nation: The Philippines," *1975 Convention Summaries, Abstracts, and Research Reports.* Washington, D.C.: American Personnel and Guidance Association.

Ravich, Diane. 1979. "Are Truth-in-Testing Laws a Fraud? Yes!" *Phi Delta Kappan* 61, no. 3, pp. 189–190.

Rayman, Jack R.; Bryson, Doris C.; and Bowlsbey, Joann H. 1978. "The Field Trial of DISCOVER: A New Computerized Interactive Guidance System." *Vocational Guidance Quarterly* 26, no. 4, pp. 349–360.

Reardon, Robert C., and Burck, Harmon D. 1980. "Training of the Career Development Specialist within Counselor Education." *Counselor Education and Supervision* 19, no. 3, pp. 210–215.

Reardon, Robert; Domkowski, Dorothy; and Jackson, Erwin. 1980. "Career Center Evaluation Methods: A Case Study." *Vocational Guidance Quarterly* 29, no. 2, pp. 150–158.

Reardon, Robert; Zunker, Vernon; and Dyal, Mary Ann. 1979. "The Status of Career Planning Centers in Colleges and Universities." *Vocational Guidance Quarterly* 28, no. 2, pp. 154–159.

Renzulli, Joseph S. 1978. "What Makes Giftedness." *Phi Delta Kappan* 60, no. 3, pp. 180–184, 261.

Riccio, Anthony C., and Barnes, Keith D. 1973. "Counselor Preferences of Senior High School Students." *Counselor Education and Supervision* 13, no. 1, pp. 36–40.

Riese, Harlan C., and Stoner, William G. 1969. "Perceptions of the Role and Function of the School Counselor." *School Counselor* 17, no. 2, pp. 126–130.

Riggar, Theodore F., and Riggar, Susan W. 1978. "The Rehabilitation Counselor in an Educational Setting." *Personnel and Guidance Journal* 57, no. 1, pp. 58–60.

Robin, Stanley S., and Wagenfeld, Morton O. 1977. "The Community Mental Health Worker: Organizational and Personal Sources of Role Discrepancy." *Journal of Health and Social Behavior* 18, no. 1, pp. 16–27.

Robinson, Carol M. 1978. "Developmental Counseling Approach to Death and Dying Education." *Elementary School Guidance and Counseling* 12, no. 3, pp. 178–187.

Rockwell, Perry J., and Rothney, John W. M. 1961. "Some Social Ideas of Pioneers in the Guidance Movement." *Personnel and Guidance Journal* 40, pp. 349–354.

Rockwell, Robert F. 1980. "Theories Underlying Student Personnel Development." In *Student Development in Higher Education,* edited by Don G. Creamer, pp. 10–95. Cincinnati: American College Personnel Association.

Rodgers, Robert F. 1980. "Theories Underlying Student Personnel Development." In *Student Development in Higher Education,* edited by Don G. Creamer, pp. 10–95. Cincinnati: American College Personnel Association.

Rogers, Carl R. 1942. *Counseling and Psychotherapy.* Boston: Houghton Mifflin.

———. 1951. *Client Centered Therapy.* Boston: Houghton Mifflin.

———. 1954. "An Overview of the Research and Some Questions for the Future." In *Psychotherapy and Personality,* edited by Carl R. Rogers and Rosalind F. Dymond, pp. 413–434. Chicago: University of Chicago Press.

———. 1975. "Empathic: An Unappreciated Way of Being." *Counseling Psychologist* 5, no. 2, pp. 2–10.

Rogers, Carl R. and Dymond, Rosalind F. (eds) 1954. *Psychotherapy and Personality Change.* Chicago: University of Chicago Press.

Rogers, Carl R., and Wallen, John L. 1946. *Counseling with Returned Servicemen.* New York: McGraw-Hill.

Romero, Dan, and Pinkney, James. 1980. "Role Swapping: An Antidote to Professional Burnout." *Counselor Education and Supervision* 20, no. 1, pp. 6–14.

Roney, Anne M. 1975. "TA and Sex Stereotypes." *Personnel and Guidance Journal* 54, no. 3, pp. 165–170.

Rosen, Albert. 1967. "Client Preferences: An Overview of the Literature." *Personnel and Guidance Journal* 45, no. 8, pp. 785–789.

Rosen, Gerald M. 1976. "The Development and Use of Nonprescription Behavior Therapies." *American Psychologist* 31, no. 2, pp. 139–141.

Rosenfeld, Anne H. 1978. *New Views on Older Lives.* Washington, D.C.: U.S. Government Printing Office.

Ross, Doris. 1976. "Compulsory Education, Not Compulsory Attendance." In *New*

Dimensions for Educating Youth, edited by John Chaffee, Jr., and James P. Clark, pp. 19–20. Reston, Va.: National Association of Secondary School Principals.

Ross, Robert I., and Gendreau, Paul, eds. 1980. *Effective Correctional Treatment.* Toronto: Butterworth and Company.

Rossi, Robert J.; Bartlett, Wendy B.; Campbell, Emily A.; Wise, Lauress L.; and McLaughlin, Donald H. 1975. *Using the Talent Profiles in Counseling.* Palo Alto, Calif.: American Institutes for Research.

Rossman, Howard M. J., and Kahnweiler, Jennifer Boretz. 1977. "Relaxation Training with Intermediate Grade Students." *Elementary School Guidance and Counseling* 11, no. 4, pp. 259–266.

Rothney, John W. M. 1958. *Guidance Practices and Results.* New York: Harper and Brothers.

———. 1970. "Some Not-So-Sacred Cows." *Personnel and Guidance Journal* 48, no. 10, pp. 803–808.

Rothney, John W. M., and Roens, Bert A. 1952. *Guidance of American Youth.* Cambridge, Mass.: Harvard University Press.

Rotter, Joe, and Crunk, Bill. 1975. "It's a Child's Right." *Elementary School Guidance and Counseling* 9, no. 4, pp. 263–269.

Ruiz, Rene A., and Padilla, Amado M. 1977. "Counseling Latinos." *Personnel and Guidance Journal* 55, no. 7, pp. 401–408.

Rule, Shelia. 1980. "The Educated Black: Caught in a Self-Fulfilling Prophecy." *New York Times.* 20 April, Section 12, p. 25.

Russel, John H., and Sullivan, Thomas. 1979. "Student Acquisition of Career Decision-Making Skills as a Result of Faculty Advisor Intervention." *Journal of College Student Personnel* 20, no. 4, pp. 291–296.

Russell Sage Foundation. 1970. "Proposed Principles for the Management of School Records: Excerpts." *Personnel and Guidance Journal* 49, no. 1, pp. 21–23.

Ryan, Charles W.; Drummond, Robert J.; and Shannon, Michael D. 1980. "Guidance Information System: An Analysis of Impact on School Counseling." *School Counselor* 28, no. 2, pp. 93–97.

Ryerson, Margaret S. 1977. "Death Education and Counseling for Children." *Elementary School Guidance and Counseling* 11, no. 3, pp. 165–174.

Ryscavage, Paul. 1979. "More Wives in the Labor Force Have Husbands with 'Above Average' Incomes." *Monthly Labor Review* 102 no. 6, pp. 40–42.

Sarason, Irwin G. 1968. "Verbal Learning, Modeling, and Juvenile Delinquency." *American Psychologist* 23, no. 4, pp. 254–266.

Sauber, S. Richard. 1975. "Multiple-Family Group Counseling." In *The Consulting Process,* edited by Jon Carlson, Howard Spelte, and Roy Kern, pp. 310–316. Washington, D.C.: American Personnel and Guidance Association.

Schmidt, Marlin R. 1975. "Introduction." *Journal of College Student Personnel,* vol. 16, no. 5, pp. 354–355.

Scholz, Nelle Tumlin; Prince, Judith Sosebee; and Miller, Gordon Porter. 1975. *How to Decide.* New York: College Entrance Examination Board.

"School Consolidation: Is Bigger Always Better?" 1976. *NIE Information.* Winter, pp. 1, 8.

Schreiber, Penny. 1980. *Marriage Counseling.* Ann Arbor, Mich.: ERIC Counseling and Personnel Services Clearinghouse.

Schwartz, Gary E. 1973. "Biofeedback as Therapy." *American Psychologist* 28, no. 8, pp. 666–673.

Schweisheimer, William, and Walberg, Herbert J. 1976. "A Peer Counseling Experiment: High School Students as Small-Group Leaders." *Journal of Counseling Psychology* 23, no. 4, pp. 398–401.

Schwenk, Mary Ann. 1979. "Reality Orientation for the Institutionalized Aged: Does It Help?" *Gerontologist* 19, no. 4, pp. 373–377.

Sears, Robert R. 1977. "Sources of Life Satisfactions of the Terman Gifted Men." *American Psychologist* 32, no. 2, pp. 119–128.

Seidman, E., et al. 1970. "The Child Development Consultant: An Experiment." *Personnel and Guidance Journal* 49, no. 1, pp. 29–34.

Sessions, John A. 1975. "Misdirecting Career Education: A Union View." *Vocational Guidance Quarterly* 23, no. 4, pp. 311–316.

Shane, Harold G. 1976. "America's Next 25 Years: Some Implications for Education." *Phi Delta Kappan* 58, no. 1, pp. 78–83.

Shapiro, Michelle, and Asher, William. 1972. "Students Who Seldom Discuss Their Post-High School Plans." *School Counselor* 20, no. 2, pp. 103–108.

Sharf, Richard S. 1974. "Interest Inventory Interpretation: Implications for Research and Practice." *Measurement and Evaluation in Guidance* 7, no. 1, pp. 16–23.

Shaw, Merville C. 1968. "The Feasibility of Parent Group Counseling in Elementary Schools." *Elementary School Guidance and Counseling* 2, no. 4, pp. 276–285.

——. 1973. *School Guidance Systems.* Boston: Houghton Mifflin.

Shertzer, Bruce, and Stone, Shelley C. 1974. *Fundamentals of Counseling.* Boston: Houghton Mifflin.

——. 1976. *Fundamentals of Guidance.* 3rd ed. Boston: Houghton Mifflin.

——. 1981. *Fundamentals of Guidance.* 4th ed. Boston: Houghton Mifflin.

Shoben, Edward Joseph, Jr. 1962. "The Counselor's Theory as a Personal Trait." *Personnel and Guidance Journal* 40, no. 7, pp. 617–621.

——. 1969. "Stray Thoughts on Revisited Eclecticism." *Personnel and Guidance Journal* 48, no. 3, pp. 198–200.

Siegel, Adelaide. 1972. "1921 to 1971: 50 Years of the *P & G.*" *Personnel and Guidance Journal* 50, no. 6, pp. 513–521.

Simon, Sidney B. 1973. "Values Clarification." *Personnel and Guidance Journal* 51, no. 9, pp. 614–618.

Sinick, Daniel. 1979. "Professional Development in Counseling Older Persons." *Counselor Education and Supervision* 19, no. 1, pp. 4–12.

Smallwood, Kathie Beckman. 1980. "What Do Adult Women College Students Really Need?" *Journal of College Student Personnel* 21, no. 1, pp. 65–73.

Smith, Darrell, and Peterson, James A. 1977. "Counseling and Values in a Time Perspective." *Personnel and Guidance Journal* 55, no. 6, pp. 309–318.

Smith, Elise J. 1980. "Career Development of Minorities in Nontraditional Fields." *Journal of Non-White Concerns* 8, no. 3, pp. 141–156.

Smith, Gloria S.; Barnes, Edward; and Scales, Alice. 1974. "Counseling the Black Child." *Elementary School Guidance and Counseling* 8, no. 4, pp. 245–253.

Smith, Robert R.; Petko, Charles M.; Jenkins, W. O.; and Warner, Jr., Richard W. 1979. "An Experimental Application and Evaluation of Rational Behavior

Therapy in a Work Release Setting." *Journal of Counseling Psychology* 26, no. 6, pp. 519–525.

Spang, Alonzo T., Jr. 1971. "Understanding the Indian." *Personnel and Guidance Journal* 50, no. 2, pp. 97–102.

Sparacino, Jack. 1979. "Individual Psychotherapy with the Aged: A Selective Review." *International Journal of Aging and Human Development* 9, no. 3, pp. 197–215.

Sparks, Dennis, and Ingram, Marjorie J. 1979. "Stress Prevention and Management: A Workshop Approach." *Personnel and Guidance Journal* 58, no. 3, pp. 197–200.

Spence, Donald P. 1973. "Analog and Digital Descriptions of Behavior." *American Psychologist* 28, no. 6, pp. 479–488.

Spencer, Barbara G.; Windham, Gerald O.; and Peterson, John H., Jr. 1975. "Occupational Orientations of an American Indian Group." In *Career Behavior of Special Groups,* edited by J. Steven Picou and Robert E. Campbell, pp. 199–223. Columbus, Ohio: Charles E. Merrill.

Splete, Howard H. 1980. "Community and School Involvement in Career Development." *Elementary School Guidance and Counseling* 14, no. 4, pp. 254–257.

Splete, Howard, and Rasmussen, Jeanette. 1977. "Aiding the Mobile Child." *Elementary School Guidance and Counseling* 11, no. 3, pp. 225–228.

Spooner, Susan E. 1979. "Preparing the Student Development Specialist: The Process-Outcome Model Applied." *Journal of College Student Personnel* 20, no. 1, pp. 45–53.

Stadler, Holly A., and Stahl, Earl. 1979. "Trends in Community Counselor Training." *Counselor Education and Supervision* 19, no. 1, pp. 42–48.

Stahl, Earl, and Havens, Robert I. 1978. "The Case for ACES Program Accreditation." *Counselor Education and Supervision* 17, no. 3, pp. 180–187.

Stamm, Martin L., and Nissman, Blossom S. 1979. *Improving Middle School Guidance.* Boston: Allyn and Bacon.

"Standardized Tests: Sexy, Sexless, or Sexist?" 1975. *1975 Convention Summaries, Abstracts, and Research Reports.* Washington, D.C.: American Personnel and Guidance Association, pp. 253–254.

Staudenmeier, James J. 1967. "Student Perceptions of Counselor Behavior Contributing to a Helping Relationship." *School Counselor* 15, no. 2, pp. 113–117.

Steele, Larry. 1980. "APGA to Fund Accreditation Body." *Guidepost* 23, no. 2, pp. 1–2, 12.

Stephens, W. Richard. 1970. *Social Reform and the Origins of Vocational Guidance,* National Vocational Guidance Association, Washington, D.C.

———. 1974. "New Light on Junior High School History." In *The American Intermediate School,* edited by Max E. Brough and Russell L. Hamm, pp. 9–18. Danville, Ill.: Interstate Printers and Publishers.

Stevens, Clarice N. 1973. "Counseling the Aged in a Public Housing Project." *Personnel and Guidance Journal* 52, no. 3, pp. 189–193.

Stillwell, Larry, and Collison, Brooke B. 1974. "A Career Development Program for a Small School." *Vocational Guidance Quarterly* 23, no. 2, pp. 174–177.

Stilwell, William E. 1976. "A Systems Approach for Implementing an Affective Education Program." *Counselor Education and Supervision* 15, no. 3, pp. 200–210.

Stinzi, Vernon L., and Hutcheson, William R. 1972. "We Have a Problem — Can You Help Us?" *School Counselor* 19, no. 5, pp. 329–334.

Stolz, Stephanie B.; Wienckowski, Louis A.; and Brown, Bertram S. 1975. "Behavior Modification." *American Psychologist* 30, no. 11, pp. 1027–1048.

Stubbins, Joseph. 1970. "The Politics of Counseling." *Personnel and Guidance Journal* 48, no. 8, pp. 611–618.

Stude, E. W., and Goodyear, Don L. 1975. *Ethics and the Counselor.* Fullerton: California Personnel and Guidance Association.

Stufflebeam, D. L. 1968. "Evaluation as Enlightenment for Decision-Making." Address sponsored by the Commission on Assessment of Educational Outcomes and Association for Supervision and Curriculum Development. Sarasota, Florida, January 1968.

Sue, Derald Wing. 1975a. "Asian-Americans: Social-Psychological Forces Affecting Their Life Styles." In *Career Behavior of Special Groups,* edited by J. Steven Picou and Robert E. Campbell, pp. 97–121. Columbus, Ohio: Charles E. Merrill.

———. 1975b. "New Directions." *Personnel and Guidance Journal* 53, no. 8, p. 550.

———. 1975c. "What Do We Stand For?" *Personnel and Guidance Journal* 54, no. 1, p. 6.

———. 1977. "Counseling at the Crossroads." *Personnel and Guidance Journal* 55, no. 6, pp. 285–286.

———. 1979. "Ethnic Identity. The Impact of Two Cultures on the Psychological Development of Asians in America." In *Counseling American Minorities,* edited by Donald R. Atkinson, George Morten, and Derald Wing Sue, pp. 83–194. Dubuque, Iowa: William C. Brown and Company.

Sue, Stanley, and Kitano, Harry H. L. 1969. "Stereotypes as a Measure of Success." In *Counseling American Minorities,* edited by Donald R. Atkinson, George Morten, and Derald Wing Sue, pp. 69–82. Dubuque, Iowa: William C. Brown and Company.

Sullivan, Howard J., and O'Hare, Robert W., eds. 1971. *Accountability in Pupil Personnel Services: A Process Guide for the Development of Objectives.* Fullerton: California Personnel and Guidance Association.

Sunbury, James F., and Cochran, John R. 1980. "Counselor Education: If It Isn't Fresh, We're Out of Business." *Counselor Education and Supervision* 20, no. 2, pp. 132–138.

Super, Donald E. 1969. "Vocational Development Theory: Persons, Positions, and Processes." *Counseling Psychologist* 1, no. 1, pp. 2–9.

———. 1970. *Computer-Assisted Counseling.* New York: Teachers College Press.

———. 1977. "The Identity Crises of Counseling Psychologist." *Counseling Psychologist* 7, no. 2, pp. 13–15.

Super, Donald E., and Bohn, Martin J., Jr. 1970. *Occupational Psychology.* Belmont, Calif.: Wadsworth.

Sweeney, T. J. 1966. "The School Counselor as Perceived by School Counselors and their Principals," *Personnel and Guidance Journal,* 44, no. 8, pp. 844–849.

Sweeney, Thomas J., and Sturdevant, Alan D. 1974. "Licensure in the Helping Professions: Anatomy of an Issue." *Personnel and Guidance Journal* 52, no. 9, pp. 575–580.

Tanney, Mary Faith. 1975. "Face Validity of Interest Measures: Sex Role Stereotyping." In *Issues of Sex Bias and Sex Fairness in Career Interest Measurement*, edited by Esther E. Drummond, pp. 89–99. Washington, D.C.: U.S. Department of Health, Education, and Welfare.

———. 1979. "Private Practice with Female Clients/Patients." *Counseling Psychologist* 8, no. 1, pp. 46–47.

Tanney, Mary Faith, and Birk, Janice M. 1978. "Women Counselors for Women Clients? A Review of the Research." In *Counseling Women*, edited by Lenore W. Harmon, Janice M. Birk, Laurine E. Fitzgerald, and Mary Faith Tanney, pp. 208–217. Monterey, Calif.: Brooks/Cole Publishing Company.

Teague, Gerald V., and Crites, Thomas G. 1980. "Faculty Contracts and Academic Advising." *Journal of College Student Personnel* 21, no. 1, pp. 40–44.

Thoresen, Carl E.; Hosford, Ray E.; and Krumboltz, John D. 1970. "Determining Effective Models for Counseling Clients of Varying Competencies." *Journal of Counseling Psychology* 17, no. 4, pp. 369–375.

Thorne, Frederick C. 1973. "Eclectic Psychotherapy," in Raymond Corsini (ed) *Current Psychotherapies*, Itasca, Illinois: F. E. Peacock Publishers, Inc. pp. 445–486.

Tidwell, Romeria. 1980. "Counseling in a Multicultural School Setting." *Journal of Non-White Concerns* 8, no. 2, pp. 84–90.

Time Share, *Everything You Want to Know About G15*. West Hartford, Connecticut. (not dated)

Tindall, Judy. 1976. "Middle/Junior High Counseling." *ASCA Newsletter* 14, no. 1, pp. 5, 8.

Toews, Jay M. 1969. "The Counselor as a Contingency Manager." *Personnel and Guidance Journal* 48, no. 2, pp. 127–134.

Toffler, Alvin. 1980. "A New Kind of Man in the Making." *New York Times Magazine*. 9 March, pp. 24–54.

Tolbert, E. L. 1959. *Introduction to Counseling*. New York: McGraw-Hill.

———. 1972. Introduction to Counseling. 2nd ed. New York: McGraw-Hill.

———. 1974. *Counseling for Career Development*. Boston: Houghton Mifflin.

———. 1976. "Guest Editor's Introduction." *Vocational Guidance Quarterly* 24, no. 4, pp. 294–297.

———. 1980. *Counseling for Career Development*. 2nd ed. Boston: Houghton Mifflin. 1980.

Tolsma, Robert J., and Marks, Stephen E. 1979. "Counselor Training in a School Center." *Counselor Education and Supervision* 18, no. 3, pp. 232–238.

Tolsma, Robert J.; Menne, John W.; and Hopper, Gordon. 1976. "The High School Characteristics Index as an Individual and Aggregate Response Measure." *Measurement and Evaluation in Guidance* 9, no. 1, pp. 5–14.

Trotzer, James P., and Kassera, Wayne J. 1971. "Do Counselors Do What They Are Taught?" *School Counselor* 18, no. 5, pp. 335–341.

Troy, Warwick G., and Magoon, Thomas M. 1979. "Activity Analysis in a University Counseling Center: Daily Time Recording or Time Estimates." *Journal of Counseling Psychology* 26, no. 1, pp. 58–63.

Truax, Charles B. 1963. "Effective Ingredients in Psychotherapy: An Approach to Unraveling the Patient-Therapist Interaction." *Journal of Counseling Psychology* 10, no. 3, pp. 256–262.

Tseng, Michael, and Thompson, Donald L. 1968. "Differences Between Adolescents

Who Seek Counseling and Those Who Do Not." *Personnel and Guidance Journal* 47, no. 4, pp. 333–336.

Tucker, Carolyn M. 1979. "Underutilization of Mental Health Services by Blacks: Strategies for Change." In *Counseling Blacks: Issues and Strategies,* edited by Woodrow M. Parker and Paul G. Schauble, pp. 1–13. Gainesville, Fla.: Psychological and Vocational Counseling Center.

Tuma, Abdul H., and Gustad, John W. 1957. "The Effects of Client and Counselor Personality Characteristics on Client Learning in Counseling." *Journal of Counseling Psychology* 4, no. 2, pp. 136–141.

Tuma, Margaret R. 1974. "Implementing a Program in Developmental Guidance and Counseling." *Personnel and Guidance Journal* 52, no. 6, pp. 376–381.

Tyler, Leona E. 1958. "Theoretical Principles Underlying the Counseling Process." *Journal of Counseling Psychology* 5, no. 1, pp. 3–8.

_____. 1960. "Minimum Change Therapy." *Personnel and Guidance Journal* 38, no. 6, pp. 475–479.

_____. 1969. *The Work of the Counselor.* 3rd ed. New York: Appleton-Century-Crofts.

Ullmann, Charles A. 1976. "Preretirement Planning: Does It Prevent Postretirement Shock?" *Personnel and Guidance Journal* 55, no. 3, pp. 115–118.

Update. 1976. *Experience Based Career Education News,* 1, no. 1, pp. 2, 4.

U.S. Department of Labor. 1977. *Dictionary of Occupational Titles.* 4th ed. Washington, D.C.: U.S. Government Printing Office.

_____. 1979. *Guide for Occupational Exploration.* Washington, D.C.: U.S. Government Printing Office.

_____. 1980a. *Exploring Careers.* Washington, D.C.: U.S. Government Printing Office.

_____. 1980b. *Occupational Outlook Handbook.* Washington, D.C.: U.S. Government Printing Office.

Vannote, Vance G. 1974. "A Practical Approach to Behavior Modification Programs." *School Counselor* 21, no. 5, pp. 350–355.

Varenhorst, Barbara B. 1974. "Training Adolescents as Peer Counselors." *Personnel and Guidance Journal* 53, no. 4, pp. 271–275.

Vener, A. M., and Krupka, L. R. 1980. "Academic Advising/Career Counseling and the 'New' College Student." *Journal of College Student Personnel* 21, no. 3, pp. 270–274.

Vernon, McCay, and Ottinger, Paula. 1980. "Counseling the Hearing-Impaired Child in a Mainstreamed Setting." In *Counseling Exceptional People,* edited by Libby Benjamin and Garry R. Walz, pp. 113–142. Ann Arbor, Mich.: ERIC Counseling and Personnel Services Clearinghouse.

Vocational Counseling the Disadvantaged Students. 1980. Ann Arbor, Mich.: ERIC Counseling and Personnel Services Clearinghouse.

von der Embse, Thomas, and Childs, Judith M. 1979. "Adults in Transition: A Profile of the Older College Student." *Journal of College Student Personnel* 20, no. 6, pp. 475–479.

Walberg, Herbert J., Schiller, Diane and Haertel, Geneva D., 1979. "The Quiet Revolution in Educational Research," *Phi Delta Kappan,* 61, no. 3, pp. 179–183.

Wall, Judy. 1974. "Getting into Print in *P&G*: How It's Done." *Personnel and Guidance Journal* 53, no. 9, pp. 594–602.

Wallach, Howard F.; Kelley, Frances; and Abrahams, Joel Peter. 1979. "Psychosocial Rehabilitation for Chronic Geriatric Patients: An Intergenerational Approach." *Gerontologist* 19, no. 5, pp. 464–470.

Walsh, Joseph A., and Melton, Joan. 1978. "Intake Dispersal Patterns: A Community Mental Health Study." *American Journal of Community Psychology* 6, no. 1, pp. 97–103.

Walz, Garry R., and Benjamin, Libby. 1974. "The Life Career Development System." In *A Comprehensive View of Career Development,* edited by Garry R. Walz, Robert L. Smith, and Libby Benjamin, pp. 71–79. Washington, D.C.: American Personnel and Guidance Association.

————. 1977. *On Becoming a Change Agent.* Ann Arbor, Mich.: ERIC Counseling and Personnel Services Clearinghouse.

————. 1978. "Counselors on the Bubble." In *New Imperatives for Guidance,* edited by Garry R. Walz and Libby Benjamin, pp. 422–454. Ann Arbor, Mich.: ERIC Counseling and Personnel Services Clearinghouse.

————. 1979. *A Futuristic Perspective for Counselors.* Ann Arbor, Mich.: ERIC Counseling and Personnel Services Clearinghouse.

Walz, Garry R., and Leu, Jane. not dated. *Futuristic Images of Guidance and Student Services.* Ann Arbor, Mich.: ERIC Counseling and Personnel Services Clearinghouse.

Walz, Garry R., and Miller, Juliet. 1969. "School Climate and Student Behavior: Implications for Counselor Role." *Personnel and Guidance Journal* 47, no. 9, pp. 859–866.

Wandt, Edwin A. 1965. *A Cross-Section of Educational Research.* New York: David McKay.

Ward, Patricia, and Rouzer, David L. 1974. "The Nature of Pathological Functioning from a Gestalt Perspective." *Counseling Psychologist* 4, no. 4, pp. 24–27.

Ward, Russell A. 1977. "Services for Older People: An Integrated Framework for Research." *Journal of Health and Social Behavior* 18, no. 1, pp. 61–70.

Ware, Martha L. 1971. "The Law and Counselor Ethics." *Personnel and Guidance Journal* 50, no. 4, pp. 305–317.

Warman, R. E. 1960. "Differential Perceptions of Counseling Role," *Journal of Counseling Psychology,* 7, no. 4, pp. 269–274.

Warnath, Charles F., ed. 1973a. *New Directions of College Counselors.* San Francisco: Jossey-Bass.

————. 1973b. "The School Counselors as Institutional Agent." *School Counselor* 20, no. 3, pp. 202–208.

Warner, Richard W. 1974. "Consulting with Parents." *Personnel and Guidance Journal* 53, no. 1, pp. 68–70.

————. 1974. "Research in Counseling." *Personnel and Guidance Journal* 53, no. 1, pp. 68–70.

Washburn, George, and Schmaljohn, Phyllis. 1975. "What Do You Want to Be When You Grow Up? A Pilot Project in Career Awareness." *Elementary School Guidance and Counseling* 10, no. 2, pp. 142–147.

Watts, A. G. 1973. "Counselling and Career Education in the United States: A Visitor's View." *Vocational Guidance Quarterly,* 21, no. 4, pp. 254–261.

Wegmann, Robert G. 1979. "Job-Search Assistance Programs: Implications for the Schools." *Phi Delta Kappan* 61, no. 4, pp. 271–273.

Weinrach, Stephen G. 1975. "How Effective Am I? Five Easy Steps to Self-Evaluation." *School Counselor* 22, no. 3, pp. 202–205.

Welbourne, Ann K. 1975. "A Peer Approach to Adolescent Sexual Information and Help." *Counseling Psychologist* 5, no. 1, pp. 77–80.

Werner, John L. 1978. "Community Mental Health Consultation with Agencies." *Personnel and Guidance Journal* 56, no. 6, pp. 364–368.

Wesman, Alexander G. 1972. "Testing and Counseling: Fact and Fancy." *Measurement and Evaluation in Guidance,* 5, no. 3, pp. 397–402.

Wesman, Alexander G. 1968. "Intelligent Testing." *American Psychologist* 23, no. 4, pp. 267–274.

Westbrook, Bert W. 1974. "Content Analysis of Six Career Development Tests." *Measurement and Evaluation in Guidance* 7, no. 3, pp. 172–180.

Westbrook, Franklin D.; Johnson, Frank; Hunt, Stanley M., Jr.; Leonard, Mary M.; Boyd, Vivian Stallworth; and McDermott, Michael T. 1978. "University Campus Consultation Through the Formation of Collaborative Dyads." *Personnel and Guidance Journal* 56, no. 6, pp. 359–363.

Westervelt, Esther Manning. 1973. "A Tide in the Affairs of Women: The Psychological Impact of Feminism on Educated Women." *Counseling Psychologist* 4, no. 1, pp. 3–26.

Wheeler, Paul T. 1980b. Mental Health Practitioners' Perceptions of Their Preparation in Program Evaluation." *American Mental Health Counselors Association Journal* 2, no. 2, pp. 88–96.

Wheeler, R. Michele. 1980a "Emergency Care for the Young." *Personnel and Guidance Journal* 58, no. 8, pp. 535–537.

White, Paul; Reardon, Sandra Barker; and Carlson, Arthur. 1979. "Increasing Career Center Accessibility for the Blind." *Personnel and Guidance Journal* 58, no. 4, pp. 292–295.

Whiteley, John and Whiteley, Rita. 1977. "California Court Expands Privilege Rebate," *APA Monitor,* 8, no. 2, pp. 5–6, 18.

Wilhelm, Charles D., and Case, Madelyn. 1975. "Telling It Like It Is — Improving School Records." *School Counselor* 23, no. 2, pp. 84–90.

Wilkinson, Gary S., and Bleck, Robert T. 1977. "Children's Divorce Groups." *Elementary School Guidance and Counseling* 11, no. 3, pp. 205–213.

Williams, Dennis A.; Masindorf, Martin; McGuire, Stryker; Copeland, Jeff B.; Donosky, Lea; and Hager, Mary. 1979. "Chicanos on the Move." *Newsweek.* 1 January, pp. 22–26.

Williams, James H. 1979. "Career Counseling for the Minority Student: Should it be Different?" *Journal of Non-White Concerns,* 7, no. 4, pp. 176–182.

Williams, Robert I. 1970. "Black Pride, Academic Relevence and Individual Achievement." *Counseling Psychologist* 2, no. 1, pp. 18–22.

Williamson, E. G. 1950. *Counseling Adolescents.* New York: McGraw-Hill.

_____. 1961. *Student Personnel Services in Colleges and Universities.* New York: McGraw-Hill.

_____. 1965. *Vocational Counseling: Some Historical, Philosophical, and Theoretical Perspectives.* New York: McGraw-Hill.

Williamson, E. G., and Biggs, Donald A. 1975. *Student Personnel Work.* New York: John Wiley and Sons.

Wilson, Sandra Reitz, and Wise, Lauress L. 1975. *The American Citizen: 11 Years After High School.* Palo Alto, Calif.: American Institutes for Research.

Winter, Jeanne, and Schmidt, Jerry A. 1974. "A Replicable Career Program for Junior High." *Vocational Guidance Quarterly* 23, no. 2, pp. 177–179.

Wirtz, Willard. 1976. "Education/Work Policy: A New Imperative, a New Prospect." *Phi Delta Kappan* 58, no. 1, pp. 99–103.

Wittmer, Joe; Lanier, James E.; and Parker, Max. 1976. "Race Relations Training with Correctional Officers." *Personnel and Guidance Journal* 54, no. 6, pp. 302–306.

Wolff, Alfred R., and Meyer, Goldye W. 1979. "Counseling Older Adults: Suggested Approaches." In *Counseling the Aged,* edited by Mary L. Ganikos, Kathleen A. Grady, and Jane B. Olson, pp. 173–194. Falls Church, Va.: American Personnel and Guidance Association.

Wolleat, Patricia L. 1979. "School-Age Girls." *Counseling Psychologist* 8, no. 1, pp. 22–23.

"Women at Work: Still Fighting 'Stereotyped Roles.'" 1979. *U.S. News and World Report.* 15 January, pp. 73–74.

Woodburn, Lawrence T., and Barnhill, Lawrence N. 1977. "Applying Family Systems Therapy Principles to Couples Counseling." *Personnel and Guidance Journal* 55, no. 9, pp. 510–514.

Woody, Robert H. 1968. "Vocational Counseling with Behavioral Techniques." *Vocational Guidance Quarterly* 17, no. 2, pp. 97–103.

Worthington, Robert M. 1974. *Career Education in the United States Today: What It Is, Where, and the Results So Far.* Flagstaff: Northern Arizona University.

Wortman, Paul M. 1975. "Evaluation Research." *American Psychologist* 30, no. 5, pp. 562–575.

Worzbyt, John C. 1976. "Pupil Records: A Crisis in Perspective." *School Counselor* 23, no. 5, pp. 358–361.

Wrenn, C. Gilbert, 1976. "Values and Counseling in Different Countries and Cultures," *School Counselor,* no. 1, pp. 6–14.

———. 1970. "The Three Worlds of the Counselor." *Personnel and Guidance Journal* 49, no. 2, pp. 91–96.

———. 1978. "Personal Perspectives — Past and Present." In *New Imperatives for Guidance,* edited by Garry R. Walz and Libby Benjamin, pp. 455–491. Ann Arbor, Mich.: ERIC Counseling and Personnel Services Clearinghouse.

———. 1980. "Observations on What Counseling Psychologists Will Be Doing During the Next 20 Years." *Counseling Psychologist* 8, no. 4, pp. 32–35.

Wright, Brenda Johnson, and Isenstein, Vivian. 1977. *Psychological Tests and Minorities.* Washington, D.C.: U.S. Government Printing Office.

Wubbolding, Robert E. 1975. "Practicing Reality Therapy." *Personnel and Guidance Journal* 54, no. 3, pp. 164–165.

Wubbolding, Robert E., and Osborne, Sally. 1974. "Education and the World of Work." *Elementary School Guidance and Counseling* 9, no. 1, pp. 49–51.

Wyatt, Ouida L. 1969. "Comment." *Personnel and Guidance Journal* 47, no. 6, p. 599.

Wysong, H. Eugene. 1974. *Objectives of a Guidance Program.* Columbus, Ohio: Ohio Department of Education.

Yates, Coy; Johnson, Norbert; and Johnson, Jerome. 1979. "Effects of the Use of the

Vocational Exploration Group on Career Maturity." *Journal of Counseling Psychology* 26, no. 4, pp. 368–370.

Young, Anne McDougall. 1980. *Back to School at 35 and Over.* October 1980 Special Labor Force Report 227, U.S. Department of Labor.

Young, Jerry W., and Harris, Kenneth A. 1977. "A Community College Model of Counseling." *Journal of College Student Personnel* 18, no. 2, pp. 133–137.

Youngman, Geraldine and Sandongei, Margaret. 1974. "Counseling the American Indian Child," *Personnel and Guidance Journal*, 8, no. 4, pp. 273–277.

"Youth, Unemployment: Guidance Is a Must." 1979. *Guidepost* 22, no. 8, pp. 1, 5.

Zaffrann, Ronald T., and Colangelo, Nicholas. 1980. "Counseling with Gifted Students: A Planned Program Approach." In *Counseling Exceptional People*, edited by Libby Benjamin and Garry R. Walz, pp. 165–192. Ann Arbor, Mich.: ERIC Counseling and Personnel Services Clearinghouse.

Zautra, Alex, and Simons, Lynn Stanley. 1978. "An Assessment of a Community's Mental Health Needs." *American Journal of Community Psychology* 6, no. 4, pp. 351–362.

Zax, Melvin, and Specter, Gerald A. 1974. *An Introduction to Community Psychology.* New York: John Wiley and Sons.

Zifferblatt, Steven M. 1972. "Analysis and Design of Counselor Training Systems: An Operant and Operations Research Perspective." *Counseling Psychologist* 3, no. 4, part 2, pp. 12–31.

Zimpfer, David; Frederickson, Ronald; Salim, Mitchell; and Sanford, Alpheus. 1971. *Support Personnel in School Guidance Programs.* Washington, D.C.: American Personnel and Guidance Association.

Ziv, Avner. 1974. "From Israel." *Personnel and Guidance Journal* 53, no. 1, pp. 55–56.

Zytowski, Donald G. 1967. "Some Notes on the History of Vocational Counseling." *Vocational Guidance Quarterly* 16, no. 1, pp. 53–55.

_____. 1972. "Four Hundred Years Before Parsons." *Personnel and Guidance Journal* 50, no. 6, pp. 443–450.

454

ACKNOWLEDGMENTS (continued from page iv)

The list on page 65 is from Donald R. Buckner, "Restructuring Residence Hall Programming: Resident Hall Educators with a Curriculum," *Journal of College Student Personnel,* vol. 18 (1977). Copyright 1977 American Personnel and Guidance Association. Reprinted with permission.

Table 3-3 on page 69 is from Andrew M. Hendry, "Student Services in Five Alberta Colleges: A Measure of Quality," *Journal of College Student Personnel,* vol. 18 (1977). Copyright 1977 American Personnel and Guidance Association. Reprinted with permission.

Table 4-1 on page 76 is from Judith A. Lewis and Michael D. Lewis, *Community Counseling: A Human Services Approach* (New York: John Wiley & Sons, 1977). Reprinted by permission.

Tables 4-2 and 4-3 and summaries on pages 81 and 82 are adapted from Francis T. Miller, Noel A. Mazade, Sally M. Muller and Dennis P. Andrulis, "Trends in Community Mental Health Programming," *American Journal of Community Psychology,* Vol. 6 (1978). Reprinted by permission of Plenum Publishing Corporation.

Material summarized on pages 85–86 is adapted from Donald H. Miller, *Community Mental Health* (Lexington, Mass.: Lexington Books, 1974). Copyright © 1974 by Donald H. Miller. Reprinted by permission of the author.

On pages 139–140, the summary of material is from *Developmental Tasks and Education,* Third Edition by Robert J. Havighurst. Copyright © 1972 by Longman Inc. Reprinted by permission of Longman Inc., New York.

Data summarized in Table 7-1 on page 157 are from Ray E. Hosford and Antoinette Ryan, "Systems Design in the Development of Counseling and Guidance Programs," *Personnel and Guidance Journal,* vol. 49 (1970). Copyright 1970 American Personnel and Guidance Association. Reprinted with permission.

The problem described on pages 159–160 is from John D. Krumboltz, "An Accountability Model for Counselors," *Personnel and Guidance Journal,* vol. 52 (1974). Copyright 1974 American Personnel and Guidance Association. Reprinted with permission.

Figures 7–1 and 7–2 on pages 156 and 158 are from R. E. Hosford and T. A. Ryan, "Systems Design in the Development of Counseling and Guidance Programs," *Personnel and Guidance Journal,* vol. 49 (1970). Copyright 1970 American Personnel and Guidance Association. Reprinted with permission.

Figure 7–3 on page 160 is from W. H. Morrill, E. R. Oetting, and J. C. Hurst, "Dimensions of Counselor Functioning," *Personnel and Guidance Journal,* vol. 52 (1974). Copyright 1974 American Personnel and Guidance Association. Reprinted with permission.

The list on pages 168–169 is from Edgar F. Huse, "Organization Development," *Personnel and Guidance Journal,* vol. 56 (1978). Copyright 1978 American Personnel and Guidance Association. Reprinted with permission.

The table of *t*-values on page 211 is from J. C. Hansen, T. M. Niland, and L. P. Zani, "Model Reinforcement in Group Counseling with Elementary School Children," *Personnel and Guidance Journal,* vol. 47 (1969). Copyright 1969 American Personnel and Guidance Association. Reprinted with permission.

The list on pages 236–237 is adapted from Thomas Fagan and Anne Wallace, "Who Are the Handicapped?" *Personnel and Guidance Journal,* vol. 58 (1979). Reprinted with permission.

Excerpts on page 239 are from Joseph S. Renzulli, "What Makes Giftedness," *Phi Delta Kappan,* vol. 60 (1978). Reprinted by permission.

The bias test results on page 255 are from Philip J. Lauver, Richard M. Gastellum, and Marilyn Sheehy, "Bias in OOH Illustrations," *Vocational Guidance Quarterly,* vol. 23 (1975). Copyright 1975 American Personnel and Guidance Association. Reprinted with permission.

The table on page 266 is from Thomas J. Jacobsen, *A Study of Career Centers in the State of California, Final Report* (1975). Reprinted by permission of the author.

The policy statement on page 272 is from American Personnel and Guidance Association, "Policy Statement: Responsibilities of Users of Standardized Tests," *Guidepost*, vol. 21 (1978). Copyright 1978 American Personnel and Guidance Association. Reprinted with permission.

The excerpt on page 286 is from Dale J. Prediger, "The Marriage Between Tests and Career Counseling: An Intimate Report," *Vocational Guidance Quarterly*, vol. 28 (1980). Copyright 1980 American Personnel and Guidance Association. Reprinted with permission.

Table 12-1 on page 298 and other information summarized on page 297 are from Joseph D. Dameron, ed., *The Professional Counselor: Competencies, Performance Guidelines, and Assessment.* Copyright 1980 American Personnel and Guidance Association. Reprinted with permission.

The ethical issues case on pages 316–317 is from E. L. Stude and D. L. Goodyear, *Ethics and the Counselor* (Fullerton, CA: California Personnel and Guidance Association, 1975). Reprinted by permission.

The evaluation standards summarized on pages 338–339 are from Joint Committee for Standards for Educational Evaluation, *Standards for Evaluations of Educational Programs, Projects, and Materials* (New York: McGraw-Hill, 1981). Reprinted by permission.

The table and summary on page 343 are from *A Cross-Section of Educational Research* by Edwin Wandt. Copyright © 1965 by Longman Inc. Reprinted by permission of Longman Inc.

The text excerpt and questions on page 349 are from Walz, G. R. & Benjamin, L., *A futuristic perspective for counselors* (Ann Arbor, MI: ERIC/CAPS, University of Michigan, 1979). Reprinted by permission.

The excerpt on page 349 is from Walz, G. R. & Leu, J., *Futuristic Images of guidance and student services* (Ann Arbor, MI: ERIC/CAPS, University of Michigan, undated. Reprinted by permission.

The quote on page 349 is from Hays, D. G., *Counseling and the future: Concepts, issues, and strategies* (Ann Arbor, MI: ERIC/CAPS, University of Michigan, 1981). Reprinted by permission.

Appendix A on pages 363–378 is from American Personnel and Guidance Association brochure, *APGA Membership*.

Name Index

Subject Index